CRITICAL
PATH

R. Buckminster Fuller

Adjuvant: Kiyoshi Kuromiya

CRITICAL PATH

ST. MARTIN'S PRESS·*New York*

For information, write: St. Martin's Press,
175 Fifth Avenue, New York, N.Y. 10010

Manufactured in the United States of America

Library of Congress Cataloging in Publication Data

Fuller, Richard Buckminster, 1895-
    Critical path.

    1. Civilization, Modern—1950-   2. Civilization——History.   I.   Title.
CB428.F84   909.82   80-21881
ISBN 0-312-17491-8

Design by Dennis J. Grastorf

Fig. 6 Dhow, p. 24, photograph by Mirella Ricciardi, reproduced from "The World of the Dhows," Part II, *Yachting World*, December 1974.

Fig. 8 Erathosthenes' Map, p. 36, reproduced from *The Story of Maps* by Lloyd Brown, Dover Publications, Inc., 1979.

Fig. 12 Ptolemy's Map, p. 45, reproduced from *Maps & Man: An Examination of Cartography in Relation to Culture and Civilization* by Norman J. W. Thrower, Prentice-Hall, 1972.

Fig. 17 Price Index for All Items, p. 107, is based on information found in the *1913–1970 Historical Statistics of the United States* and the *Statistical Abstract of the United States, 1979*.

Fig. 18 Total National Debt, p. 115, is based on information found in the *1918–1970 Historical Statistics of the United States*, the *1970–1978 Statistical Abstract*, and the *Survey of Current Business 1979*.

Fig. 36 The Birthrate and Energy Production, p. 207, is reproduced from *Ho-Ping: Food for Everyone* by Medard Gabel, Anchor Press, 1979.

"Those whom God hath joined together let no one put asunder."
To ANNE HEWLETT FULLER *on this, our 63rd Wedding Anniversary and my 85th Birthday—July 12, 1980*

ACKNOWLEDGMENTS

We wish to express our thanks for their help in preparing this book to: Tom Vinetz, E.J. Applewhite, Michael Denneny, John Berseth, Paul Dinas, Janet Bregman-Taney, Shirley Sharkey, and Ann Mintz.

R.B.F.
K.K.

CONVENTIONAL CRITICAL-PATH CONCEPTIONING is linear and self-under-informative. Only spherically expanding and contracting, spinning, polarly involuting and evoluting orbital-system feedbacks are both comprehensively and incisively informative. Spherical-orbital critical-feedback circuits are pulsative, tidal, importing and exporting. Critical-path elements are not overlapping linear modules in a plane: they are systemically interspiraling complexes of omni-interrelevant regenerative feedback circuits.

—*Synergetics 2* [revised]

CONTENTS

Foreword

IT IS THE AUTHOR'S working assumption that the words *good* and *bad* are meaningless. This is based on science and not on opinion. In 1922 physicists discovered a fundamental complementarity of disparate individual phenomena to be operative in physical Universe. This was fundamentally amplified with the subsequent discovery of the always-and-only-different, always-co-existing proton and neutron which, with their always-coexistent electrons, positrons, neutrinos, and antineutrinos, are eternally intertransformable.

No longer was valid *the* "building block" of the Universe. It was discovered that unity was plural and at minimum sixfold. All the intercomplementations are essential to the successful accomplishment of eternally regenerative Universe. Science's discovery of fundamental complementarity has frequently occasioned individual scientists' realization that the word *negative* used as the opposite of the word *positive* is at best carelessly and misinformedly employed.

Since complementarity is essential to the success of eternally regenerative Universe, the phenomenon identified as the opposite of *positive* cannot be *negative,* nor can it be *bad,* since the interopposed phenomena known heretofore as *good* and *bad* are essential to the 100-percent success of eternally regenerative Universe. They are both *good* for the Universe.

Science recognizes many fundamentally complementary aspects of Universe. The black hole is not a negative. As implosion is to explosion, the black hole phenomenon is to the inside-out, expanding Universe. The black hole is the inverse phase—the outside-inning phase—of cosmic evolution. What humans have spontaneously identified as good and bad—or as positive and negative—are evolutionary complementations in need of more accurate identifications.

If you want to sail your ship to windward through a narrow passage, you have to do what sailors call "beating to windward"—first you sail on your port tack, then on your starboard tack, then port, then starboard, again and again, not on your "good tack" and your "bad tack." We walk right foot, left foot, not right foot, wrong foot.

This book is written with the conviction that there are no "good" or "bad" people, no matter how offensive or eccentric to society they may seem. I am confident that if I were born and reared under the same circumstances as any other known humans, I would have behaved much as they have.

There's a short verse written long ago by an English poet and teacher, Elizabeth Wordsworth:

> *If all good people were clever,*
> *And all clever people were good,*
> *The world would be nicer than ever*
> *We thought that it possibly could.*
> *But somehow, 'tis seldom or never*
> *That the two hit it off as they should;*
> *For the good are so harsh to the clever,*
> *The clever so rude to the good.*

If you think you identify with anybody in this book, be sure to remember that I don't have any "good" or "bad" people. You and I didn't design people. God designed people. What I am trying to do is to discover why God included humans in Universe.

I'm trying to find out what God permits us progressively to know and preferably to do if we humans are to continue in Universe.

For many years I hesitated about writing this book. God has introduced me to many, many thousands of humans. Quite a few of those I have known have had decision-making powers that could, and often did, affect human affairs in major ways. Much of their decision-making integrated with thousands of decisions made by other Earthians. The integrated thousands of decisions inadvertently were compounded with a myriad of unforeseen technological, exploratory, and environmental happenings. The individual decision-makings and unforeseen happenings around the world and in Universe at large altogether synergetically produced historical results not contemplated by any. Such noncontemplated-by-any results constitute evolution—the will of God.

In my eighty-five years I have often been privy to what was at the time secret, critical information. Time and change have "declassified" those secrets. In piecing together the significant components of world-around humanity's evolutionary trending, my insights have frequently been illumined by information confided in me by others. In recollecting once-confidential information, which is now essential to an adequate comprehension of relevant evolutionary trendings, I hope no one will make the mistake of thinking that I am being a traitor to my friends. Not only am I being loyal to all my friends but to all humanity—without whom there would be no life.

My reasons for writing this book are fourfold:

(A) Because I am convinced that human knowledge by others of what this book has to say is essential to human survival.

(B) Because of my driving conviction that all of humanity is in peril of extinction if each one of us does not dare, now and henceforth, always to tell only the truth, and all the truth, and to do so promptly—right now.

(C) Because I am convinced that humanity's fitness for continuance in the cosmic scheme no longer depends on the validity of political, religious, economic, or social organizations, which altogether heretofore have been assumed to represent the many.

(D) Because, contrary to (C), I am convinced that human continuance now depends entirely upon:

(1) The intuitive wisdom of each and every individual.

(2) The individual's comprehensive informedness.

(3) The individual's integrity of speaking and acting only on the individual's own within-self-intuited and reasoned initiative.

(4) The individual's joining action with others, as motivated only by the individually conceived consequences of so doing.

(5) The individual's never-joining action with others, as motivated only by crowd-engendered emotionalism, or by a sense of the crowd's power to overwhelm, or in fear of holding to the course indicated by one's own intellectual convictions.

We all see things differently. Seeing is sensing. Hearing is sensing. Touching is sensing. Smelling is sensing. What each of us happens to sense is different. And our different senses are differently effective under ever-differing circumstances. Our individual brains coordinatingly integrate all the ever-different sensings of our different faculties. The integrated product of our multifold individual sensings produces awareness. Only through our sensings are we aware of the complementary "otherness."

Awareness of the "otherness" is information. The complex of successively experienced informations produces interweaving episodes—and the complex of special-case-episode-interweavings produces the scenario that our brain's memory banks identify as our individual being's "life."

The way only-our-own, individual integrity of being responds spontaneously only to our own exclusive sensing of any given otherness episode is what I mean when I use the word *feeling:* How do I feel about life? How do I feel about it now? . . . and again now? Our feelings often change. What do I feel that I need to do about what I am feeling?

One of the many wonderful human beings that I've known who has affected other human beings in a markedly inspiring degree was e. e. cummings, the poet.

He wrote a piece called "A Poet's Advice," which I feel elucidates why "little I," fifty-three years ago at age thirty-two, jettisoned all that I had ever been taught to believe and proceeded thereafter to reason and act only on the basis of direct personal experience. Cummings's poem also explains why, acting entirely on my own initiative, I sought to discover what, if anything, can be effectively accomplished by a penniless, unknown individual—operating only on behalf of all humanity—in attempting to produce sustainingly favorable physical and metaphysical advancement of the integrity of all human life on our planet, which omnihuman advantaging task, attemptable by the individual, is inherently impossible of accomplishment by any nation, private enterprise, religion, or other multipeopled, bias-fostering combination thereof.

A POET'S ADVICE

A poet is somebody who feels, and who expresses his feelings through words. This may sound easy. It isn't.

A lot of people think or believe or know they feel—but that's thinking or believing or knowing; not feeling. And poetry is feeling—not knowing or believing or thinking.

Almost anybody can learn to think or believe or know, but not a single human being can be taught to feel. Why? Because whenever you think or you believe or you know, you're a lot of other people: but the moment you feel, you're nobody-but-yourself.

To be nobody-but-yourself—in a world which is doing its best, night and day, to make you everybody else—means to fight the hardest battle which any human being can fight; and never stop fighting.

As for expressing nobody-but-yourself in words, that means working just a little harder than anybody who isn't a poet can possibly imagine. Why? Because nothing is quite as easy as using words like somebody else. We all of us do exactly this nearly all of the time—and whenever we do it, we are not poets.

If, at the end of your first ten or fifteen years of fighting and working and feeling, you find you've written one line of one poem, you'll be very lucky indeed.

And so my advice to all young people who wish to become poets is: do something easy, like learning how to blow up the world—unless you're not only willing, but glad, to feel and work and fight till you die.

Does this sound dismal? It isn't.
It's the most wonderful life on earth.
Or so I feel.

—e. e. cummings

Exploring, experiencing, feeling, and—to the best of my ability—acting strictly and only on my individual intuition, I became impelled to write this book.

I'm not claiming to be a poet or that this book is poetry, but I knew cummings well enough to be confident that he would feel happy that I had written it.

CRITICAL PATH

INTRODUCTION:

Twilight of the World's Power Structures

H UMANITY IS MOVING EVER DEEPER into crisis—a crisis without precedent.

First, it is a crisis brought about by cosmic evolution irrevocably intent upon completely transforming omnidisintegrated humanity from a complex of around-the-world, remotely-deployed-from-one-another, differently colored, differently credoed, differently cultured, differently communicating, and differently competing entities into a completely integrated, comprehensively interconsiderate, harmonious whole.

Second, we are in an unprecedented crisis because cosmic evolution is also irrevocably intent upon making omni-integrated humanity omnisuccessful, able to live sustainingly at an unprecedentedly higher standard of living for all Earthians than has ever been experienced by any; able to live entirely within its cosmic-energy income instead of spending its cosmic-energy savings account (i.e., the fossil fuels) or spending its cosmic-capital plant and equipment account (i.e., atomic energy)—the atoms with which our Spaceship Earth and its biosphere are structured and equipped—a spending folly no less illogical than burning your house-and-home to keep the family warm on an unprecedentedly cold midwinter night.

Humanity's cosmic-energy income account consists entirely of our gravity- and star (99 percent Sun)-distributed cosmic dividends of waterpower, tidal power, wavepower, windpower, vegetation-produced alcohols, methane gas, vulcanism, and so on. Humanity's present rate of total energy consumption amounts to only one four-millionth of one percent of the rate of its energy income.

Tax-hungry government and profit-hungry business, for the moment, find it insurmountably difficult to arrange to put meters between humanity and its cosmic-energy income, and thus they do nothing realistic to help humanity enjoy its fabulous energy-income wealth—in fact, they send their government "revenooers" out into the mountain forest to fine and to destroy the equipment of any civilian so "treacherous" as to apply private enterprise in the alcohol-from-Sun-energy-photosynthesis harvesting to personal advantaging. If any citizens start making their own automobile-powering alcohol, the "revenooers" will have to pounce on them just as they do on those making moonshine "likker."

Ninety-nine percent of humanity does not know that we have the option to "make it" economically on this planet and in the Universe. We do. It can only be accomplished, however, through a design science initiative and technological revolution.

For three-quarters of all the trillions of nights humans have been on board planet Earth, the Moon has been their most intimate sky companion. For millions of years humans assumed it to be obvious that no one would really touch the Moon. Those who did not assume that to be obvious were obviously loony—lunatics, "Moon touchers."

In the battle of human power systems to see who is to control the world's people and their economies, the communist U.S.S.R. and the capitalist U.S.A. had been taught by World War II that whoever could fly the highest would gain the observational advantage for controlling the firepower of their guns and thus win the military supremacy of the world. In the "cold" Third World War the U.S.S.R. and U.S.A., inspired by the German rocketry, saw that whoever could maintain the greatest number of around-the-world-outer-space-platforms could control around-the-Earth firepower. The Moon was just such a "permanent" sky advantage.

Greatly challenged by the Russians' initially most successful space-operating accomplishments, President John Kennedy authorized the funds for the Apollo Project, which had first to do all of the tasks here on Earth preparatory to getting a team of humans ferried over to the Moon, to land, and then to return safely to Earth.

There were obvious first things first to be accomplished—second things before third things and 7308 things before 7309 things. Some were going to take longer than others. There would be a pattern of start-ups and lead-ins of differing time lengths. This complex, shad-bone-like pattern would be known as "the critical path." The critical path of overall human history's technological evolution involved two million* things that had to be done before blast-off of the first Earth-to-Moon ferrying-over-and-back.

Fortunately early humans, having no knowledge that what they were do-

---

*This is only a magnitude figure. It obviously is not exact.

ing would someday lead to humans physically, safely visiting the Moon, had already accomplished one million of those essential tasks before President John Kennedy allocated the federal funds to accomplish the remaining one million. Suddenly it was evident—but only to those few students who cared about the overall significance of such nonobvious, vast-time-scale inventories of evolutionary, historical, technological accomplishments—that without the million items already accomplished, it would be impossible to realize any of the Apollo Project's one million additional technical requirements—let alone accomplish them within the critically "effective" U.S.A. vs. U.S.S.R. competition time limit. Evolution is methodically synergetic and omnimeaningful.

Now, in 1980, a large number of all humans ten years of age and under, all of whom were born after humans reached the Moon, have learned so much about the Apollo Project as to be quite familiar with its critical-path accomplishment. They have entered the evolutionary scenario at a spontaneous conceptual level twice as well informed initially as were any pre–Apollo Project humans, and they find it logical to think about the solution of major evolutionary challenges in the comprehensive terms of both the all-history critical-path lessons as well as those of the as-yet-clearly-remembered and -documented special-case lessons of the Apollo Project's one million additionally accomplished, *critical-path* tasks. The under-ten-year-old post-Moon-landers are saying, "Humans can do anything they need to do." They are writing me letters saying so and asking why we don't make our world work satisfactorily for all humans. This is encouraging.

By 1989 those successful Moon-ferry-over conditioned, thoughtful young ones will be twenty. That's just the right age for commanding and executing the 1989 world-embracing design science revolution, which will result in the conversion of all humanity into an integrated, omniharmonious, economically successful, one-world family.

As of 1980 the successful solution of the myriad of social-economic-psychological problems now existent is obviously a more difficult task for humanity to address than was the achieving of the Apollo Project. For those who care to know how we're going to accomplish the 1989 omnisuccess of humans on Spaceship Earth, it is necessary to invest the rest of this hour in reading this Introduction, which contains the minimum information leading to ultimate comprehension of the fact that humanity now—for the first time in history—has the realistic opportunity to help evolution do what it is inexorably intent on doing—converting all humanity into one harmonious world family and making that family sustainingly, economically successful.

It will take all the evenings of one week to read the *Critical Path* book itself. This is the minimum time investment necessary to discover what roles may be effectively performed by humans individually in support of the 1989 design science realization of the success of humanity.

History shows that, only when the leaders of the world's great power structures have become convinced that their power structures are in danger of being destroyed, have the gargantuanly large, adequate funds been appropriated for accomplishing the necessary epoch-opening new technologies. It took preparation for World War III to make available the funds that have given us computers, transistors, rockets, and satellites to realistically explore the Universe. In the one hour of concentrated introductory reading about the critical path that must be accomplished in order to achieve understanding that we have the option to "make it," the first thing first is to understand what the world power structures are and of what their unique technical levers and strategies consist.

*   *   *

Throughout the history of land and sea transport those who have gained and held control of the *world's lines of vital supply* have done so only by becoming *the masters* in the game of establishing supreme human power over all other subpowerful organizations—ergo, invisibly over all humanity.

The historical development of massively keeled and ribbed, deep-bellied ships, which came into human use in the 3000–1000 B.C. era of the Phoenicians, Cretans, and Mycenaeans, altogether altered and vastly enlarged the interregional and international physical-transporting means of the world's lines of supply. The change was the shift over from that of the armed-horsemen-escorted, way-station-fortressed, twixt-city-states, overland, mule-horse-and-camel-borne caravaning to the thousandfold-greater cargo- and armaments-carrying capacity of the fighting-crew-manned fleets of those massively built, wind-sailing and slave-rowed, seagoing ships.

Ancient Troy was a powerful city-state and commanded much of the overland traffic between Asia and Europe. The Mycenaeans' siege of Troy—when their supplies were continually replenished by their fleet of those heavily ribbed, deep-bellied ships—reversed the city-state's former supremacy over invaders, whose brought-with-them food had theretofore become exhausted long before exhaustion of the food supplies stored in the great granaries of those inside the walls. The fall of Troy saw the supremacy over human affairs pass from the masters of the overland, Asia-to-Europe, inland-sea ferrying and caravaning lines of supply to the masters of the high-seas, maritime lines of supply.

The center of the stage of history's most critical events moved ever westward and mildly northward. Thus unfortified Venice became in due course the headquarters of the masters of the Mediterranean lines of supply.

The fifteenth-century Europeans' adoption of Arabic numerals and their computation-facilitating "positioning-of-numbers" altogether made possible Columbus's navigational calculations and Copernicus's discovery of the operational patterning of the solar system and its planets. Facile calculation so improved both the building of the ships and their navigation that the ever-larger ships of the Mediterranean ventured out into the North and South Atlantic to round Africa and reach the Orient. With Magellan's crew's completion of his planned circumnavigation, the planet Earth's predominantly water-covered sphericity was proven. The struggle for supreme mastery of human affairs thus passed out of the Mediterranean and into the world's oceans. Ships could carry vastly greater cargoes of the fabulous riches of the Orient to the European market than could the overland caravaning. One European ship completing one successful round trip to the Orient could realize a great fortune for its owners.

In 1600 Queen Elizabeth I and a few intimates founded the East India Company. Exercising her crown privileges, the queen granted the company limited liability for losses on the part of the enterprise backers. They could lose their money if the ship were lost, but they could not be held liable for the lives of the sailors who were drowned. While the owners could insure and very greatly limit the magnitude of their losses, the sailors and their families could not. "Ltd."—limited, in England—and "Inc."—incorporated, in the U.S.A.—and other similar legal definitions in all capitalist countries constitute "for ages uncontested"—ergo, custom-validated and legal-judgments-upheld—royal decrees greatly favoring big-money capitalism over the mortal, breadwinner-loss-taking vast majority of the poor.

Elizabeth's East India Company scheme was to have her national navy (and armies) first win mastery of the world's sea-lanes. This advantage would thereafter be exploited by her privately owned enterprise. This scheme became one of the first of such national power structure bids for establishing and maintaining world-trade supremacy through dominance of the world's high seas', ocean currents', trade winds', critical straits', and only-seasonably-favorable passages' world-around line of vital and desirable supplies. All the other world-power-stature individuals who vied for supreme mastery of the world's high seas lines of supply also operated invisibly through monarchs and nations over whom they had sufficient influence. Through such behind-the-throne influence the influenced nation's resources could be politically maneuvered into paying for the building and operation of the navies and armies that would seek to establish and protect their respective privately owned enterprises.

With the Battle of Trafalgar in 1805 the British Empire won "the world's power structures championship" and became historically the first empire "upon which," it was said, "the sun never sets." This is because it was the first empire in history to embrace the entire spherical planet Earth's 71-percent maritime, 29-percent landed, wealth-producing activities. All previous empires—Genghis Khan's, Alexander the Great's, the Romans', et al.— were unified European, North African, and Asian-continental, river-, lake-, and sea-embracing, flat-out land areas completely surrounded in all lateral directions by the infinitely unknown. All earlier empires were infinite systems—open systems. The British Empire was history's first spherically closed, finite system. Building and maintaining the world's most powerful navy, the 1805 supremely victorious British Empire was to maintain its sovereignty over the world's oceans and seas for 113 years.

Concurrently with its 1600 A.D.–initiated two centuries of maritime and military struggle for world dominance, England was also developing a civilian army of the world's best-informed and Empire-backed scientific, economic, and managerial personnel for the most economically profitable realization of its grand, world-embracing strategies. To educate the army of civil servants was the responsibility of the East India Company College located just outside of London. (In 1980 it is as yet operating.) Its graduates went to all known parts of the planet to gather all possible data on the physical and human culture resources to be exploited as well as information on the local customs of all the countries, large and small, with whom Great Britain and the East India Company must successfully cope and trade.

In 1800 Thomas Malthus, later professor of political economics of the East India Company College, was the first human in history to receive a comprehensively complete inventory of the world's vital and economic statistics. The accuracy of the pre-Trafalgar 1800 inventory was verified by a similar world inventory taken by the East India Company in 1810. In a later—post-Trafalgar—book Malthus confirmed in 1810 his 1800 finding that world-around humanity was increasing its numbers at a geometrical progression rate while increasing its life-support production at only an arithmetical progression rate, ergo, an increasing majority of humans would have to live out their short years in want and misery.

"Pray all you want," said Malthus, "it will do you no good. There is no more!"

A half-century later Darwin expounded his theory of evolution, assuming that nature's inexorable processes were the consequence of the "survival only of the fittest species and individuals within those species."

Karl Marx compounded Malthus's and Darwin's scientifically convincing conclusions and said, in effect, "The worker is obviously the fittest to survive. He is the one who knows how to handle the tools and seeds to produce the life support. The opulent others are 'parasites.'" The opulent others said, "We are opulent and on top of the heap because we demonstrate Darwin's 'fittest to survive.' The workers are dull and visionless. What is needed in this world is big-thinking enterprise, courage, cunning, and fighting skill." For the last century these two ideologies, *communism* and *free enterprise,* have dominated the political affairs of world-around humanity. Each side says, "You may not like our system, but we are convinced that we have the fittest, fairest, most ingenious way of coping with the lethal inadequacy of life support operative on our planet, *but* because there are those who disagree diametrically on how to cope, only all-out war can resolve which system is fittest to survive."

Those in supreme power politically and economically as of 1980 are as yet convinced that our planet Earth has nowhere nearly enough life support for all humanity. All books on economics have only one basic tenet—the fundamental scarcity of life support. The supreme political and economic powers as yet assume that it has to be either you *or* me. Not enough for both. That is why (1) those in financial advantage fortify themselves even further, reasoning that unselfishness is suicidal. That is why (2) the annual military expenditures by the U.S.S.R., representing socialism, and the U.S.A., representing private enterprise, have averaged over $200 billion a year for the last thirty years, doubling it last year to $400 billion—making a thus-far total of six trillion, 400 billion dollars spent in developing the ability to kill ever-more people, at ever-greater distances, in ever-shorter time.

* * *

Weighing only fifty-five pounds, with a wingspan of ninety-six feet, the human-powered *Gossamer Albatross* was able to fly across the English Channel because the structural materials of which it was built were many times tensilely stronger than an equal weight of the highest-strength aircraft aluminum. The tensile strengths of the *Albatross's* structural materials were sixty times stronger per equivalent weight than the strongest structural materials available to Leonardo da Vinci for realizing the design of his proposed human-powered flying machine. The *Albatross's* high-strength carbon-fiber and Mylar materials were all developed only a short time ago—since World War II.

A one-quarter-ton communication satellite is now outperforming the previously used 175,000 tons of transatlantic copper cables, with this 700,000-fold reduction in system-equipment weight providing greater message-carrying capacity and transmission fidelity, as well as using vastly fewer kilowatts of operational energy.

Continuing to attempt to fit our late-twentieth-century astronautical man-on-Moon-visiting capability into a nineteenth-century horse-and-buggy street pattern, house-to-house-yoo-hooing life-style (and a land baron racket) is so inefficient that the overall design of humanity's present social, economic, and political structuring and the physical technology it uses wastes ninety-five out of every 100 units of the energy it consumes. (Our automobiles' reciprocating engines are only 15-percent efficient, whereas turbines are 30 percent, jet engines 60 percent, and fuel cells used by astronauts 80 percent.) In the United States, throughout all twenty-four hours of every day of the year—year after year—we have an average of two million automobiles standing in front of red stoplights with their engines going, the energy for which amounts to that generated by the full efforts of 200 million horses being completely wasted as they jump up and down going nowhere.

Environment-controlling buildings gain or lose their energy as "heat or cool" only through their containing surfaces. Spheres contain the most volume with the least surface—i.e., have the least possible surface-to-volume ratio. Every time we double the diameter of a spherical structure, we increase its contained atmosphere eightfold and its enclosing surface only fourfold. When doubling the diameter of our sphere, we are not changing the size of the contained molecules of atmosphere. Therefore, every time we double a spherical structure's diameter, we halve the amount of enclosing surface through which an interior molecule of atmosphere can gain or lose energy as "heat or cool." Flat slabs have a high surface-to-volume ratio, and so flat slab fins make good air-cooling motorcycle and light-airplane engines. Tubes have the highest surface-to-volume ratios. Triangular- or square-sectioned tubes have higher surface-to-volume ratios than have round-sectioned tubes. Tall slab buildings and vertical, square-sectioned, tubular-tower skyscrapers have the maximum possible energy (as heat or cool)- losing capability.

One two-mile-diameter dome enclosing all the mid-Manhattan buildings between Twenty-second and Sixty-second streets and between the Hudson and East rivers, having a surface that is only one eighty-fourth that of all the buildings now standing in that midtown area, would reduce the heating and cooling energy requirements of that area eighty-four-fold.

The human pedal-powered airplane and the communication satellite are only two out of hundreds of thousands of instances that can now be cited of the accomplishment of much greater performance with much less material. The inefficiency of automobiles' reciprocating engines—and their traffic-system-wasted fuel—and the energy inefficiency of today's buildings, are only two of hundreds of thousands of instances that can be cited of the design-avoidable energy wastage. But the technical raison d'être for either the energy-effectiveness gains or losses is all completely invisible to human eyes. Thus, the significance of their omni-integratable potentialities is uncomprehended by either the world's leaders or the led.

Neither the great political and financial power structures of the world, nor the specialization-blinded professionals, nor the population in general realize that sum-totally the omni-engineering-integratable, invisible revolution in the metallurgical, chemical, and electronic arts now makes it possible to do so much more with ever fewer pounds and volumes of material, ergs of energy, and seconds of time per given technological function that it is now highly feasible to take care of everybody on Earth at a "higher standard of living than any have ever known."

It no longer has to be you or me. Selfishness is unnecessary and henceforth unrationalizable as mandated by survival. War is obsolete.

It could never have been done before. Only ten years ago the more-with-less technology reached the point where it could be done. Since then the invisible technological-capability revolution has made it ever easier so to do. It is a matter of converting the high technology from weaponry to livingry. The essence of livingry is human-life advantaging and environment controlling. With the highest aeronautical and engineering facilities of the world redirected from weaponry to livingry production, all humanity would have the option of becoming enduringly successful.

All previous revolutions have been political—in them the have-not majority has attempted revengefully to pull down the economically advantaged minority. If realized, this historically greatest design revolution will joyously elevate all humanity to unprecedented heights.

The architectural profession—civil, naval, aeronautical, and astronautical—has always been the place where the most competent thinking is conducted regarding livingry, as opposed to weaponry. Now is the time for the comprehensive architectural profession to reorient itself from the six-months-per-one-residence work schedule to the millions-per-day, air-deliverable, sewer-and-water-mains-emancipated, energy-harvesting, dwelling-machine-production world with its unpurchasable, air-deliverable dwelling machines only rentable from a Hertz-Hilton-Bell-Tel service industry, able to accommodate at unprecedentedly high standards of living all humanity's remote-from-one-another living accommodations. Now is also the time for the architectural profession to reorient itself from the years-to-build, human-need-exploiting cities to the all-in-one-day-air-deliverable-or-removable, human-need-serving, singly-domed-over cities. We have to satisfactorily rehouse the alternately convergent and divergent shuttling phases of four billion uprooting, around-the-world-integrating, sometimes transient, sometimes resident, sometimes in cities, sometimes in the country humans—before 2000 A.D.

Technologically we now have four billion billionaires on board Spaceship Earth who are entirely unaware of their good fortune. Unbeknownst to them their legacy is being held in probate by general ignorance, fear, selfishness, and a myriad of paralyzing professional, licensing, zoning, building laws and the like, as bureaucratically maintained by the incumbent power structures.

Dismaying as all this paralysis may be, it will lead eventually to such crisis that comprehensive dissemination of the foregoing truths ultimately will be accomplished through (1) the world-around-integrated electronic media broadcasting and (2) the computerized switchover from the inherently-in-adequate-life-support accounting assumption of yesterday to the adequate-for-everyone-and-everything, time-energy accounting comprehensively employed by the multibillion-galaxied, eternally regenerative Universe itself. An exclusively-to-be-accomplished, world-around-integrated, computer-facilitated, cosmically compatible accounting switchover will make it popularly comprehensible that we do indeed have four billion billionaires on our planet, thereby publicizing that fact and thereby inducing the systematic release of their heritage to all Earthian humans. All this accounting switchover must also be accomplished before 2000 A.D.

Those who make money with money deliberately keep it scarce. Money is not wealth. Wealth is the accomplished technological ability to protect, nurture, support, and accommodate all growful needs of life. Money is only an expediency-adopted means of interexchanging disparately sized, nonequatable items of real wealth.

A shoemaker has ten milk-drinking children. He wants to acquire a milk cow to convert grass into milk to take care of his children. The shoemaker makes his shoes out of cowhide, but that is not the reason he wants the cow. If and when the cow gets too old for milk production, he can butcher it for its meat and obtain a goodly supply of cowhide for his shoemaking.

A cow breeder wants a pair of shoes. He and the shoemaker agree that it takes much more time and individual inputs to produce a milk cow than it does to make a pair of shoes. They agree that you can't cut the cow up and still milk it. So they employ metal, which, being scarce and physically useful, has high and known exchange value and which could be cut apart into whatever fractions are necessary to implement the disparate values of interexchanging. That's how we got money.

Computers do not have to see or feel anything. Computers do not deal in opinion judgments; they simply store, retrieve, and integrate all the information given them. The more relevant the information they are given and the more accurate that information, the better the answers that the computer can give as to the consequences of doing thus and so under a given set of circumstances. Only the computer can cope with the astronomical complexity of integrating the unpredicted potentials of the millions of invisible technology gains in physical capabilities already accomplished. Only world-considerate computer accounting will be able to produce the figures that will persuade all humanity to divert high-science technology from weaponry to livingry. Computer capability will clearly manifest that we indeed now have four billion real-wealth billionaires.

Computer capability will distribute only-computer-readable credit cards to all humanity, whose constant living, travel, and development use will continually integrate all the production starts and holds on world-wide co-ordinated supplying of the needs of a world-around dynamically dwelling humanity. Computers will relegate all gold to its exclusively functional uses as a supreme electromagnetic conduction-and-reflection medium—with its supremacy amongst metals also manifest as rated in weight and bulk per ac-complished function. The computer will relegate all physical substances to their uniquely best functional uses.

All the foregoing considerations demonstrate clearly why the computer accounting switchover is not only possible but mandatory and must be ac-complished before the fear and ignorance of the billions of humans involved in the power structure's bureaucracies panic and push the atomic-bomb re-lease buttons. What makes us say "panic" of the major political, religious, and business bureaucracies? Bureaucracies will panic because all the great political, religious, and—most of all—big-business systems would find their activities devastated by the universal physical success of all humanity. All the strengths of all great politics and religion and most of business are de-rived from the promises they give of assuaging humanity's seemingly tragic dilemma of existing in an unalterable state of fundamental inadequacy of life support.

There are two more prime obstacles to all humanity's realization of its op-tion to "make it." One is the fact that humanity does not understand the language of science. Therefore it does not know that all that science has ever found out is that the physical Universe consists entirely of the most exqui-sitely interreciprocating technology. Ninety-nine percent of humanity thinks technology is a "new" phenomenon. The world populace identifies technol-ogy with (1) weapons and (2) machines that compete with them for their jobs. Most people therefore think they are against technology, not knowing that the technology they don't understand is their only means of exercising their option to "make it" on this planet and in this life.

Fortunately the mathematical coordinate system that has been and as yet is employed by science is *not* the coordinate system employed by the phys-ical Universe. Nature is always most economical. Science's coordinate sys-tem is not most economical and is therefore *difficult*. Nature never has to stop to calculate before behaving in the most economical manner. Scientists do. Also, fortunately, we have discovered nature's coordinate system, which is elegantly simple and popularly comprehensible. (See *Synergetics,* vols. 1 and 2—Macmillan, 1975, 1979.) Synergetics will make it possible for all humanity to comprehend that physical Universe is technology and that the technology does make possible all humanity's option to endure successfully.

The other prime obstacle to realization of the "great option" is the fact that the world's power structures have always "divided to conquer" and have always "kept divided to keep conquered." As a consequence the power structure has so divided humanity—not only into special function categories but into religious and language and color categories—that individual humans are now helplessly inarticulate in the face of the present crisis. They consider their political representation to be completely corrupted, therefore they feel almost utterly helpless.

Asking a computer "What shall I do?" is useless. You can get an informative answer, however, if you program your question into the computer as follows: "Under the following set of operative circumstances, each having a positive or negative number value in an only-one-value system, which of only two possible results will be obtained if I do so and so? And by how much?"

In 1953 my friend the late Walter Reuther, then president of the United Auto Workers, was about to meet with the board of directors of General Motors to form a new and timely post-World-War-II-oriented labor pact. At that time the first of the "new-scientists"-prototyped computers ever to be industrially manufactured were being assembled, put in running order, and fine-tuned by Walter Reuther's skilled machinists. Walter had all his fine-tuning machinists put the following problem into their computers: "In view of the fact that most of General Motors' workers are also its customers, if I demand of General Motors that they grant an unheard-of wage advance plus unprecedented vacation, health, and all conceivable lifetime benefits for all of its workers, amounting sum-totally to so many dollars, which way will General Motors make the most money: by granting or refusing?" All the computers said, "General Motors will make the most profit by granting."

Thus fortified, Walter Reuther made his unprecedented demands on General Motors' directors, who were elected to their position of authority only by the stockholders and who were naturally concerned only with the welfare of those stockholders. Reuther said to the assembled General Motors board of directors: "You are going to grant these demands, not because you now favor labor (which, in fact, you consider to be your enemy), but because by so granting, General Motors will make vastly greater profits. If you will put the problem into your new computers, you will learn that I am right."

The directors said, "Hah-hah! You obviously have used the wrong computers or have misstated the problem to the computers." Soon, however, all their own computers told the directors that Walter was right. They granted his demands. Within three years General Motors was the first corporation in history to net a billion-dollar profit after paying all government taxes— with their profits increasing steadily thereafter for twenty years.

* * *

In the electrical-power and light-generating industry the privately owned "public" utilities' largest customers are the industries. The public utilities must always generate enough electricity to ensure their customers' never having a shortage and that electricity be cheap; otherwise the industrial customers would install their own generating equipment. What the customers don't use of the surplus generated power is pure loss to the "public" utilities. To cope efficiently with the foregoing variables, each utility has plotted the peak and valley patterns for each second of each day of all the years since the "public" utilities entered the business. The utilities have many stand-by generators, most of which are in operation for only a small fraction of the time. All of each company's past peak-and-valley history is combined with probability mathematics to determine how many generators to have in operation at any given time of any given day of each newly evolving year.

In the 1930s Wendell Willkie was first to discover that with integration of the electrical-generating networks of neighboring localities, whose peaks and valleys inherently differ to some degree, the excess of any of the network's member utilities at any one moment is frequently used by other grid members' peaks. When this happens, it brings pure profit to the excess-power-generating seller.

The practical limit on the distance of electrical power delivery from the time of World War I until twenty years ago was 350 miles. However, 350 miles could not span the distances between any two of the continent's four national time zones. Twenty years ago, as a consequence of the new technologies of the space age, ultrahigh-voltage, superconductivity, and other technical developments occurred that made 1500-mile delivery of electricity possible, practical, and economical. This reach provided the ability to span continental time zones, whose peaks and valleys obviously differed greatly from one another, and this meant greater profits to be derived from across-time-zone-integrated electrical-energy networks.

Responding to 1929's Great Crash, the New Deal set up the Tennessee Valley Authority, which built many huge dams and enormous hydroelectric-power-generating capability. This solved all the flood problems of that area. It also greatly irritated the "private sector," which said government had no right to enter into competition with "private enterprise." Subsequently the government set up its Rural Electrification Administration (REA). The government was interested in rehabilitating the country's Depression-ruined farms. The private sector's electrical-generating industry was not interested. They thought it could be done only at a great loss. The electrical grids financed and administered by the REA interspersed all the great urban centers' electric grids in the United States. When the 1500-mile electrical-delivery reach unpredictably occurred and potential grid integratings across the time zones loomed, the government-administered rural grids became strategically involved. The boards of directors of all the private-sector "public" utilities said they would never integrate electrically with government—they were completely against government being in their game. However, they obviously could not integrate across the time zones except by employing the government's Rural-Electrification-established-and-financed grid.

The problem, with all its pro and con data, was put into the computer by the engineers of both the government and the private sector. The question was asked: "In which way would the private sector make the most money—by integrating with the government's network, or not?" The computer said the private sector would make 30-percent greater profit by integrating with government. The private sector undertook to do so. When both sides found that great profit would occur for the private sector—which for many years had been the prime financial backer of the Republican party— great political barriers developed in the Democratic administration which had to be overcome. President Lyndon Johnson, acting on behalf of the federal government, used his power over the Democratic party to remove enough barriers to permit the government to agree to integrate with the private sector. The "private sector," which theretofore had always backed the Republican presidential candidates, apparently became confused and backed Democrat Lyndon Johnson's successful bid for re-election.

Time and again in their short history computers have demonstrated their ability to reverse historically assumed-to-be-unalterable positions of both sides of the opposed political/economic power structure's directorates or committees. Computers can remember accurately and can cope with and integrate the vast amounts of all known, relevant information on complex problems, uncopeable-with prior to the computer. What we had prior to the computer were respected opinions and only-selfishness-conditioned reflexes on how to cope. Though an opinion might be wrong, there was no practical and convincing way to prove it. Unchallenged, the opinions became *respected precedent,* then *exceptionless concepts,* and sometimes even civil and academically accepted *social law.*

Computers will be used more and more to produce the opinion-obsoleting answers to progressive crises-provoked questions about which way world society as a whole will enduringly profit the most. Computers will correct misinformed and disadvantaged conditioned reflexes, not only of the few officials who have heretofore blocked comprehensive techno-economic and political evolutionary advancement, but also of the vast majorities of heretofore-ignorant total humanity.

Within the crises times immediately ahead—into which we have already entered—the computer is soon to respond: "We must integrate the world's electrical-energy networks." We must be able to continually integrate the progressive night-into-day and day-into-night hemispheres of our revolving planet. With all the world's electric energy needs being supplied by a twenty-four-hour-around, omni-integrated network, all of yesterday's, one-half-the-time-unemployed, standby generators will be usable all the time, thus swiftly doubling the operating capacity of the world's electrical energy grid.

A half-century ago I discovered with my nonvisibly distorted, one-world-island-in-one-world-ocean, 90° longitude-meridian-backbone, north-south-oriented, sky-ocean world map that a world energy network grid would be possible if we could develop the delivery reach. Since I was on the watch for it, when the 1500-mile-reach capability was technically established twenty years ago, it was immediately evident to me that we could carry our American electrical network grid across the Bering Straits from our Alaska grid to reach the extreme northeastern Russian grid, where the U.S.S.R. had completed a program of installing dams and hydroelectric-power-generating stations on all their northerly flowing rivers all the way into eastern Kamchatka. About 1500 miles could interconnect the Russians' Asiatic continent electric integrated power grid with the Alaskan grid of the industrial North American electric energy grid.

In the early years of Trudeau's premiership of Canada, when he was about to make his first visit to Russia, I gave him my world energy network grid plan, which he presented to Brezhnev, who turned it over to his experts. On his return to Canada Trudeau reported to me that the experts had come back to Brezhnev with: "feasible . . . desirable."

I therefore predict that before the end of the 1980s the computer's politically unbiased problem-solving prestige will have brought about the world's completely integrated electrical-energy network grid. This world electric grid, with its omni-integrated advantage, will deliver its electric energy anywhere, to anyone, at any one time, at one common rate. This will make possible a world-around uniform costing and pricing system for all goods and services based realistically on the time-energy metabolic accounting system of Universe.

In this cosmically uniform, common energy-value system for all human-

FIGURE 1.   Ultra-High-Voltage World Electric Grid

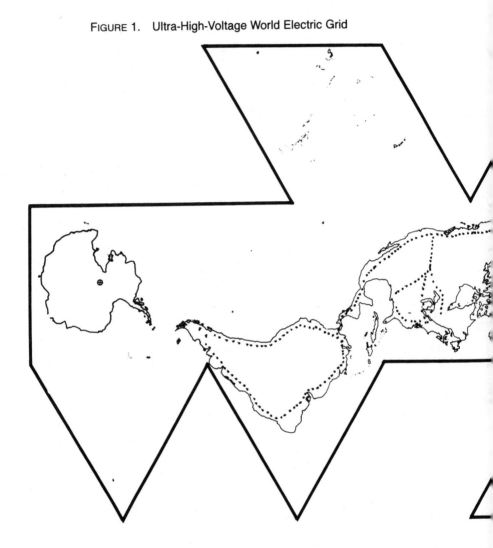

..................Grid line of world's ultra-high-voltage, 1500-mile, intergenerator connection reach

Establishing electric current currency for whole world: 1¢ = 1 kwh

B. Fuller's Dymaxion Sky-Ocean World Map

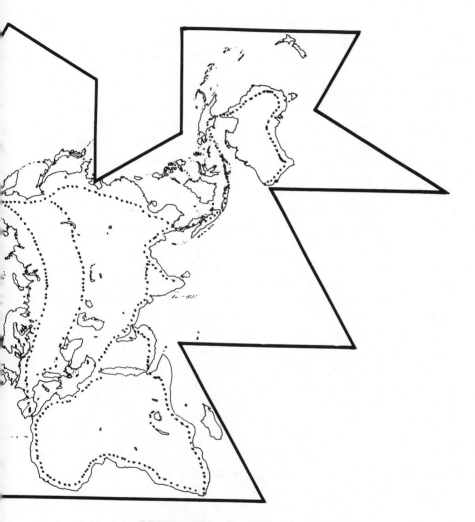

PERCENTAGE OF WORLD POPULATION

South America	6%
Central America	1%
North America	7%
Africa	11%
Europe	16%
Asia (54% land, 7% water)	61%
	100%

ity, costing will be expressed in kilowatt-hours, watt-hours, and watt-seconds of work. Kilowatt-hours will become the prime criteria of costing the production of the complex of metabolic involvements per each function or item. These uniform energy valuations will replace all the world's wildly intervarying, opinion-gambled-upon, top-power-system-manipulatable monetary systems. The time-energy world accounting system will do away with all the inequities now occurring in regard to the arbitrarily maneuverable international shipping of goods and the top economic power structure's banker-invented, international balance-of-trade accountings. It will eliminate all the tricky banking and securities-markets exploitations of all the around-the-world-time-zone activities differences in operation today, all unbeknownst to the at-all-times two billion humans who are sleeping.

The world energy network grid will be responsible for the swift disappearance of planet Earth's 150 different nationalities. We now have 150 supreme admirals, all trying to command the same ship to go in different directions, with the result that the ship is going around in circles—getting nowhere. The 150 nations act as 150 blood clots in blocking the flow of recirculating metals and other traffic essential to realization of the design science revolution.

In treating with the many immediate, most important survival problems, each question will be programmed into the computer asking which way society will experience the lowest-cost optimum living: by giving all humans handsome fellowships, with an income adequate for a high standard of living, or by having them go on *earning* their livings. The computer will show that 70 percent of all jobs in America and probably an equivalently high percentage of the jobs in other Western private-enterprise countries are preoccupied with work that is not producing any wealth or life support—inspectors of inspectors, reunderwriters of insurance reinsurers, Obnoxico* promoters, spies and counterspies, military personnel, gunmakers, etc.

The computer will also have verified both of the important findings of the brilliant Denver, Colorado, oil geologist, François de Chardenèdes: (1) the script of his scenario of "Nature's Production of Petroleum," and (2) his economic findings regarding the amount of energy employed as heat and pressure, for the length of time initially that it took nature to photosynthetically process Sun radiation into the myriad of hydrocarbon molecules that comprise all the vegetation and algae, which later are consumed and growthfully multiplied by a myriad of other biological species, a large percentage of which Sun-energy-nurtured-and-multiplied molecules are ultimately processed into petroleum.

---

*See description of Obnoxico in Chapter 6, pp. 225–26.

The script of de Chardenèdes's "Scenario of Petroleum Production" makes it clear that, with all that cosmic-energy processing (as rain, wind, and gravitational pressure) and processing time (paid for at the rates you and I pay for household electrical energy), it costs nature well over a million dollars to produce each gallon of petroleum. To say "I didn't know that" doesn't alter the inexorable energy accounting of eternally regenerative, 100-percent-efficient—ergo, 100-percent-concerned—physical-energy Universe.

We find all the no-life-support-wealth-producing people going to their 1980 jobs in their cars or buses, spending trillions of dollars' worth of petroleum daily to get to their no-wealth-producing jobs. It doesn't take a computer to tell you that it will save both Universe and humanity trillions of dollars a day to pay them handsomely to stay at home.

History's political and economic power structures have always fearfully abhorred "idle people" as potential troublemakers. Yet nature never abhors seemingly idle trees, grass, snails, coral reefs, and clouds in the sky.

One would hope the at-home-staying humans will start thinking—"What was it I was thinking about when they told me I had to 'earn my living'—doing what someone else had decided needed to be done? What do I see that needs to be done that nobody else is attending to? What do I need to learn to be effective in attending to it in a highly efficient and inoffensive-to-others manner?"

Comprehensively and incisively programmed with all the relevant data regarding education, it will be evidenced that the physical and social costs will be far less for individual, at-home-initiated, research-and-development-interned self-teaching than having individual students going to schools, being bused, and so on. This mass-production baby-sitting is only continued because of the union-organized response to the fear of the teachers about losing their jobs. Their political clout has for long been strong enough to guarantee continuance of this inefficiency to the present moment.

The computer will make it clear that by far the most effective educational system for human beings—all the way from birth through early childhood and on—is that to be derived from the home video cassette system and its supporting books, the pages of which are also to be called forth on world-satellite-interlinked video "library" screens as published in any language. The computer will also make it very clear that, freed of the necessity to earn a living, all humanity will want to exercise its fundamental drive first to comprehend "what it is all about" and second to demonstrate competence in respect to the challenges. The greatest privilege in human affairs will be to be allowed to join any one of the real wealth-production or maintenance teams.

Fortunately, the computer-directable design science revolution option does exist by which all looming problems can and may be effectively solved. Evolution does seem intent upon making humans a success.

*   *   *

Critical Path comprehensively traces all the important trends of history that have led to this moment of humanity's potential first-stage success and its opening of a whole new chapter of humanity's ever functioning in local support of the integrity of eternally regenerative Universe.

To know now what we could never have known before 1969—that we now have an option for all humanity to "make it" successfully on this planet in this lifetime—is not to be optimistic. It is only a validation of hope, a hope that had no operationally foreseeable validity before 1969. Whether it is to be Utopia or Oblivion will be a touch-and-go relay race right up to the final moment. The race is between a better-informed, hopefully inspired young world versus a running-scared, misinformedly brain-conditioned, older world. Humanity is in "final exam" as to whether or not it qualifies for continuance in Universe as *mind,* with the latter's access to the design laws—called by science "the generalized principles"—governing eternally regenerative Universe.

Human minds have a unique cosmic function not identifiable with any other phenomenon—the capability to act as local Universe information-harvesters and local Universe problem-solvers in support of the integrity of eternally regenerative Universe.

At the present cosmic moment, muscle, cunning, fear, and selfishness are in powerful control of human affairs. We humans are here in Universe to exercise the Universe-functioning of mind. Only mind can apprehend, abide by, and be led by truth. If human mind comes into control of human affairs, the first thing it will do is exercise our option to "make it."

If you read the entire *Critical Path* book carefully, including its sometimes long but essentially detailed considerations, and pay realistically close attention to these considerations, you will be able to throw your weight into the balancing of humanity's fate. While you could be "the straw that breaks the camel's back," compressively you can also be the "straw"—straw of intellect, initiative, unselfishness, comprehensive integrity, competence, and love—whose ephemerally effective tension saves us.

The invisibly tensive straws that can save us *are* those of individual human integrities—in daring to steer the individual's course only by truth, strange as the realized truth may often seem—wherever and whenever the truths are evidenced to the individual—wherever they may lead, unfamiliar as the way may be.

The integrity of the individual's enthusiasm for the now-possible success of all humanity is critical to successful exercise of our option. Are you spontaneously enthusiastic about everyone having everything *you* can have?

For only a short time, in most countries, has the individual human had the right of trial by jury. To make humanity's chances for a fair trial better, all those testifying must swear "to tell the truth, all the truth, and nothing but the truth." But humans have learned scientifically that the *exact* truth can never be attained or told. We can reduce the degree of tolerated error, but we have learned physically, as Heisenberg discovered, that exactitude is prohibited, because most exquisite physical experiment has shown that "the act of measuring always alters that which is measured."

We can sense that only God is the perfect—the exact truth. We can come ever nearer to God by progressively eliminating residual errors. The nearest each of us can come to God is by loving the truth. If we don't program the computer truthfully with all the truth and nothing but the truth, we won't get the answers that allow us to "make it."

When we speak of the integrity of the individual, we speak of that which life has taught the individual by direct experience. We are not talking about loyalty to your mother, your friends, your college fraternity, or your boss, who told you how to behave or think. In speaking of truth we are not talking about the position to take that seems to put you in the most favorable light.

It was the 1927 realization of the foregoing that brought the author to reorganize his life to discover what, if anything, the little, penniless, unknown individual, with dependent wife and child, might be able to do effectively on behalf of all humanity that would be inherently impossible for great nations or great corporate enterprises to do. This occasioned what is described in my "Self-Disciplines," Chapter 4.

With world-around contact with youth, generated by invitations to speak to the students of over 500 universities and colleges during the last half-century, I can conclude at the outset of 1980 that the world public has become disenchanted with both the political and financial leadership, which it no longer trusts to solve the problems of historical crisis. Furthermore, all the individuals of humanity are looking for the answer to what the little individual can do that can't be done by great nations and great enterprises.

The author thought that it would be highly relevant to the purpose of this book to enumerate those self-disciplines that he had adopted and used during those fifty years. Only those self-disciplines can cogently explain why he adopted the design science revolution and not the political revolutions (the strategy of all history). Only by understanding those disciplines can we understand the strategy governing the development of the artifacts, which strategy is called "critical path"—ergo, the name of this book.

Each year I receive and answer many hundreds of unsolicited letters from youth anxious to know what the little individual can do. One such letter from a young man named Michael—who is ten years old—asks whether I am a "doer or a thinker." Although I never "tell" anyone what to do, I feel it quite relevant at this point to quote my letter to him explaining what I have been trying to do in the years since my adoption of my 1927-inaugurated self-disciplinary resolves. The letter, dated February 16, 1970, reads:

Dear Michael,

Thank you very much for your recent letter concerning "thinkers and doers."

The things to do are: the things that need doing: that *you* see need to be done, and that no one else seems to see need to be done. Then you will conceive your own way of doing that which needs to be done—that no one else has told you to do or how to do it. This will bring out the real you that often gets buried inside a character that has acquired a superficial array of behaviors induced or imposed by others on the individual.

Try making experiments of anything you conceive and are intensely interested in. Don't be disappointed if something doesn't work. That is what you want to know—the truth about everything—and then the truth about combinations of things. Some combinations have such logic and integrity that they can work coherently despite non-working elements embraced by their system.

Whenever you come to a word with which you are not familiar, find it in the dictionary and write a sentence which uses that new word. Words are tools—and once you have learned how to use a tool you will never forget it. Just looking for the meaning of the word is not enough. If your vocabulary is comprehensive, you can comprehend both fine and large patterns of experience.

You have what is most important in life—initiative. Because of it, you wrote to me. I am answering to the best of my capability. You will find the world responding to your earnest initiative.

Sincerely yours,

Buckminster Fuller

The political and economic systems and the political and economic leaders of humanity are not in final examination; it is the integrity of each individual human that is in final examination. On personal integrity hangs humanity's fate. You can deceive others, you can deceive your brain-self, but you can't deceive your mind-self—for mind deals only in the discovery of truth and the interrelationship of all the truths. The cosmic laws with which mind deals are noncorruptible.

Cosmic evolution is omniscient God comprehensively articulate.

PART I

CHAPTER 1

Speculative Prehistory of Humanity

T HE DYMAXION WORLD MAP shows one world island in one world ocean with no breaks in the continental contours and with no visible distortion of the relative size or shape of any of the cartographic patterning. (See map on page 169.) The coloring on the full-size map is that of the optical spectrum, with red representing the hottest climates and dark blue representing the coldest climates. The borderline between yellow and green is the freezing line. The color shown for any area of the map represents the coldest conditions for that geographic area. Verkhoyansk, in northeastern Siberia, is the cold pole of planet Earth's northern hemisphere. Yet, sometimes in August at noonday, Verkhoyansk is as hot as equatorial Africa. Frequently in midwinter Verkhoyansk's temperature falls to sixty-five degrees below zero Fahrenheit. Equatorial Africa rarely has a temperature at midwinter of less than seventy degrees above zero Fahrenheit. The annual temperature variation between the hottest and coolest in equatorial Africa is only twenty degrees Fahrenheit, while the annual variation at Verkhoyansk is 120 degrees Fahrenheit.

The vital factor that determines social patterns, human preoccupations, and economic customs of those dwelling in different geographic environments depends on how cold it gets, not on how hot. With their shade-making artifacts humans can live nakedly under the hottest of Earth's weather conditions. Consisting physically of 60 percent water, humans cannot live nakedly where it is cold—not below the freezing line of thirty-two degrees above zero Fahrenheit.

The Dymaxion Map shows that (1) the colder an area gets, the more the annual temperature variation, and (2) the more the geographical temperature varies annually, the more inventive the humans who live in those areas

3

have to be to survive. If you live by Lake Victoria in eastern Africa and you wish to cross it, you will invent a wooden boat. If you live beside Lake Baikal in central Siberia and you wish to cross that body of water, you will invent a wooden boat in the summer and skates and sleds in the winter. The people who live in the colder areas are not more inventive—they simply have many more environment-caused occasions in which to employ all humans' innate inventiveness. Move humans from a hot country into a cold country, and they become as inventive as those who live there—or they perish.

*   *   *

As flying insects are hit by the windshields of our speeding automobiles, their intricate wings, legs, sensors, and bodies splash out as flat, yellow-green blobs. More than 50 percent by both volume and weight of the average physical structure and mechanics of all biological species consists of water. Humans' structuring and integral organic equipping is over 60 percent water. Earthians are hydraulically designed technologies.

All structures consist of a balanced interaction between tensive and compressive forces. Nature services all her tension functions rigidly with three crystalline, maximum-cohesion bonds, and services her compression-resisting functions with double-bonded, flexibly hinged, variously viscous hydraulics. These are noncompressible, but being flexible, they distribute their loads evenly to all the surfaces of their triple-bonded, tensional-container systems. As long as the triple-bonded tensional crystalline's containers are strong enough, the hydraulic structural system will hold its tensionally predesigned, optimally extended shapes because the contained liquids, which entirely fill the designed container, are noncompressible.

Because water is essential to all the biological organisms' ecological system of regeneration on our planet, the major facts about it are vitally relevant.

Vital fact number one (as already stated) is that biological life is 50 percent water.

Vital fact number two is that we don't know of any water in Universe other than that on our planet Earth. Almost three-quarters of the Earth's surface is covered with water. The water coverage averages in depth the length of a vertically suspended chain consisting of 2000 head-to-foot-linked humans. The world's oceans seem so deep to people that the amount of water in Universe is thought of by them as unlimited. But on a twelve-inch-diameter Earth globe the proportional depth of the ocean to Earth's diameter would be only three one-thousandths of an inch, which means that the absorption depth of the blue ink into the thin paper cover of the globe upon which the oceans are printed is far deeper in respect to the miniature Earth globe than is the real world ocean in respect to the real Earth's globe.

Vital fact number three is that water freezes and boils within close limits. Anywhere in Universe except inside Earth's biosphere the water (of which we too consist) would be either frozen, boiling, evaporated, or incandescent.

These facts integrate to tell us that our terrestrial biosphere is a unique environment essential to the survival of human organisms, not only on our planet, but anywhere within the thus-far-discovered Universe. To keep humans alive outside our biosphere requires reproducing and maintaining our exact biospherical conditions within a physically powerful and superbly insulated, into-space-rocketable container.

Before the continental networks of reinforced-concrete highways commenced half a century ago, human civilization, as seen from a low-flying airplane, was always strung out along the brooks, rivers, ponds, lakes, seas, and oceanfronts. Vast real estate developments and their underground-hidden, long-distance pipelines now tend to obscure this absolute dependence of humans upon water.

Vital fact number four is that water gains and loses heat more slowly than any other known profusely available substance. The South Pacific and Indian Ocean atolls were formed on the ocean-surface rims of both extinct and active volcanoes, broken through the ocean-bottom crust of the Earth. The volcanoes and the radiation from the Sun brought the water temperature to a level compatible with humans' normal 98.6 degrees Fahrenheit, and the tropical ocean's temperature was maintainable thereafter by the Sun alone. The world ocean's thermal stability keeps the world's temperature changes at minimum.

All humans in all history have always been born naked, helpless for months, hungry, thirsty, curious, and ignorant. They could not have survived if born where they would freeze, be dehydrated, or burn to death. The most logically propitious place for humans to survive and prosper within our planetary biosphere was on the coral atolls of the South Pacific and North Indian oceans. Here the barrier reefs effectively intercepted the great seas. The temperature of the almost-still water inside the lagoons was so compatible with life that head-above-water humans could stay in them continuously without any unfavorable effect. The lagoons abounded in fish, and there were mildly sloping, easy-to-walk-in-or-out-upon beaches of white sand. Crystal fresh waters poured down the mountainsides, and coconuts full of milk fell to the ground around the humans. Fruits were plentiful, and there were no wild animals threatening to eat the helpless baby humans.

Discovering that they themselves could not drink the salt water, these island-atoll people soon learned that the edible vegetation and fruits grew only from fresh water and Sunlight. Noting that the fresh water came either from the sky or from springs, the atollers came to invent shoal, freshwater-paddies-filling, parallelly contoured, intertiered-one-above-the-other terraces at human-waist-height distances above one another. This terraced water-ditching started high on the hillsides. Down and through this inter-dammed valving the fresh waters slowly flowed—so slowly as to usually appear to be motionless. Ultimately they leached into the sea.

The atollers made small and large freshwater vessels of animal skins, wood, and stone—vessels that held water inside and dug-out log vessels that excluded the water. Living half in the water, they became natural hydraulic inventors.

* * *

It is relevant to our speculative prehistory reviewing of all known clues that, in common only with water-dwelling mammals such as whales and porpoises, humans shed salt water tears, as do none of the other primates.

Marrying a fast-running horse with another fast-running horse increases the mathematical probability of "concentrating" the fast-running genes—ergo, has high probability of producing an even faster-running horse, which high-bred needs much care, having lost its general capability to cope with the wide range of hostile environmental events.

Through the mathematical probability consequent to sorting out and concentrating special behavioral-capability genes and isolated pairing and inbreeding of parents manifestly rich in those special physical capabilities, we humans have learned how to accomplish the development of ever-more-highly-specialized biological species. We note that inbreeding of special, frequently employed capabilities has always been accomplished only at the cost of outbreeding general adaptability to cope with the infrequently occurring, high-energy-concentrating events. Humans geographically isolated for many generations (for instance, in a high-mountains-enclosed valley), inevitably inbreed those of their numbers most successfully and lengthily surviving under those special environmental conditions because the surviving types are the only ones left with which to cohabitate. This automatically concentrates the most favorable genes for local survival. The highly inbred progeny become specialists in surviving under the locally prevailing special-environmental conditions.

We have no experimental evidence of successfully interbreeding highly divergent special biological species and their unique capabilities to produce completely effective general adaptability. If, on the other hand, we continued successively to inbreed generation after generation of champion Olympic gymnasts, we would soon come to super-inter-tree-jumping-and-swinging monkeys with no more intellectual talent and general-adaptability usefulness than that of the bright chimpanzees.

For this and other persuasive reasons my speculative prehistory has assumed (since 1927) Darwin's evolution of life from the simple to the complex, accomplished through progressive agglomeration of single-cell amoebas, to be in reverse of the facts.

When Darwin was a young man, at the time of the voyage of the *Beagle,* Dalton was among the world's leading physicists. Mendeleyev's periodic table of the elements had not as yet been conceived of. Dalton favored the concept that all atoms were produced by combinations of the hydrogen atoms. This concept and Darwin's single-cell concept fitted neatly into humanity's propensity for looking for "THE building block of the Universe"— people's imagination is childishly stimulated at the idea of finding "THE KEY." Spontaneously, we are simplistically inclined—it feeds the ego. "Oh, boy! If I had the key—what couldn't I do?"

Today it is eminently clear that human beings' physiological composition consists of a relative abundance of the ninety-two regenerative chemical elements' atoms similar to the relative abundance of chemical elements in Universe, which Universe consists of a plurality of individually unique generalized principles. In 1922 came physics' demonstration of a fundamental complementarity of inherently different components of physical phenomena. In 1956 the Nobel Prize in physics was given for the proof that the complementaries were not "mirror images"—one of the other. The number of chemical elements present in the amoeba will not accommodate the chemical elements' complexity of Universe. Universe is inherently complex and eternally regenerative. It can have no "beginning" or "ending." Vast numbers of scientists as yet labor vainly to account for the misconception of beginnings and endings. We have at minimum the neutron and the proton, which always and only coexist, the electron and the positron, the neutrino, antineutrino, and all. There is no single building block—there are only complexes of complex systems.

As the great mathematician Leonhard Euler discovered with his topology, all visual experiences consist of three inherently different and unique phenomena: (1) lines; (2) when lines cross, we get vertexes (corners, fixes, points); (3) when several lines intercross, we get an area (window or face), or, as we call them in synergetics: (1) trajectories, (2) crossings, (3) openings. (See §§ 1007.11–15, *Synergetics,* vol. 1; §§ 1007.22–31, *Synergetics,* vol. 2.) A system divides all of the Universe into (*a*) all of the Universe outside the system, (*b*) all of the Universe inside the system, and (*c*) the little bit of remaining Universe which comprises the system that separates the macrocosm from the microcosm. The minimum system of Universe (4) is com-

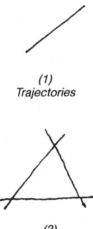

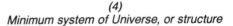

(1)
Trajectories

(2)
Crossings

(3)
Openings

(4)
Minimum system of Universe, or structure

FIGURE 2.

plex—four corners, four windows, and six edges. "Thank you, Euler—that will do, Darwin."

We see it as highly feasible to have telescanned from elsewhere in Universe the DNA-RNA-like coding of a complex angle-and-frequency programming together of terrestrially occurring chemical elements into their molecule-combining chemistries to successively produce a variety of species such as trilobites, dinosaurs, etc., as a progression of elsewhere-controlled Earth-landing tests. We see it as also highly feasible that these landings were used to discover the most suitable types of local-in-Universe information-harvesters and problem-solvers. The critical-limit experiences of the successive creature landings we see thereafter being sent back to some cosmic headquarters, thereby to guide the improvement of the design of the landings of thick-skinned creatures able to cope with greater annual temperature ranges than are humanly tolerable. And after further millions of years have passed and the environmental conditions have become auspicious, we see it becoming feasible to telescan the assembling of humans on Earth, thereafter inbreeding some of them into the ape stages.

We can comprehend how South Sea–atoll, lagoon-frolicking male and female human swimmers gradually inbred pairs of underwater swimmers who held their breath in their lungs for ever-longer periods, and after many inbreedings of largest lungers and as many outbreedings of general adaptability organic equipment, the progeny evolved into porpoises and later into whales.

Intimately relevant to these fundamental reorientings of our speculative prehistory of humans present aboard planet Earth, we have the following hard-fact scientific discoveries:

1. Vitamin D from Sunlight is essential to humans because milk-provided calcium is essential to the human bone structure. Vitamin D functions in the conversion of calcium into bone structure.
2. Humans synthesize vitamin D through the action of the Sun's ultraviolet rays on the skin. This biochemical function is a zoological counterpart of botanical photosynthesis of Sun radiation into hydrocarbon molecules.
3. But vitamin D is one of those vitamins of which humans can have an *overdose.*
4. In warmer and tropical climes, where vitamin D from the Sun is adequate or excessive, humans' subconsciously functioning organisms, employing their chemical process options, develop Sunlight filters in the skin consisting of darker and darker pigments, which prevent excess absorption of radiation and avoid the overdose of vitamin D.
5. Where there is not much Sunlight, as in the Far North, human organisms had to progressively remove their skin pigment filters, which left only blond skin permitting maximum synthesis of vitamin D from the Sun.
6. Vitamin D is not naturally present in most foods. The one food in which it is significantly present is whale blubber—a food of the Eskimos. Because of long periods of darkness and the large amounts of clothing the Eskimos wear to protect them from the cold, Sunlight-synthesized vitamin D is not available in enough quantity to the Eskimos.
7. The two chief, human-organism-supplied skin pigments that filter the Sun's rays are:
    Melanin: brown and black skin
    Carotin: oriental (yellow) skin*

In confirmation of all the foregoing we note the white and pink skin bottoms of the feet and palms of hands of otherwise dark or black-skinned individuals—white because not exposed to Sun and therefore unable to photosynthesize vitamin D from the Sun, therefore not protectively colored by melanin or carotin filters.

---

*See W. Farnsworth Loomis, "Skin Pigment Regulation of Vitamin D Biosynthesis in Man," *Science* (Aug. 4, 1967), vol. 157, pp. 501–506.

Biology demonstrates a botanical counterpart of the foregoing zoological Sun-utilizing and -filtering strategies for the Sun-intensity filtering strategies manifest in the Earth's hardwoods. The most northerly are white oak, southward of which we come to the pink oak and light-yellow birch. As we go farther south, we see the pink pearl maple and gray ash, then the deep red-yellow southern pine, south of which occur the brown mahoganies and dark-gray teak, and farther south the dark-brown rosewoods, with the spectrum change terminating at the Equator in the black ebony.

Compound this information with the fact that only for the last short decade in all of human history have we learned through incontrovertible scientific evidence that undernourishment of a child during its gestation in the womb or in its first year of life most frequently results in damage to the human brain. The damage may often be just a mild dulling or slowness of wit of an otherwise seemingly healthy human.

Throughout all known history the powerful fighting kings and noble stock reserved exclusively to themselves all animal flesh derived from their hunting. The poor people had to make do with the local roots, nuts, and fruits, which, due to vagaries of special environments, often contained a range of chemical ingredients inadequate to healthy nourishment. The animals, on the other hand, ate of the vegetation in general and of other animals' flesh, sum-totally acquiring a comprehensively broad input of the full gamut of chemistries essential to a healthy diet.

Karl Marx, bespeaking the workers, assumed the working class to be innately different from the noble class. He and the other defenders of the working class assumed that the workers and the nobles were of different organic and blood stock. The nobles also assumed this to be true and required that the nobles intermarry with other nobles. Both nobles and workers assumed that experience taught them that there is a fundamental inadequacy of life support in this world.

The workers' leaders assumed that the spontaneous familiarization of the workers with tools and farming made them the fittest to survive. They considered the nobles to be parasites. Finding themselves on the "top of the heap," the nobles assumed that their venturesomeness, wit, courage, muscle, and skill at arms had obviously rendered them the "fittest to survive." The workers' leaders assumed that if the workers could successfully organize themselves to be the class to survive, they must exterminate all those of the aristocratic blood.

Since the discovery that infantile undernourishment was alone responsible for the dulling of the human workers' brains, we have discovered that there is no organic blood class or species differentiation of humans. Compounding the latter information and that governing skin pigmentation, we discover that, by scientific evidence, there is neither race nor class differentiation of humans. All humans are of the same family.

All physiognomic and other physiological differentiations in human appearance are the exclusive consequences of multigenerations of unplanned inbreeding of those types that survived most successfully under unique environmental conditions, within which local geographies, tribes or nations dwelt for protracted periods. The U.S.S.R. had 146 different nations to integrate into their republic. Those "nations" had been geographically isolated and inbred so long that their local survival types looked physically different from members of the other nations.

* * *

We have had four known ice ages. They average a million years apiece. The intervals between them average a quarter of a million years. Together they cover a known total of four and three-quarter million years. The Leakey family's proofs of the presence of humans on our planet for over three million years take us back through two ice ages and two inter-ice-age intervals to the end of the second ice age.

As an ice age develops, more and more of the Earth's water is frozen, which greatly lowers the ocean level and reveals previously hidden, interconnecting land masses. At the time of the last ice age's occurrence the sea-hidden, interisland connections revealed themselves as continental isthmuses and peninsulas. The great islands of Java, Sumatra, Borneo, the Philippines, Sulawesi, and Bali became integral parts of the Malay Peninsula. New Guinea was part of continental Australia. Alaska and Siberia were connected.

The expanding ice mantle drove the northern continents' fur-skinned wild animals southward into the new peninsular *extensions* of the Asiatic mainland. The surprised once-islanded natives learned gradually to cope with these animals—hunted some, domesticated others (such as sheep and goats), and mounted, rode, or directed some, such as horses, mules, elephants, and water buffaloes. As the ice age withdrew, melting ice filled the oceans and seas, and the islands became once more isolated, but they were now inhabited with wild animals. Tigers as yet are found in western Bali.

At great mountain altitudes, where the temperatures were low, the ice caps remained, most notably on the High Himalaya range. In the vast ice cap of the Himalayas water melted to produce great rivers that flowed seaward from the five-mile-high frozen reservoir.

Because the atoll-incubated original human life had come naturally to invent rafts and boats that became their natural transport, when the waters receded they used those boats to bridge the increasing distance between the

once-interconnected lands. Boats being their natural transport, they dug canals into the muddy mainland coast as it became progressively uncovered.
Flying above the coast of Thailand and Cambodia today one can see the
myriad of geometrically neat ancient canals that penetrated their seacoast.

These two primitive conditions, (A) ocean water covering or permeating
the land and (B) the melted waters flowing seaward from the ice-topped
mountains, produced in the course of history two very different kinds of hy-
drocultures—those of the islanded sea-people and those of the inland and
upland traveled and settled people. The sea-people's major waters were
salty; the inland and upland peoples' major waters were fresh. The inland
people frequently came to fresh water, whereas the boat and island people
only infrequently came upon freshwater sources. The sea, boat, and island
people tended to anticipate their freshwater needs more than the inland and
mountain people.

The atoll people, it must be remembered, had an absolute necessity for
potable fresh water, and fortunately, from time to time, they found it cours-
ing down their mountainsides from high-altitude, rain-filled lakes. We note
that the island people were the original, planet-landed peoples who explored
widely with their paddled canoes and gradually settled inland and upland,
being able to cope with the mountain coldness because of their new animal-
skin clothing and tents fashioned from the skins of wild animals that
roamed into their peninsula-interbridged "islands" during the last ice age.

The great architectural feature of Bali is that of the narrow vertical gap

Bali—gateway

FIGURE 3.

in the gateways of their walled-in dwelling compounds, a gap they explain as representing the gap that occurred long ago between once-united Bali and Java. This occurred only 30,000 years ago, when the last ice age began to melt away and its waters once again separated the islands. The Balinese architectural legend-supported memory thus goes back 30,000 years.

Whenever I fly over Cambodia and Thailand and see the canal patterns penetrating for hundreds of miles into the land, I cannot suppress the intuition that, in addition to being the atoll-water-people's first entry into the main river mouths, these canals were also where these people began to work the mainlands. Having learned so much about hydraulic flows with the come and go of tides into island lagoons and basins, those first inland and upland paddlers were able to carry their hydraulic thinking up into the mainland hills and mountains.

Of course, the Sun also was always elevating fresh water into the sky, first by evaporation and then by "condensation" at the cold heights, whereafter gravity pulled it again earthward, distributing it over wide areas as wind-propelled rain clouds. "Condensation" is electrolytic.

The atoll-water-people learned millions of years ago that wood floated, that one log rolled over in the water, and that two logs with their branches intertwined no longer rolled in the water. From this they learned that two parallel logs properly boomed and tied together at a little distance not only produced a stable craft but one that, with the leaves of its branches sewn together and intuitively angled, would sail almost into the wind. In learning to tie their logs and spars together to withstand great strains imposed by winds and waves, those atoll people learned that triangles are the only structurally stable patterns for the interbracings, outriggings, and sparring of their sailing canoes and catamarans.

These fishing people had great need for strong baskets to contain their fish and other vital supplies when trafficking between islands—and later to capture and secure the animals when the latter invaded them during the ice ages. It is historically noteworthy that amongst all the South Pacific islands peoples and all the coastal peoples from Japan southward to Burma, all their baskets, small and large, are triangularly sixty-degree (three-way) woven, while all the basketry of all the rest of the world is square, or ninety-degree (two-way) woven. The sole exception is the three-way woven baskets found at the northern end of the Andes in South America just inland from where the Japanese current would have carried the water-peoples' drifting rafts.

None of these same water-people (as a great Austronesian observer, Austin Coates,* brilliantly discovered) understand the Western world's bank-

---

*Austin Coates, *Islands of the South* (London, Heinemann, 1974).

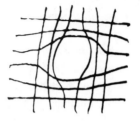

*Two-way weaves
are spreadable,
ergo distortable,
ergo unstable.*

FIGURE 4.   Two-way versus three-way weave.

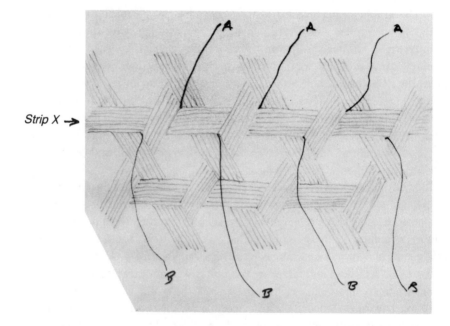

Strip X →

FIGURE 4a.   Strip *X* cannot be spread above *A* points nor lowered below *B* points—ergo, three-way weaves are unspreadable, therefore provide stable pattern and stable structure.

ing- and credit-financed business. As a consequence four Chinese families run all the banking businesses of Java and Sumatra and Indonesia in general. These Southeast Asians say the banker cannot lend them the wind before the wind blows. They are right, as the world's bankers are about to learn to the unprecedented discomfort of all humanity.

Everyone who has visited the rice cultures of Japan and Southeast Asia has witnessed the vast and meticulous hydraulic engineering of the mountain- and valley-side rice paddy system flowing horizontally and multidirectionally at each level as the waters are gradually brought seaward from great heights with never a chance missed to make foods and flowers grow along the way. These beautiful levelings and infinitely delicate controllings of water flow must have been of the greatest importance to human survival over many millennia, if not for millions of years.

* * *

Our "speculative prehistory" identifies the terraced rice paddy development as the most complete in the world, occurring as a consequence of there being boat and island people who have learned by experience the critical function fresh water plays in life. Their experience has taught them to become most anticipatorily effective through artifacts (the rice paddy being an artifact) in avoiding lack of fresh water. This leads to our prognostication that the next era of important anthropological research will occur in coral reefs.

Up to a decade ago archeologists, anthropologists, geologists, biologists, and historians of world-around affairs placed the beginnings of human life on Earth (and Scriptures' Garden of Eden) somewhere east of Suez, close to but aeons before ancient Babylon, which itself is in the heart of the great valley of the Tigris and Euphrates rivers in ancient Mesopotamia.

The historical experts assumed that humanity's graduation from the Stone Age into the Bronze Age also occurred in Asia Minor. This assumption rested largely on the copper found on the large, historically strategic island of Cyprus lying just off the eastern Mediterranean coast of Asia Minor.

The name "Cyprus" comes from the Latin *cuprus,* meaning "copper." Bronze, however, is made of copper *and* tin. Copper as a metal is soft and not very good for weapons or tools; so, too, is tin. Bronze is hard, resilient, and excellent for weapons and tools. Historians and archeologists seem to be extraordinarily poor metallurgists. Because early bronze items were found in Asia Minor in the vicinity of Cyprus, they misconcluded that it was there that the Bronze Age began. But the oldest metals-discovering, -developing, and -trading records known to humanity on our planet are the meticulously accurate data of the Phoenicians. Their detailed records tell us that they had to sail hundreds of miles westward out of the Mediterranean into the Atlantic and thence northward for more hundreds of miles to what we call today the British Isles to get the tin occurring exclusively on those islands, then bringing it back to Asia Minor, where it was combined with Cyprus copper to make bronze.

Until 1950 there is no historical record of humanity inventing metallurgical alloys. All metallurgical alloys have always been accidentally discovered. The alloys occur as symmetrically stable arrangements of atoms—invisible to naked human eyes—happen to come into critical proximity under the right heat conditions to produce their common liquidity. No one could foresee that combining soft copper with even softer tin could and would produce stiff, hard, resilient bronze. Tin and copper had to co-occur geologically in the same geographical area to be subject to accidental melting together.

To me it is absolutely impossible that the beginnings of the Bronze Age could have occurred in Asia Minor. That bronze was produced there tells us that some Asia Minor people learned about bronze-making from others, who earlier and elsewhere had discovered it accidentally. Overland caravans from the Orient to Asia Minor experienced the uses of bronze and learned that it was an alloy of copper and tin. Then, having learned from overseas explorers and traders that tin occurred in the British Isles, the Cyprus-neighboring Phoenicians set about to import it to Asia Minor. It was, incidentally, the tin in the British Isles that induced Julius Caesar to build a highway all the way from Rome to the English Channel and, thereafter, to settle Romans in England until the tin was nearly exhausted. In this connection it is importantly relevant to note that we now know that much earlier in history the Phoenicians navigated and traded the Indian Ocean and visited Thailand, which as we now know was where bronze was first produced.

Approximately seventeen years ago (1964) highly artful bronze castings were discovered in northeast Thailand, in an area called Ban Chiang. In that area tin and copper co-occur abundantly. There the two could have been melted together accidentally. In Ban Chiang we have found early pottery of unprecedented and artfully delighting design. This pottery required the magnitude of heat necessary to alloy copper and tin (both have low melting points). The same metallurgically naïve historians already mentioned had assumed the Bronze Age civilization to have traveled eastward from Asia Minor all the way to China. Thereafter the Chinese, whom those mistaken historians admit were very smart and apparently caught on fast to the cultural attainments of Asia Minor, swiftly developed a highly cultivated civilization of their own involving an enormous production of fine art bronzes.

Then, said yesterday's experts, the bronze artists of northern China found their way down into Southeast Asia—a region considered by them to be a cultural Johnnie-come-lately!

You cannot use carbon 14 to prove the age of bronzes, but in 1977 metallurgists discovered ways of dating the ages of bronzes. In 1975 the Thai government placed the diggings at Ban Chiang in the charge of the Museum of the University of Pennsylvania, with the latter's archeologist Dr. Chet Gorman in command. Dr. Gorman took many of the bronzes to Philadelphia and in due course developed ingenious means for arriving at the age of bronze objects—and did so to the satisfaction of metallurgical scientists in general. These proofs showed that the bronzes of Ban Chiang are the earliest known on planet Earth. This news was published on the front page of *The New York Times* in the summer of 1977. We now know that the Bronze Age began in Southeast Asia. This reversal of historical theory greatly enhances our own speculative hypothesis that humanity originated in the Austronesian islands and came out into the (Asian) mainland in separate stages, each occurring after one of the last ice ages. This reversal of the basic history of civilization also lends further credence to my reversed Darwinian theory of evolution on planet Earth.

* * *

The last human exodus from the islands of Austronesia onto the mainland occurred after the last ice age, about 30,000 years ago. On the first such exodus, two ice ages ago (which was two and one-half million years ago), those humans who had mastered horses mounted them and, leaving their on-foot rice-growing, sheep-and-goat-herding, and on-foot hunting brethren behind, rode northwest to hunt wild animals, until the next ice age forced them to endure survival in caves of nonglaciated Western Europe. With skin and hair all bleached they emerged and mounted horses 30,000 years ago to confront the westward on-foot or on-camel caravaning of the earliest Egyptian and Mesopotamian civilizations of written history. The latter civilization probably developed from the Indian Ocean and Austronesian island-atoll people blown westward on rafts to (A) Queen Hatshepsut's source of pitches for her Egyptian shipbuilding, which source the Egyptians called the "Land of Pun"—which we now know to have been Somaliland (the Leakeys' Olduvai Gorge country)—and (B) to Arabia, blown by the tween-monsoon easterlies of the Indian Ocean and the Arabian Sea. (The word *pun* in South African coloreds' language means "red"—the Red Sea is the Pun Sea, the *Pun* as the *Pun* of Pun-icians, or later Phoenicians, of Carthage's and Rome's Pun-ic Wars.)

If you look at my Dymaxion World Map (in which, as we have noted be-

FIGURE 5. Dymaxion Map with 100 Population Dots

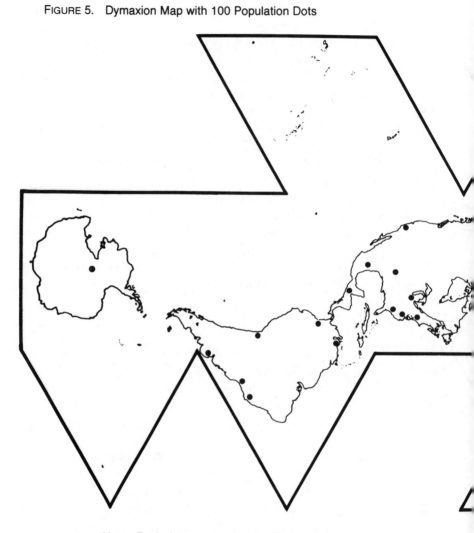

Note: Each dot represents 44 million people

South America	6%
Central America	1%
North America	7%
Africa	11%
Europe	16%
Asia (Land 54%, Water 7%)	61%

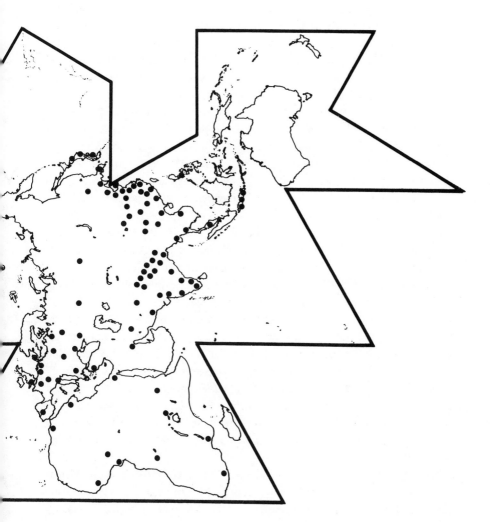

fore, there is no visible distortion of the relative shape or size of any of the
land or water patterning), you will find one hundred dots, each representing
1 percent of humanity as of 1980 A.D.; that is, each dot represents forty-
four million human beings. Each 1 percent is carefully located in the demographic center of each forty-four-million grouping of the Earth's total
people. You can see on my map that within an area that is only about 8
percent of the Earth's total surface, known as the Orient (which contains
India, China, and Southeast Asia), 54 percent of humanity exists; of this 54
percent, 8 percent are the as-yet-islanded (or peninsulaed) water-people: Japan, 3 percent; Philippines, 1 percent; Java, Sumatra, etc., 3 percent; Singapore and the lower Malay Peninsula, 1 percent. Going on the globe
westward, "following the Sun" and facing into the prevailing north and
southwesterly winds, we observe Asia Minor, Africa, and Europe with
32 percent, and then "the West," the Americas, with 14 percent of all humanity.

Kipling wrote in 1900, "East is East, and West is West, and never the
twain shall meet." All who read him thought Kipling was obviously correct.
No one in 1900 could foresee the as-yet-uninvented airplanes, let alone 350-
passenger-carrying, 500-mph, intercontinental and around-the-world-flying
jet airplanes, nor satellite-relayed intercontinental telephony, etc.

You can see on my map the enormous concentration of humanity in Java,
Malaysia, and the Indonesian islands, as well as along the original "waterfront" areas of the Asian mainland. Together Burma, Thailand, Cambodia,
Laos, and Vietnam are the beachheads of Austronesian islanders "landing"
upon the Asian continent. Clearly that is where humanity first went inland
and upland to the Himalayas, exploring the Mekong River toward its
source. This extraordinary fact relates also to the last ice age and uniquely
to the 8 percent of my world map known as the Orient, which contains the
54 percent of humanity.

Looking closely at this area we see the Indus River rising in the Himalayas and flowing westward to Karachi and then into the Arabian Sea.
Then, starting in almost the same High Himalayan place as the Indus, we
see the Ganges flowing initially westward, then turning eastward and flowing south of the Himalayas to the Bay of Bengal. Next we note the Brah-
maputra River, originating within 100 miles of the sources of the Indus and
Ganges and flowing first eastward, then southward, to penetrate the Himalayas, whence it flows also to the Bay of Bengal. Then we note the Sal-
ween, the Mekong, the Yangtze, and the Yellow rivers, all starting from
approximately the same geographical source atop the Himalaya Mountains
(an area so small that my forefinger tip can cover it on my map). Thus 54
percent of humanity (over eight times the population of North America) is

"watered" from the same "reservoir"—the frozen Himalayan reservoir, which melts just fast enough to keep things growing and life going on through ages and ages and ages.

As the water-people came out of the ocean-island habitats and began to ascend those rivers and "carried aloft" their "canoes" around and above the rapids and waterfalls, they could not help eventually discovering the common regional source of this comprehensive life-support water.

In the present critical unrest of our world, where we find the greatest ideologically warring powers on our planet puppeting, through Vietnam, the dissensions into warrings of Cambodians, Laotians, Thais, and Burmese, it is clearly seen that the only differences between those Southeast Asian peoples are the rivers by which they go inland and upland—to the same source of life-supporting water. It is easy to understand why the Dalai Lama was located in Tibet, at the source of all their water. That source epitomized God as the physical life-giver and -taker.

* * *

Looking at Southeast Asia on a metallurgical resource display map and coming north in the Gulf of Siam to the mouth of the Chao Phraya River, we note that in the Malay Peninsula there are vast amounts of tin ore all the way from Singapore to Burma and northward inland in Thailand along the Chao Phraya River to northern Thailand. Then, altering our direction, we go a short way eastward and descend from the mountains of Laos, which are everywhere rich in copper ore. Everywhere along the east bank of the Chao Phraya River lies copper ore, and everywhere along its west bank lies tin ore.

At Bangkok, on the Chao Phraya River, I find the most extraordinary history of the development of wooden boatbuilding as yet manifest on our planet. I remember how back in 1958, as I went along canals leading off from the Chao Phraya River, I kept discovering shipyards. In all America there are less than fifty boatbuilding yards now in operation. But in Greater Bangkok alone I saw more than 100 boatyards.

To the boatyards of the Chao Phraya River and its canals the logging people inland and upstream bring seaward (with the current and tides) great teak logs, which are towed together in enormous intertied rafts. As we get into the Bangkok region, we see the great teak log rafts moored wherever there is spare waterfront.

The shipbuilders usually keep the logs soaking for up to 100 years before using them in their ships' hulls. After a century of soaking the teak becomes highly stabilized structurally. They then haul out and dry the logs sufficiently for their shipbuilders to work them into long planks and frames with their

metal tools. In all my boatbuilding experience—of which I have had a lot—
I have not found any craftsman sawing out long, delicately curved ship's
plankings and planing them with greater accuracy than in Bangkok. They
make their planks so carefully that they fit watertightly together without
any caulking. They dry the teak just enough to fashion it into ship's planks,
but the minute the ships are launched (for instance, as great rice-freighting
hulls), enough moisture gets back into the wood to swell the planks watertightly together. (What also fascinates is the incredible amount of rice being
brought out to feed civilization—stored sometimes for months in boats' bel-
lyholds, which are absolutely *dry-tight and never painted.*)

The Thais have had thousands of years of such boatbuilding experience.
The entire evolutionary history of great boatbuilding is as yet manifestly
alive on the Chao Phraya River. Every instance of the progressive stages of
its evolution—from watertight teak bins mounted on rafts to the big-ribbed,
deep-belly ships found in use there today—is in live operation.

Anyone who is a sailor knows that ships have to have powerful and enduring fastenings of many kinds—nails, screws, and rivets—to hold fast the
teak planking to the ribs, and myriads of rope cleatings, chain plates, etc.
Nothing could better serve as fastenings than nonrusting bronze. Those
Thai sailors and boatbuilders were the first to accidentally marry copper
and tin to produce bronze and thereafter to use it purposefully in shipbuilding. Copper's first great structural functioning came when combined with
tin as bronze fastenings in ships.

I am absolutely confident that Bangkok is the center of the beginnings of
the best ship technology and design engineering of world-around civilization. Prototypes of every type of hull from gondolas to barges are there, including the prototypes of the powerfully ribbed, deep-bellied ships that the
Phoenicians sailed across the Indian Ocean and to Mesopotamia, where the
"Garden of Eden" story is played. When they attained big-rib ships, their
sailors went readily out to sea whence their islanded forebears came. These
improvements allowed them to go more directly into the wind. They could
"beat" at a twenty-two-and-one-half-degree angle either side of the wind
and "work to windward" rapidly.

The sea-going traffic extended at first to the Malay Straits, then spread
out into the Indian Ocean. As the interchange between different nationalities increased, so also each began to copy the best features of the others'
craft. The ships became composites of the sum-total experience gained
throughout that general area. The merchants moved westward into the Indian Ocean (which has reverse winds during the monsoon), but by this time
they could go counter to the breeze.

Thus it was that the dhow of the western Indian Ocean reached the Persian Gulf, the Red Sea, and the east coast of Africa. The men who as yet handle these dhows are extraordinary. They assume that their trade has been in continuous existence for at least 10,000 years. Their navigation must be meticulous. Considering the period that it would of necessity take to develop such vessels as theirs and to establish such a circulation, there is no reason at all to doubt their estimates.

Among ships the dhow still sails the sharpest angle into the wind. This is the advantage of the triangular lateen sail, with its long spar attached to its short mast in such a manner that their angle of incidence is forty-five degrees. The front of the spar is heavier than the rear end, which projects into the sky. The balance is so exacting, however, that the sheeting does not have to be very rigid and the mast can act as a fulcrum.

The dhow enabled sailors to go against the wind to a greater degree than they had ever done before. They could now sail to westward over great distances—against prevailing currents. Out of this remarkable skill came a new phase of "world" seafarers. No longer subject to the vagaries of the elements, they could make headway against them.

After many thousands of years eastbound man became westbound. The former gave rise to the Eastern philosophy of "acceptance," which still persists. The latter was a new development and fundamentally altered humanity's thinking. To the sailor God seems to be the prevailing winds and currents that carry one in a particular direction. To go against the wind or current, to "beat to windward," is therefore a deliberate act against Him. Here began a concept of man being contrary to his God.

In the early drifting-with-the-current-and-prevailing-wind days a large migrating of humanity occurred within the Pacific. The rafting colonists were swept along the coast of China into the Bering Straits by the Japan Current. There a bridge of land between the continents contributed considerably to the overland migration from the Orient to the coast of North America. The Japan Current carried the rafters to Alaska. It carried them to Mexico and Central America. It carried them to Colombia, Bolivia, and Peru. Thereafter the same current swept them back westward across the Pacific back to Austronesia, as Thor Heyerdahl proved with his raft *Kon Tiki*.

As sailing-into-the-wind people headed westward from the Malay Straits, they crossed the Indian Ocean, arriving in Mesopotamia and on the east coast of Africa. From there they traveled overland to the Nile. Over 10,000 years of continuous voyaging across the Indian Ocean by the dhow sea captains evidences the deep-bellied, heavily keeled and ribbed engineering of their craft and its seaworthiness—and locates the origins of sea technology in the area of Ban Chiang.

All civilization had its origins in the network of maritime interlinkages

FIGURE 6.   Dhow—ship with a continuous 10,000-year history of Indian Ocean crossings.

of early cultures. Tension-capability is newly manifest in seagoing-born tensional skill and intellectual capability. Compressional capability is manifest of the land-born stone ages and the inertia of stone walls. At sea humanity entered into true technology—that of powerful tension-interfastening capability. Bangkok itself is the prototype of all canal cities developed by later water-people around the world—for example, Venice and Amsterdam. Sampans are prototypes of Venetian gondolas later brought, covered, by the Phoenicians to Venice. (See map, page 42.) Bangkok seems to be the prototyping locale of the big-keel, big-ribbed, deep-bellied ships of both the China Sea and the Indian Ocean.

CHAPTER 2

Humans in Universe

B EFORE THE PICTORIALLY GRAPHIC RECORD of the presence of human-ity aboard our planet began, there was no way for individuals to record their feelings and thoughts except as manifest in their tool-inventing. People must have been in critical life-sustaining need to have invented words. Words are tools, but their sounds could not be made to last under early history's conditions. Individually identifiable humans had no line of communication reaching directly to us today, other than the evidence of humanity's massive group work in carving, shaping, and building with stones, plus the nonidentifiable individual's profuse handicrafting of small artifacts such as pottery, arrowheads, and beads.

From the beginning of the pictorially recorded history—on walls, vases, jewelry—we gain more and more information regarding general human experiences, capabilities, thoughts, and motivations. For instance, it is evidenced that throughout all earlier times until yesterday, the ruling social powers assumed the human masses to be universally ignorant and accredited them with having only muscle and dexterity value. The illiteracy of the masses was mistakenly interpreted as meaning that the commoner was inherently lacking in intellect—just a "poor wretch." As "the exception that proved the rule," once in a rare while—by command of some "god"—a commoner apparently was endowed with creative powers and insights. The ease with which the erroneous assumption could be made that the masses are *stupid* is manifest when we realize how easily present-day humans, conditioned to speak only Americanese, could deceive themselves into mistaking for an "inherently illiterate Mongol" an ill-clothed, war-bruised, Chinese communist Ph.D. physicist, unable to speak Americanese or the local dialect.

During only the last few decades of the three and a half million years within which humans now are known to have been living aboard our planet Earth have the behavioral clues been increasingly sufficient to suggest that all humans, including the assumed-to-be "illiterates" and "spastics," are born with a comprehensive and superb inventory of subjectively apprehending and synergetically comprehending faculties—as well as objectively articulating capabilities. This has not yet been formally acknowledged to be the case by the present educational establishments' "capability accrediting boards." Awareness of the foregoing has not as yet dawned amongst the politico-social pressure groups such as the labor unions, veterans' organizations, or parent-teacher associations.

We may soon discover that all babies are born geniuses and only become degeniused by the erosive effects of unthinkingly maintained false assumptions of the grown-ups, with their conventional ways of "bringing up" and "educating" their young. We now know that schools are the least favorable environment for learning. The home TV is far more effective, but we are allowing the big money-making advertisers to poison the information children assimilate in their four to five hours a day of spontaneous turning-on, looking at and listening to the TV.

It is possible to identify some of the known faculties that we generally assumed to be coordinate in those whom society does concede to be adult geniuses. The publicly accredited characteristics of genius consist, for instance, of an actively self-attended intuition. The intuition, in turn, opens the conceptual and perceptual doors. With those doors self-opened, the innate faculties frequently combine and employ the individual's scientific, artistic, philosophical, and idealistic imaginings in producing physically talented, logical, far-sighted, and practical articulations. Leonardo da Vinci, who fortunately weathered the genius-eroding susceptibilities of childhood, manifested and coordinatingly employed all and more of such conceptual faculties and articulative capabilities.

In the graphically recorded history of the last eight millennia, as well as in the dim twilight of pre-Indo-Chinese, Mesopotamian, Egyptian, and South and Central American graphic documentations of history, there have appeared, from time to time, individuals who grew to maturity without losing the full inventory of their innate, intuitive, and spontaneously coordinate faculties. These unscathed individuals inaugurated whole new eras of physical environmental transformation so important as, in due course, to affect the lives of all ensuing humanity. We shall hereafter identify such unscathed, comprehensively effective, and largely unidentified individual articulators as the artist-scientists of history.

Since the dawn of the most meagerly revealed human history there have been a number of importantly distinct periods of historical transformation of both the physical and cosmological environments of society. Each of these eras has been opened by the artist-scientist. The invisible power structures behind-the-visible-king first patronize and help to develop the artist-scientists' advanced-environment breakthroughs, but always go on, ever more selfishly, to overexploit the breakthroughs.

The environment—everything that is "not me"—is subdivisible into two parts, physical and metaphysical. The metaphysical environment consists of human thoughts, generalized principles and customs. The artist-scientist types seem to have avoided attempting to reform the metaphysical environment. They are documented only by their employment of the cosmic laws—generalized principles—to reorganize the *physical* constituents of the livingry and the scenery. The artist-scientists apparently assumed intuitively that a more man-favoring rearrangement of the environment would be conducive to humanity's spontaneous self-realization of its higher potentials. Human travelers coming to a river and finding a bridge across it spontaneously use the bridge instead of hazarding themselves in the torrents.

Scientist-artists originally conceived and designed the bridges. The power-structure-behind-the-king, seeing great exploitability of the bridge for their own advantaging, accredited the workers and materials to build the bridges.

Physiology and biology make it clear that at the outset of graphically recorded history a universally illiterate—but probably *not* unintelligent—humanity was endowed with innate and spontaneously self-regenerative drives of hunger, thirst, and species regeneration. The a priori chemical, electromagnetic, atomistic, genetic, and synergetic designing of these innate drives apparently was instituted by a wisdom—a formulative capability inherent in Universe—higher than that possessed by any known living humans. These drives probably were designed into humans to ensure that human life and the human mind—long unacknowledged as humanity's highest faculty—ultimately would discover its own significance and would become established and most importantly operative not only aboard planet Earth, but also in respect to vast, locally evidenced aspects of Universe. As such, mind may come not only to demonstrate supremacy over humanity's physical muscle but also to render forevermore utterly innocuous and impotent the muscle-augmented weapons and the latter's ballistic hitting powers. Mind possibly may serve as the essential, anti-entropic (syntropic) function for eternally conserving the omni-interaccommodative, nonsimultaneous, and only partially overlapping, omni-intertransforming, self-regenerating scenario—which we speak of as "Universe."

Mind, operative aboard our planet Earth and probably elsewhere in Universe in a myriad of effective circumstances, can and may perform the paramount function of conserving the scenario "Universe." If so, it will have to be accomplished by apprehending, comprehending, and teleologically employing the metaphysical, weightless, omni-intercooperative generalized principles of Universe in strategically effective degree and within a critical time limit.

This can be accomplished in progressively more effective ways—for instance, by Earthians competently "fielding" all those physical energy increments entropically broadcast by the stars, which happen to impinge kinetically upon our Earth as it orbits the Sun. Employing the appropriate biological and physiological principles, these receipts must be collected, sorted, analyzed, synergetically comprehended, and symmetrically combined into complex but orderly, macro-and-micro-cohering aggregates. Therewith, they must be added into the Earth biosphere's resource-conserving and -storing inventory. It is seemingly manifest by the comprehensively considered record that the task of metaphysical intellect is to cooperate with evolution as a major syntropic factor by collecting, sorting, and symmetrically combining information into ever more advantageous and orderly patterns, i.e., designs, to offset the physical Universe's macrocosmic proclivities of becoming locally ever more dissynchronous, asymmetric, diffuse, and multiplyingly expansive.

The kinetic intercomplementarity of finite Universe requires that what disassociates here must associate there—and also there. High-pressure conditions at one point are balanced by low pressures elsewhere. The stars are all radiantly dissipating energy. The Earth, however, is a celestial center where energies from the stars are being collected and photosynthetically combined in an orderly molecular assembly as hydrocarbons, which are consumed by orderly designed species, and then self-multiply to make these biological species grow, undergo transformations, and eventually be buried deeply beneath the Earth's surface. When, after many billions of years, enough orderly-molecule energy has been impounded aboard our spherical space vehicle Earth, the Earth itself will become a radiant star, as the discards of other burned-out and dissipated stars are concurrently aggregated in billions of local elsewheres—some trillions of years hence also to become stars.

No factor operative aboard our planet is so effective in aggregating, reorganizing, concentrating, and refining the disorderly, random resource receipts as is the human mind. Human mind has discovered a number of cosmic laws—generalized scientific principles. Objectively employing a plurality of the cosmic laws, human mind developed the computer, whose combined information storage and retrieval vastly augmented human brain's information storing, retrieving, and formulative disclosings—ergo, magnificently augmenting human mind's local Universe problem-solving task and rendering that cosmic functioning of human mind highly effective.

Mathematics constitutes human mind's most cosmically powerful faculty. How did human mind develop progressively its mathematical functioning?

* * *

Trigonometry had to start with sea-people. It is the conclusion of British, German, and U.S.A. navies' experts that celestial—offshore—navigation began with the South Pacific's island peoples. Much has been published on this subject. What is not as well published is the fact that the navigators on all those islands live entirely apart from the other humans in their native groups.

When the supposedly God-ordained chieftain of those islands finds his prestige and popular credence declining, he can go to the navigator and ask him to produce a miracle. The chieftain does not know of the navigator as such. The chieftain knows naught of navigation. He thinks of the navigator as a magician or miracle-maker. All the chieftain knows is that his miracle-producer goes off to sea sailing his catamaran out of sight on the ocean. The navigator, using his well remembered, unique patternings of the stars and the ocean currents, water temperatures, and major "old-seas" patterns, goes to another far-off island where there exist shells or trees or stones or other items such as have never been and probably never will be found on the home island. The navigator brings this foreign item back to the island king-chieftain, who displays it before the people, who spontaneously assume that the chieftain has conjured the strange object into existence with his divine powers—and the chieftain's accreditation as being divinely instituted is restored.

We can now comprehend the succession of events by which, generations later, prehistory's successors of the ancient navigators eventually became the high priests of Egypt, Babylon, and other great civilizations. Both their evolutingly developed mathematical calculating capability and their navigational intuiting ultimately led to their discovery that the Earth is a circumnavigatable sphere. This knowledge made them more powerful than the physically powerful fighting kings.

Offshore, with no familiar landmarks to guide them, early water-peoples learned through necessity and invention how to sail their ships on courses running between any two well-recognized stars co-occurring diametrically opposite one another above the sky's circular horizon at various given times of the night and reliably reappearing in the same pattern in any geographical area on any given day of the year. Any two prominent, easy-to-recognize stars in the sky gave the unique course for the ship to follow. The point on the mast, B, at which the bright star in the sky toward which they sailed occurred at any given time of observation, and the point C, at which the boom of their sail contacted the mast, and the point A, at which the stern-

standing or -sitting helmsman's eye occurs, gave the three corner points of
a right triangle whose three angles, A, B, and C, always sum-totalled 180
degrees. This 180-degree sum-total angular constancy of any plane triangle
formed the basis of all *plane trigonometry.*

If one of the three angles of a triangle is a right angle, then all the variation takes place only between the two other angles, whose angular sum will
always equal that of the constant right angle (ninety degrees).

With their ship's (or raft's) masts mounted perpendicularly (at right angles, vertically) to their ship's or hull's waterline, they steered the ship at
night by keeping the mast always lined on the approached star—as long as
the Earth's rotation allowed the sight of that star to remain in a usable
line of sight. The angle of elevation of the approached star could be sightingly measured by the helmsman observing, from the stern, the star's ever-
changing height on the mast as sightingly identified, for instance, by the
mast's sail-luff rings, which elevation altered as the Earth revolved during
the night within the spheric array of Universe stars. With days, months,
years, and lifetimes of such observing, measuring, and calculating, the sea-
people gradually evolved trigonometry. (See Fig. 7.)

Their ten fingers and ten toes, the ankles of their two legs, the slender
wrists of their two arms and their necks served as rods on which to slide
bracelets or necklaces or rings of bone, rope, bent wood, or dried seaweed.
The number of bracelets on their right-side ankles, wrists, and fingers could
be made to correspond to the human-foot-length-spaced-apart vertical intervals on their masts occurring between the rings holding their sails to the
mast, and the number of bracelets on their left-side ankles, wrists, and fingers could be made to correspond to the number of ribs of their ship, which
also occurred horizontally a foot-length apart, between the foot of the mast
and where the observing helmsman sat in the stern of the ship or raft. That's
one of the ways in which sailors learned how to calculate the relative lengths
of the two right-angle-forming edges of their triangular sail. The right angle
of their triangle occurred between the mast and the ship's horizontal plane.
The vertical and horizontal lines represented the two measurable sides *a* and
b of the right triangle.

You and I learned at school that if we multiply a number by itself we obtain the second power of that number ($N \times N = N^2$). We also learned that
the sum of the second power of sides *a* and *b* of our right triangle always
equals the second power of the third side *c*—the hypotenuse of our right triangle.

With this information and the ankle, wrist, and finger rings with which
to multiply and divide, the sailor-navigator could learn the exact lengths of
all three edges of his right triangle, and he soon learned that the angles opposite each edge of the triangle were proportioned to the angles opposite

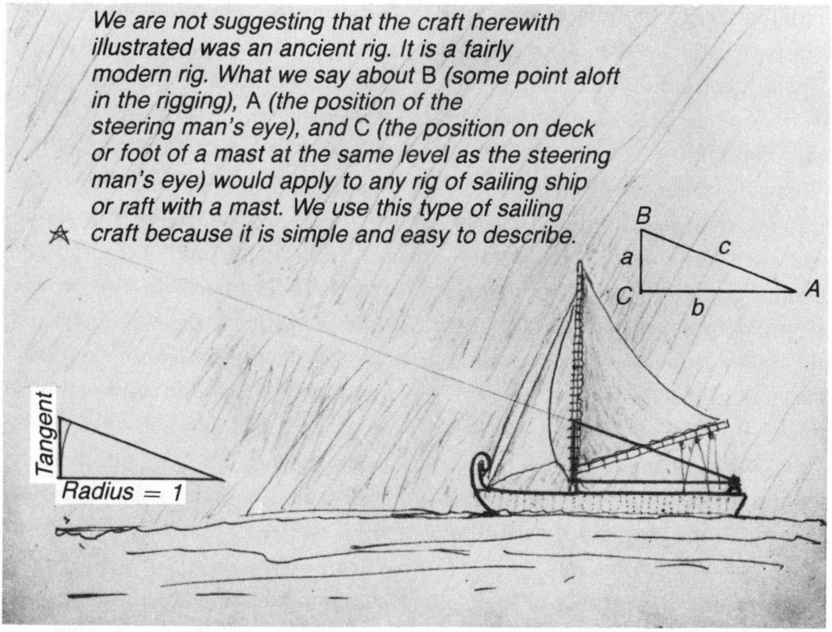

We are not suggesting that the craft herewith
illustrated was an ancient rig. It is a fairly
modern rig. What we say about B (some point aloft
in the rigging), A (the position of the
steering man's eye), and C (the position on deck
or foot of a mast at the same level as the steering
man's eye) would apply to any rig of sailing ship
or raft with a mast. We use this type of sailing
craft because it is simple and easy to describe.

FIGURE 7.   Using Ship Mast for Navigational Trigonometry.

them ($A/a = B/b = C/c$). Thus, these sailor-navigators learned of the constancy of the angle above the horizon of any given observed star as seen from any given geographical position at any given time of any given night of the year. From these crude beginnings they gradually evolved formalized frames of shell beads mounted slidably on wooden rods with which to record their observed measurement numbers and to carry out the calculations. These devices eventually developed into the abacus, with which they could swiftly multiply and divide.

The earliest sailor-navigators also made complex ocean maps by superimposing straight bamboo sticks on one another, horizontally in a flat plane, each stick representing the North-Star-referenced ocean-course direction running between any two known geographical points as progressively referenced to the prominent star points visible at the beginning of their voyage. The complex of sticks showed the relative angular interrelationships of the different ocean courses running between the well-known stars sightable above the circular horizon and opposite one another.

In its westward voyaging-trendings from its South Pacific and Indian

Ocean beginnings (among water-peoples) to overland traveling in India and caravaning in China and Southeast Asia, mathematics gradually lost much of its earlier natural cosmic grandeur and that grandeur's intuition-inspiring discovery of relevant environment interrelationships.

Subsequently the abacus provided a facile means of accumulating progressive products of multiplication by moving those products ever further leftward, column-by-column, as the operator filled the available bead spaces one by one and moved the excess over ten into the successive right-to-leftward columns.

Obviously, number products in even tens (such as the number 20) leave the first right-hand column empty. When the expert abacus-user lost his abacus overboard or by accidental burial in the desert sand, he could remember and visualize its operation so clearly that all he needed to know was the problem-developed content of each column in order to develop any multiplication or division. He then invented symbols for the content of each column to replace drawing a picture of the number of beads—the symbol 3 was quicker than making three pictures. Having developed symbols to express the contents of each column, he had to invent a symbol for the numberless content of the empty column—that symbol became known to the Arabs as the *sifr;* to the Romans as *cifra;* and to the English as *cipher* (our modern zero).

Prior to the appearance of the cipher, Roman numerals had been invented to enable completely illiterate servants to keep "scores" of one-by-one occurring events—for example, a man would stand by a gate and make a mark every time a lamb was driven through the lamb-size gate. The more complex Roman numerals were those used by the supervisors, keeping count by their fingers—a V for five (the angle between his thumb and the other four fingers) and X for ten (representing the supervisor's crossed index fingers.) Since one cannot see "no sheep" and cannot eat "no sheep," the Roman world seemingly had no need for a symbol for nothing. Only an abacus's empty column could produce the human experience that called for the invention of the *ciphra*—the symbol for "nothing."

When I first attended school, the older tradespeople in my town—the drugstore man, the butcher, the hardware man—who had known me since my babyhood and were my natural friends, each asked me, "Have you learned to do your ciphers yet?" The discovery of the symbol for nothing became everything to humanity. The cipher alone made possible humanity's escape from the 1700-year monopoly of all its calculating functions by the power structure operating invisibly behind the church's ordained few.

The from-the-Indian-Ocean-landed navigator-priests' 3000 B.C. Babylonian geometry is spherical—omnidirectional. Apparently seeking to discover nature's time-inclusive, four-dimensionally comprehensive, mathematical coordinate system, the Babylonians failed only in their early attempt to correlate their 360-degree great circle's central-angle-determined arcs' subdivisions into degrees, minutes, and seconds with time's hours, minutes, and seconds, but they did discover that the cosmically generalized, closed-spherical-surface system was maximally divisible into 120 spherical right triangles, 60 positive and 60 negative. This greatest-common-denominator sixtyness probably occasioned the Babylonians' adoption of 60 minutes and 60 seconds as the arithmetically absolute, numerically maximum common divisor of all finite systems and of their subsystems. It was factorable by all four of the first prime numbers, 1, 2, 3, 5.

For reasons unknown to us a retrogression in mathematical conceptioning emerges, possibly as a consequence of the navigator-priests foreseeing that their power would deteriorate if the kings or other people caught on to too much of their calculating capability. Egypt's artists visually portrayed all humans and animals only as one-plane, flat silhouettes. In a similar way the Greek and Egyptian geometers—as, for instance, Euclid in 300 B.C.— retrogressed into two-dimensional plane geometry from the Babylonians' omnidimensional, finite-system, experience-invoked time dimension. The Greeks and Egyptians became concerned only with omnilaterally, infinitely extensible plane geometry and its "square"-unit of areal subdivision. Superimposed upon this plane, two-dimensional base the Greek and Egyptian geometers subsequently developed a timeless, weightless, temperatureless, three-dimensional, cubical coordinate system whose squares and cubes were geometrically irreconcilable with a spherical Earth and all the other radiationally and gravitationally divergent-convergent, inherently nucleated, finite, spherical systems' growths and shrinkages—electromagnetic and acoustical, spherically gradient wave propagations.

All geometrical proofs of the Euclidean Greeks had to originate in the two-dimensional plane geometry and not in the three-dimensional configuration or four-dimensional temperatured, weighted, and lengthed reality.

While some individual scholars were evolving their geometry, others were evolving nongeometrical methods of communication.

The ability of humans to write in vertical or horizontal lines of symbolic forms—i.e., Tartarian picto-linguistic, hieroglyphics, cuneiform, Linear A, Linear B, and so on—required great expertise and was not commonly useful. In 1500 B.C. the Phoenicians invented letters for each known mouth-and-lungs-articulated sound. Having developed phonetic pronunciation of each letter, they therefrom evolved combined pronunciation of each word. Five hundred years later, in 1000 B.C., the Greek language, employing the Phoenician phonetic spelling concept, developed the twenty-four pronounceable letters which are the same as those used in the Greek writing of present-day—late-twentieth-century-A.D.—Greece. This phonetic form made practical the individual scientists' own recording of their own thoughts as well as the thoughts of others.

As yet convergently-divergently omniconsiderate, in the manner of the Babylonians, and thinking microcosmically, the Greek Democritus in 460 B.C. was the first known human to conceive of a smallest cosmic entity. He named it the "atom."

Thinking macrocosmically, the Greek Pythagorean scientists of 600 to 400 B.C., situated to the north of Athens, were the first people known and recorded to think of our world as a spherical entity. In 410 B.C. the Pythagorean Philolaeus was the first to describe the Earth as a spherical body in motion around a central cosmic fire. He also conceived of the stars, the Sun, the Moon, and five planets—Venus, Mercury, Mars, Jupiter, and Saturn— as spherical bodies. His Sun was not at the center of the planetary system's motion. There is a possibility that he was thinking in galactic, rather than in solar-centered, terms.

In 350 B.C. the latter-day Pythagorean Heraclides was the first to conceive of the Earth sphere as spinning west to east. But Heraclides' cosmos was as yet geocentric. His Earth spun at the center of the fixed-stars Universe.

Another Greek, Aristarchus, conceived around 200 B.C. of the spherical Sun as the center of the spherical planets' orbital system as each planet revolved individually around its own axis at its own unique rate while also orbiting the Sun in greater orbital time periods. For him all the stars were fixed, and the Moon revolved around the Earth. His unprecedented thoughts almost got him killed.

Eratosthenes, in 200 B.C., measuringly calculated the circumference of Earth within 1.5-percent accuracy. He also made a map of the world running from clearly identifiable England on the northwest to the (not so convincingly identified) mouth of the Ganges in the southeast. His map included all of Africa on the south (with a reasonably accurate foreshortened profiling of South Africa, which outline could not have been included by him had not such an around-Africa-voyaging been already accomplished and reported).

It was also around 200 B.C.—as we learned authoritatively only five years ago—that the Phoenicians sailed from the Aegean Sea to both the east and west coasts of South America. Because of the prevailing winds the west coast of South America would be much more naturally reached from the Mediterranean by first sailing southward, rounding the southern tip of Africa, crossing the Indian Ocean northeastwardly on its main current to pass just north of Australia, then turning northward with the Japan Current and the prevailing winds to transit China, Japan, and the Aleutian Islands to Alaska, and then on the same current southwardly to the west coasts of both North and South America, where the most recent deciphering of the prephonetic Phoenician code makes clear that the Phoenicians had landed. Locally documented in stone carving, this occurred circa 200 B.C.—ergo, was contemporary with Eratosthenes' map-making. Then, after stopping on the west coast of South America, the Phoenicians probably followed the coast southward until the "Roaring Forties" winds and current swept them around the Horn into the South Atlantic, whence the northerly current took them along South America's east coast. Here they made another stone-carving-recorded stop. Thereafter the Atlantic Gulf Stream swept them northwardly, then westwardly, along the northern coast of South America, through the Lesser and Greater Antilles, all the way westward to the Panama Isthmus, then north from Yucatán into the Gulf of Mexico, then southward north of Cuba around Florida, then with the Gulf Stream, diverted northward by the Virgin and Bahama islands into the swiftly flowing North Atlantic Gulf Stream, past Cape Hatteras, Nova Scotia, south of Greenland, Iceland, and Spitzbergen, where the ice forced them to go westward until they discovered their familiar Scandinavia, British Isles, etc., from which they returned home to the Mediterranean and to Carthage on the north coast of Africa or to their capital port of Biblos on the eastern Mediterranean shore.

I feel confident that Eratosthenes had knowledge of their circumnavigation. Without a magnetic compass, sextant, or chronometer the Phoenicians were guided only by their familiarity with star constellations and driven by prevailing ocean currents, trade winds, and angular-pattern-informative-following-of-coastlines. They kept recorded accounts of all changes in their course angularly as plotted against the star pattern and of the whole sky.

The Phoenicians obviously had to subsist on fish and rainwater.

As a sailor-navigator myself, I am confident that Eratosthenes would not have closed his map along its top edge if he had no knowledge of the fact that the Earth had been circumnavigated. The almost-closed, circular bay shown along the top edge of his map, which showed that such an experience occurred midway on the trips, is probably occasioned by the fact that the South and North Atlantic Gulf Stream sweeps deeply into the Caribbean Sea all the way to the isthmus of Panama and then through the Gulf of Mexico, as already recounted. (See Figs. 8 and 9.)

Around the same year, 200 B.C., the Stoic philosopher Crates developed the first *terrestrial* globe—celestial globes preceded it.

It is clear that a special chain of Greek scientist-philosopher-cosmologists consisting of Philolaeus (410 B.C.), Heraclides (350 B.C.), and Aristarchus (200 B.C.) had successively evolved a concept of the solar system that was

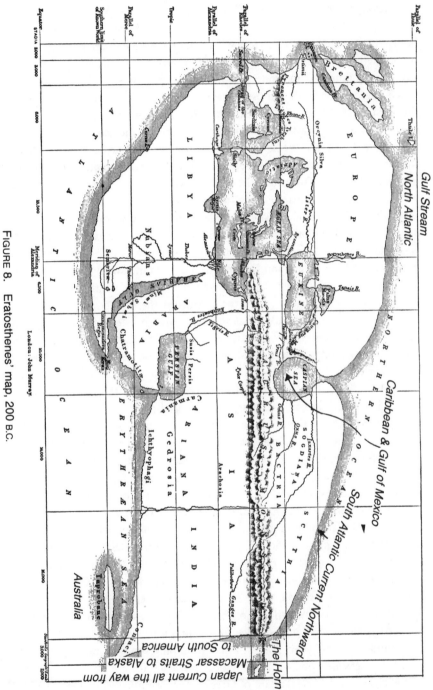

FIGURE 8. Eratosthenes' map, 200 B.C.

in fair agreement with that of Copernicus and Kepler 1700 years later (1543 A.D.) and even with our late-twentieth-century conceptioning.

It is also clear that beginning with Plato's pupil Aristotle (384–322 B.C.) and the latter's *practical* philosophy, the geocentric concept of the celestial system was, after 200 B.C., becoming more and more formally adopted by the "world's" flat-minded power-structure "authorities," despite contradictory complexities. The difficultly explained geocentric cosmic systems' planetary behaviors and Sun motion was not considered by the authorities to be an objection since, as they rationalized it, these matters seemingly had no "practical" bearing on everyday affairs. It seems almost equally clear that between 200 B.C. and 200 A.D. a deliberately planned policy was adopted by the combined supreme political and religious power structure of that period, which undertook the conditioning of the human reflexes to misconceive and mis-see (or mostly not see at all) the macro-micro-cosmic systems in which we live. Their success drew the curtains on science for 1700 years—until 1500 A.D. That curtain would never again have been raised had it not been for the discovery of that something-called-nothing—the cipher. Because it was "nothing," the information-monopolizing, physical-property-coveting power structure had overlooked it.

Only the learned-from-others knowledge of the unlimited multiplying and dividing—and thereby ratioing—and the relative-experiences-evaluating capability provided exclusively by the cipher and its leftward positioning of numbers in increments of ten integers, could make possible individual human's knowledge of how to escape from the prison of ignorance successfully established by the church-state hierarchy. If you have never been taught about the cipher and its functioning, there is almost no possibility of your accidentally discovering the computationally operative functioning of "nothing"—much less feel the necessity of inventing a symbol for that invisible, senseless nothingness. If the positioning of numbers and its computation-facilitating capability had been known by the Alexandrian Greeks, all chances that you might discover this were seemingly banished when the emperors of the Roman Empire usurped and amalgamated the vast religious priesthood power with their already-established military supremacy.

It was the Asiatic, 800 A.D. publishing of the function of the cipher by al-Khwarizmi the Arab that ultimately saved the day when, in about 1200 A.D., knowledge of it reached northern Italy and southern Germany by way of Carthage in North Africa.

Following the death of Christ and the preaching by his disciples, the promised prospect of salvation for all believers raised the Christian priesthood to unprecedentedly powerful popularity. The combined religious and martial emperorship found its authoritarianly formulated *credo* (meaning "I

FIGURE 9. Probable voyage in 200 B.C. of Phoenicians going with prevailing ocean currents and trade winds before days of magnetic compass-using, using only interstar lines of interrelationships.

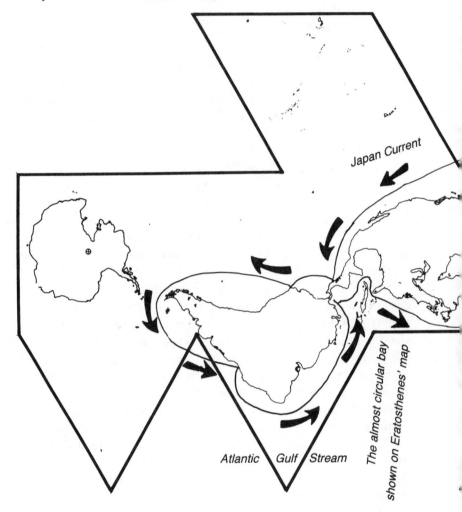

Japan Current

Atlantic   Gulf   Stream

The almost circular bay
shown on Eratosthenes' map

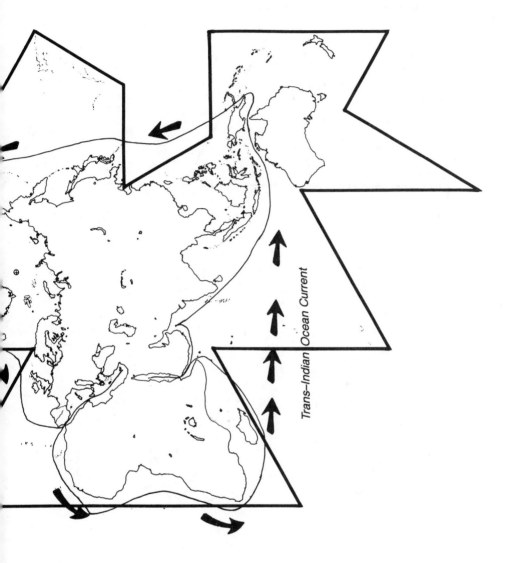

Trans–Indian Ocean Current

39

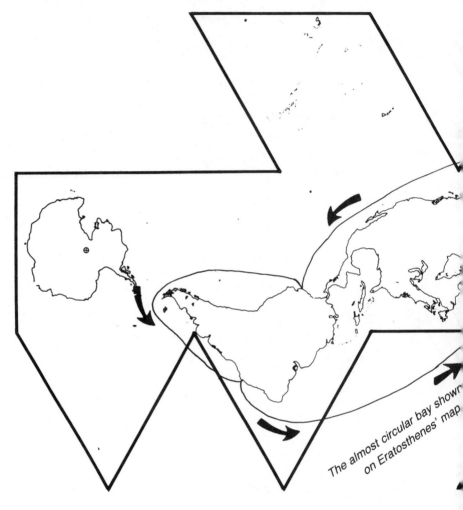

FIGURE 10. Possible if not probable voyaging of Phoenicians in 250 B.C. to both west and east coasts of South America from Levantine Biblos.

The almost circular bay shown on Eratosthenes' map

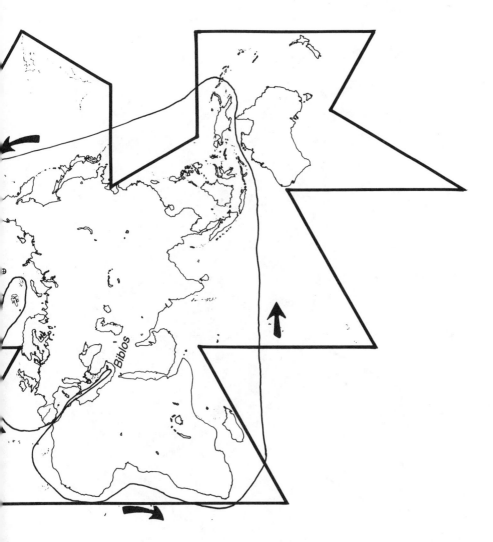

FIGURE 11. Early Circumnavigations

Phoenicians 230 B.C.

Phoenicians 500–200 B.C.

Columbus 1492 A.D.

Vikings 1000 A.D.

Phoenicians 550 B.C.

believe") threatened by the B.C. Greek scientists' ever-unorthodox thinking and discovering. "Science," as Sir James Jeans said two millennia later, "is the earnest attempt to set in order the facts of experience." Scientific thinking constantly discovered experimental evidence of the erroneous conceptioning of nonscientific authority. The emperor-pope did not want any of *his* subjects "attempting to set in order the facts of their own experiences."

To cope with the scientists' persuasive, experience-supported logic, the emperor needed popularly plausible divine authority. Though all acknowledged the emperor to be the unquestioned military leader, with absolute *physical* power, he needed also the only-by-God-to-be-given *metaphysical* dispensation assertedly relayed to the ordained priests by the succession of popes, an authority that was originally received from the disciples and by the disciples from the son of God and his direct authority from God. Thus "officially authorized," the pope-emperor could require all believers to secretly confess their sins to *his* officials. He could also ordain universal adoption of the most-useful-to-him explanations of the causality of all human experiences. The emperor-pope could tell his people how to behave, how to gain God's favor.

If the emperor-pope accredited the Alexandrian Greeks' development of the Sun-centered planetary system, he obviously could not maintain the logic of the concept of a two-dimensional, flat-out world sandwiched in parallel between Heaven above and Hell below. The concept of God in Heaven above, with a seat beside Him to which Christ had ascended, could not be maintained except in a world of commonly parallel-to-one-another, up-and-down, perpendicular trees and people on an infinitely, omnilaterally extended, flat-world plane—around which the Sun and stars set and rose. This cosmology put the emperor-pope and his God at the center of Universe.

The total overall evolutionary events of 400 to 200 B.C. in the eastern Mediterranean world saw all the extraordinary Greek intellectual activity transpiring almost exclusively in the city of Alexandria—founded by Alexander the Great in 332 B.C. on the delta at the westernmost mouth of Egypt's River Nile. In 100 B.C. the Alexandrian library was said to have contained 700,000 volumes, or manuscript scrolls. Fortunately some of those volumes in Alexandria were meticulously copied and distributed to libraries around the civilized world of that time, for over 40,000 volumes of the Alexandrian library were burned in 47 B.C. during a siege in the war between Caesar and Pompey.

In the second century A.D. Ptolemy conceived his conic, latitude-and-longitude world map, reading from the British Isles in the west to China in the east. His *Almagest* publication contained a storehouse of navigational data. In the *Almagest* Ptolemy published his catalog of over 1000 stars.

In 272 A.D. a Roman emperor burned the Alexandrian library for a second time. The third burning of the Alexandrian library was accomplished by a later Roman emperor in 391 A.D. In 529 A.D. all the Mediterranean universities were closed. In 642 A.D. occurred the final complete burning of the library of Alexandria by Muslims.

As we have already described, the earliest known world maps are Eratosthenes' surprisingly informative 200 B.C. map and the 200 A.D., latitude-and-longitude-divided, fanlike, cylindrical stretch-out of Ptolemy, which dropped out the south African territory of Eratosthenes but included China, Arabia, and India.

We have studied Eratosthenes' world map of 200 B.C. in connection with the fact that we now know reliably that the Phoenicians reached both coasts of South America at about that time and that the Phoenicians sailed from and returned to Carthage on the north coast of Africa, or to their sovereign's eastern Mediterranean port just north of Beirut, Lebanon. From there cedars were shipped to Eratosthenes' Alexandria in Egypt, to build the big-bellied, stoutly ribbed sailing ships. It is quite evident to us that Eratosthenes had great confidence that his world had been circumnavigated. He knew that we live on a spherical planet. Why else would he have been inspired to make his remarkably accurate measurement of the Earth's circumference, etc.?

The 200 B.C. coincidence of Eratosthenes' world map, Crates' world globe, and the Phoenicians' sky-star-globe-advantaged circumnavigation is highly visible only when using my Dymaxion world map. Using Mercator's, the polyconics, or other world projections, it would never have been logically revealed. Of course, neither Eratosthenes nor the Phoenicians used the geographical names I employ.

With the exception of the B.C. Greek, spherically informed world mapping, all the post-Roman emperor-pope's and pre–1500 A.D. comprehensive maps show the world as a flat-out system surrounded by an infinitely extendable, planar wilderness.

All the great pre-sixteenth-century empires—such as those of Genghis Khan, Alexander the Great, and Rome—employed that flat concept, with civilization centered around the Mediterranean, which means "sea in the middle of the land." The people, in the times of Alexander the Great or of Caesar or of Saladin, all thought in that flat way. As yet today "simple, elementary, plane geometry" is used by and taught to beginners; "solid" is considered more difficult, and "spherical trig" even more advanced and difficult.

The real consequences of that—psychologically, philosophically, and mathematically—are devastating. It means that "inside" the empire we have

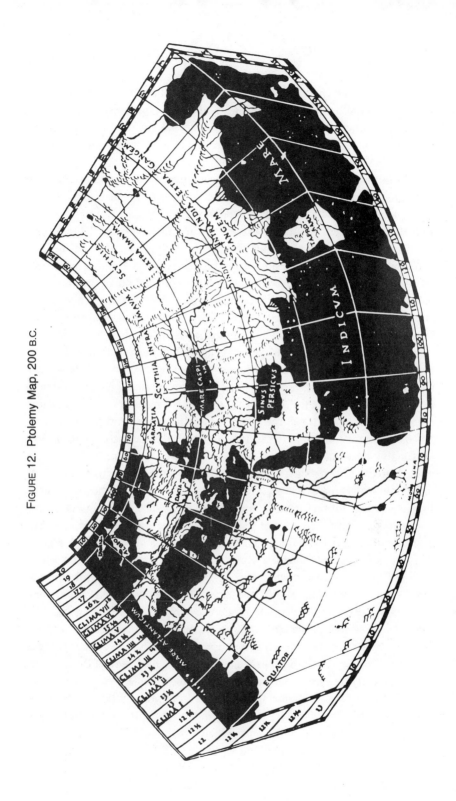

Figure 12. Ptolemy Map, 200 b.c.

45

something we call civilization, while "outside" the empire begins the unknown wilderness peopled with brutes and worse, and outside of that, live dragons, and beyond the dragons, flat infinity. What we have in flat-land is an only local definability, surrounded by flat-outward infinity—undefinability.

This meant, then, that the Greeks, in attempting to communicate their mathematical conceptioning, defined the circle as "an area bound by a closed line of equal radius from one point," the triangle as "an area bound by a closed line of three angles, three edges, and three vertices." The Greeks talked only of the area that was "bound" as having validity and identity, while outside (on the other side of the boundary) existed only treacherous terrain leading outward to boundless infinity—an unknown and unknowable wilderness. The feedback from this world view has ingrained fundamental biases into our present-day thinking. We can conceive only of *one* side of a line as definable, organized, and valid. "Our side" is natural and right—"God's country"—and vice versa. All humanity has thought of its own local area as being familiar, organized, and a priori, with all else remote and unthinkable. The Greeks oversimplified conceptioning with their misassumption that geometry could begin with plane geometry which they said employed only three tools: the straightedge, the scribe, and dividers. They failed altogether to include the surface on which they scribed as constituting an equally essential component of their otherwise experimentally demonstrated proofs of their various propositions. Because the earth of the Earth on which they scribed was so large and its limits were unknown to them, they concluded that it was an infinitely extended surface. They failed altogether to recognize the fact that you cannot have a surface of nothing. Any surface on which they scribed had to be a topological feature of a system. They obviously knew naught of Euler's topology nor of my systems geometry (see Chapter 4, *Synergetics*, vol. 1). Systems always divide all Universe outside the system from all of the Universe inside the system. All systems are finite subdividers of macro- and micro-Universe. Not knowing that they were always scribing on a closed, finite system, the Greeks defined a plane geometrical polygon as "an area bound by a closed line of so many angles and edges." They assumed that the area on the "outer" side of the line continued laterally to infinity and was therefore undefinable. What their closed lines always did was to divide all the finite surface area of the polyhedronal system on which they scribed into two finite areas both of which were exactly bound by the surface-drawn polygon's perimeter. Draw a triangle on the sand of a beach. You inadvertently divide all the surface of planet Earth into two areas, A and B—"A" the triangle which you consciously and visually drew and "B" the enormous area on the "outside" of the consciously drawn triangle, consisting of all the rest of the surface of our spherical plan-et Earth. All that remaining surface of our spherical-surface Earth is bound by the closed-perimeter figure of "three angles and three edges" which you scribed in the sand. Unbeknownst to them, the Greek Euclideans were al-ways dealing in polyhedra of "system geometry." Humans could not make a local Earth-surface triangle without inherently making a vast terrestrial-size triangle. The two terrestrial triangles, little A and vast B, in turn brought inherently into play the almost spherical, vastly high-frequency-tri-angulated polyhedronal system on whose surface they were scribing. This in turn and unbeknownst to them affected the rest of the Universe—the macro-Universe outside the system upon which they scribed and the micro-Universe inside the system upon which they scribed. Thus humans have al-ways unknowingly affected all Universe by every act and thought they articulate or even consider.

Fortunately the unrealistic thinking of humans has had little effect on Universe and evolution whereas realistic thinking has cosmic effectiveness in pure principle. Realistic, comprehensively responsible, omnisystem-con-siderate, unselfish thinking on the part of humans does absolutely affect hu-man destiny. If the realistic thinking can conceive of technically feasible options facilitating satisfactorily effective human fulfillment of its designed functioning as local Universe information inventorying and local Universe problem-solving in support of the integrity of eternally regenerative Uni-verse, then the accomplishment of that realistic conceptioning is realistically effective in satisfying Universe that human mind is accomplishing its de-signed evolutionary role.

* * *

In our comprehensive reviewing of published, academically accepted his-tory we continually explore for the *invisible power structure* behind the vis-ible kings, prime ministers, czars, emperors, presidents, and other official head men, as well as for the underlying, hidden causes of individual wars and their long, drawn-out compaigns not disclosed by the widely published and popularly accepted causes of those wars.

There may be great significance in the fact that Pythagoras in Greece and Buddha in the Orient occur at the same time—in the sixth century B.C. Both are powerfully, perceptively thinking and acting human individuals who, coming out of a past in which only the mystically ordained kings counted and humans were omniexpendable pawns, produced mathematical tools and philosophic breakthroughs for individual humans forever thereafter to em-ploy. Their scientific and philosophic gifts to humanity were in marked con-trast to the self-advantaging military conquests of kings. Pythagoras, in a little town north of Athens in the Near East, and Buddha, in the Far East, utterly unknown to one another, co-occur as a vast amount of moral and spiritual thinking is taking place in the Near East as recorded in the Old Testament of the "prophets." Historical research indicates a succession of "Isaiahs" starting at about the same time as Pythagoras and Buddha and as the Greek school of scientists and scientific thinkers, running to 200 B.C. Isaiah the Second speaks of "turning the swords into plowshares and spears into pruning knives" and "leopard lying down with the lamb" and prophesies "a little child shall lead them."

Nonrural, nonmilitary humans had words and mathematical tools and writing ability with which to initiate a breakthrough toward ultimate emancipation of all humans.

Such individuals as Pythagoras and Buddha were unanticipated by the behind-the-scenes physical power structures. They were probably unnoticed at first. The ever-advancing scientific conceptioning of the Greeks between 600 B.C. and 200 B.C., as well as the comprehension and thoroughness of the scriptural writers, suggest that not until about 200 B.C. did the great power structures operating behind the official states' officers begin to find ways of putting brakes on the individual's metaphysical breakthrough. The power structure then began to enter into the cosmological formulations and began to cut the ramifications of human conceptioning and cope-with-able magnitude. Humans had found that each one had a private "hotline" to God. What the power structures needed was a way to put in a control switchboard so that the individuals would have to "call up" God only through officialdom's censor-supervised switchboard.

For example, the Roman Catholic church, fortifying its proclaimed "divine mandate" as intermediary between the individual and God, attacked technology because it could eliminate the stresses of poverty, and much of Roman Catholic business and prosperity was founded on the exploitation of misery. The business strategists of the Vatican were inherently against abortion—pregnancy being the single greatest source of confessional and donation money to the Church. Herein lies the source of the Church's persistent maintenance of its dogma and authority in the face of a technologically emergent and potentially powerful humanity.

*   *   *

As described, before recording graphically its presence aboard our planet, humanity had no line of communication reaching directly to us today other than the physical sea and land building arts and handicrafting of small artifacts, as well as their "designed" interrelationships to be read in the burial positions of the skeletons and their artifacts, etc.

Everyone "knows" that as one goes inland from the sea, one comes to ever-higher mountains. It was thought that if one went far enough inland, one would come to a mountain reaching to Heaven—and occupied at its highest point by God. More and more durable cosmological models of this world view were built—with living god-kings assumedly to occupy the lesser heights after their death. How strong the king might be would govern the height of his mountain as surmounted by ever-higher central "mountain" pinnacles. These square-based cosmological models are the gats and wats of Southeast Asia, the pyramids of Central American Mayas and Incas, the Babylonian ziggurats and Egyptian pyramids.

The design authority for the wats was probably that of the priest-navigators, whose architectural skills derived from their knowledge of the principles of boatbuilding. The world-around priest-navigator's cosmological authority was responsible for the astronomical observatory structures as yet standing in India, Mesopotamia, Crete, Egypt, England, and Central America.

In the early dawning of graphically chronicled civilization the wats involve gods of the sea and gods of the sky as well as gods of the underground land. The fire, smoke, and lava of volcanoes, well known to men, indicated that "down" led through the horizontal plane of the world into a Hell of brimstone and fire, just as "up" led everywhere exclusively toward the serene blue Heaven of the highest God. These cosmological-symbol edifices—the wats and gats—had no interior spaces for religious or royal-court ceremonies or for occupation by any living human except as an astronomer. They were developed by designer-priests and constructed by slaves only for the convenience of the livingly visible god-king's after-death physical reascension from Earth to become once more an invisible god of Heaven, capable of returning at any future time to resume human or any other convenient form. Like animals, ordinary humans (and human life) were absolutely expendable (either as slaves or as sacrifices).

As recorded in the stone carvings of Egypt and Mesopotamia, the history of world society begins with humanity at large knowing nothing of physics, chemistry, or biology. Humans recognized but few safe edibles. Humans had witnessed many lethal poisonings by superficially attractive items plucked from the mysterious scenery. Infection was rampant. Average survival was in the neighborhood of twenty-two years, or about one-third of the once-in-a-rare-while-demonstrated, biblically mentioned "three score and ten"-year life-span. Life was so fundamentally awful that no logic could persuade humanity to believe that the living experience was intended by the great God of Universe to be desirable in its own right. The only tenable assumption was that life on Earth was suffered only in preparation for a life hereafter. It was reasoned that the worse life on Earth proved to be, the better would be the suffering-earned life hereafter. Experience seemed to show that adequate sustenance in general was so fundamentally scarce that even in the hereafter none could conceive of there being adequate life support for other than the pharaoh.

This being evident to all, it was commonly assumed that if the pharaoh—the people's leader—could be safely delivered into the next world with all his sovereign equipment, thereafter he might be able to get all his people safely delivered to him in the afterlife paradise.

Because life in this world was so torturously devoid of life support, desperation drove humans to thievery and vandalism as a general way of life. To get the pharaoh and all his equipment and riches safely into the next world involved building a stone mountain on top of his burial chamber in the superstable form of the pyramid. This called for supreme engineering, designing, and large-scale building capability. Thus it came about that the *economic-authority/patronage* that employed and subsidized the pyramid-designing, architectural, engineering, and building efforts of the intuitive artist-scientist, poet, inventor, engineer, and initiator of the early Egyptian pyramid was exclusively the *life hereafter of the pharaoh*.

The authority—to employ whatever technological capabilities he could muster from the nonobvious but intellectually conceptual resources hidden in the scenery—went to the artist-scientist-inventor to support his reorganization of environmental potentials for the advantage of the life hereafter of the pharaoh—and his most faithful servants.

With all building there is a temporary, "make-ready," structural scaffolding. The artist-scientist-inventors existing in the times of the earliest pharaoh needed to elevate and move gargantuan, rectilinearly chiseled stone blocks into place. They could readily see that the thousands of slaves available could shovel together great-approach hills of rock and sand, upon which they could first lay parallel tracks of delimbed tree trunks and thereafter, with other tree trunks, could pry forward the wood-roller-mounted blocks of stone. The pharaoh's creative architect may have been the first human in history to conceive of the principle of the lever and its ability to move great rocks. Whoever he was, he proved that with ever longer and stouter levers he could vastly augment the musclework of whole armies of slaves; moreover, he discovered that the degree of work-advantage to be realized with various-size levers could be mathematically calculated. The pharaoh died. They entombed him, and he supposedly went to the world of eternal hereafter accompanied by all his riches. When the pharaoh died, his artist-scientist-inventor was rewarded by being entombed with the pharaoh (along with the other most faithful servants) so that they could be the first of the pharaoh's people to enjoy the blessings of the "hereafter." But knowledge of the levering effectiveness remained in this world.

The next architect-engineer genius for the next pharaoh, using the levers, wood-log rollers, and wood-log tracks invented by his predecessors, discovered that many of his army of slave workers were dying or unable to work for lack of adequate food. To correct this condition he conceived of shunting the waters of the Nile into slave-produced irrigation ditches, which led the Nile into the potentially fertile floodlands bordering the river. The artist-scientist rearranged the living environment in ways that technologically increased the human advantage of the "antechamber," make-ready for the hereafter world.

After each pharaoh's entombment the principles first discovered and objectively employed by the succession of Leonardo-type architect-engineers of the pyramids, the "scaffold"-phase tools such as the lever, were not forgotten amongst the as-yet-living people. The departed architect-engineers left behind the irrigation ditches, which continued to irrigate and grow more food in this "antechamber-to-Heaven" world. The irrigation ditches did not disappear by going over into the hereafter. Use of these physical "scaffolding" capabilities in this pre-Heaven world by the living society persisted and multiplied, pharaoh by pharaoh. The technological inventiveness of the pharaohs' respective scientist-artist-architects became evolution's comprehensive environment advancers.

Finally, the inventory of technological "scaffolding equipment" employed in this rearranged-environment world in the predeath days of the pharaoh altered the spontaneous thinking of the living. The work effectiveness of the living slaves, as inventively led by the era's artist-scientists, became so prodigious that it became obviously possible not only to prepare magnificently for the most favorable afterlife of the living pharaoh but also to prepare magnificent, vandal-thwarting, stone-edifice-covered tombs for guarding the sub-pharaoh nobles' entry into the afterlife. During the next succession of dynasties the progressively ever more prodigious inventory of environment-controlling technology, currently available in this world to serve as scaffolding for enshrinement of the eternal afterlife of the pharaoh and nobles, multiplied to such accelerating degree that in due course it became spontaneously apparent to all concerned that the total of now-workable technology made possible accommodating the safe entry into the afterlife of the rich, middle-class society.

The afterlife enshrinement of the prosperous middle class that occurred in the Greek and early Roman B.C. period brought about the development of carved marble mausoleums and burial urns.

Eventually the environment-altering technological capability in this (for-

99-percent-of-humanity-miserable) temporal activity, being conducted in this life to ensure the exclusive afterlife enjoyment only of kings, nobles, and middle-class-wealthy, became so vast that new human perception inspired the prophets Buddha, Christ, and Mohammed and probably vast numbers of other unknown, intelligent, and inspired humans to assume that there now existed adequate technical know-how and materials to build in-this-world-physical-"scaffolding" structures that would provide for safe entry into the afterlife not only of the king, nobles, and middle class, but also of all humanity, including the most lowly commoners and slaves.

This did not occur in one day. There was a gradual dawning awareness on the part of a few that the changing technological capability vis-à-vis the environment promised a vast change in human affairs. This bred an era of prophets and thinkers heralding general human qualifications in this life for entry into the next life. The Old Testament is dramatic manifest of this period.

For millennia, the progeny of the South Pacific island navigators, the navigator-priests of the Persian Gulf, Mesopotamia and Egypt had only the pharaohs to ferry over into Heaven. For another millennium they had only the nobles and the rich middle class to prepare for safe entry into the afterlife. The priests' beneficiaries constituted less than 1 percent of humanity. But, when everybody had potential entry into Heaven, we see the long-ago South Seas navigator-priests' successors becoming very powerful popular authorities.

The by-word-of-mouth news swiftly went round that all humanity could now be accommodated in the next world and would be welcomed there if individually qualifying in this world through devout acts and thoughts. The officially accredited representatives of God in this world gained enormous power through their function of tutoring for and passing on the qualifications of individual humans in this world for passage into Heaven—the alternative being Hell. This power became swiftly annexed by the Holy Roman emperor-pope and, as we earlier described, gave rise to the vast European church-state empire and 1500 years of the Dark Ages.

During the Dark Ages those individuals endowed with creative powers and insights seem by and large to have carefully avoided attempting to reform the political, religious, or scientific status quo. The record shows the original thinkers and skilled artists to have employed only architecture, painting, sculpture, poetry, music, and dance to express their inspiration by their intuitively conceived, metaphysically generalized principles. The inventive individuals seem to have confined their inventiveness to technically facilitating the accepted customs—for instance, the development of movable type to augment the religious publishing.

The highly organized physical-resource capabilities—to house the priests' activities of getting everyone worthy into the next world—witnessed the construction of chapels, churches, cathedrals, synagogues, mosques, temples, and vast monasteries in Europe and Asia Minor. Eventually the magnitude of in-this-life-physical-"scaffolding" 's technological development proliferated to such an extent that society began to realize that not only the afterlife of the king, the nobles, the rich middle class, and all the people, but also the *living* life of the king in this world, could be accommodated—and thus developed the divine-right-of-kings time.

Next, the accommodation of living-life enjoyment, as well as of a glorious afterlife, was extended to certain invisible behind-the-throne-power-structure individuals as well as the king.

Next, the bounteous this-life as well as guaranteed next-life glory was extended to the nobles—the Magna Carta time.

With ever-accelerating technological development in preparing for everyone's next life as well as the king's and nobles' this-life enjoyment, the time arrived when it became evident and was spontaneously realized that in addition to attending to getting everyone but the unfortunate "to-Hell-bound sinners" into Heaven and providing the enjoyment of this life by both the king and the nobles, it was possible to take care of the enjoyment of this life by the rich middle-class society. This gave rise to the Victorian Age. Sometimes spoken of as the Industrial Revolution, this technological advantaging of the rich middle class was enormously advantaged by the circa-1500 A.D. introduction of the cipher-permitted-engineering-and-scientific calculation.

All the foregoing human-mind-invented scaffolding, technological advantaging, and the all-history recording of the total accumulated inventory of artifacts and scientific discoveries, led to the opening of the twentieth century, when a handful of perceptive individuals, such as Henry Ford, saw that the total environment-advantaging technology had become so effectively developed that it made possible the advantaging not only of the afterlives but also of the lives of all humanity. Through the use of inanimate-power-driven industrial tools and mass-production techniques, the end products of these perceptive individuals' designing could be made to advantage all humanity.

Henry Ford, inspired by the farmer's transportation needs, inaugurated the mass use of the invisible and ever-higher-performance-per-pound alloys and the invisible controls of ever-closer measuring of invisibly operating parts of the machinery, structure, and production tooling of his automobiles. Ford developed the use of moving assembly lines. He concerned himself directly as the prime designer not only of his end product—the automobile—but also of his evolving machinery and structural technology and all the other supporting activities of final pertinence to the success of the massively reproductive industry—factories, tools, mining, transporting of raw materials all around the world, his own railroads and ships, massive-objects-loading equipment, communications, and information handling.

All the foregoing physical-environmental rearrangements—advantaging both the afterlife and the living lives of all humanity—occurred under the conditions of humanity's thinking of reality as consisting only of the phenomena that could be apprehended directly by humanity's senses of sight, touch, hearing, smelling, and tasting. All invisible occurrences and phenomena were considered to be either mystical, magical, or trickery.

Then came man's discovery of electromagnetics, atomic physics, metallurgy, and chemistry, and the whole new world of invisible, nonsensorially contactable—ergo, only instrumentally or only mathematically apprehensible—reality. Thereby, all of previous time's mysteries were either logically explained or dismissed. Technology expanded reality 999-fold to include the whole range of the invisible events of Universe. These had been held previously by humans to be magical and superstitiously mystical. Now they had become the realities of everyday pure and applied science. With the inclusion of this 99-percent invisible world of reality, along with its as yet myriad of unsolved problems, into our everyday strictly sensual reality came the radio-introduced concepts of tuning-in and tuning-out. In yesterday's two-universe—(1) life and (2) Heaven—thinking we had *things* and *nothings.* Things and space. "Life" and "Death." Now we have tuned-in and tuned-out. "Tuned-out" does not mean dead. Without anyone saying so humanity's need for two universes, "This Life" and ";The Afterlife," began to fade out as it realized that this life and its vast mysteries were all one.

*   *   *

In all the cosmological models of early civilizations, a wide, four-cornered planar Earth was surrounded by infinitely extensive waters, surmounted by ever-higher central "mountain" pinnacles. This discloses how the early humans explained to themselves the sum of their experiences regarding the structure and operating scheme of their real world from out of whose eastern watery extremity the Sun and stars rose, passed over, descended, plunged in under and out—then repeated. Because the Sun and stars quite obviously passed "over," and returned "under," it, the world was implied to be a thick but penetrable watery slab extending horizontally to infinity in all planar directions. All the perpendiculars then were extended in only two directions in relation to man's erroneously conceived flat Earth. Those two exactly opposite, positive and negative, exclusively perpendicular directions in respect to the horizontal Earth plane were the seemingly obvious concepts of "up" and "down."

This flat conceptioning is manifest right up to the present in such everyday expressions as "the wide, wide world" and "the four corners of the Earth." As mentioned before, "up" and "down" are the parallel perpendiculars impinging upon this flat-out world. Only a flat-out world could have a Heaven to which to ascend and a Hell into which to descend. Both Christ and Mohammed, their followers said, ascended into Heaven from Jerusalem.

Scientifically speaking (which is truthfully speaking), there are no directions of "up" or "down" in Universe—there are only the angularly specifiable directions "in," "out," and "around." Out from Earth and into the Moon—or into Mars. IN is always a specific direction—IN is point-to-able. OUT is any direction.

Don't let these facts of comprehensive, human misorientation give you a personal inferiority complex. My own direct questioning of many large scientific audiences proves that all scientists as yet realistically "see" the Sun going "down" in the evening—though science has known for 500 years that this is untrue. Around the world nothing has ever been formally instituted in our educational systems to gear the human senses into spontaneous accord with our scientific knowledge. In fact, much has been done and much has been left undone by powerful world institutions that prevents such reorientation of our misconditioned reflexes. Our own misconditioned reflexes are powerful deterrents to our successful self-reorientation of our apprehending faculties to accord with the emerging truths. Though I have been trying for fifty-three years to rid myself of the words *up* and *down,* I find them popping out in my speech.

We now know that we do not live on a flat-slab Earth. We do live on board an 8000-mile-in-diameter spherical spaceship speeding around the Sun at 60,000 miles per hour, spinning axially as it orbits. None of the perpendiculars to a sphere are parallel to one another. The first aviators flying completely around the Earth within its atmospheric mantle and gravitationally cohered to the planet, having completed half their circuit, did not feel "up-side-down." They had to employ other words to correctly explain their experiences. So, aviators evolved the terms "coming-*in*" for a landing and "going-*out,*" not "down" and "up." Those are the scientifically accreditable words—*in* and *out.* We can go only in, out, and around.

The Astrodome of Houston has a spherical diameter of 800 feet. The planet Earth has a diameter of about 8000 miles. A nautical mile is approximately 6000 feet. So, the Earth's diameter is forty-eight million feet, which is 60,000 times the diameter of the sphere of which the Astrodome's spherical roof is a segment. The height of the Earth's highest mountain, Mt. Everest, is only one sixteen-hundredths the diameter of the real Earth.

Houston's Astrodome may be considered to be a one sixty-thousandth—

1/60,000th—scale model of a corresponding spherical segment of the real Earth. Mount Everest at the same 1/60,000th scale would make only a six-inch-high mound on the Astrodome. At the same scale a human being standing on the Astrodome would be only one two-thousandths of an inch high—i.e., .002 inch. The smallest dimension you and I can see (with our naked eye) is one one-hundredth, .01, of an inch. So you and I are only one-fifth of the height necessary to be visible at the scale of the Astrodome, used as a 1/60,000 scale model of a corresponding central-angle spherical section of the planet Earth's surface. It would require a dome five times the diameter of the Astrodome to make a scale model of the Earth on which you and I would appear as the smallest speck you and I can see. The Earth is

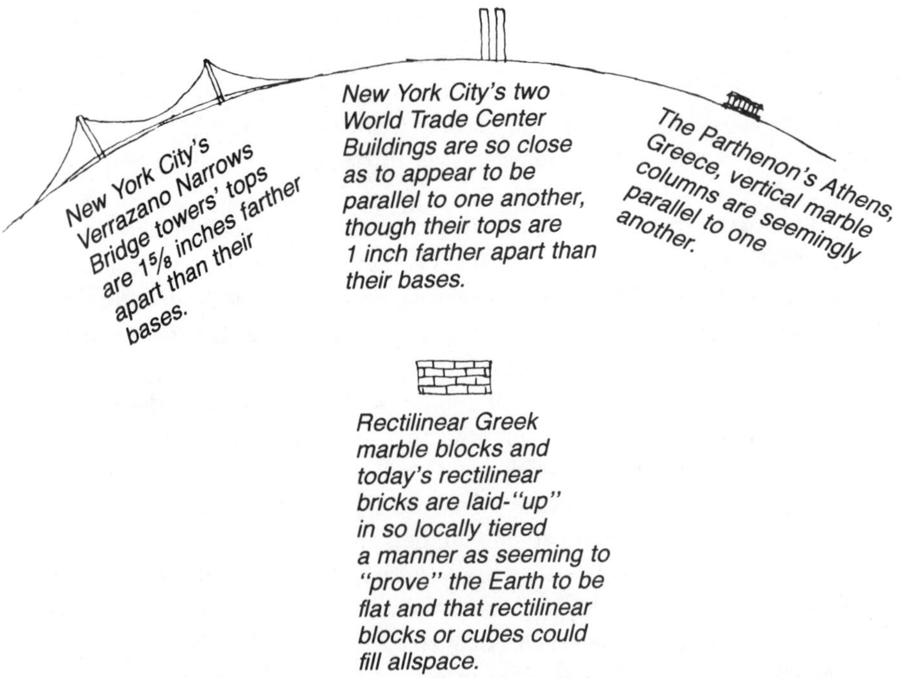

New York City's two
World Trade Center
Buildings are so close
as to appear to be
parallel to one another,
though their tops are
1 inch farther apart than
their bases.

New York City's
Verrazano Narrows
Bridge towers' tops
are 1⅝ inches farther
apart than their
bases.

The Parthenon's Athens,
Greece, vertical marble
columns are seemingly
parallel to one
another.

Rectilinear Greek
marble blocks and
today's rectilinear
bricks are laid-"up"
in so locally tiered
a manner as seeming to
"prove" the Earth to be
flat and that rectilinear
blocks or cubes could
fill allspace.

FIGURE 13.   Bridge, Trade Center, Parthenon

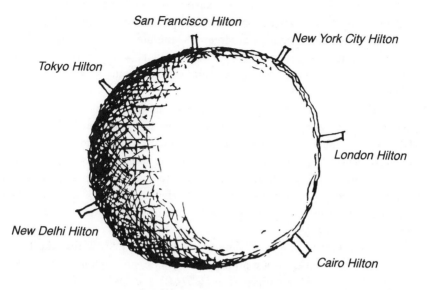

FIGURE 14.   The around-the-world Hilton Hotels are clearly not parallel to one another.

so big in comparison to you and me that it is physically impossible for humans to see their Earth as other than flat.

I have now flown entirely around the Earth forty-seven times by many different airline routes, and looking out the plane's windows at the circular horizon and having never felt myself to be upside-down, I am beginning to realistically feel our Earth to be a sphere—but a very, very big sphere.

*   *   *

I clearly remember New Year's Eve, December 31, 1899. I was four and a half. I had just received my eyeglasses and was deeply excited at all that I could now see. At 11:45 P.M. my father opened a window of our New England home to let in the twentieth century. I remember with what earnest thinking he tried to envision the coming years in which I would live beyond his time. The British Empire was at its height of power and splendor. The "world," as we know of it in 1980 after two official world wars and a third much more prolonged and ruthlessly vicious, unofficial world war, was utterly inconceivable. H. G. Wells was writing about a war in the air but he did not conceive of automobiles or electrons. About 99 percent of humanity was illiterate. Few, if any, individuals thought in world terms because the conceptual world of humanity at large was "infinite"—ergo, realistically un-think-about-able. Everyone "knew" that humans would never reach the Moon. Any who wasted their time thinking about doing so were dismissed as luna-tics.

The British Empire was commanded from the British Isles by great busi-ness venturers—the world men who ruled the world's oceans. The British Isles were found to be the most easily defendable shipbuilding bases and were conveniently positioned to rule the whole waterfront of all the Euro-pean customers of the venturers' Oriental booty. Observing so many ships loaded with so many British sailors (shanghaied out of the British pubs), the world came to identify history's most successful world-outlaw organization as "the British Empire."

This was the first empire of man to occur after we knew that the Earth was a sphere. A sphere is a mathematically finite, omnisymmetrical, closed system. A sphere is finite unity. (See §§ 224.07 *Synergetics,* vol. 1.)

As we described in our Introduction, Thomas Malthus, professor of po-litical economics of the East India Company College, was the first econo-mist ever to receive all the vital statistics and economic data from a closed-system world. Once the world is conceived of as a sphere—a finitely closed system—there was no longer an infinite number of possibilities, such as ac-companied the misconception of the infinitely extended flat-out world. In an infinite world, with its infinity of possibilities, praying was felt to be "worthwhile."

Because Earth had been discovered by its high-seas masters to be a closed and finite system, the great pirate venturers who controlled the seas took their scientists around the world to discover and disclose to them its exploit-able resources. Only because the Earth constituted a closed system could the scientists inspect, in effect, *all* the species, and only thus was Charles Dar-win able to develop the closed-system theory of "evolution of species." Such a theory could not have existed before that. It would have had to include dragons and sea serpents. All the people in all the previous open-edged em-pires lived in a system within whose infinity anything could happen or exist. Paganism (or peasantism) wasn't illogical. Geometrically speaking, the pa-gans could have an infinite number of gods. There were also an infinite number of chances of upsetting the local pattern, which was a most satis-fying idea if it happened that the individual didn't like the prevailing local pattern.

It seems strange that we were not taught about the historical, philosophi-cal, and economic significance of the foregoing transition from an open-flat to a closed-sphere world system. Because the churches were strong and the great pirates wished to obscure both their monopoly of the riches of the now limited system and their grand world ocean strategy for its control, the significance of the concept of a closed world system was popularly unrealized. The power structure and its patronized educational systems "let well enough alone."

CHAPTER 3

Legally Piggily

I'M GOING TO REVIEW my prehistory's speculative assumptions regarding the origins of human power structures.

In a herd of wild horses there's a king stallion. Once in a while a young stallion is born bigger than the others. Immediately upon his attaining full growth, the king stallion gives him battle. Whichever one wins inseminates the herd. Darwin saw this as the way in which nature contrives to keep the strongest strains going. This battling for herd kingship is operative amongst almost all species of animal herds as well as in the "pecking order" of flocking bird types.

I'm sure that amongst the earliest of human beings, every once in a while a man was born much bigger than the others. He didn't ask to be—but there he was. And because he was bigger, people would say—each in their own esoteric language—"Mister, will you please reach one of those bananas for me, because I can't reach them." The big one obliges. Later the little people would say, "Mister, people over there have lost all of their bananas and they are dying of starvation, and they say they are going to come over here and kill us to get our bananas. You're big—you get out in front and protect us." And he would say, "OK," and successfully protect them.

The big one found his bigness continually being exploited. He would say to the littles, "Between these battles protecting you, I would like to get ready for the next battle. We could make up some weapons and things." The people said, "All right. We'll make you king. Now you tell us what to do." So the big man becomes king quite logically. He could have become so in either a bullying or good-natured way, but the fact is that he was king simply because he was not only the biggest and the most physically powerful but also the most skillful and clever big one.

Every once in a while along would come another big man. "Mr. King, you've got things too easy around here. I'm going to take it away from you." A big battle ensues between the two, and after the king has his challenger pinned down on his back, he says, "Mister, you were trying to kill me to take away my kingdom. But I'm not going to kill you because you'd make a good fighter, and I need fighters around here to cope with the enemies who keep coming. So I'm going to let you up now if you promise to fight for me. But don't you ever forget—I can kill you. OK?" The man assents, so the king lets him up.

But instinctively the king says secretly to himself, "I mustn't ever allow two of those big guys to come at me together. I can lick any one of them, but only one by one." The most important initial instinct of the most powerful individual or of his organized power structure is, "Divide to conquer, and to keep conquered, keep divided."

So our special-case king has now successfully defended his position against two or more big guys who are all good fighters. He makes one the "Duke of Hill A," the second "Duke of Hill B," and the third "Duke of Hill C," and tells each one to "mind your own business" because "only the king minds everybody's business," and he has his spies watch them so that they can't gang up on him. Thus, our considered king is doing very well in his tribe-defending battles.

However, there are a lot of little nonfighting people who are not obeying the king regarding preparations for the next fighting period. The king says to his henchmen, "Seize that mischievous little character over there who is really being a nuisance around here." To the prisoner the king says, "I'm going to have to cut your head off." The man says, "Mr. King, you'd make a big mistake to cut my head off." The king asks, "Why?" "Well, I'll tell you, Mr. King, I understand the language of your enemy over the hill, and you don't. And I heard him say what he is going to do to you and when he's going to do it." "Young man, you've got a good idea at last. You let me know every day what my enemy over the hill says he is going to do and so forth, and your head is going to stay on. In addition, you're going to do something else you've never done before. You're going to eat regularly right up here in the castle near me. And I'm going to have you wear a royal purple jacket (so that I can keep track of you)." The king now has that little man under control and useful. Then another little man makes trouble for the king. As he is about to be beheaded, he shows the king that he understands metallurgy and can make better swords than anybody else. The king says, "You better make a good sword in a hurry." The man makes a beautiful, superstrong, and sharp sword—there's no question about that. So the king says, "OK, your head stays on. You, too, are to live here at the castle."

Next, under the threat of beheadment, another man making trouble for the king says, "The reason I am able to steal from you is because I understand arithmetic, which you don't. If I do the arithmetic around here, people won't be able to steal from you." The king makes him court mathematician.

As each of these men are given those special tasks to do for life, the king says to all of them, "Each of you mind only your own business. You, Mr. Languageman, mind only your own business; and you, Mr. Swordmaker, mind only your own business; and you, Mr. Arithmetic, mind only your own business. Each one minds only his own business. I'm the only one that minds everyone's business. Is that perfectly clear?" "Yes sir." "Yes sir." "Yes sir."

The king now has his kingdom operating very well. He has great fighters, superior metallurgy, better arithmetic and logistics, better spying and intelligence. His kingdom is growing ever bigger. Years go by, and these experts are getting old. The king says, "I want to leave this kingdom to my grandson. Mr. Languageman, I want you to pick out and teach some younger person about language. You, Mr. Swordmaker, I want you to pick out and teach somebody about metallurgy. You, Mr. Arithmetic, I want you to pick out and teach someone about arithmetic." And his total strategy became the pattern for the ultimate founding of Oxford University.

The way the power structure keeps the wit and cunning of the intelligentsia—who are not musclemen, who cannot do the physical fighting—from making trouble for the power structure (if the intelligentsia are too broadly informed, unwatched, and with time of their own in which to think) is to make each one a specialist with tools and an office or lab. That is exactly why bright people today have become streamlined into specialists.

Nobody is born a specialist. Every child is born with comprehensive interests, asking the most comprehensively logical and relevant questions. Pointing to the logs burning in the fireplace, one child asked me, "What is fire?" I answered, "Fire is the Sun unwinding from the tree's log. The Earth revolves and the trees revolve as the radiation from the Sun's flame reaches the revolving planet Earth. By photosynthesis the green buds and leaves of the tree convert that Sun radiation into hydrocarbon molecules, which form into the bio-cells of the green, outer, cambium layer of the tree. The tree is a tetrahedron that makes a cone as it revolves. The tree's three tetrahedral roots spread out into the ground to anchor the tree and get water. Each year the new, outer-layer, green-tree cone revolves 365 turns, and every year the tree grows its new tender-green, bio-cell cone layer just under the bark and over the accumulating cones of previous years. Each ring of the many rings of the saw-cut log is one year's Sun-energy impoundment. So the fire is the many-years-of-Sun-flame-winding now unwinding from the tree. When the log fire pop-sparks, it is letting go a very sunny day long ago, and doing so in a hurry." Conventionally educated grown-ups rarely know how to answer such questions. They're all too specialized.

If nature wanted humans to be specialists, she would, for instance, have given them a microscope on one eye, which is what nature has done with all other living organisms—other than humans. Each has special, organically integral equipment with which to cope successfully with special conditions in special environments. The low-slung hound to follow the Earth-top scent of another creature through the thickets and woods . . . the little vine that can grow only along certain stretches of the Amazon River . . . the bird with beautiful wings with which to fly, which bird however, when landed and in need of walking, is greatly hampered by its integral but now useless wings.

Humans are not unique in possessing brains that always and only are co-ordinating and storing for later retrieval the integrated information coming in from each and all the creature's senses—visual, aural, tactile, and olfactory. Humans are unique in respect to all other creatures in that they also have minds that can discover constantly varying interrelationships existing only between a number of special case experiences as individually apprehended by their brains, which covarying interrelationship rates can only be expressed mathematically. For example, human minds discovered the law of relative interattractiveness of celestial bodies, whose initial intensity is the product of the masses of any two such celestial bodies, while the force of whose interattractiveness varies inversely as the second power of the arithmetical interdistancing increases.

The human mind of Bernoulli discovered the mathematical expression of the laws of intercovarying pressure differentials in gases under varying conditions of shape and velocity of gas flow around and by interfering bodies. The Wright brothers' wing foils provided human flight, but not the information controlling the mathematics of varying wing foil conformations. Bernoulli's work made possible the mathematical improvement in speed and energy efficiency of various wing designs. Human mind's access to the mathematics of generalized scientific laws governing physical phenomena in general made possible humanity's production of its own detached-from-self wings to outfly all birds in speed and altitude, while being able to loan one another those wings and modify them to produce even better wings.

* * *

I'm sure our human forebears went through quite a period of giants and giant-affairs evolution. These probably led to all sorts of truth-founded legends from which fairy stories were developed, many of which are probably quite close to the facts of unwritten history. Then humans developed to the point at which a small man made a weapon, a stone-slinger, such as in the story of David and Goliath, with which the little man slays the big man by virtue of a muscle-impelled missile. At the U.S. Naval Academy "ballistics" is defined as: the art and science of controlling the trajectory of an explosively hurled missile. After the sling and spear we got the bow and arrow with which a small man could kill a big man at much greater distance than with spear or sling. So skill and human-muscle-impelled weapons ended the era of giants.

Discovery of energetic principles, and human inventiveness in using those principles, such as the invention of catapults and mechanically contracted, steel-spring-coil arrow impelment, advanced the art of weapons. The human power structures that could best organize and marshal the complex of interessential "best" weapons and support an army of best-trained people with each of the special types of weapons were the ones who now won the battles and ran the big human "show." The discovery of gunpowder by the Chinese and the invention of guns introduced the era of ballistics, or as the Navy terms it, "explosively hurled missiles."   .

Going back to the stone-sling, bow-and-arrow, spear, club, and knife era of weapons, we find that territorial battles between American Indian nations were fought over the local hunting and fishing rights, but the land itself always belonged to the Great Spirit. To the Indians it was obvious that humans could not own the land. There was never any idea that the people could own land—owning was an eternal, omniscient omnipotence unique to the greatness, universality, and integrity of the forever-to-humans-mysterious Great Spirit. Until a special human-produced change in the evolution of power structures occurred, the ownership of anything being unique to the Great Spirit—in whatever way that might be designated by local humans—was held by all people around our planet.

In 1851 Seattle, chief of the Suquamish and other Indian tribes around Washington's Puget Sound, delivered what is considered to be one of the most beautiful and profound environmental statements ever made. The city of Seattle is named for the chief, whose speech was in response to a proposed treaty under which the Indians were persuaded to sell two million acres of land for $150,000.

> How can you buy or sell the sky, the warmth of the land? The idea is strange to us.
> If we do not own the freshness of the air and the sparkle of the water, how can you buy them?
> Every part of this earth is sacred to my people. Every shining pine needle, every sandy shore, every mist in the dark woods, every clearing and humming insect is holy in the memory and experience of my people. The sap which courses through the trees carries the memories of the red man.

The white man's dead forget the country of their birth when they go to walk among the stars. Our dead never forget this beautiful earth, for it is the mother of the red man. We are part of the earth and it is part of us. The perfumed flowers are our sisters; the deer, the horse, the great eagle, these are our brothers. The rocky crests, the juices in the meadows, the body heat of the pony, and man—all belong to the same family.

So, when the Great Chief in Washington sends word that he wishes to buy our land, he asks much of us. The Great Chief sends word he will reserve us a place so that we can live comfortably to ourselves. He will be our father and we will be his children.

So we will consider your offer to buy our land. But it will not be easy. For this land is sacred to us. This shining water that moves in the streams and rivers is not just water but the blood of our ancestors. If we sell you land, you must remember that it is sacred, and you must teach your children that it is sacred and that each ghostly reflection in the clear water of the lakes tells of events and memories in the life of my people. The water's murmur is the voice of my father's father.

The rivers are our brothers, they quench our thirst. The rivers carry our canoes, and feed our children. If we sell you our land, you must remember, and teach your children, that the rivers are our brothers and yours, and you must henceforth give the rivers the kindness you would give any brother.

We know that the white man does not understand our ways. One portion of land is the same to him as the next, for he is a stranger who comes in the night and takes from the land whatever he needs. The earth is not his brother, but his enemy, and when he has conquered it, he moves on. He leaves his father's grave behind, and he does not care. He kidnaps the earth from his children, and he does not care. His father's grave, and his children's birthright are forgotten. He treats his mother, the earth, and his brother, the sky, as things to be bought, plundered, sold like sheep or bright beads. His appetite will devour the earth and leave behind only a desert.

I do not know. Our ways are different from your ways. The sight of your cities pains the eyes of the red man. There is no quiet place in the white man's cities. No place to hear the unfurling of leaves in spring or the rustle of the insect's wings. The clatter only seems to insult the ears. And what is there to life if a man cannot hear the lonely cry of the whippoorwill or the arguments of the frogs around the pond at night? I am a red man and do not understand. The Indian prefers the soft sound of the wind darting over the face of a pond and the smell of the wind itself, cleansed by a midday rain, or scented with piñon pine.

The air is precious to the red man for all things share the same breath, the beast, the tree, the man, they all share the same breath. The white man does not seem to notice the air he breathes. Like a man dying for many days he is numb to the stench. But if we sell you our land, you must remember that the air is precious to us, that the air shares its spirit with all the life it supports.

The wind that gave our grandfather his first breath also receives his last sigh. And if we sell you our land, you must keep it apart and sacred as a place where even the white man can go to taste the wind that is sweetened by the meadow's flowers.

You must teach your children that the ground beneath their feet is the ashes of our grandfathers. So that they will respect the land, tell your children that the earth is rich with the lives of our kin. Teach your children that we have taught our children that the earth is our mother. Whatever befalls the earth befalls the sons of the earth. If men spit upon the ground, they spit upon themselves.

This we know: the earth does not belong to man; man belongs to the earth. All things are connected. We may be brothers after all. We shall see. One thing we know which the white man may one day discover: our God is the same God.

You may think now that you own Him as you wish to own our land; but you cannot. He is the God of man, and His compassion is equal for the red man and the white. This earth is precious to Him, and to harm the earth is to heap contempt on its creator. The whites too shall pass; perhaps sooner than all other tribes. Contaminate your bed and you will one night suffocate in your own waste.

But in your perishing you will shine brightly fired by the strength of the God who brought you to this land and for some special purpose gave you dominion over this land and over the red man.

That destiny is a mystery to us, for we do not understand when the buffalo are all slaughtered, the wild horses are tame, the secret corners of the forest heavy with scent of many men and the view of the ripe hills blotted by talking wires.

Where is the thicket? Gone. Where is the eagle? Gone.

The end of living and the beginning of survival."*

* * *

In my prehistory accounting I talk about the time when each ice age is engaging an enormous amount of the oceans' water, lowering the waterfront and bringing together the islands of Borneo, the Philippines, and others, all to become part of the Malay Peninsula. I also spoke of the ice cap pushing the furry animals southward until they were suddenly pushed into the land of the previous islands now formed into the new peninsula—into land they could never before reach. This is how animals like tigers got out to now-reislanded places like Bali. Human beings suddenly confronted with these wild animals learned how to cope, hunting some and taming others. In following the evolution of human power structures we are now particularly interested in the humans who found themselves confronted with a tidal wave of wild animals. Those who were overwhelmed became aggressive hunters, and those who were not overwhelmed became peaceful domesticators of the animals. Some of the most aggressive men mounted horses, moved faster than all others, and went out to seek the beasts.

---

*Chief Seattle's speech was submitted by Dr. Glenn T. Olds at Alaska's Future Frontiers conference in 1979.

We have learned in the last decade from our behavioral science studies that aggression is a secondary behavior of humans—that when they get what they need, when they need it, and are not overwhelmed, they are spontaneously benevolent; it is only when they become desperate that they become aggressive because what they have relied on is no longer working. There are two kinds of social behavior manifest today around the world—the benign and the aggressive. It is probable that this dichotomy occurred in the human-versus-animal confrontation in the ice age time.

When an ice age starts to recede, the horsemen start north—hunting with clubs and spears. At the same time, moving much more slowly, we have the beginnings of great tribes of humans following their flocks of goats and sheep as the latter lead them to the best pastures—sometimes high on mountainsides, sometimes on great plains. With the *big man* as king—the head shepherd—we have humanity migrating off into a wilderness that seemed to have no limits. The land belonged to the Great Spirit. The people lived on the flesh of their animals and the encountered fruits, berries, nuts, and herbs. They kept themselves warm with clothing made of the skins of the animals and also with environment-controlling tents made of local saplings and the animal skins.

We have a king shepherd, from the day of the giants, tending his people and his flock, when along comes a little man on a horse, with a club hanging by his side. He rides up to the king shepherd and, towering above him, says, "Well, Mr. Shepherd, those are very beautiful sheep you have there. You know, it's very dangerous to have such beautiful sheep out here in the wilderness. The wilderness is very dangerous." The shepherd responds, "We've been out in the wilderness for generations and we've had no trouble at all."

Night after night thereafter sheep begin to disappear. Each day along comes the man on the horse. He says, "Isn't that too bad. I told you it was very dangerous out here. Sheep disappear out in the wilderness, you know." Finally, there is so much trouble that the shepherd agrees to accept and pay in sheep for the horseman's "protection" and to operate exclusively within the horseman's self-claimed land.

No one dared question the horseman's claim that he owned the land on which the horseman said the shepherd was trespassing. The horseman had his club with which to prove that he was the power structure of that locale; he stood high above the shepherd and could ride in at speed to strike the shepherd's head with his club. This was how, multimillennia ago, twentieth-century racketeers' "protection" and territorial "ownership" began. For the first time little people learned how to become the power structure and how thereby to live on the productivity of others.

Then there came great battles between other individuals on horses to determine who could realistically say, "I own this land." Ownership changed frequently. The ownership-claiming strategy soon evolved into horse-mounted warfare as each gang sought to overwhelm the other. Then the horse-mounted gangs, led by a most wily leader, used easily captured human prisoners to build them stone citadels at strategic points. Surrounded by prisoner-built moats rigged with drawbridges and drawgates, they would come pouring out to overwhelm caravans and others crossing their domains. "Deeds" to land evolved from deeds of arms. Then came enormous battles of gangs of gangs, and the beginning of the great land barons. Finally we get to power-structure mergers and acquisitions, topped by the most wily and powerful of all—the great emperor.

This is how humans came to own land. The sovereign paid off his promises to powerful supporters by signing deeds to land earned by the physical deeds of fighting in shrewd support of the right leader. Thereafter emperors psychologically fortified the cosmic aspect of their awesome power by having priests of the prevailing religions sanctify their land-claiming as accounted simply either by discovery or by arms.

In another set of events that opportuned the power structure the land barons discovered the most geographically logical trading points for caravaning: a place where one caravan trail would cross another caravan trail; where, for instance, the caravaners came to an oasis or maybe to a seaport harbor and transfer some of their goods from the camel caravans to the boats. The caravaners would say, "Let's exchange goods right here. Fine. You need something; I have it."

One day they're exchanging goods when along comes a troop of armed brigands on horseback. The head horseman says, "It's pretty dangerous exchanging valuable things out here in the wilderness." The caravaners' leader says, "No, we never have any trouble out here. We have been doing this for many generations." Then their goods begin to be stolen nightly, and finally the merchants agree to accept and pay for "protection." That was the beginning of the walled city. The horse-mounted gangsters brought prisoners along to build the city's walls and saw to it that all trading was carried on inside the walls. The lead baron then gave each of his supporters control of different parts of that city so that each could collect his share of the "taxes."

This is how we came to what is called, archeologically, the city-state, which was to become a very powerful affair. There were two kinds: the agrarian-productivity-exploiting type and the trade-route-confluence-exploiting type. These produced all the great walled cities such as Jericho and Babylon.

The agrarian-supported city-state works in the following manner: For example, we have Mycenae in Greece, a beautiful and fertile valley. It is ringed around with mountains. You can see the mountain passes from the high hill in the center of the valley. At the foot of the high central hill there is a very good well. So they build a wall around the citadel on the top of that mid-valley hill and walls leading down to and around the well so that they can get their water. When they see the enemy coming through the passes, the Mycenaeans bring all the food inside their walls and into their already-built masonry grain bins. What they can't bring inside the walls, they burn—which act was called "scorching the fields." The enemy enters the fertile valley, but there's nothing left for them to eat. The enemy army has to "live on its belly"—which means on the foods found along their route of travel—and is hungry on arrival in the valley. The people inside have all the food. The people outside try to break into the walled city, but they are over-whelmed by its height and its successfully defended walls. Finally the people outside—only able to go for about thirty days without food—get weaker and weaker, then the people inside come out and decimate them.

This was the city-state. It was a successful invention for a very long period in history. At the trade-route convergences city-states operated in much the same way but on a much larger scale with the siege-resisting supplies brought in by caravans or ships. The city-states were approximately invincible until the siege of Troy. Troy was the city-state controlling the integrated water-and-caravaning traffic between Asia and Europe near the Bosporus. It had marvelous walls. Everything seemed to be favorable for its people.

Meanwhile in history, we have millennia of people venturing forth on the world's waters—developing the first rafts, which had to go where the ocean currents took them; then the dugouts, with which they paddled or catama-raned and sailed in preferred directions; and finally the ribbed-and-planked ship, suggested to them by the stout spine and rib cage of the whales, seals and humans—stoutly keeled and ribbed, deep-bellied ships. With their large ships made possible by this type of construction, sailors came to cross the great seas carrying enormous cargoes—vastly greater cargoes than could be carried on the backs of humans or animals. Ships could take the short across-the-bay route instead of the around-the-bay mountain route.

The Phoenicians, Cretans, and the Mycenaeans, together, in fleets of these big-ribbed and heavily planked ships, went to Troy and besieged it. Up to this time the besiegers of Troy had come overland, and they soon ran out of food. But the Troy-besieging Greeks and Cretans came to Troy in ships, which they could send back for more supplies. This terminally-turned-around voyaging back to the supply sources and return to the line of battle was called their "line of supply." The new line-of-supply masters—the Greeks—starved out the Trojans. The Trojans thought they had enough food but had not reckoned on the people besieging them having these large ships. The Trojan horse was the large wooden ship—that did the task of horses—out of whose belly poured armed troops.

At this time the *power structure of world affairs* shifts from control by the city-state to the masters of the lines of supply. At this point in the history of swiftly evolving, multibanked, oar- and sail-driven fighting ships, the world power-structure control shifts westward to Italy. While historians place prime emphasis on the Roman legions as establishing the power of the Roman Empire, it was in fact the development of ships and the overseas line of supply upon which its power was built—by transporting those legions and keeping them supplied. Go to Italy, and you will see all the incredibly lovely valleys and great *castellos* commanding each of those valleys such as you saw in the typical city-states, and you can see that none of those walls has ever been breached. Also in Italy—in the northeastern corner—is Venice, the headquarters of the water-people. The Phoenicians—phonetically the Venetians—had their south Mediterranean headquarters in Carthage in northern Africa. In their western Mediterranean and Atlantic venturings the Phoenicians became the Veekings. The Phoenicians—Venetians—in their ships voyaged around the whole coast of Italy and sent in their people to each *castello*, one by one. The Venetians had an unlimited line of supply, and the people inside each *castello* did not. The people inside were starved out. Thus, all of the regional masters of the people in Italy hated the Venetians-Phoenicians-Veekings who were able to do this.

There being as yet no Suez Canal, the new world power structure centered in the ship mastery of the line of supply finally forcing the Roman Empire to shift its headquarters to Constantinople some ten centuries after the fall of Troy. The Roman emperor-pope's bodyguards were the Veekings-Vikings, the water-peoples' most powerful frontier fighters. The line of supply from Asia to Constantinople was partially caravan-borne and partially water-borne via Sinkiang–Khyber Pass–Afghanistan or via the Sea of Azov, the Caspian and the Black seas. From Constantinople, the western Europe-bound traffic was rerouted from overland to waterway routes. Because the Asia-to-Constantinople half of the trading was more land-borne-via-caravans, whose routes were dominated by the city-state–mastering Turks, Constantinople in due course was taken over by the Turks who established the Byzantine Empire in the Aegean Sea and Asia Minor.

Before leaving the subject of the great power-structure struggle for control of the most important, greatest cargo-tonnage-transporting, most profitable, Asia-to-Europe trade routes, we must note that the strength of the Egyptian Empire was predicated upon its pre-Suez function as a trade route link between Asia and Europe via the Indian Ocean, the Red Sea, overland

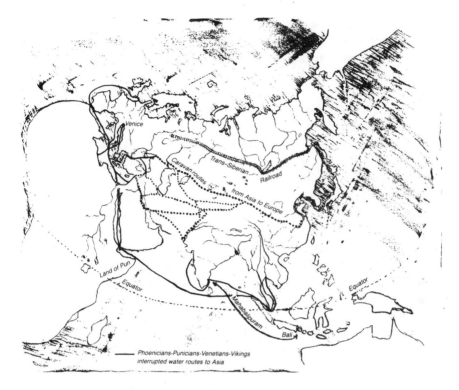

FIGURE 15.   Water and caravan routes between Asia and Europe

caravan to the Nile, and then water-borne to Alexandria, or via Somaliland, overland to the headwaters of the Nile, and thence to Alexandria. The latter route was not economically competitive but was the route of travel of the ship-designing and -building arts that in due course brought the stoutly keeled, heavily ribbed, big-bellied ships into the Mediterranean.

We have seen the Greek Alexander the Great crossing Persia and reaching the Indian Ocean, thus connecting with the Phoenician trading to Asia. A thousand years later the Crusaders—ostensibly fighting for holy reasons—were the Indian Ocean–Phoenician-Venetian-Veeking water-borne power structure fighting the older overland–Khyber Pass power structure over mastery of the trade route between Asia and Europe.

In our "Humans in Universe" chapter we spoke about the 600–200 B.C. Greeks' discovery that our Earth is a sphere and a planet of the solar system. This was the typical scientific product of a water-navigation people.

We witnessed also the originally horse-mounted Roman Empire's destruction of such knowledge, as their earlier grand strategy sought to reestablish the Asia-to-Europe trade pattern via Constantinople and the inland, overland, Khyber Pass route. This explains why the power structure saw fit to Dark-Age-out the mariners' spherical concept. It explains Ptolemy's 200 A.D. conic map's cutting off the around-Africa route mapped by Eratosthenes 400 years earlier.

With the world three-quarters water the bigger ship-producing capability was the beginning of a complete change in the control of human affairs. Bigger and better engineering was developed. The rival power structures were focused on the water supply lines. The Romans' overland road to England became obsolete. The Phoenician ships sailing out through Gibraltar into the Atlantic outperformed them. This shifted the battles among the world trade-route power structures from on-the-land popular visibility to popularly unwitnessed seascape. Long years of great battles of the corsairs, the pirates of the Barbary Coast, and so forth were unwitnessed and unknown to the land people. Who the power structures might be became popularly invisible.

Finally, bigger ships got out of the Mediterranean and into the Atlantic, around Africa to the Orient, and then around the world. Thus, "those in the know" rediscovered that the world is a sphere and not an infinitely extended lateral plane. Great battles ensued—waged under the flags of England, France, and Spain—to determine who would become supreme master of the world's high-seas line of supply. These great nations were simply the operating fronts of behind-the-scenes, vastly ambitious individuals who had become so effectively powerful because of their ability to remain invisible while operating behind the national scenery. Always their victories were in the name of some powerful sovereign-ruled country. The real power structures were always the invisible ones behind the visible sovereign powers.

Because the building of superior fleets of ships involved a complex of materials to produce not only the wooden hulls but the metal fastenings and the iron anchors and chains and the fiber ropes and cloth sails, and because woods from many parts of the world excelled in various functions of hull, masts, spars, oars, etc., large money credits for foreign purchase of these and other critical supplies brought control of the sea enterprising into the hands of international bankers.

The building of invisible world-power-structure controls operates in the following manner. Suppose you know how and have the ambition, vision, and daring to build one of these great ships. You have the mathematics. You have the positioning of numbers that enables you—or your servants— to calculate the engineering data governing the design of hulls, spars, rigging, etc., and all the other necessary calculations for the building of a ship capable of sailing all the way to the Orient and returning with the incredible treasures that you have learned from travelers are to be found there. One trip to the Orient—and a safe return to Europe—could make you a fortune. "There are fabulous stores of treasures in the Orient to be cashed in—*if* my ship comes in!"

The building of a ship required that you be so physically powerful a fighting man—commanding so many other fighting men as to have a large regiment of people under your control—that you must have the acknowledged power to command all the people in your nation who are carpenters to work on your ship; all your nation's metalworkers to work on the fastenings, chain plates, chains, and anchors of your ship; all those who can make rope and all the people who grow fibers for your rope; all the people who grow, spin, and weave together the fabrics for your sails. Thus, all the skilled people of the nation had to be employed in the building and outfitting of your ship. In addition you had to command all the farmers who produced the food to feed not only themselves but also to feed all those skilled people while they built the ship—and to feed all your army and all your court. So there was no way you could possibly produce one of these great ships unless you were very, very powerful.

Even then, in building ships, there were many essential materials that you didn't have in your own nation and so had to purchase from others. You also needed working cash—money to cope with any and all unforeseen events that could not be coped with by use of muscle or the sword—money to trade with. It was at this stage of your enterprise that the banker entered into the equation of power.

Up until 1500 B.C. all money was cattle, lambs, goats, or pigs—*live money* that was real life-support wealth, wealth you could actually eat. Steers were by far the biggest food animal, and so they were the highest denomination of money. The Phoenicians carried their cattle with them for trading, but these big creatures proved to be very cumbersome on long voyages. This was the time when Crete was the headquarters of the big-boat people and their new supreme weapon—the lines-of-supply-control ship. Crete was called the Minoan civilization, the bull civilization, worshippers of the male fertility god.

The pair of joined bull's horns symbolized that the particular ship carried real-wealth traders—that there were cattle on board to be exchanged for local-wealth items. The Norsemen with their paired-horn headdress were the Phoenician, Veenetian, Veeking (spelled Viking but pronounced "Veeking" by the Vikings). Veenetians, Phoenicians. (Punitians, Puntits, Pundits. Punic Wars. Punt = boat = the boat people. *Pun* in some African Colored languages means "red," as in Red Sea.). The Veekings were simply the northernmost European traders. The Veekings, Veenitians, Feenicians, Friesians—i.e., Phoenicians, Portuguese—were cross-breeding water-world people.

Graduating from carrying cattle along for trading in 1500 B.C. the Phoenicians invented metal money, which they first formed into iron half-rings that looked like a pair of bull's horns. (Many today mistake them for bracelets.) Soon the traders found that those in previously unvisited foreign countries had no memory of the cattle-on-board trading days and didn't recognize the miniature iron bull horn. If metal was being used for trading, then there were other kinds of metal they preferred trading with people—

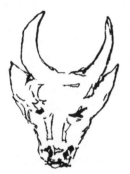

Minoan Bull

Viking

Phoenician Money

FIGURE 16.

silver, copper, and gold were easy to judge by hefting and were more aesthetically pleasing than the forged iron bull horn symbols.

This soon brought metal coinage into the game of world trading, with the first coin bearing the image of the sovereign of the homeland of the Phoenicians.

This switch to coinage occurred coincidentally at just about the same time as the great changeover from city-state dominance to line-of-supply dominance of the power-structure group controlling most of world affairs. This was the time when the Phoenicians began trading with people of so many different languages that, in need of a means of recording the different word sounds made by people around the world, the Phoenicians invented phonetic spelling—Phoenician spelling—which pronounced each successive sound separately and invented letter symbols for each sound. With phonetic spelling human written communication changed very much—from the visual-metaphor-concept writing of the Orient, accomplished with complex ideagraphics (ideographs), several of which frequently experienced, generalized cartoons told the whole story visually. It was a big change from ideographs to the Phoenicians' phonetic spelling, wherein each letter is a single sound—having no meaning in itself—and whereby it took several sounds to make a whole word and many such words to make any sense—i.e., a sentence. This is the historical event that Ezra Pound says coincides with the story of the Tower of Babel. Pound says that humanity was split into a babble of individually meaningless sounds while losing the conceptual symbols of whole ideas—powerful generalizations. You had to become an expert to understand the phonetic letter code. The spelling of words excluded a great many people from communicating, people who had been doing so successfully with ideographs.

This gradual alteration of world trading devices from cattle to gold brought about the world-around development of pirates who, building small but swift craft, could on a dark night board one of the great merchant ships just before it reached home, richly laden after a two-year trip to the Orient, and take over the ship and, above all, its gold. With the gold captured, the pirates often burned the vanquished ship.

As already mentioned in our Introduction, it was in 1805, 200 years after the founding of the East India Company, that the British won the Battle of Trafalgar, giving them dominance of all the world's lines of supply. They now controlled the seas of the world. It was said by world people that the British Empire became the first empire in history upon which "the sun never set." In order to get their gold off the sea and out of reach of the pirates, the British made deals with the sovereigns of all the countries around the world with whom they traded, by which it was agreed from then on to keep annual accounts of their intertrading and at the end of the year to move the gold from the debtor's bank in London to the creditor's bank in London to balance the accounts. In this way they kept the gold off the ocean and immune to sea pirate raiding. This brought about what is now called the "balance of trade" accounting.

The international trading became the most profitable of all enterprises, and great land-"owners" with clear-cut king's "deeds" to their land went often to international gold moneylenders. The great land barons underwrote the building of enterprisers' ships with their cattle or other real wealth, the regenerative products of their lands, turned over to the lender as collateral.

If the ship did come back, both the enterpriser and the bankers realized a great gain. The successful ship venturer paid the banker back, and the banker who had been holding the cattle as collateral returned them to their original proprietor. But during the voyage (usually two years to the Orient and back to Europe) the pledged cattle had calves, "kind" (German for "child"), and this is where the concept of interest originated, which was payable "in kind"—the cattle that were born while the collateral was held by the banker were to belong to the banker.

When the Phoenicians shifted their trading strategy from carrying cattle to carrying metal money, the metal money didn't have little money—"kind"—but the idea of earned interest persisted. This meant that the interest was deducted from the original money value, and this of course depreciated the capital equity of the borrower. Thus, metallic equity banking became a different kind of game from the original concept.

In twentieth-century banking the depositors assume that their money is safely guarded in the vaulted bank, especially so in a savings bank, whereas their money is loaned out, within seconds after its depositing, at interest payable to the banker which is greater than the interest paid to the savings account depositor and, since the metal or paper money does not produce children—"kind"—the banker's so-called earned share must, in reality, be deducted from the depositor's true-wealth deposit.

The merchant bankers of Venice came to underwrite the Venetians' (the Phoenicians') voyaging ventures. Such international trade financing swiftly became the big thing in the banking game. The "Merchant of Venice"—Shylock and his "pound of flesh forfeit" of the debtor—was Shakespeare's way of calling attention to the fact that the bankers' "interest" was in reality depleting the life-support equity of both the depositors and the borrowers.

It was the financing of such international voyaging, trading, and individual travel as well as of vaster games of governmental takeovers that built the enormous wealth-controlling fortunes of early European private banking families. It was under analogous circumstances of financing inter-American-European trade that, in the late nineteenth century, J. P. Morgan became a man of great power. By having his banking houses in Paris and London, Philadelphia and New York, he was able not only to finance people's foreign travel, all their intershipment of goods, and to give letters of credit, but also to finance and control major "new era" railroading, shipbuilding, mining, manufacturing, and energy-generating enterprises in general.

Such powerful banking gave insights regarding the degrees of risks that could be taken. The people doing the risking came to the banker for advice. In such a manner J. P. Morgan developed the most powerful financing position in America, as society went from wooden ships to steel ships and the concomitant iron mining, blast furnace building, and steel rolling mill development, as well as the making of boilers and engines, electric generators, and air conditioning systems.

To better understand the coming of world power structure into North American affairs, we will switch back from the nineteenth to the seventeenth and eighteenth centuries, to the opening up of North America and the American socioeconomic scene. The European colonization occurred in several major ways.

The Spanish way was accomplished with vast haciendas—grants from the king to powerful supporters. The hacienda development began in Central America and Mexico and expanded northward into California.

The British king also gave vast plantation grants to royal favorites on the North American southeastern coast, below the freezing line.

The French came to two parts of North America: (1) to the Gulf of Mexico–Mississippi delta, where exiled prisoners were dumped, and (2) to the St. Lawrence area of Canada, whence they moved westward via the Great Lakes, then southward on the Mississippi to join with these lower Mississippi colonists exploring northward and westward on the Mississippi.

British sovereign grants were also being given on the northeastern coast, where it was much colder and where existence was much more difficult. Because it was much more difficult to colonize, the royal favorites who received large land grants from the British king in the north did everything they could to encourage colonization of any kind by others, who bought their land from their landlords. The Pilgrims and other people of religious conviction found the freedom of thought-and-act to warrant hazarding their lives in that cold-winter wilderness. On the northeast coast of North America the individuals who did the colonizing were not the landowners, who remained safely in Europe. In the south the royal-favorite landowners themselves occupied and personally operated many of the great plantations.

Though motivated by distinctly different northern and southern reasons for doing so, we have the east-coast North American British-blood people breaking away from the Old World through the American Revolution.

In our tracing of the now completely invisible world power structures it is important to note that, while the British Empire as a world government lost the American Revolution, the power structure behind it did not lose the war. The most visible of the power-structure identities was the East India Company, an entirely private enterprise whose flag as adopted by Queen Elizabeth in 1600 happened to have thirteen red and white horizontal stripes with a blue rectangle in its upper lefthand corner. The blue rectangle bore in red and white the superimposed crosses of St. Andrew and St. George. When the Boston Tea Party occurred, the colonists dressed as Indians boarded the East India Company's three ships and threw overboard their entire cargoes of high-tax tea. They also took the flag from the masthead of the largest of the "East Indiamen"—the *Dartmouth.*

George Washington took command of the U.S. Continental Army under an elm tree in Cambridge, Massachusetts. The flag used for that occasion was the East India Company's flag, which by pure coincidence had the thirteen red and white stripes. Though it was only coincidence, most of those present thought the thirteen red and white stripes did represent the thirteen American colonies—ergo, was very appropriate—but they complained about the included British flag's superimposed crosses in the blue rectangle in the top corner. George Washington conferred with Betsy Ross, after which came the thirteen white, five-pointed stars in the blue field with the thirteen red and white horizontal stripes. While the British government lost the 1776 war, the East India Company's owners who constituted the invisible power structure behind the British government not only did not lose but moved right into the new U.S.A. economy along with the latter's most powerful landowners.

By pure chance I happened to uncover this popularly unknown episode of American history. Commissioned in 1970 by the Indian government to design new airports in Bombay, New Delhi, and Madras, I was visiting the grand palace of the British fortress in Madras, where the English first established themselves in India in 1600. There I saw a picture of Queen Elizabeth I and the flag of the East India Company of 1600 A.D., with its thirteen red and white horizontal stripes and its superimposed crosses in the upper corner. What astonished me was that this flag (which seemed to be the American flag) was apparently being used in 1600 A.D., 175 years before the American Revolution. Displayed on the stairway landing wall together with the portrait of Queen Elizabeth I painted on canvas, the flag was painted on the wall itself, as was the seal of the East India Company.

The supreme leaders of the American Revolution were of the southern type—George Washington and Thomas Jefferson. Both were great landowners with direct royal grants for their lands, in contradistinction to the relatively meager individual landholdings of the individual northern Puritan colonists.

With the Revolution over we have Alexander Hamilton arguing before the Congress that it was not the intention of the signers of the Declaration of Independence that the nation so formed should have any wealth. Wealth, Hamilton argued—as supported by Adam Smith—is the land, which is something that belonged entirely to private individuals, preponderantly the great landowners with king-granted deeds to hundreds and sometimes thousands of square miles, as contrasted to the ordinary colonists' few hundreds of acres of homestead farms.

Hamilton went on to argue that the United States government so formed would, of course, need money from time to time and must borrow that money from the rich landowners' banks and must pay the banks back with interest. Assuming that the people would be benefited by what their representative government did with the money it borrowed, the people gladly would be taxed in order to pay the money back to the landowners with interest. This is where a century-and-a-half-long game of "wealth"-poker began—with the cards dealt only to the great landowners by the world power structure.

Obviously, very powerful people had their land given to them by the king and not by God, but the king, with the church's approbation, asserted it was with God's blessing. This deed-processing produced a vast number of court decisions and legal precedent based on centuries and centuries of deed inheritances. Thus, landlord's deeds evolved from deeds originally dispensed from deeds of war. Then the great landlords loaned parcels of their lands to sharecropping farmers, who had to pay the landlord a tithe, or rent, and "interest" out of the wealth produced by nature within the confines of the deeded land. The landlord had his "tithing" barn within which to store the grains collected in the baskets (*fiscus* is Latin for "basket"; thus the fiscal year is that which winds up within the basketed measuring of the net grains harvested). The real payoff, of course, was in regenerative metabolic increments of the botanical photosynthetic impoundment of Sun radiation and hydrocarbon molecules' structuring and proliferation through other hydrogenic and biological interaccommodations. Obviously none of this natural wealth-regenerating and -multiplying process was accreditable to the landlords.

When I was young, there were people whom everybody knew to be very "wealthy." Nobody had the slightest idea of what that "wealth" consisted, other than the visible land and the complex of buildings in which the wealthy lived, plus their horses, carriages and yachts. The only thing that counted was that they were "known to be" enormously wealthy. The wealthy could do approximately anything they wanted to do. Many owned cargo ships. However, the richest were often prone to live in very unostentatious ways.

Of course, money was coined and the paper equivalents of metallic coinage were issued by the officers of banks of variously ventured private-capital-banking-type land systems. Enterprises were underwritten by wealthy landowners, to whom shares in the enterprises were issued and, when fortunate, dividends were paid. "Rich" people sometimes had their own private banks—as, for instance, J. P. Morgan and Company. Ordinary people rushed to deposit their earnings in the wealthy people's banks.

For all the foregoing reasons nobody knew of what the wealth of the wealthy really consisted, nor how much there was of it. There were no income taxes until after World War I. But the income tax did not disclose capital wealth. It disclosed only the declared income of the wealthy. The banks were *capitalized* in various substantial amounts considered obviously adequate to cover any and all deposits by other than the bankers involved in proclaiming the capital values. These capital values were agreed upon privately between great landowners based on equities well within the marketable values of small fractions of their vast king-deeded landholdings.

"The rich get richer and the poor get children" was a popular song of the early 1920s. Wages were incredibly low, and the rich could get their buildings built for a song and people them with many servants for another song. But, as with uncalled poker hands, nobody ever knew what the "wealthy" really had. I was a boy in a "comfortably off" family, not a "wealthy" family—not wealthy enough to buy and own horses and carriages. To me the wealthy seemed to be just "fantastically so."

This brings us to World War I. Why was it called the First *World* War? All wars until this time had been fought in the era when land was the primary wealth. The land was the wealth because it produced the food essential to life. In the land-wealth era of warring the opposing forces took the farmers from the farms and made soldiers of them. They exhausted the farm-produced food supplies and trampled down the farms. War was local.

In 1810, only five years after Malthus's pronouncement of the fundamental inadequacy of life support on planet Earth, the telegraph was invented. It used copper wires to carry its messages. This was the beginning of a new age of advancing technology. The applied findings of science brought about an era in which there was a great increase of metals being interalloyed or interemployed mechanically, chemically, and electrolytically. Metals greatly increased the effectiveness of the land-produced foods. The development of nonrusting, hermetically sealed tin cans made possible preservation and distribution of foods to all inhabited portions of our planet Earth. All the new technology of all the advancing industry, which was inaugurated by the production of steel in the mid-nineteenth century, required the use of all the known primary metallic elements in various intercomplementary alloyings.

For instance tin cans involved tin from the Malay straits, iron from West Virginia mines, and manganese from southern Russia.

The metals were rarely found under the farmlands or in the lands that belonged to the old lords of the food-productive lands. Metals were found—often, but not always, in mountains—all around the world, in lands of countries remote from one another. Mine ownerships were granted by governments to the first to file claims.

It was the high-seas, intercontinental, international trafficking in these metals that made possible the life-support effectiveness of both farming and fishing. The high-seas trafficking was mastered by the world-around line-of-supply controllers—the venturers and pirates known collectively as the British Empire. This world-around traffic was in turn financed, accounted, and maximally profited in by the international bankers and their letters of credit, bills of exchange, and similar pieces of paper. International banking greatly reduced the necessity for businessmen to travel with their exported goods to collect at the importer's end. Because the world-around-occurring metals were at the heart of this advance in standards of living for increasing numbers of humans all around the world, the struggle for mastery of this trade by the invisible, behind-the-scenes-contending world power structures ultimately brought about the breakout of the visible, international World War I.

The war was the consequence of the world-power-structure "outs" becoming realistically ambitious to take away from the British "ins" the control of the world's high-seas lines of supply. The "outs" saw that the British Navy was guarding only the surface of the sea and that there were proven new inventions—the submarine, which could go under the water, and the airplane, which could fly above the water—so the behind-the-scenes world-power-structure "outs" adopted their multidimensional offensive strategy against the two-dimensional world-power-structure "ins." The invisible-power-structure "outs" puppeted the Germans and their allies. The invisible-power-structure "ins" puppeted Great Britain and her allies. With their underwater strategies the "outs" did severely break down the "ins' " line of supply.

J. P. Morgan was the visible fiscal agent for the "in" power structure, operating through Great Britain and her allies. The 1914 industrial productivity in America was enormous, with an even more enormous amount of untapped U.S. metallic resources, particularly of iron and copper, as backup.

Throughout the nineteenth century all the contending invisible world power structures invested heavily in U.S.A.-enterprise equities. Throughout that nineteenth century, the vast resources of the U.S.A. plus the new array of imported European industrial tooling, the North American economy established productivity. The U.S.A. economy took all the industrial machinery that had been invented in England, Germany, France, and Europe in general and reproduced it in America with obvious experience-suggested improvements.

In 1914 World War I started in the Balkans and was "joined" in Belgium and France on the European continent. The British Isles represented the "unsinkable flagship" of the high-seas navy of the masters of the world oceans' lines of supply. The "unsinkable flagship" commanded the harbors of the European customers of the high-seas-line-of-supply control. If the line of supply that kept the war joined on the European continent broke down completely, then the "outs" would be able to take the British Isles themselves, which, as the "flagship" of the "ins," would mean the latter's defeat.

In 1914, three years before the U.S.A. entered the war, J. P. Morgan, as the "Allies' " fiscal agent, began to buy in the U.S.A. to offset the line-of-supply losses accomplished by the enemy submarines. Morgan kept buying and buying, but finally, on the basis of sound world-banking finance, which was predicated on the available gold reserve, came the point at which Morgan had bought for the British and their allies an amount of goods from the U.S.A. equaling all the monetary bullion gold in the world available to the "ins' " power structure. Despite this historically unprecedented magnitude of the Allied purchasing it had only fractionally tapped the productivity of the U.S.A. So Morgan, buying on behalf of England and her allies, exercised their borrowing "credit" to an extent that bought a total of goods worth twice the amount of gold and silver in the world available to the "ins." As yet the potential productivity of the U.S.A. was but fractionally articulated. Because the "ability to pay later" credit of the Allied nations could not be stretched any further, the only way to keep the U.S.A. productivity flowing and increasing was to get the U.S.A. itself into the war on the "ins' " side, so that it would buy its own productivity in support of its own war effort as well as that of its allies.

By skillful psychology and propaganda the "ins" persuaded America that they were fighting "to save democracy." I recall, as one of the youth of those times, how enthusiastic everyone became about "saving democracy." Immediately the U.S.A. government asked the British and their allies, "What do you need over there?" The "ins" replied, "A million trained and armed men, and the ships to carry them to France, and many, many new ships to replace the ships that have been sunk by submarines. We need them desperately to keep carrying the tanks and airplanes, weapons, and munitions to France." The "ins" also urgently requested that the U.S. Navy be increased in strength to equal the strength of the British Navy and therewith to cope with the German submarines, "while our British Navy keeps the German high-seas fleet bottled up. We want all of this from America."

America went to work, took over and newly implemented many of the U.S. industries, such as the telephone, telegraph, and power companies, and produced all that was wanted. For the first time in history, from 1914 to 1918, humanity entered upon a comprehensive program of industrial transformation and went from wire to wireless communications; from tracked to trackless transportation; from two-dimensional transport to four-dimensional; from visible structuring and mechanical techniques to invisible—atomic and molecular—structuring and mechanics.

Within one year the million armed and trained U.S.A. soldiers were safely transported to France without the loss of one soldier to the submarines. Arrived in France, they entered the line of battle. With the line of supply once more powerfully re-established by the U.S. Navy and its merchant fleet, it became clear that the "ins" were soon going to win.

J. P. Morgan, now representing the "allied" power structures' capitalist system's banks as well as serving as the Allies' purchasing agent, said to the American Congress, "How are you going to pay for it all?" The American Congress said, "What do you mean, pay for it? This is our own wealth. This is our war to save democracy. We will win the war and then stop the armaments production." Morgan said, "You have forgotten Alexander Hamilton. The U.S. government doesn't have any money. You're going to pay for it all right, but since you don't have any money, you're going to have to borrow it all from the banks. You're going to borrow from me, Mr. Morgan, in order to pay these vast war bills. Then you must raise the money by taxes to pay me back."

To finance these enormous payments Mr. Morgan and his army of lawyers invented—for the U.S. government—the Liberty Loans and Victory Loans. Then the U.S. Congress invented the income tax.

With the U.S. Congress's formulating of the legislation that set up the scheme of the annual income tax, "we the people" had, for the first time, a little peek into the poker hands of the wealthy. But only into the amount of their taxable income, not into the principal wealth cards of their poker game.

During World War I, U.S. industrial production had gone to $178 billion. With only $30 billion of monetary gold in the world, this monetary magnitude greatly exceeded any previously experienced controllability of the behind-the-scenes finance power structure of the European "Allies."

World War I over, won by the Allies, all the countries on both sides of the warring countries are deeply in debt to America. Because the debt to the U.S.A. was twice that of all the gold in the "ins'" world, all the countries involved in World War I paid all their gold to the U.S.A. Despite those enormous payments in gold all the countries were as yet deeply in debt to the U.S.A. Thereafter all those countries went off the gold standard.

All the monetary gold bullion paid to the U.S.A. was stored in the mountain vaults of Fort Knox, Kentucky. International trade became completely immobilized, and the U.S.A. found itself having unwittingly become the world's new financial master. Swiftly it arranged vast trading account loans to the foreign countries. This financing of foreign countries' purchasing by the U.S.A. credit loans started an import-export boom in the U.S.A., followed by an early 1920s recession and another boom; then, the Great Crash of 1929.

The reasons for the Great Crash go back to the swift technological evolution occurring in the U.S.A. between 1900 and the 1914 beginning of World War I and the U.S.A.'s entry into it in 1917. Most important amongst those techno-economic evolution events are those relating to electrical power. Gold is the most efficient conductor of electricity, silver is the next, and copper is a close third. Of these three gold is the scarcest, silver the next, then copper. Though relatively scarce, copper is the most plentiful of the good electrical conductors. Copper is also nonsparking and therefore makes a safe casing for gunpowder-packed bullets and big gun shells. As a consequence of these conditions, in the one year, 1917, more copper was mined, refined, and manufactured into wire, tubing, sheet, and other end products than in the total cumulative production of all the years of all human history before 1917.

With the war over all the copper that had been mined and put into generators and conductors did not go back into the mines nor did it rot.

World War I was not an agrarian, but an inanimate-energy and power-driven, industrial-production war—with the generating power coming from Niagara and other waterfalls as well as from coal and petroleum. For the first time the U.S.A. was generating power with oil-burning steam turbines.

When the war was over, all this power-production equipment was still in prime operating condition. There was enormous potential productivity—a wealth of wealth-producing capability that had never before existed, let alone as a consequence of war. The production capacity that had been established was so great as to have been able to produce, within a two-year span, all those ships, trucks, and armaments. What was the U.S.A. economy going to do with its new industrial gianthood? It was the vastness of this unexpected, government-funded production wealth and its ownership by corporate stockholders that generated many negative thoughts about the moral validity of war profiteering.

There were many desirable and useful items that could be mass-produced and successfully marketed. Young people wanted automobiles, but automobiles were capital equipment. In 1920 capital equipment was sold only for cash. There were enough affluent people in post-World-War-I U.S.A. to provide an easy market for a limited production of automobiles. In 1920 there were no bank-supported time payment sales in the retail trade. The banks would accept chattel mortgages and time payments on large mobile capital goods, such as trucking equipment, for large, rich corporations. Banks would not consider risking their money on such perishable, run-away-with-able capital equipment as the privately owned automobile.

Because the banks would not finance the buying of automobiles and so many money-earning but capital-less young people wanted them, shyster loaners appeared who were tough followers of their borrowers when they were in arrears. Between the ever-increasing time-payment patronage and the affluent, a market for automobiles was opening that could support mass production.

In 1922 there were about 125 independent automobile companies. They were mostly headed by colorful automobile-designing and -racing individuals for whom most of the companies were named. They survived by individually striving each year to produce an entirely new and better automobile, most of which were costly. Many accepted orders for more than they had the mechanical capability to produce. Their hometown financiers would back these auto-designing geniuses so that they could buy better production tooling and build larger factories. Wall Street sold swiftly increasing numbers of shares in auto companies. More and more of them went broke for lack of production, distribution, and maintenance experience on the part of the auto-designer managements.

In 1926 the Wall Street brokerage house of Dillon, Read and Co. made a comprehensive cost study of the auto-production field. They found that 130,000 cars a year was, in 1926, the minimum that could be accounted as *mass* production and sold at production prices. Any less production had to carry a much higher price tag. To warrant the latter, the cars had to be superlatively excellent. The English-built Rolls-Royce brought the highest price on the American market. There was fierce competition among Packard, Peerless, Cadillac, Pierce-Arrow, Locomobile, Lozier, Leland, and others for the top American car. All of those premium cars' frames, bodies, engines, and parts were manufactured within their own factories. There were several in-between classes, such as that of the Buick. Most of the 100 or so cars in this intermediate range were assembled from special engines, frames, and other parts made by independent manufacturers.

The mortality in auto companies was great. Dillon, Read led Wall Street out of its dilemma by buying several almost bankrupt companies, closely located to one another, such as those of the Dodge family, whose joint production capacity topped the 130,000 units per year mass-production figure.

They named their new venture the Chrysler Company. Dillon, Read fired the auto company presidents, who were primarily interested in new-car-designing, and replaced them with production engineers. Wall Street followed suit and put in production engineers as presidents of all the auto companies—except Ford, who owned his company outright and had no obligation to Wall Street and its legion of stock buyers. Old Henry himself was already the conceiver, initiator, and artist-master of mass production.

Because the American public was in love with the annual automobile shows, the Wall Street financiers who had thrown out all the colorful auto-designer presidents started a new game by setting up the Madison Avenue advertising industry, which hired artists who knew how to use the new (1920) airbrush to make beautiful drawings of only superficially—not mechanically—*new* dream cars. They made drawings of the new models, which required only superficial mudguard and radiator changes with no design changes in the hidden parts. Parts were purchased by the big companies from smaller, highly competitive parts manufacturers operating in the vicinity of Detroit.

This was the beginning of the downfall of the world-esteemed integrity of Yankee ingenuity, which was frequently, forthrightly, and often naïvely manifest in American business. Big business in the U.S.A. set out to make money deceitfully—by fake "new models"—and *engineering design advance* was replaced by *"style" design change.*

In the late twenties first Ford and then General Motors instituted their own time-financing corporations. The bankers of America said, "Let them have it, they'll be sorry—autos, phew! We don't want to go around trying to recover these banged-up autos when the borrower is in default." The bankers said, "It is very immoral to buy automobiles 'on time.' They are just a luxury."

What the bankers did like to support in the new mass productivity was tractor-driven farm machinery. Farm machinery was easy to sell. As the farmer sat atop the demonstration plowing or harvesting equipment, with its power to go through the fields doing an amount of work in a day equal to what had previously taken him weeks, he said to himself, "I can make more money and also take it a little easier." So the bankers approved the financing of the production and marketing of the farm machinery. They held a chattel mortgage on the machinery and a mortgage on the farmland itself and all its buildings. The bankers loved that. There was enthusiastic bank acceptance of the selling of such equipment "on time" to the farmers. The bankers did not consider this "immoral." The farmer was "producing food wealth." The automobilist was "just joy riding."

Then there came a very bad hog market in 1926. Many farmers were unable to make the payments on their power-driven equipment. The local country banks foreclosed on the delinquent farmers' mortgages and took away their farms and machinery. The bankers had assumed that the farms were going to be readily saleable. It turned out, however, that there were not so many nonfarmers waiting to become farmers, and most of the real farmers had been put out of business by the bank foreclosures so they couldn't buy back their own farms. There were no city people eager to go out and buy one of those farms. "How you gonna keep them down on the farm, after they've seen Paree?" were the words of a popular World War I song.

So the dust bowls developed as the upturned, unsown soil began to blow off the farms. It is relevant to note that, in 1900, 90 percent of U.S.A. citizens were living and working on the farms; in 1979 only 7 percent were on the farms, mostly as local supervisors for big, absent-ownership corporations. The owners of the farmlands today are no longer "farmers" or even individual humans—they are the great business conglomerates. What began in 1934 as government subsidies and loans to farmers for farm machinery, later to keep acreage out of production, would by 1978 result in President Carter making enormous payments to appease big corporations for cutting off vital grain and other strategic shipments to Russia. Next, the U.S. government would make enormous subsidies to bail out large corporations such as Lockheed and Chrysler, which as basic military suppliers the U.S. government could not allow to go bankrupt. Eventually the U.S. taxpayers will be asked to make "free-of-risk" bail-outs of "private" enterprises, corporations with initial physical assets worth over a billion dollars classifed as risk enterprises.

We now return to the 1926-'27-'28-'29 sequence of events developing from selling the farmers' machinery on the bankers' drop-dead terms (*mortgage* means "on death terms"). In 1927 and 1928 the bigger Western city banks began to foreclose on their local country banks that had financed the farm machinery sales and had been borrowing from the bigger city banks to cover their unprecedentedly expanded loaning. First the little and then the successively bigger banks found that they had foreclosed on farmhouses that had no indoor toilets, many with roofs falling in, barns in poor condition, with the replevined farm machinery rusting out in the open—and no customers.

Word of the bad news gradually went around; small bank "runs" began; and in 1929 came the Great Crash in the stock market. All business went from worse to worser. Unemployment multiplied. Prices steadily dropped. Nobody had money with which to buy. Bigger and bigger banks had to foreclose on smaller banks, until finally in early 1933 there came one day in which 5000 banks closed their doors to stop "the run" on their funds.

People were dismayed and both individually and collectively helpless to do anything to combat the economic collapse. The economy had gone to pieces. People did not parade and protest. They became so low in spirit and listless that they just sat around silently in their homes or in public places. The New York subway stations were filled with people sleeping on the concrete platforms and stairways. No religious organizations were willing to let people sleep in their churches.

There came a "pecking-order" point when the central Chicago banks foreclosed on all the other big Western city banks—followed by the big New York City central banks foreclosing on Chicago's central banks. Finally came the denouement, when the big New York banks found themselves about to close because they were already behind-the-scenes insolvent. This occasioned the U.S. Congress voting to accelerate by four months the presidential inauguration of Franklin Delano Roosevelt who, minutes after taking his oath of office, signed the Bank Moratorium, which momentarily suspended the acknowledgment of the death of the wealthy landowners' banking system that had lost all or much of its depositors' money. About a month later Congress voted to the President of the U.S.A. the ability to control all money. Months later again the U.S. Supreme Court upheld that legislation. The U.S.A. citizens themselves and their government had become the wealth resource "of last recourse." The underwriting wealth belongs to all the people and not to the few. That happened also to be the description of socialism.

The 150-year-long "infinite wealth" poker hand and its uncalled bluffing was over. The called hands were suddenly down. It turned out that the "wealthys'" wealth was nonexistent. Their marble-walled, steel-barred, visibly vaulted banks had been psychologically attractive to the depositors, who preferred to have their earnings and savings deposited along with the wealth of the powerfully rich. What the banks had been doing was to loan the people's deposits to other people. The banks had no money themselves. What they had done was to capitalize their land at their self-asserted value and had been credited with that value of stock in the bank's ownership.

In 1933, for the first time ever, the hands of the U.S. American wealthy were exposed (and by inference, all land-based capitalism everywhere around the world)—most were money empty. Their land and multiservanted mansion values dropped to almost nothing. Nobody had the almost-nothing amount of money to buy those richly housed estates. There was one exception to the last statement—the Vatican-administered Roman Catholic Church's world organization, which for a pittance acquired many extraordinary properties at that time, which it converted into monasteries and convents, colleges and schools.

The game of "deedable land wealth" had been a bluff from its very beginning—multimillennia ago, when that little man on a horse, armed with a club, first rode up to the giant shepherd leader of a tribe and said, bluffingly, "It's very dangerous out here in the wilderness for beautiful sheep such as yours," and the shepherd leader's ultimate coercion into accepting "protection" from the claiming and proclaiming "owner" of the land.

Landownership did not go back to an act of God. All the kings always had their priests present when the land claimage was made by their explorers. The priests planted their crosses to confirm that the king's ownership was blessed by God. The Roman Catholic Church, starting in its emperor-pope days, has been in the deeded-land business for "going on" 2000 years. It is as yet the world's largest real estate owner. *Real,* a Spanish word, means "royal"—the succession of king-deeded estate lands.

With the bluff of wealth over in March 1933, almost all business in America stopped. On the inauguration of Franklin Delano Roosevelt the emergency was so absolute that Congress voted unanimously for whatever corrective measures the New Deal administration prescribed.

Roosevelt and his advisors said, "One thing is clear. Despite the emergency America abhors socialism. Americans don't like the assumption that everybody is equal. Americans are so independent, they don't feel at all equal. They don't like socialism, but," said the New Deal leaders, "the fact is that we, the American people, are going to have to guarantee our own bank accounts. People don't like to keep their money under their mattresses and prefer to put it into a bank, so we will have to do what we can to rehabilitate the banks. We the people acting unanimously through our government are going to have to guarantee the safety of each deposit in the banks to a convincingly substantial amount—$5000. We will leave the bank in ownership of the management of the stockholders of those banks that, by virtue of the presidential moratorium, are as yet theoretically alive, and hope that, with our guaranteeing, regulation, and supervising, many of them will reopen and will be able to progressively accredit their depositors with some percentage of their original deposits.

"But let us not deceive ourselves. With the government of the people guaranteeing the bank accounts, it becomes, in operating fact, *socialism.* On the other hand people themselves know so little about banking, credit concepts, and the history of power structures that they will not know that they have adopted socialism, since the government has not taken 'possession' of the banks. Society will think well of 'we the people' as the government, guaranteeing the new deposits in the banks up to $5000."

Society likes the idea of a bank as a safekeeping device. People have always believed that when they put their money in the bank, it stayed there. They had no idea it went out on loan within minutes after it came in. They were completely hoodwinked by the appearance of the banks as safe, fire-proof, and robberproof depositories of their earnings. Even today, in the last twenty years of the twentieth century, people know little more about banks than they did during the 1929 Crash or at the depth of the Depression in 1932, when all they knew was that they had lost their deposits in most of them.

In 1933, '34, '35, and '36 the New Deal and the U.S. Congress diligently investigated the banking system and the practices of its most powerful lead-ers. They found many malpractices, which we will discuss later. Most prominently they found the banks loaded with worthless mortgages on properties that were unsaleable because uninhabitable—mortgages on build-ings without roofs, bathrooms, etc.

The government said, "The first thing we must do is make those mort-gages we've inherited worth something." At this point the American gov-ernment dictated the banking strategy and started refinancing of the building industry. The so-called building "industry" was already 2000 years behind the arts of building ships of the sea and sky, which ships of the sea and sky are, in fact, environment-controlling structures in exactly the same sense that land buildings are environment-controlling structures.

While the design of the seagoing and airgoing environment controls are floatably and flyably weight-considerate and semiautonomous because they generate their own power, desalinate their own water, etc., there is no weight consideration in the designing of the land-anchored environment controls. They don't have to float or fly. They are utterly dependent on sew-ers, waterlines, electric lines, highway maintenance. They are utterly con-trolled by the prime landowners, their building codes and readily imposable legal restrictions—all based on the real estates' ownership and control of the highways-sewers-waterlines—the metabolic "guts" of all U.S.A. towns and cities.

When the government owns the wealth and controls the issuance of its money, it is socialism. The New Deal was not trying to deceive the people but was engaged in a rescue operation of the first order and was hopeful of not irritating the people psychologically by what it seemed was critically mandatory to accomplish.

Paradoxically, the first people they irritated—greatly—were yesterday's rich, in particular those who were as yet living on the dividends and interest of as yet solvent industrial corporations' stocks and bonds. In fear of the New Deal they sought to discredit Roosevelt by a word-of-mouth campaign. From 1933 to 1940 individual members of rich gentlemen's clubs of New York were ostracized from membership in the rudest manner by "the mem-bers" if they were not heard to speak frequently of "that son-of-a-bitch in the White House."

Franklin Roosevelt and his advisors said, in effect, "We've got to do what we feel is best for the people by whatever name the 'best' may bear. We've got them depositing again in the banks and are rehabilitating all those mortgaged properties which we have inherited by loaning the new owners of the properties funds at negative interest provided they will rehabilitate the property—reroof or put in a bathroom, etc."

To those who understood some of its intricacies, everything was now out in the open about the world of banking. The New Deal said it was going to prohibit usurious rates of interest—"the banks must earn enough to keep themselves going, but only can charge 1½ percent for interest." Banks were regulated just like the Post Office. No banker had authority beyond that of a postmaster. The New Deal completely separated from banking what Morgan and many of the private banks had been doing—taking deposit money and putting it into common stocks and even into the bankers' own highly speculative private ventures. Thus came the New Deal's Securities and Exchange Commission and the complete separation of banking and initial risk financing—or, at least, supposedly so. Banks' trust departments could as yet buy and sell corporate venture stocks for clients' accounts however.

There were a number of individual bankers who went far beyond unwise banking practices and who, as individuals, took personal advantage of the information they had of individual depositors' affairs and of their privilege as top bank officers to do truly inimical things to enrich their own positions. Few today remember that a half-century ago a number of New York and Chicago's top bankers were sentenced into penitentiaries—the New Yorkers into Sing Sing—the senior partner of J. P. Morgan and Company, the president of the National City Bank, the president of Chase Bank. Every one of them had been found to be doing reprehensible financial tricks. They were selling their own friends short. They were opening their friends' mail and manipulating the stock market. They were manipulating everybody. They were way overstepping the moral limits of the privileges ethically existent for officers in the banking game, so a great housecleaning was done by the New Deal.

The banking story is best told by a poem that was, at that time, allegedly composed by Ogden Nash but was never to my knowledge formally published and copyrighted. It was, however, memorized and widely recited from copies often typewritten by those who remembered it:

"BUTCHER, BAKER, CANDLESTICK MAKER"

I'm an autocratic figure in these democratic states,
A dandy demonstration of hereditary traits.
As the children of the baker bake the most delicious breads,
As the sons of Casanova fill the most exclusive beds,

As the Barrymores and Roosevelts and others I could name
Inherited the talents that perpetuate their fame,
My position in the structure of society I owe
To the qualities my parents bequeathed me long ago.
My father was a gentleman and musical to boot.
He used to play piano in a house of ill repute.
The Madam was a lady and a credit to her cult,
She enjoyed my father's playing and I was the result.
So my Daddy and my Mummy are the ones I have to thank
That I'm Chairman of the Board of the National Silly Bank.

CHORUS: *Oh, our parents forgot to get married.*
          Our parents forgot to get wed.
          Did a wedding bell chime, it was always a time
          When our parents were somewhere in bed.
          Then all thanks to our kind loving parents.
          We are kings in the land of the free.
          Your banker, your broker, your Washington joker,
          Three prominent bastards are we, tra la,
          Three prominent bastards are we!

In a cozy little farmhouse in a cozy little dell
A dear old-fashioned farmer and his daughter used to dwell.
She was pretty, she was charming, she was tender, she was mild,
And her sympathy was such that she was frequently with child.
The year her hospitality attained a record high
She became a happy mother of an infant which was I.
Whenever she was gloomy, I could always make her grin,
By childishly inquiring who my daddy could have been.
The hired man was favored by the girls in Mummy's set,
And a traveling man from Scranton was an even money bet.
But such were Mother's motives and such was her allure,
That even Roger Babson wasn't absolutely sure.
Well, I took my mother's morals and I took my daddy's crust,
And I grew to be the founder of the New York Blankers Trust.

CHORUS: *Oh, our parents forgot, etc.*

In a torrid penal chain gang on a dusty southern road
My late lamented daddy had his permanent abode.
Now some were there for stealing, but my daddy's only fault
Was an overwhelming tendency for criminal assault.
His philosophy was simple and quite free from moral taint;

Seduction is for sissies, but a he-man wants his rape.
Daddy's total list of victims was embarrassingly rich,
And one of them was Mother, but he couldn't tell me which.
Well, I didn't go to college but I got me a degree.
I reckon I'm the model of a perfect S.O.B.,
I'm a debit to my country but a credit to my Dad,
The most expensive senator the country ever had.
I remember Daddy's warning—that raping is a crime,
Unless you rape the voters, a million at a time.

CHORUS: *Oh, our parents forgot, etc.*

I'm an ordinary figure in these democratic states,
A pathetic demonstration of hereditary traits.
As the children of the cop possess the flattest kind of feet,
As the daughter of the floozie has a waggle to her seat,
My position at the bottom of society I owe
To the qualities my parents bequeathed me long ago.
My father was a married man and, what is even more,
He was married to my mother—a fact which I deplore.
I was born in holy wedlock, consequently by and by,
I was rooked by every bastard who had plunder in his eye.
I invested, I deposited, I voted every fall,
And I saved up every penny and the bastards took it all.
At last I've learned my lesson, and I'm on the proper track,
I'm a self-appointed bastard and I'M GOING TO GET IT
    BACK.

CHORUS: *Oh, our parents forgot to get married.*
          Our parents forgot to get wed.
          Did a wedding bell chime, it was always a time
          When our parents were somewhere in bed.
          Then all thanks to our kind loving parents.
          We are kings in the land of the free.
          Your banker, your broker, your Washington joker,
          Three prominent bastards are we, tra la,
          Three prominent bastards are we!

*   *   *

To accomplish their restartings in all areas of the U.S.A. economic system
the New Deal also set up the Works Progress Administration (to get people
jobs) and the Reconstruction Finance Corporation (to get the big industries
going).

Amongst the first of the New Deal's emergency acts of 1933 was the establishment of the Works Progress Administration, which provided jobs for approximately anyone who wanted them—artists, mathematicians, etc., as well as all white- and blue-collar workers and, of course, all day laborers and such.

Then, pressed by the labor unions and the political urge to avoid the characteristics of socialism and get the heretofore unemployed millions off WPA—the New Deal's Works Progress Administration—the government financed new buildings and granted mortgages for longer and longer periods to encourage people to undertake the production of much-needed homes and other buildings. It must be noted that the rejuvenated building industry was reset in motion as a concession to the building trades and a move to increase employment, not as a much-needed evolutionary advance in the art of human environment controlling. The unions were so strong as to be able to push the New Deal very hard in the direction of resuming only yesterday's multifoldedly inefficient "one-off" building design techniques and materials as the activity in which they could establish maximum employment. Technically ignorant bank officers became the authorities who alone judged the design validity of the structures and architectural acceptability of the building projects, funds for the building of which they authorized as mortgage-secured loans of their bank depositors' money.

The New Deal went on to rationalize its strategic acts by arguing to itself, "In order to continue as a nation we must have our national defense. Since it is established that there is nowhere nearly enough life support to go around in this world, if we don't have a formidable national defense, we're going to be successfully attacked by hungry enemies. Our national defense can't carry on without steel and the generation of electricity, the production of chemicals, and other imperative industrial items."

The FDR team soon concluded that the industries producing those absolute "defense" necessities were to be called our "prime contractors." The prime contractors *must* be kept going at any cost. "So we'll give war-production orders to the prime contractors to produce such-and-such goods. The contractors with signed government contracts can then go to the banks and borrow the money to pay their overhead and to buy the materials and power and to pay the wages to produce the goods. Then we the government will pay the producers for those finished goods and services, and they can pay off their loans from the bank. The money paid by the prime contractors as wages will give people buying power, which will allow them to start other economic production systems going." This became a monetary irrigation system (still in use today in 1980 U.S.A. affairs), which works at a rate providing about ten recirculations in a year following upon each major war order initiated by and paid for by the government.

In the depths of the Depression in 1932, when you could buy a meal for five cents and the finest of shirts for one dollar, the Reconstruction Finance Corporation went much further. It gave U.S. Steel $85 million worth of new rolling equipment (in 1980 U.S. currency that would be close to a billion dollars), etc., etc.

The U.S.A.'s Reconstruction Finance Corporation had a secondary government machinery-owning outfit that loaned all these prime contracting companies new equipment with which to fill their government orders. What the New Deal did in fact was to socialize the prime contractor corporations instead of the people. This hid the fact of socialism from the world in general. Socializing the prime contractor corporations indirectly benefited the people themselves. In this way the New Deal seemingly didn't *give* money to the corporations—just orders. The U.S.A.-established and -financed RFC loaned the prime contractors all the money they needed to buy all the equipment. But in the end the government rarely collected on the loans and finally just forgave the machinery borrowers altogether, selling them the equipment for very low "nominal" sums.

The New Deal had also pledged itself at outset to take care of the "forgotten man." The government voted minimum-wage limits of a substantial magnitude. The economy was going again. People were getting more and more jobs—how many depended upon how many prime contracts the government gave out. World War II was clearly looming ahead. The New Deal said, "We have to be prepared" . . . and their "preparedness" ordering increased. Jobs increased rapidly. Empty buildings filled.

There were a number of great corporations whose businesses had practically stopped by 1933, but those businesses had now been set in healthy motion once more under the New Deal's socializing of the prime contractors. Franklin Roosevelt said to the heads of the great corporations that had not gone "bust," "Every one of you has a large surplus that you held on to, in fear, through the Depression. We want you to spend your surpluses in research and development of new equipment. Since the early clipper ship days, it has always been a function of a 'fundamental risk enterprise' that the enterprise use some of its profits to buy itself new and better equipment—a new and better ship—with the enterprise that is doing the prime risk-taking by investing in the new equipment, thereby requalifying for the privileges and rewards granted by governments for wise risking, daring execution, and good *management*."

FDR said, "We want you enterprisers to 'modernize.' " But U.S.A. big corporate management said, in unison, "We won't do that. It is much too risky a time to use any of our surplus." They knew the oncoming World War II was forcing the government to see that their plants were modernized, so by holding out they forced the government to take over both the risk and cost of modernizing. Heretofore in the history of private enterprise research and development—of more efficient new plants and equipment— had been funded from the enterprise's "surplus" earnings—i.e., from earnings prudently withheld from distribution to stockholders to ensure the continuing strength of the enterprise.

Then FDR's U.S.A. Treasury, with all FDR's lawyers' advice, ruled that the large private-enterprise corporations could make their new *plant expansion* and *equipment improvements* and *charge the costs to operating expenses,* which expenses were then to be deducted from new earnings before calculating income taxes. This amounted, in fact, to an indirect subsidy to cover all new-equipment acquisition. The U.S.A. Treasury next ruled that all *research* and *development*—"R and D"—was thereafter also to be considered by the U.S.A. Treasury Department as "an operating expense" and also to be deducted from income before calculating income taxes. The U.S.A. thereby eliminated almost all the "risks" of private enterprise.

Next Henry Luce, representing news publishers in America—the newspapers and magazines—went to Roosevelt and said, "Your democracy needs its news. You have to have some way for the people to know what's going on." "Yes," said FDR. Luce went on, "We publishers can't afford to publish the news. The prices people are willing to pay for the news won't pay for the publications. The newspapers and magazines are only paid for by advertising, and the New Deal has no allowance for advertising in its operating procedures." The New Deal then ruled that advertising was henceforth to be classified as research and development, therefore deductible from gross income as an operating expense before calculating taxes. Thus advertising became a hidden subsidy of very great size—about $7 billion a year at that time—hidden in tax-calculation procedures. The subsidy was so great as to cover the founding of what has come to be known as "Madison Avenue."

While the government was doing all this, the Congress passed strict and comprehensive rent controls, bank-loan-interest controls, and price controls of every kind. It was pure socialism. It had to be done that way. There was no question.

The Securities and Exchange Commission reforms removed J. P. Morgan's two directors from the boards of almost every one of the U.S.A.'s great corporations—except Henry Ford's—whose interlocking directorships had formerly given Morgan prime control over U.S.A. industry. With the termination of Morgan's control of all the major corporation boards such as those of U.S. Steel and General Motors, these great corporations' managements found that they were no longer beholden to J. P. Morgan, and only to their stockholders. "All we have to do now to hold our jobs is to make money for the stockholders."

At this moment the U.S.A. had evolved into a *managerial capitalism,* in contradistinction to the now-defunct, invisible "finance capitalism" of which J. P. Morgan had been the master.

What became noticeable at this time was the uniformity of position taken by all the great corporation managements in respect to actions taken by the New Deal—for instance, the great corporations' across-the-board refusal to expend surplus on research and development.

To discover how that came about it first must be realized that the industrial-enterprise underwriting and expansion-financing of the private banking houses of Wall Street could not have been carried on without the advice, contract-writing services, and legal planning of the world's most powerful and most widely informed legal brains. As a consequence the corporation law firms of Wall Street, New York, were peopled with the most astute thinkers and tacticians of America—if not of the whole world. When the Great Crash of 1929 came and events of the Depression occurred, as already related (and the great poker hands were called, and the New Deal had prosecuted the guilty and housecleaned the system and socialized the prime contractors, etc.), it was the counsel of Wall Street lawyers that governed the positions taken by the new, self-perpetuating, industrial-giants' managements. It was the former J. P. Morgan's and other financiers' lawyers who now counseled all the as-yet-solvent big-industry managements to guard their surplus and refuse to cooperate with the New Deal.

Furthermore the Wall Street lawyers could see clearly what the public couldn't see—i.e., that while the New Deal was unilaterally socializing the system, it was doing so without exacting any contractual obligation on the corporations to acknowledge the government's economic recovery strategies. The corporations gave no legal acknowledgment of their socialized status. It was clear to the Wall Street lawyers that without such contractual acknowledgment the government socializing was a one-sided, voluntary commitment on the part of the political party in power. Therefore, in fact, none of the big corporations had lost their free-enterprise independence by accepting the enormous government rehabilitation expenditures.

Since the Wall Street lawyers and brethren in other parts of the country were called upon to fill the Supreme Court bench from which body they could determine the province of "free enterprise," the lawyers reasoned somewhat as follows: "A socialized system—as clearly manifest by the U.S.S.R.—cannot tolerate free enterprise's freedom of initiative. There is no lucrative law practice in socialized states—ergo, if we are to survive, we lawyers on Wall Street had best figure out how to go about keeping the fundamentals of capitalism alive amongst the few great industrial corporations that as yet remain solvent despite the 1929 and 1933 Depression events."

The Wall Street lawyers saw clearly that it was those surviving corporations' undistributed surplus which certified that capitalism had not gone entirely bankrupt despite its banking system's failure.

Operating invisibly behind the "skirts" of the as-yet-live corporations, the Wall Street lawyers very informally, but very seriously, organized far-ahead-in-time research-and-study teams consisting of the most astute corporation lawyers to be found in America. From these teams' realistic conceptioning they formulated a grand strategy that would keep capitalism's private enterprise alive and prospering indefinitely *as run invisibly but absolutely legally by the lawyers.*

The latter's research discovered that they would not soon be able to popularly and legally overthrow the New Deal. It was clear that not until World War II was over might they find conditions suitable for untying all the economic controls established by the New Deal.

It is appropriate at this point to do some reviewing of evolutionary changes that had been transpiring in the nature of capitalism.

It all starts with the *land-based capitalism,* a capitalism maintained by whoever seized, successfully defended, and controlled the land—ergo, owned the land. Those producing food and life support on the lands were all subservient to, and paid tribute to, the great landowners. In land capitalism whoever owned the fertile fields controlled all the wealth to be made from that land. Land capitalism dealt with nature's own metabolic productivity.

Then private enterprise and finance capitalism came to discover what could be done with mass-produced metals to multiply the value of the land-produced, life-support metabolics.

In the mid-nineteenth century mass production of steel, for the first time in history, suddenly gave humans the capability of producing long-span beams, whereby they were able to produce large-enough, semifireproof, and powerful structures to move more and more wealth-production work under cover. Western-world capitalism began to produce wealth under cover in addition to that produced out in the field. To make the tin cans in the factory to can the food produced in the fields, or to take the cotton produced in the fields and mass-produce cotton cloth, became known as "value-added-by-manufacture." Value-added-by-manufacturing was accomplished primarily with metals—metal buildings, metal machinery, metal tools, metal sea and land transportation systems, and, ofttimes, metal end products.

As already mentioned, it was the new, world-around, metals sources that brought about the name *World* War I.

Suddenly we had a completely new form of capitalism, which required both the large-scale financing and integration of metals, mines and mine-owners, metals refining and shaping into wholesaleable forms, all to be established around the world by the world masters of the great line of supply. The world line of metals-and-alloy supply was essential in producing all the extraordinarily productive new machinery and that machinery's delivery system, as was the generation and delivery of the unprecedentedly vast amounts of inanimate energy as electricity.

This new form of the world power structure's capitalism—by *ownership of the mines and metals* working all around the world—we call the *metals and mining capitalism.* Whoever owned the mines had incredible power, but never as great as those who controlled the line of their supply. Combining the two, (1) the mines and metals-producing industry and (2) the line of supply, we have the world power structure that operated as the first supranational, world-around-integrated, metals cartels. They were out of reach of the laws of any one country, in a *metals cartels capitalism.* Combining these two with (3) the absolute need of the large financing and credit at magnitudes rarely affordable by any one individual, we find *finance capitalism* integrating the world operation.

At any rate we now understand why the 1914–18 war was called *World War I.* It was inherently a war for mastery of the world's metallic resources and their world-around physical integration, controlling, and exploitation.

The amount of metal productivity of World War I was so great that, after the war, as the arms products became obsolete and were displaced by new design products, the metal contained in the ever vaster amounts of obsolete products began to come back into circulation as scrap. The scrap resources swiftly increased. The Morgan-escaped managerial capitalists said, "I'm going to keep my job if we pay our stockholders dividends—the rate at which we can pay dividends is directly dependent upon the rate at which our production wheels go around. To keep our wheels going around, we don't care whether we are using scrap metals or mined metals. As a matter of fact, the metals-as-scrap are usually more refined than the metals coming out of the mines. They cost less, so we're better off using the scrap—whether from obsolete buildings, machinery, armaments, railways, or ships." Formerly Morgan had insisted on all his controlled manufacturing corporations acquiring all their metal stocks only from newly mined, refined, and wholesale "shaped" stocks.

The mining companies found that industry would not buy ingots of their metals. They found that they had to turn their metals into tubes, bars, sheet, plate, wire, and a great variety of sizes and shapes. Wall Street's finance capitalism, therefore, underwrote the development of a host of metals-shaping industries who were the automatic customers of the only-ingot-producing, metals-mining corporations.

The post–World War I mineowner-capitalists began gradually to be washed out of the game by virtue of the Morgan-emancipated managerial capitalists saying, "Our job is to keep the wheels going around." Wheels-going-around producing saleable goods from scrap metals became strategic.

Up to the time of World War I the owners of the factories (Mr. Morgan et al.) said, "We put you in as management to make a profit out of this factory." If the management said, "Give us a new piece of machinery," the owners said, "New piece of machinery! What are you talking about? We put you in to make money out of our machinery. You are fired." Change was anathema to the J. P. Morgan-type of financier. Scientists would come to Mr. Morgan and say, "Mr. Morgan, I can show you how to make steel so that it won't rust." "Young man! The more it rusts, the more I sell. How crazy you must be! Get the doctor to look this man over, he's obviously a lunatic—take those mad papers out of his pocket and put them in my desk drawer."

But change was welcomed by the late-1930s' managerial capitalism. New designs called for more whirling of their production wheels. The change came in the form of many new armament designs for the clearly approaching World War II. The new designs released as "scrap" the metals from obsolete designs.

Concurrently, with the New Deal's reforms and controls, the wage-earners were now getting a fairer share of the national income, and the economy was prospering—particularly so as the New Deal began officially to remember the "forgotten man." Congress put a dollar cellar under the wages and elevated worker earnings enough to produce minor affluence and security for labor in general.

Just before the U.S.A. entered World War II, the Wall Street lawyers instructed the heads of great corporations to say to Roosevelt, "We heads of the corporations of America were not elected by the American people. We were chosen by our stockholders. Our job is to make profits for our stockholders. At the time of World War I a lot of business people were called 'profiteers.' As we enter into World War II war production, we don't want to be called 'immoral profiteers.' If you want cooperation from us, Mr. Roosevelt, you as government are going to have to be the one to initiate our corporations' being properly rewarded for our cooperation."

Mr. Roosevelt said, "I agree. You are beholden to your stockholders, so you are going to have to pay them dividends." Coping with this dilemma, the United States Treasury Department agreed that it was legitimate for the industrial corporations to make up to 12-percent profit per each product turnover. The New Deal said, "We the people, as government, are, however, going to renegotiate with you all the time, continually inspect you, to be sure you are really earning your profits." As a consequence of all the continuous renegotiation by the government, those U.S.A. corporations earned an average of 10 percent on every turnover. This meant that in World War II for every annual war budget—running at first at $70 billion per year—10 percent, or $7 billion, was earmarked for distribution to the stockholders of the corporations. Complete socialization of the stockholders of the prime U.S.A. corporations was accomplished.

Amongst the prime contractors identified by the New Deal were all the leading automobile companies. For example, Chrysler was picked out to produce the war tanks. With their powerful position established with the government, the U.S.A. automobile manufacturers, on being asked to convert all of their productivity to war armaments, agreed amongst themselves to put into storage all of their production tooling and to resume their postwar auto production with the models they were last producing at outset of war. New production tooling would cost them several billions of dollars. They had their Madison Avenue companies grind out advertisements showing the G.I. soldiers saying, "Please keep everything the same at home until I return."

Because Germany's, Italy's, and Japan's production equipment was destroyed during World War II, they were free after the war to start using the newest war-advanced technology in both the designing and the production of their automobiles. That was the beginning of the end for the U.S.A.'s prestige as the world's technological leader. The U.S.A. post–World War II cars were inherently seven years passé in contrast to the smaller, faster foreign cars. The "Big Three" American auto producers undertook to manufacture while keeping the foreign cars off the market and while they themselves exploited America's market need for a geographically expanding economy's transportation.

In the late 1960s the "Big Three" automobile companies of America found that their distributors were disenchanted with decreasing financial returns and with frequent bankruptcy. To hold their distributors G.M., Ford and Chrysler deliberately manufactured a few of their mechanically well-designed parts with inferior materials that were guaranteed to deteriorate electrolytically or otherwise. The replacement of these parts guaranteed that all the distributors' car buyers would have to return to them for service on a high-frequency basis, at which time the distributor would replace the parts catalogue-priced so high that the distributor was guaranteed a profitable business. This continuing deceit of the customers—we the people—was the beginning of the end of the American automobile business and the once-great world esteem for Uncle Sam. U.S.A. discreditation has been brought about without the U.S.A. people's knowledge of the money-maker-world's invisible cheating.

Throughout all pre–World War II years employers had maintained that unemployed people were unemployed because they were unqualified for survival, socially expendable. Then World War II saw young people deployed on war tasks all around the world. In view of this loss of labor vast amounts of automation were incorporated in the U.S.A.'s home-front war production. With the war over, the government found the cream of its youth all unemployed, and because of the automation there were no jobs in sight. Because they were the proven "cream of the youth," no one could say they were unemployed because they were unqualified, so the as-yet-operative New Deal created the G.I. Bill, which sent all those young people to prepaid college and university educations.

By World War II's end labor was earning so much that, for the first time, it was feeling truly secure, affluent, and successful. Emulating the pattern of the rich, individuals of labor were becoming little capitalists, with many enjoying the realization of their own home and land, with two shiny new post–World War II cars in the garage, their kids going to college, and some savings in the bank. The workers began buying shares in IBM and other superpromising private enterprise companies.

The Wall Street lawyers, being astute observers of such matters, realized that this labor affluence had brought about a psychological reorientation of the body politic. People no longer remembered or felt the depression of spirit that was experienced in the Great Depression of social economics following the Great Crash. The Wall Street lawyers' grand strategists saw this as the time for breaking through the New Deal's hold on government, an event which, up to that time, seemed impossible. The lawyers said, "Whoever can get the victorious, supreme-command American general of World War II as their candidate for President will be able to get the presidency." They captured Eisenhower. Eisenhower had no political conviction, one way or the other. His vanity was excited at the idea of becoming president of his country.

The Wall Street lawyers explained to Eisenhower the prevailing new psychology of affluence and convinced him that the new affluent majority would elect a Republican. Thus they successfully persuaded him to be a Republican. With the healthy economy the new wage-earner capitalists, with a vested interest in maintaining the status quo, readily voted for Eisenhower on the Republican ticket. Eisenhower's Wall Street lawyer-managers explained to him that he had been able to win the war because of the vision, courage, and ingenuity and the productive power of American free enterprise. They convinced Eisenhower that "the U.S.A. is, in fact, free enterprise." They also convinced him that the Democrats' New Deal was socialism and therefore the inherent enemy of free enterprise.

As soon as the Wall Street lawyers had Eisenhower in office in 1952, they instructed him to break loose all the economic controls of the New Deal. They had him cut all price controls, all rent controls, all interest-rate controls; they had him terminate anything that was stymieing the making of big money by big business. For instance, they persuaded Eisenhower to allow the insurance companies to invest their vast funds in common stocks. Before Ike's liberation of the insurance companies they were allowed to put their funds only in "Class A" bonds and similar investments. Cheered by the capitalist-owned sector of the press, his Wall Street lawyer-advisors for a long time had Ike feeling like a great liberator.

The Wall Street lawyers' grand strategists put the Wall Street lawyer John Foster Dulles in as Ike's Secretary of State to dictate the American foreign policy of "Soviet containment," and Foster Dulles's Wall Street lawyer brother Allen Dulles was put in as head of a new brand of absolutely invisible, U.S.A.-financed, capitalistic welfare department, the CIA, established ostensibly to cold-war-cope with the secret-agent operations of our enemies. So secret was their operation that the people of the United States and its Congressional lawmakers had no idea of the size of the unlimited funds given to the CIA, nor for what those unknown funds were expended. The CIA and Allen Dulles had a U.S.A.-signed blank check for X amount of money to do X tasks. I call the CIA, "Capitalism's Invisible Army."

The great U.S.A. corporations, having been saved in 1933 by being only "unilaterally socialized," and having in the subsequent fifteen years become powerfully healthy from enormous war orders, immediately after Eisenhower's election started escalating prices. Their logic was that the first corporation head to increase prices in a given field of production would be the first to be able to distribute that "upping" as profits to his stockholders and thereby to gain for himself greater economic management status and personal wealth.

* * *

As a long-time student of foreign investment I saw a pattern developing. Between 1938 and 1940 I was on the editorial staff of *Fortune* magazine as its science and technology consultant, and my researchers harvested all the statistics for *Fortune*'s tenth-anniversary issue, "U.S.A. and the World." In that issue I uncovered and was able to prove several new socioeconomic facts—for the first time in the history of industrial economics: (1) the economic health of the American—or any industrial—economy was no longer disclosed (as in the past) by the total tonnage of its product output, but by the amount of electrical energy generated by that activity; tonnage had ceased to be the criterion because (2) we were doing so much more given work with so much less pounds of materials, ergs of energy, and seconds of time per given function as to occasion ever newer, lighter, and stronger metallic alloys, chemicals, and electronics. Though at that time universally used as the number-one guide to the state of economic health of any world nation, tonnage no longer represented prosperity. The amount of energy being electrically generated and consumed became the most sensitive telltale of economic health. Furthermore, I was able in that issue to study carefully all the foreign investments made in America all the way back to its colonization in the early seventeenth century.

The ramifications of my studies in foreign investments in America and elsewhere are wide. An example of my findings included discovery of the swift, post–American Revolution investment in U.S.A. ventures by the British (East India Company–advised) financial world as already mentioned.

I found a similar situation to be existent in World War II. As head mechanical engineer of the U.S.A. Board of Economic Warfare I had available to me copies of any so-called intercepts I wanted. Those were transcriptions of censor-listened-to intercontinental telephone conversations, along with letters and cables that were opened by the censor and often deciphered, and so forth. As a student of patents I asked for and received all the intercept information relating to strategic patents held by both our enemies and our own big corporations, and I found the same money was often operative on both sides in World War II.

The East India Company, whose flag I have shown to be the origin of ours, was a private enterprise chartered by the British. Quite clearly the East India Company didn't lose the American Revolution. The British government lost the Revolution, and the East India Company swiftly moved large amounts of its capital into U.S. America.

With World War II over I began to watch very closely the foreign investments patterning and the strategic metals movements, especially of copper, but those of silver and gold as well. In 1942 America had all the monetary bullion gold in the world in the Kentucky hills. During World War II what was called "the China Bloc"—which was the Sung family and others backing Chiang Kai-shek—were able to persuade the American Congress that China had always been corrupt and was eternally corruptible; to completely avoid communism in China Congress should let them have $100 million worth of gold bullion ($2 billion at January 1980 gold pricing) to be taken out of the Kentucky hills. Personally I don't think that gold ever went anywhere near China. I think it went right into the Swiss bank accounts of some clever thieves. But with that much gold out of the Pandora's box of the U.S.A. Kentucky hills vaults, it provided a "gold lever" with which to progressively pry loose more and more gold to be reintroduced into the "lifeblood" of world economic accounting.

After World War II, with only the one exception of the $100 million worth of monetary gold bullion of the China Bloc, all the rest of the world's international monetary gold bullion was residing in the Kentucky hills, U.S.A., vaults. All countries outside America had gone off the gold standard. In the course of international monetary negotiating that accompanied the U.S.A.'s post–World War I inadvertent ascendency into being the master economic state, and the U.S.A.'s post–World War II attempts to rehabilitate the leading economies around the world by rehabilitating the economies of its vanquished nations and thereby increasing international trading, the U.S.A. was persuaded to re-establish the gold standard for accounting the international balances of trade.

Gold is the super-helicopter of the open world-market-trading stratagems of the makers-of-money-for-self by the legalized manipulation of the money equity of others, all unbeknownst to the initial wealth equity-owning others. In 1934 Roosevelt's New Deal prohibited the further use of gold by U.S.A. citizens or U.S.A. businesses.

By 1953 it became apparent that the Wall Street lawyers were moving the major American corporations out of America. Of the 100 largest corporations in America four out of five of their annual investment dollars in new machinery and buildings for 1953 went exclusively into their foreign operations. This four-fifths rate persisted for a score of years.

The Wall Street lawyers told Mr. Eisenhower that they didn't like the overaltruistic social viewpoint of the Marshall Plan for helping underdeveloped countries. They liked foreign aid, but not exclusively for the development of underdeveloped countries. The Wall Street lawyers approved of the "foreign aid" wherefore the U.S.A. continued with annual *foreign-aid* commitments by Congress. The average annual foreign-aid appropriation has been $4 billion (1950 value) per year over the twenty-seven-year period from 1952 to 1979, which amounted to a $100 billion total. Each new year's foreign-aid bill had a rider that said that if American companies were present in the country being aided, the money had to be spent through those American companies. In the foreign countries the corporations and individuals could again deal in gold.

Foreign aid paid for all the new factories and machinery of all the American corporations moving out of America. This became a fundamental pattern: first the 100 largest corporations, then the 200 largest corporations followed, then what *Fortune* calls the 500 largest corporations. Moving out of America could be done readily because a corporation is only a legal entity—it is not a human being. It had no physical body to pass through immigration or emigration. You and I cannot move out of America because we are physical—we need a passport. A corporation does not.

So the Wall Street lawyers simply moved their prime corporate operations

elsewhere. It was clearly evident that with only 7 percent of the world's population in the U.S.A., and with two cars already in many U.S.A. garages,
by far the major portion of further exploitation of the world's peoples' needs
and desires would develop outside of the U.S. of America. But the main objective of the Wall Street lawyers was for the corporations to get out from
under the tax control of the American government. In 1933 the American
people had saved the corporations by subsidizing them; then, twenty years
later, the Wall Street lawyers moved them out of America, getting the
American people to pay for the move. This allowed the corporations to acquire gold equities while the U.S.A. citizens and small domestic businesses
could not do so.

Soon after Eisenhower's 1952 election to the presidency, the lawyers reminded him once more that America clearly had won the war only through
his brilliant generalship backed up by American free enterprise, and said,
"We want you to stop the welfare-state-inclined American government from
competing with free enterprise. You must cut out all the navy yards and the
arsenals. They compete against the free-enterprise corporations, which are
quite capable of doing the same work as the navy yards, but of doing it
much more efficiently. You must turn all such production over to private
industry, cut out the U.S.A. post office and turn that over to private enterprise, cut out the Federal Deposit Insurance Corporation and turn that over
to the insurance industry." Although much of this transfer of production
from government to private enterprise control was never completed, Eisenhower goaded on by his lawyers initiated the flow of taxpayer-financed,
highly trained personnel and especially their technical know-how to private
enterprise. This irreversible trend continues on to the present day, as can
be shown by the history of the whole of the atomic energy field.

Those acquainted with the story of the atomic bomb development remember the momentous occasion when theoretical fission was discovered in 1939
by Hahn and Stresemann in Germany and secretly communicated by them
to American physicists, who checked out their calculations and found them
correct and then persuaded Einstein to go to Roosevelt to tell him that this
was so and that Hitler's scientists were hot on the trail.

Franklin Roosevelt, exercising war powers given him by Congress, in effect instantly appropriated $80 billion for what became known later as the
Manhattan Project. Later, that initial $80 billion appropriation was supple-
mented by an additional $75 billion for a total of $155 billion of the American people's money that went into developing atomic energy.

The Wall Street lawyers' grand strategists sent a man named Lewis
Strauss to Washington to "join in the World War II effort." Strauss was a
partner in the Wall Street banking house of Kuhn, Loeb. He was also a bril-

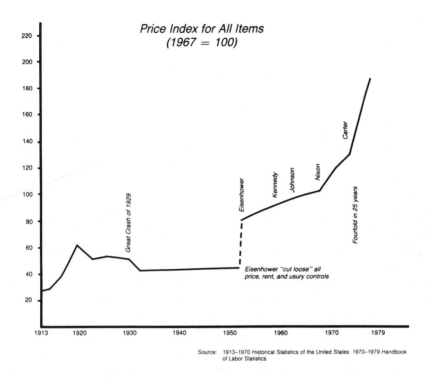

Price Index for All Items
(1967 = 100)

Source: 1913–1970 Historical Statistics of the United States. 1970–1979 Handbook of Labor Statistics

FIGURE 17. Price Index for All Items

liant son-in-law of Adolph Ochs, president of *The New York Times.* Strauss was made an admiral in gratitude for his forsaking Wall Street to help America win the war. After the war Admiral Strauss was appointed to the Atomic Energy Commission; in 1953 Eisenhower named him commission chairman. Strauss and the Wall Street lawyers persuaded Eisenhower that the Atomic Energy Commission must not be in competition with capitalism and must be turned over to private enterprise. So it was—$155 billion worth of it, all of which had been paid for by the American public—but it consisted of work so secret that only the scientists who were intimate with the work understood it.

All that was necessary to correct the situation was to give contracts to private enterprise to carry on the atomic work and to let the government's scientists go to work for the private-enterprise corporations.

At this point the Wall Street lawyers and Strauss persuaded Eisenhower that the United States Bureau of Standards' scientists were in competition with private enterprise and must be curbed. Strauss assured Eisenhower that the corporations would take on all the bureau's discarded scientists. What the Wall Street lawyers' grand strategists realized was something momentous—to wit . . . that in the new 99.9-percent invisible reality of alloys, chemistry, electronics, and atomics, *scientific and technical know-how was everything*. Physical land and buildings were of no further interest to capitalism. Metaphysical know-how was the magic wand of the second half of the twentieth-century world power structures. Physical properties were subject to deterioration, taxable, and cumbersome. Advised to do so by their lawyers, capitalism and private enterprise set about after World War II to monopolize all strategic technological know-how—i.e., all metaphysical properties—and to dump all physical properties. They called for an economic program by which people would be forced to buy the apartments and houses—to get all physical properties off capitalism's hands.

The post-Eisenhower era becomes most suitably identified as that of *lawyer capitalism* and of "no-risk," sure-thing, free enterprise.

The whole of atomic development was know-how. Scientists had the know-how, and anybody without their technical information could not even speak their language. The Know-How Club, monopolized by lawyer capitalism, was a very tight club. Furthermore, the nonmember four billion plus human beings on planet Earth knew nothing about the invisible micro-macro, non-sensorially-tune-in-able reality. Large private enterprise had now hired all the know-how scientists and engineers. They seemingly could keep the public out of their affairs forever. The world power structure had the U.S. government completely emasculate the Bureau of Standards. There was an earnest and concerned battle by a few responsible scientists to keep the bureau intact, but they were overwhelmed. Henceforth all science must be done by the private corporations themselves or under their subsidized university-college and private laboratory work. To appreciate the extent of this know-how monopoly of the big corporations, one need only look over the wording of the scientist and engineering help-wanted advertisements of the big corporations in the many pages of *The New York Times* Sunday business section or of their counterpart publications in other big cities.

In the invisible, esoteric world of today's science there is no way for the American government or public, without the U.S.A. Bureau of Standards' scientists, to follow the closely held technical secrets of the big, profit-oriented corporations. To a small extent such popular journals as *Scientific American* help people follow details of this-and-that special case science without learning of the significance of the information in respect to comprehensive socioeconomic evolution.

No economic accounting books list metaphysical assets. Metaphysics is held to be insubstantial—meaning in Latin "nothing on which to stand." Patents can be granted only for special cases—i.e., limited *physical-practice* applications of abstract generalized principles, which principles alone are inherently metaphysical and unpatentable, being only "discovered" and not "invented." But physical patents are capital.

We have two fundamental realities in our Universe—the physical and the metaphysical. Physicists identify all physical phenomena as the exclusive manifest of energy: energy associative as *matter* or disassociative as electromagnetic behavior, *radiation*. Both of these energy states are reconvertible one into the other. Because there is no experimental evidence of energy being either created or lost, world scientist-philosophers now concede it to be in evidence that Universe is eternally regenerative.

The physicists have found that energy will always articulate levers electromagnetically, gravitationally, chemically by reactive forces, by vibratory waves, etc. Metaphysics consists only of weightless, dimensionless, abstract thoughts and mathematical principles that cannot lever physical needles in respect to instrument dials. Energy in either of its states, being physical, can be entered into the capital account ledgers.

The large issue today is the technical know-how that governs the transformations of energy between its two states. "Know-how" is metaphysics. Metaphysics now rules. When the head of one of the U.S.A.'s largest banks was asked what "commodities" were involved in that bank's import-export dealings with the rest of the world on behalf of the Chinese government, he answered that know-how was the prime commodity being acquired by the Chinese through that bank.

I have spent a great deal of time since World War II in Japan, dealing with their industrialists, and have personally witnessed the Japanese acquisition by contracts of a whole complex of exquisitely specific packages of industrial know-how, together with the respective follow-through educational services—all acquired from, and performed by, engineering and business-administration teams of many of the leading American corporations.

The post–World War II Japanese had already perceived that they did not need to own the physical mines of metallic ores because they had learned also how to carry on exclusively with the melting down and recirculating of the world's metals, particularly those poured into the Orient and Western Pacific islands by the U.S.A. during World War II in the form of now-obsolete—ergo, "scrapped"—armaments. The essence of Japan's recent decades' economic success has been the acquisition and realization of the industrial-technology-know-how wealth existent exclusively in metaphysical know-how, in contradistinction to strictly physical land properties, tools, and end products. With all their pre–World War II machinery smashed the

Japanese and Germans acquired new, vastly improved industrial equipment with which to realize their know-how production, whereas the World-War-II-winning U.S.A. and European Allies using their old technology became more preoccupied with making money than in producing superior products.

Because of the foregoing it was now possible to maintain that hidden know-how capability within private corporate walls. Since 99 percent of humanity does not as yet understand science's mathematical language, less than 1 percent of humanity is scientifically literate—ergo, the lawyers' strategy of tight monopolization of scientific know-how within the scientifically staffed corporations was highly feasible.

In 1929, at the time of the Great Wall Street Crash, only about 1 percent of the U.S.A.'s big corporations had research departments. Now, half a century later, all the big corporations have all the powerful research departments, other than those in which pure scientists are engaged in academic work under some corporate or government subsidy. Through the national defense budget's armaments development, all the once risky research and development costs of enterprise are paid for by the public through taxation.

The big oil companies knew long ago that humanity would ultimately run out of an adequate supply of petroleum and other fossil fuels, though coal may last a thousand years. That's why, by the means we have reviewed, the oil companies acquired control of the know-how on atomic energy as well as all the atomic plants and equipment paid for originally by the U.S.A. government. The power structure's only interest is in *selling* energy—and only energy that they can run through a meter. They're not in the least interested in anyone getting windpower—except themselves. Very rich men love having their sailing yachts wind-driven to Europe or the South Seas, but this is not for the people. People's power must be piped or wired to them only through meters.

When in 1972 all the power-structure capital had converted its dollars into gold, oil, or other highly concentrated and mobile equities, then-President Richard Nixon severed the U.S.A. dollar from its government-guaranteed gold equity value of $35 per ounce, the U.S.A. people's dollar buying power plummeted—now, in 1980, being worth only 5 cents of the 1971 U.S.A. dollar.

By 1974 much of the world's buying power landed in the lap of the Arabs, who also sat atop the chief petroleum source of the world. In effect they had both the money with which to buy their petroleum and the largest reserves to be bought. If someone wanted to buy their petroleum, often they couldn't do so, because few in the world had the monetary resources remaining with which to do so. The Arabs realized they would have to lend out their money to work, but they had no experience in such investment matters. The Arabs had no knowledge of the vast industrial production and distribution technical and administrative requirements. Nor had they any experience in the exploitation of the world-energy industry prior to their own lands' exploitation by others before the onslaught of the petroleum company giants. The Arabs had not known how to discover, drill for, refine, and distribute the petroleum upon which they had been sitting unwittingly for thousands of years.

So content were the Arab monarchs with the gratification of their every physical desire—artfully heaped upon them personally by the capitalist world's foreign-oil-exploiting functionaries—that they would never have taken over the direct mastery of their petroleum affairs had not the psycho-guerilla warfare between the capitalist and communist powers deliberately aroused the Arabian peoples themselves, bringing pressure upon their leaders to take over the foreigners' operations. Since their subsequent epochal enrichment, the Arabs' political leaders as well as the monarchs and sheiks have bought everything of which they could dream, as stimulated by the affluent acquisitions patterns in other economies. After vast stock and bond investments, real estate and new building ventures in foreign countries, they found that they could expend only a fraction of their monetary wealth. The Arabs have now reached the dilemma of how to turn their monetary gold fortune to important and lasting advantage.

In 1977 the king of Saudi Arabia said to a leading American banker with large oil interests, "My banks don't know anything about international banking and major industrial accommodation." The American banker said, "Would you like me to run your banks?" The king said, "Of course." So the American banker did, and in the process he taught them international and transnational industrial-finance management.

There's no question that the few who have title to Arabian oil find it essential to amalgamate their operations with the world's great oil companies, which own the vast equipment of world-around distribution and interaccounting capabilities as well as the vast majority of refineries and petrochemical industries. The great oil companies control it all. In general they and noncommunist Arabia are one and the same. The Organization of Petroleum Exporting Countries' (OPEC) officialdom, regardless of national political differences, is very probably run entirely by the oil corporations' trillions of dollars of persuasiveness.

It is relevant at this point to note that the Arabs' inadvertent isolation of both the physical-wealth items—(1) the underlying monetary gold and (2) the prime negotiable energy commodity, petroleum—and their concurrent discovery of their utter lack of know-how, clearly differentiated out the relative values of (A) the purely physical petroleum and gold, and (B) the exclusively metaphysical know-how wealth. It turned out that B was most in demand as well as scarcest. The physical wealth was thus proved to be of approximately zero value, while the metaphysical know-how wealth proved to be the prime economic "good-health" constituent of wealth.

Moreover, those who own oil also own the atomic energy and have long ago assumed that, if humanity exhausts or abandons oil, it will automatically switch over to atomic energy. Humanity has had nothing to say about all this because the know-how was so obscure and the lawyers' stratagems so invisibly large. The lawyers' omnilegal international stratagems were and as yet are so obscure, in fact, that no government authorities—let alone the public—knew that the world energy monopoly's scientists had not taken into account earthquakes, for instance, in the construction of New England atomic energy plants, nor had the public or government anticipated that the intuitive wisdom of humanity would develop such an antipathy to atomic energy as eventually to force lawyer capitalism to fall back on its "ownable" coal mines and shale for conversion into pipable and meterable liquid fuels. It is as yet inscrutable to the public, government, and lawyer capitalism just how strong literate humanity's intuitive wisdom will be in preventing the full-scale conversion of coal and shale into liquid energy fuel when it learns, as it has now been learned in a scientifically undeniable way, that this selfishly exploitable energy fuel strategy will inexorably destroy the atmosphere's capability of supporting biological life on planet Earth. Like all fossil fuels coal gives off carbon dioxide when burned, but coal gives off 25 percent more of it per unit of energy than oil and 50 percent more than natural gas. Although carbon dioxide comprises less than 1 percent of the Earth's atmospheric gases, this concentration has risen 17 percent since preindustrial times and is expected to rise an equivalent amount in the next twenty years. The "greenhouse" effect from the Sun's heat and increasing amounts of this otherwise harmless gas could send average global temperatures soaring by as much as 6 degrees Fahrenheit within fifty years according to a U.S. government study. This unprecedented global environmental catastrophe would be virtually irreversible for centuries.

No one knows whether the cessation of the waste radiation of atomic energy exploitation or the cessation of coal and shale conversion into fluid fuel will occur in time to permit the physical continuance of humans on planet Earth. What we do know however, as we have previously stated, is (1) that, with the unselfish use of technology, it is now possible to take care of all humanity at a higher standard of living than any have ever experienced and do so on a sustaining basis by employing only our daily energy income from Sun and gravity and (2) that we can do so in time to permit the healthy continuance of humans on planet Earth.

Now things are beginning to go wrong with atomic-power generation . . . everywhere. To start off with, neither the scientists nor the atomic plant private-enterprise owners have any safe solution for what to do with radio-active atomic wastes. Humanity's intuitions are logically aroused, and public antipathy to atomic energy is rapidly expanding—despite billions of dollars being spent by the world energy cartel in propaganda campaigns to make the vast majority of people "go for" atomic energy.

The second great gasoline-line "pinch" of June 1979 was put upon the public by the invisible energy-know-how cartel to painfully divert the public concern generated by the Three Mile Island radiation accident and threat of a reactor "meltdown." Though the public had reacted strongly against atomic plants, the sudden energy supply squeeze administered by the oil companies made the general public so energy hungry again that it stopped, for the moment, listening to those who were attempting to curtail atomic energy plants. The "gas crisis" re-established "rational" public yielding to governmental support of atomic energy as the "answer" to the energy crisis.

Today's (1980) world-power-structures struggle is one between the U.S.S.R. and big capitalism, which we now call lawyer capitalism, which deliberately took the world's private-enterprise corporations out of the fundamental jurisdiction of America. They have kept their U.S.A. operations going in a seemingly normal way, so people in U.S. America haven't realized that these companies are officially situated elsewhere despite the incredible amplification of those great corporations' annual profits, whose annual totals payable to these corporations' stockholders are of the same magnitude as the annual increase in the U.S.A.'s joint internal and external debt increases.

America is utterly bankrupt externally in terms of balance of trade due to its own oil companies now operating as Arabian business. The national debt at the time of the New Deal was $33 billion—which was the cost of World War I. Before World War I we frequently had no national debt whatever. We have today a national debt that exceeds $800 billion—30 percent of that indebtedness came from underwriting of ever-longer-term mortgages. In 1934 the U.S.A. underwrote a completely obsolete building industry while Eisenhower allowed the banking world to make an incredible amount of money in interest rates and services* in support of the building and real estate game, which building industry—if it were any good—would pay the U.S.A. back handsomely. The U.S.A. cannot even pay the annual interest on its $800 billion national debt. That is why the Nixon presidency and all those since have had to enter each year with a negative budget, ac-

---

*In 1978 over $1 billion just for transferring home-ownership deeds.

knowledging that at year's end the U.S.A. will be a $100 billion-magnitude unrecoverably deeper in debt. Our foreign-trade-balance indebtedness is (as of September 1979) $104 billion ($86 billion if foreign branches of U.S. banks are taken into account). Sum-totally, what has been taken from the people of the U.S.A. runs into many trillions of dollars. In the quarter of a century since Eisenhower America has become completely bankrupt, with its world leadership, its financial credit, and its reputation for courage, vision, and human leadership gone.

* * *

None of this was the American people's doing. It was all done in an absolutely legal but utterly invisible manner by the lawyer-capitalism. Individual bankers, industrial-corporation officers, et al. have had to do what their lawyers told them to do. No bad people have been involved. The lawyers were following their survival instinct—and doing so completely legally.

Everything we have reported here has been published at one time or another, but with the individual items often so far apart from the last relevant item that the public has tended not to remember and associate the items. As a consequence the total picture presented here is approximately unknown to any but the Wall Street lawyers' grand strategists, most of whom are no longer alive.

* * *

One of my earliest books was *Nine Chains to the Moon,* written in 1935 and published by Lippincott in July 1938, and now being published by Doubleday. In it I referred so frequently to Finance Capitalism that I developed a contraction of those two words into FINCAP. FINCAP had died a lingering death between 1929 and 1934. In this book, *Critical Path,* I refer so often to the lawyer-resurrected "capitalism" that it is appropriate to refer henceforth to LAWCAP. LAWCAP's "capitalism" is paradoxically the most highly socialized organization in all history—the citizens of LAWCAP's welfare-state—the whole body of corporate stockholders—having an annual average dole of $100,000 per capita without their even having to make a pretense of getting a job.

If we take the billions of dollars given in the 1930s to the great U.S.A. defense-industries corporations by the New Deal's Reconstruction Finance Corporation . . . if we take the hidden tax-deduction subsidies to do research, development, and advertising given to all these companies in pre-1942 dollars between 1933 and 1980 . . . if we take the $100 billion in foreign aid that paid for the overseas establishment of the great corporations . . . if we take the $155 billion of atomic know-how and development taken over

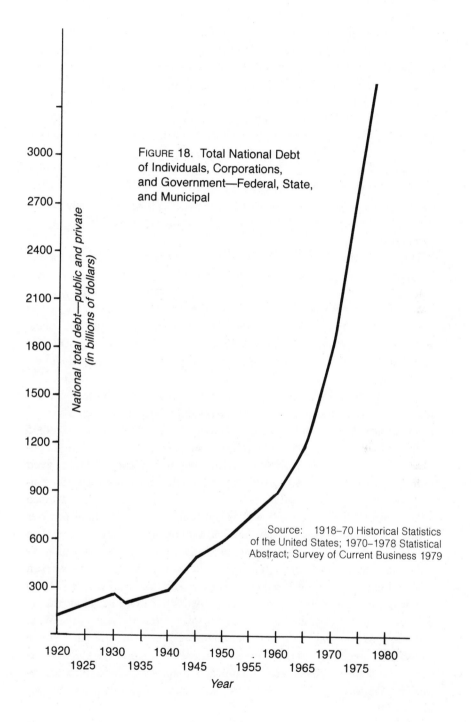

FIGURE 18. Total National Debt of Individuals, Corporations, and Government—Federal, State, and Municipal

Source: 1918–70 Historical Statistics of the United States; 1970–1978 Statistical Abstract; Survey of Current Business 1979

by the oil companies . . . and if we take the number of fine ounces of gold bullion taken out of America exclusively by the capitalist world's banking system . . . and if we take a reasonably low estimate of the unknown billions of dollars taken out of the U.S.A. by the CIA to operate exclusively on behalf of international capitalism without the knowledge or authority of the people of the U.S. of America's quasi-democracy . . . and if we multiply the sum of the foregoing figures by twenty-five, which is the amount to which our present U.S.A. dollars have been depreciated between the time of the appropriations and January 1, 1980, we come to a figure in the magnitude of *$6 trillion* that has been legally transferred from the U.S.A. people's national capital account over to the capital ownership account of the stockholders of the 1000 largest, transnational, exclusively American-flag-flying corporations.

The transnationally operating LAWCAP in the early '50s resurrected the twenty-year-dead FINCAP and its "capitalist" world and left only its American-flag-flying storefronts in the U.S.A. to cover its comprehensive financial withdrawal from the U.S.A. LAWCAP silently and invisibly moved capitalism's big-time operations into the any-legally-propitious-elsewhere. With its invisibly operating CIA (Capitalism's Invisible Army) LAWCAP exploited the unwitting citizens of the U.S.A. in order—they hoped—to destroy socialism.

The 1947–50 LAWCAP decision to start a World War III had two objectives: (1) to keep capitalism in business, and (2) to prevent the Russians from employing their industrial productivity to produce a higher standard of living for their own people than that demonstrated in the U.S.A. LAWCAP's decision to start World War III inaugurated history's greatest game of poker, with the U.S.S.R. as a very reluctant player, worried about its "home-folks'" political agitation for a few "goodies." It became a poker game that called for each side adding approximately $100 billion per year into the "killingry kitty." They have now done so for thirty years. This amounts to $6 trillion. By complete coincidence $6 trillion happens to be approximately the same magnitude as that of the total mileage per year traveled by light operating at 186,000 miles each second of the year.

Throughout those thirty years, the U.S.A.-half of this $6 trillion (that is, $3 trillion) was redeposited at various turnover rates per year in the Western-world banks, and the latter continually reloaned those dollars, at historically unprecedentedly high rates, to armaments industry. The net of it all was to convert science and technology's highest capability into accomplishing the killing of ever more people at ever greater distances in ever shorter time.

LAWCAP's comprehensive grand strategy had its Achilles' heel.

Having successfully lifted $6 trillion from the mid-twentieth-century world's leading nation—the U.S.A. and its people—LAWCAP puppeted the U.S.A.'s people into expending another of their own $6 trillion in playing "the drop-dead killingry poker game" with the U.S.S.R. exclusively on behalf of invisible LAWCAP. The latter was sure that with its complete control of all the world's money to back the U.S.A., the latter could not lose the killingry poker game with the U.S.S.R. Counting on winning the poker game, LAWCAP started planning its own post–World War III future.

LAWCAP once more deceived its so-easy-to-deceive U.S.A. puppet with the kibitzing of the U.S.A.'s playing of its killingry poker hand. LAWCAP did so through its enormous media control and its election-funding and lobbying power of the American political game. LAWCAP had its political leaders convince the U.S.A. people that they were playing the poker game so satisfactorily that the U.S.A. assumed that it was far ahead in atomic bombs, which gave it complete national security and assumedly maintained its world-around power and prestige.

LAWCAP was confident that with ownership of all money and control of all the Western world's arms-producing facilities, they could outlast the U.S.S.R.'s ability to cope with its internal pressure for shifting its productivity toward its people's life-style—as surreptitiously agitated for by the CIA's psycho-guerilla operations.

Because it was a "poker game" the Russians, realizing that intercontinentally delivered warheads with a twenty-minute lag between rocket blast-off and landing bang-off inadvertently provided a twenty-minute radar lead, that meant for the first time in the history of war that both sides would be able to see the other side shooting at them twenty minutes before the bullets would reach them, which gave both sides twenty minutes within which to get away all of both sides' atomic bombs, gases, germs, and death rays before the Big Bang, thus producing the first war in history in which both sides and all their allies would lose. To be a survivor of such a war would be worse than being killed by it. Planet Earth would be humanly untenable.

Because the Russians knew all this was so, and the American people did not seem to know it was so, the Russians assumed after the Khrushchev-Eisenhower Geneva Meeting of 1955 that atomic bomb warfare would never occur—that is the way the U.S.S.R. played their poker hand. They assumed only enough atomic bomb-making to camouflage their strategy, while they counted on conventional arms, vast divisions of armed and trained men, and the greatest ever of world history's line-of-world-supply-controlling navies. The latter featured all of their now-perfected Vertol planes, being above-the-sea-surface-emitted, vertically ascending into the sky from enormous-bellied atomic submarines, moving far more swiftly submerged—seventy knots—

than could the surface-battling, forty- to fifty-knot aircraft carriers. This the U.S.S.R. assessed to be the world-winning strategy.

The reason that LAWCAP's strategy kibitzed its U.S.A. players into holding four atomic bomb "aces" and an aircraft carrier "king" was because LAWCAP wanted to be sure that the atomic energy technology was so advanced and proliferated by World War III's end that they could employ its U.S.A.-peoples-paid-for basic equipment and widely developed uranium mines and production sources and its scientific personnel to produce the energy to run through their money-making meters after their fossil fuels were exhausted.

LAWCAP's cupidity outwitted its wisdom. LAWCAP's sense of evolutionary-event acceleration was faulty. They bluffed only the people of the U.S.A.—not the Russians.

The Russians have now attained so commanding a lead in the killingry poker game that even the U.S.A. president concedes that it would take the U.S.A. a minimum of ten years to restrategy itself so that it could in any way cope with the Russians' "conventional" naval supremacy and its vastly greater numbers of modernly armed divisions of world-around warfaring capabilities.

In the meantime as already mentioned the United States has gone completely bankrupt internally, its national indebtedness coming very close to a trillion dollars and its balance of trade debt to $109 billion—worsening at a horrendous rate due to LAWCAP's arranging to force the U.S.A. to obtain almost half its petroleum energy from the Near East. The U.S.A. has for eight years past been unable to meet even the interest on its internal debt as demonstrated by a negative balance of trade. Its future credit has been hypothecated thirty years beyond Armageddon. Nothing to stop the U.S. Treasury from issuing 2050 notes, but for how far into the future can LAWCAP keep selling U.S.A. promissory notes?

Unless God has something else in mind, it looks as though it will not be long before LAWCAP's kibitzing of the U.S.A. will have lost the $6-trillion killingry poker game. Russia will not hesitate to "call" the U.S.A. hand and rake in the winnings of omniworld, line-of-supply control—maritime, aeronautical, and astronautical.

In one way the U.S.A. and U.S.S.R. citizens are in much the same socioeconomic position. The Communist party which runs the U.S.S.R. consists of about 1 percent of their total population, while the U.S.A. is controlled by about the same 1 percent, who are the LAWCAP strategists of the great U.S.A. corporations.

The U.S.A. is not run by its would-be "democratic" government. All the latter can do is try to adjust to the initiatives already taken by LAWCAP's great corporations. Nothing could be more pathetic than the role that has to be played by the President of the United States, whose power is approximately zero. Nevertheless, the news media and most over-thirty-years-of-age U.S.A. citizens carry on as if the president had supreme power. All that he and the Congress can do is adjust to what the "free-enterprise system" has already done. They are riding on the snapping end of the power-structure dragon's tail.

If I had not been studying and working for a half-century on the assumption that this present state of affairs would come about at about this moment in history, I would have to be very pessimistic now about the human affairs of the 7 percent of the world's population situated within the national boundaries of the U.S.A. let alone critically threatened omnihumanity.

But, in fact, I have been studying and working anticipatorily throughout all those intervening fifty-three years, and I know what I am talking about. The world now has an option to become comprehensively and sustainingly successful—for all—and that is what this book is about: How to do so ... and do so expeditiously enough to succeed within the time limit. "How to do so" is implicit in the chapters that follow starting with the manner in which I came to discover the critical options and the individual self-disciplines that came naturally to disclose the grand strategy of human survival and successful functioning.

* * *

Only cosmic costing accounts for the entirely interdependent electro-chemical and ecological relationships of Earth's biological evolution and cosmic intertransformative regeneration in general. Cosmic costing accounts as well for the parts played gravitationally and radiationally in the totality within which our minuscule planet Earth and its minuscule star the Sun are interfunctionally secreted. Cosmic costing makes utterly ludicrous the selfish and fearfully contrived "wealth" games being reverentially played by humanity aboard Earth.

Fortunately, the Sun does not demand payment for all the energy that it delivers by radiation to Earth in the overall cosmic scheme, which is trying to make humanity a success despite our overwhelming ignorance and fear. The stars are trying to tell humanity to awake and prosper and to consciously assume the important cosmic responsibilities for which it was designed. Since realization and fulfillment of that responsibility involve evolutionary discovery by humanity of the cosmic stature of its mind and the inconsequentiality of its muscle, the planting of humans on Earth may not bear fruit.

When Universe is developing important functional interdependencies, she does not put all her embryos in the same proverbial "basket," (or *fiscus*). So poor is the probability of self-discovery by humans of the infinite potential of the mind and the relative triviality of human musclepower (which is not even as capable as a grasshopper's) great nature must have planted a myriad of human-function-equivalent seedlings on a myriad of planets. In order to succeed as local-in-Universe critical information-gatherers and local-in-Universe problem-solvers in support of the integrity of eternally regenerative scenario Universe, the human-function equipment for local-in-Universe information-gathering will be as variable as the varied environments in Universe. Rarely will they have the appearance of human organisms—such would be employed only under environmental conditions similar to those of planet Earth.

The first manifestation that humanity may make good on this planet will be the serious introduction of cosmic costing into the mainstream deliberations of Earthians.

Cosmic accounting completely eliminates the economic validity of bankruptcy accounting, except when humans make the mistake of trying to hoard or withdraw critical "capital" assets from production functioning. Withdrawal of capital assets is akin to attempting to withdraw one of the stars from the celestial system. Into what Universe, other than the cosmic totality, may the star be transferred? Every atom and electron is an essential part of the eternally regenerative—ergo, totally inexhaustible (but always locally ebbing and flooding)—pulsative Universe.

PART II

CHAPTER 4

Self-Disciplines of Buckminster Fuller

1 MY FATHER DIED when I was fifteen.
  "Darling, never mind what you think. Listen. We are trying to teach you!"

My mother said it. My schoolteachers said it. All grown-up authorities of any kind—the policeman, the druggist said it. "Thinking" was considered to be a process that is only teachable by the elders of the system. "That is why we have schools, dear." "Thinking" was considered to be an utterly unreliable process when spontaneously attempted by youth.

2. Grandmother taught us the Golden Rule: "Love thy neighbor as thy self—do unto others as you would they should do unto you."

3. As we became older and more experienced, our uncles began to caution us to get over our sensitivity. "Life is hard," they explained. "There is nowhere nearly enough life support for everybody on our planet, let alone enough for a comfortable life support. If you want to raise a family and have a comfortable life for them, you are going to have to deprive many others of the opportunity to survive and the sooner, the better. Your grandmother's Golden Rule is beautiful, but it doesn't work."

4. Knowing that my mother and relatives loved me, I did my best not to pay any attention to my own thinking and trained myself to learn what seemed to me "the game of life" as you would train yourself to play football. The rules are all written by others.

5. Along came World War I. I did well in the Navy. I didn't have to "make money" with my ships. But when I entered the business world and

had to make money over and above producing a good product, or when it had to be myself or somebody else who was to survive in the system, I was a spontaneous failure. I was always sure that I could cope with hardship better than the other guy, so I would yield.

6. In 1907, at the age of twelve, challenged by Robert Burns's "Oh wad some power the giftie gie us to see oursels as others see us," I sought to "see" myself as others might and to integrate that other self with my self-seen self and thereafter to deal as objectively as possible with the comprehensively integrated self. One of the techniques I adopted for doing this was to keep a come-as-it-may chronological—rather than an alphabetical or a categorical—record of my activities. In 1917, at age twenty-two, as commissioned line officer in the U.S. Navy, I named the record the "Chronofile." It consisted, and as yet consists, of all my "to and from" letters, programs, sketches, memoranda, doodles, etc., plus a few typical bills.

In 1917 Anne Hewlett and I were married. In 1918 our daughter Alexandra was born; she contracted infantile paralysis and spinal meningitis and died on her fourth birthday in 1922. Between 1922 and 1927 I developed a manufacturing and building business, designed and equipped four small factories for manufacturing new building components, and therewith successfully erected 240 residential buildings, but I failed to do so profitably and lost my friends' investments and became discredited and penniless. Coincidentally with my failure in business in 1927, our second daughter, Allegra, was born in pristine health.

7. In 1927, at age thirty-two, finding myself a "throwaway" in the business world, I sought to use myself as my scientific "guinea pig" (my most objectively considered research "subject") in a lifelong experiment designed to discover what—if anything—a healthy young male human of average size, experience, and capability with an economically dependent wife and newborn child, starting without capital or any kind of wealth, cash savings, account monies, credit, or university degree, could effectively do that could not be done by great nations or great private enterprise to lastingly improve the physical protection and support of all human lives, at the same time removing undesirable restraints and improving individual initiatives of any and all humans aboard our planet Earth.

8. In 1927 I also committed all my productivity potentials toward dealing only with our whole planet Earth and all its resources and cumulative know-how, while undertaking to comprehensively protect, support, and advantage all humanity instead of committing my efforts to the exclusive advantages of my dependents, myself, my country, my team.

This decision was not taken on a recklessly altruistic do-gooder basis, but in response to the fact that my Chronofile clearly demonstrated that in my first thirty-two years of life I had been positively effective in producing life-advantage wealth—which realistically protected, nurtured, and accommodated X numbers of human lives for Y numbers of forward days—only when I was doing so entirely for others and not for myself.

Further Chronofile observation showed that the larger the number for whom I worked, the more positively effective I became. Thus it became obvious that if I worked always and only for all humanity, I would be optimally effective.

9. I sought to do my own thinking, confining it to only experientially gained information, and with the products of my own thinking and intuition to articulate my own innate motivational integrity instead of trying to accommodate everyone else's opinions, credos, educational theories, romances, and mores, as I had in my earlier life.

10. I sought to accomplish whatever was to be accomplished for anyone in such a manner that the advantage attained for anyone would never be secured at the cost of another or others.

11. I sought to cope with all humanly unfavorable conditions, customs, and afflictions by searching for the family of relevant physical principles involved, and therewith through invention and technological development to solve all problems by physical data and devices that were so much more effective as to be spontaneously adopted by humans and thereby to result in producing more desirable life-styles and thus emancipate humans from the previously unfavorable circumstances.

I must always "reduce" my inventions to physically working models and must never talk about the inventions until physically proven—or disproven.

The new favorable-to-humans environment constituted by the technological inventions and information must demonstrate that new inanimate technology could now accomplish what heretofore could not be accomplished by social reforms. I sought to reform the environment, not the humans. I determined never to try to persuade humanity to alter its customs and viewpoints.

12. I sought never to "promote" or "sell" either my ideas or artifacts or to pay others to do so. I must never hire any agents to produce publicity for me, nor engage any lecture, literary, or "idea-selling" agents, nor hire personnel who would solicit support of any kind on my behalf. All support

must be spontaneously engendered by evolution's integrating of my inventions with the total evolution of human affairs.

13. I assumed that nature had its own unique gestation rates, not only for the birth of each new biological component of ecological intersupport, but also for each inanimate technological artifact invention of human interadvantaging.

14. I sought to develop my artifacts with ample anticipatory time margins so that they would be ready for use by society when society discovered through evolutionary emergencies that they needed just what I had developed. I realized that if the new tools I had developed could provide valid human-advantage increases, then they would inevitably be adopted by society during the successive inexorable emergencies that occur in society, which evolution of emergence only through emergencies would dictate the proper rate of regenerative gestation of spontaneously adopted social advances.

15. I sought to learn the most from my mistakes.

16. I sought to decrease time wasted in worried procrastination and to increase time invested in discovery of technological effectiveness.

17. I sought to document my development in the official records of humanity by applying for and being granted government patents.

18. Above all I sought to comprehend the principles of eternally regenerative Universe and to discover human functioning therein, thereby to discover nature's governing complexes of generalized principles and to employ these principles in the development of the specific artifacts that would benefit humanity's fulfillment of its essential functioning in the cosmic scheme.

19. I sought to educate myself comprehensively regarding nature's inventory of chemical elements, their weights, performance characteristics, relative abundances, geographical whereabouts, metallurgical interalloyabilities, chemical associabilities and disassociabilities.

I sought to comprehend the full gamut of production tool capabilities, energy resources, and all relevant geological, meteorological, demographic, and economic data, as well as to comprehend the logistics and vital statistics thus far methodically amassed by humanity as derived from its all-history experiences.

20. I sought to operate only on a do-it-yourself basis and only on the basis of intuition.

21. I oriented what I called my "comprehensive, anticipatory design science strategies" toward primarily advantaging the new life to be born within the environment-controlling devices I was designing and developing, because the new lives would be unencumbered by conditioned reflexes that might otherwise blind them to the potential advantages newly existent within the new environment-control system in which they found themselves beginning life.

As already mentioned, our second child, Allegra, was born in 1927. Five years earlier her sister, Alexandra, had died on the eve of her birthday, having gone through four years of spinal meningitis and infantile paralysis.

Allegra's birth was a mysterious, awesome, and beautiful event, for my wife Anne and I realized that not only were we being again entrusted with a new life, but this time with that of a beautifully healthy life. At that moment I was penniless and, to the relatively few who knew me, discredited. I had proved myself to be a failure in a business that had been financially backed by many of my friends. I had only a rich inventory of experience. That experience made clear to me that there were critical problems to be solved regarding total humanity aboard planet Earth—problems that would take at least a half-century to cope with successfully; problems as yet unattended to by anyone; problems that, if successfully solved, would bring lasting advantage to all humanity; problems that, if left unsolved, would find all humanity at ever-increasing disadvantage.

It was not that the problems could not be seen by others, but society was preoccupied with individual, national, state, and local business-survival problems, which forced its leaders into short-term, limited-scope considerations—with no time for total world problems. The presidents of great corporations had to make good profits within a very few years or lose their jobs. The politicians, too, were preoccupied with short-range national, state, or municipal survival matters.

It seemed also clear to me that there had opened up a new avenue of approach to humanity's survival problems, an avenue that could be traversed only by an individual operating entirely on the individual's own economic and philosophic initiative.

All the world was preoccupied with intercompetitive survival, being spontaneously motivated by the working assumption of the existence of a fundamental inadequacy of life support on our planet. The leading ideologies said, "You may not like our system, but we are convinced that we are coping most wisely, justly, and practically with fundamental inadequacy of life support. We are the fittest to survive."

What my experience taught me was that if the physical laws thus far found by science to be governing Universe were intelligently and fearlessly employed in the production of ever higher performances per each pound of material, erg of energy, and second of time invested, it would be feasible to take care of all humanity at higher standards of living than had ever been known by any humans—and to do so sustainingly. Evolution seemed to be operating in such a manner as to drive humans to inadvertent accomplishment of their own success.

Despite the fearful "you-or-me" survival preoccupations, it seemed clear to me that if an individual who had practical experience in engineering, marketing, aeronautics, vessels on the sea, building on the land, mass manufacturing arts, and naval ballistics, who also could discern the evolutionary potentials emerging in scientific discoveries and see what the priority of tasks might be in bringing about general economic success for all humanity, then if that individual were to address those problems, completely committing the balance of his life to the realization of such technical advantaging of humanity, then, if that individual was doing what nature was trying to do, he might find self—and those dependent on self—surviving and gaining in knowledge, capability, and experience relevant to the tasks to be accomplished.

Effective exploration requires effective record-keeping. I am confident of the accuracy of the record presented herewith. I am also confident that my personal record is pretty much the same as the record that would have been manifest by any healthy, well-informed individual who undertook the course I chose to steer upon the birth of Allegra in 1927. The fact that the individual who did pursue this course as a deliberate experiment (myself) found that it proved to be an economically tenable way of life and a technically effective way of approaching world problems may encourage others to address problems in the same manner.

*   *   *

As already related, in 1907 I started a chronological record of my life and in 1917 named it the "Chronofile." In 1917, at the age of twenty-two—fortified with the already-thick Chronofile—I determined to make myself "the special case guinea pig study" in a lifelong research project—i.e., documenting the life of an individual born in the "Gay Nineties"—1895, the year automobiles were introduced, the wireless telegraph and the automatic screw machine were invented, and X rays were discovered—having his boyhood around the turn of the century, and maturing during humanity's epochal graduation from the nineteenth century, which closed Sir Isaac Newton's "normally at rest" and myriadly isolated hybrid world cultures to which change was anathema, into the twentieth century and Einstein's normally "dynamic," omni-integrating world culture to which change has come to seem both essential and popularly acceptable.

Though I lived within seven miles of Boston's center, so new and rare an object was the automobile that I was seven years old when I first saw one. I first drove one when I was twelve. Operators' licenses and owners' registration certificates did not come into official use in any states until a decade later.

When I was nine years old, the airplane was invented, but I did not see one flying until I was fourteen, and I did not fly one until I was twenty-two, within which same year (1917) I heard the historically first human-voice conversation over the radio. Earlier in that extraordinary year the U.S.A. had entered World War I; I had entered the U.S. Navy; and Anne Hewlett had entered into marriage with me.

The cumulative effect of this swift succession of epochally surprising "first-ever" (for me) human and personal experiences precipitated my previously mentioned inauguration of the history of the evolution of "Guinea Pig B" ("B" for Bucky)—the Chronofile.

Along with millions of other pre–Kitty Hawk juveniles I, too, had tried to invent the airplane, first with paper dart models and then with box-kite-like multiplaned gliders. Despite our elders' doubts and engineering's down-to-earth negatives, immanent invention of the "airplane" was everywhere present in the thought world of my pre–Wright Brothers, knee-breeches years. It is interesting that our latest supersonic and 2000-mile-per-hour planes are beginning to take on the overall shape perfection of those early paper darts. Children's intuitions are keen.

My extraordinary experiences with the U.S. Navy's World War I galaxy of new tools—oil-burning turboelectric ships, aircraft, diesel-engined submarines, radios, automatic range-keepers, etc.—convinced me that the experience pattern of my generation was not to be just one more duplicate generation in a succession of millions of generations of humanity, with an approximately imperceptible degree of environmental change, as compared to the immediately previous generation. I was convinced that, unannounced by any authority, a much greater environmental and ecological change was just beginning to take place in my generation's unfolding experience than had occurred cumulatively between my father's, grandfather's, great-, and great-great-grandfather's four previous generations. I had read their diaries, expense accounts, or letters containing descriptions of their lives in their successive undergraduate days in the Harvard classes of 1883, 1843, 1801, and 1760, respectively. They all told of days-long walking or driving trips between Cambridge and Boston. I realized intuitively that the subway, which opened in my 1913 freshman year to connect Harvard Square in Cambridge to Tremont and Park streets in Boston in seven minutes, was a harbinger of an entirely new space-time relationship of the individual and the environment.

It was clearly the environment and not the humans that was changing, and though the environmental changes might not alter human genes, changes in their external conditions might permit humans to realize many more of their innate capabilities than heretofore.

Humans are tool complexes—hands for certain tasks, feet, ears, teeth, etc., for others. Using their human tool complexes, human minds, comprehending variable interrelationship principles, invent detached-from-self tools—the bucket can lift out more water from the well than can a pair of cupped human hands—that are more special-case-effective but not used as frequently as their organically integral tools. Humans invent craft tools and industrial tools. The latter are all the tools that cannot be invented or operated by one human. The first industrial tool was the spoken word. With words humans compounded their experience-won knowledge. (Most industrial tools are driven by inanimate energy rather than by human muscle.)

Dwellings are environment-controlling machines. So are automobiles. Automobiles are little part-time dwellings on wheels. Both autos and dwellings are complex tools. Both autos and dwellings are component tools within the far vaster tool complex of world-embracing industrialization. I use the word *industrialization* to include all intercoordinate humanity, all its artifacts, its evolving omni-interfunctioning and omni-integrating, omni-life-support-producing capability.

I do not demean the phenomenon of industrialization by identifying it as being the money-making business that exploits productivity for unilateral profit. I do not identify the biological complexity "cow" and its ecological support system as being a component of some dairy business. Industrialization is *not* business's mass production of weaponry and munitions for political proliferation and personal profit. Industrialization's productivity is exploited by business. But industrialization's coordinate productivity can be employed directly by spontaneous cooperation of humanity without business-profit-motivation.

Life continually alters the environment, and the altered environment in turn alters the potentials, realities, and challenges of life. Environment embraces a complex of nonsimultaneously occurring but omni-integrating mutations of humans' external, only-by-invention-realized, metabolic-regeneration organisms which we think and speak of as industrialization.

Our Harvard 1917 class of 700 had only three automobile-owning members at its 1913 freshman start, one of whom was Ray Stanley, whose father had invented and produced the Stanley Steamer. But it was even then at least wishfully clear that humans in general might sometime acquire automobiles. Since that time I have owned successively forty-three automobiles, three of which I invented and built, and have personally driven the forty-three cars a total of one and one-quarter million miles. I have lived long enough in various places to have had my cars registered in different years in ten different U.S.A. states. I have flown one and one-half million miles, part of that distance in three of my own planes. I have owned many boats, traveled in many others, and have commanded several craft in the United States Navy.

My total travel, by land, sea, and air, aggregates more than three and one-half million miles to date, and in the last twenty-two years my work has taken me completely around the world forty-seven times, making it more economical and efficient to rent automobiles locally than to own them and leave them sitting in airport parking lots. Consequently I have rented over 100 cars in addition to the forty-three I owned. This is in no wise a unique record. It is fairly average for millions of humans who have responsibilities in the general frontiers of evoluting world society. Three and one-half million is paltry mileage for any senior Pan American Airways pilot. Every astronaut with only two weeks away from Earth has traveled over three and one-half million miles.

Pre–1900 average world man covered only 30,000 miles in his entire lifetime, which is only one percent of my lifetime mileage to date.

In 1900 no human thought assumed that acceleration existed in human affairs, i.e., sociologically. In 1980 there is no longer valid dissent from the concept of an accelerating change in the affairs of humans on Earth. The average U.S.A. family now moves out of town every three years. My present official address for passports and taxation is in Maine. I have had successive voting privileges in eight states. Whether I am "in residence" or not, my land, my house, you too, and I whirl constantly around the Earth's axis together (at about 800 miles per hour in the latitude of New York City), as all the while our little Spaceship Earth zooms around the Sun at 60,000 miles per hour, while at the same time our solar system rotates in its nebular merry-go-round at hundreds of thousands of miles per hour—none of which celestial-arena traveling did I include in my previously stated lifetime mileages or in those of other Earthians.

In all reality I never "leave home." My backyard has just grown progressively bigger and more globular until now the whole world is my spherical backyard. "Where do you live?" and "What are you?" are progressively less sensible questions. "At present I am a passenger on Spaceship Earth," and "I don't know what I am. I know that I am not a category, a highbred specialization. I am not a thing—a noun. I am not flesh. At eighty-five, I have taken in over a thousand tons of air, food, and water, which temporarily became my flesh and which progressively dissassociated from me. You and I seem to be verbs—evolutionary processes. Are we not integral functions of the Universe?"

In 1917, in the U.S. Navy, I had intuited that an intermultiplicative historical acceleration of technical events was beginning that would bring about a fundamental and cataclysmic reorientation of human life in Universe. Accelerating acceleration had been discovered by Galileo circa 1600 in respect to free-falling bodies, out of which, with other discoveries, he formulated his first laws of motion. But the first laws of motion had not been conceived of, initially or since, as being applicable to human sociology—as accelerating our ecological evolution—until I intuitively hailed it as doing just that in 1917.

Discussion of "acceleration" in economic, sociologic, and ecologic evolution did not begin in the intellectual publications until more than a decade later. Also, two decades before publication by others was my 1922–1927 discovery that ever higher tool performance per unit of pounds, time, and energy input (as metallurgical and electronic fallout from the weaponry industries into the domestic consumer economy) was resulting sum-totally in providing progressively ever more energetic performances with ever less weight and volume of material per function as well as ever less energy expenditure per each unit of overall performance in the domestic economy. I discovered this when erstwhile weaponry-support contractors sought to exploit their U.S.-government-paid, scientifically instrumented, and production-tooled "new factories" when those factories and all their government-developed tools were returned to the companies after World War I's armaments contracts were terminated.

In contradistinction to the successively greater performance gains with ever less pounds and volumes of materials, ergs of energy, and seconds of time per each unit of performance strategy employed in designing ships (environment controls) of the sea and sky for the military, the dry-land building economy had theretofore been prototyped by fortress and castle building. Increased environment security was to be accomplished only with more weight and masonry massiveness—the heavier, higher, and thicker the walls, the more the security attained.

In 1917 this more performance with less weight and volume of materials, less ergs of energy, and less seconds of time investment per each accomplished unit of performance, manifested itself for the first time in the metallurgy, chemistry, and electronics of World War I sea and sky armaments developments. This newly observed phenomena seemed to me to put in question the absolute scientific validity of Malthus's 1805 discovery that humanity is multiplying its numbers at a geometrical rate while increasing its life-support capability only at an arithmetical rate, as a consequence of which it was universally concluded by all eco-political power system masters that only a few humans are destined to survive successfully. Conversely, it seemed to me that it could come to pass through more-with-lessing that all of humanity might become both physically and economically successful even within the foreseeable future.

There is not a chapter in any book in economics anywhere about doing more with less. Economists traditionally try to maximize what you have, but the idea that you could go from wire to wireless or from visible structuring to invisible alloy structuring did not occur to them at all. It was outside their point of view—beyond their range of vision. Economists are specialists trained to look only at one particular thing.

In my *Shelter* magazine of 1930–33 and in my 1938 book, *Nine Chains to the Moon,* I identified this progressive doing-more-with-less as *ephemeralization.* Though *Fortune* magazine also published my 1922 concept of *ephemeralization* in its tenth-anniversary issue of 1940 in a prominent manner, and despite *ephemeralization* having subsequently wrought epochal advancements in the standard of living for two billion previously deprived humans, *ephemeralization* is a phenomenon that in 1980 is as yet largely unknown to or overlooked by the world's professional economists. Nonetheless, the *combination of accelerating acceleration and ephemeralization** has now elevated 60 percent of all humanity from its year-1900 99-percent poverty level into realization of an everyday standard of living superior to that enjoyed by any kings, tycoons, or other power-commanding humans prior to the twentieth century.

Sailors watch for every clue nature may give to coming events—cloud formations, temperature of the water, wind direction shiftings, etc. To survive, navigators must anticipate comprehensively. The sailor's subconscious as well as conscious faculties interact to inform his anticipatory decisions. Only intuiting the subsequently realized epochal significance of *accelerating ephemeralization* to be implicit, as already noted, I decided in 1917 to scientifically document its emergent realizations as they impinged upon the daily life of an individual, his family, and his world.

---

*Someone suggested to me that *etherealization* may be a better word. However, it is disqualified for my meaning because it is founded on the no longer physically accepted concept of *ether.*

My 1917 "Project Guinea Pig B" was greatly advantaged by the Dymaxion Chronofile. As of June 1980 the Chronofile consists of 737 volumes, each containing 300–400 pages, or about 260,000 letters in all.

The first important regenerative effect upon me of keeping this active chronological record was that I learned to "see myself" as others might—and usually did—see me.

Second, it persuaded me ten years later (1927—a decade after inception of "Project Guinea Pig B," in 1917) to start my life as nearly "anew" as it is humanly possible to do.

One basic tenet of my new 1927 volition, as already mentioned, was that whatever was to be accomplished for anyone must never be at the cost of another. Robin Hood, whose story my father read aloud to me when I was very young and not long before my father died, became my most influential early-years' mythical hero. This meant that in my "first life" I had improvised methods in general to effect swift moral and romantic justice for those I found in trouble or danger. Foolishly self-confident in my "first life," I had often rushed thoughtlessly to assume responsibilities beyond my physical, monetary, or legal means to fulfill. This rashness led me into complex dilemmas, for in attempting to keep my assumption of responsibilities legal, I inadvertently involved my unwitting family, dragging them into preposterous financial sacrifices.

In inaugurating my new life I took away Robin Hood's longbow, staff, and checkbook and gave him only scientific textbooks, microscopes, calculating machines, transits, and industrialization's network of tooling in general. I made him substitute new inanimate forms for animate reforms. I did not allow Robin any public relations professionals or managers or agents to "promote" or "sell" him. It seemed obvious that if the new tools that the "new" Robin Hood developed could provide valid human-advantaging increases, they would inevitably be adopted by society during the successive, inexorable economic emergencies—which dictate the proper rate of regenerative gestations of evolution.

Along with the Dymaxion Chronofile I have kept all the tearsheets of newspapers, magazines, programs, etc., in which my work was reported. Until 1970 I could not afford to subscribe to a clipping service. Most of the clippings I have came into my hands by my own discovery or as a consequence of friends and acquaintances spontaneously sending clippings to me. This record now contains over 37,000 articles written and published by others about me or my work. It begins in 1917. Half of the 37,000 unique items have been published in the last twenty years. The record does not include the radio and television broadcasting about me or my work, which radio and TV broadcastings, both local and national, are ever increasing, averaging in 1979 at two per week for an annual total of 100 broadcasts, varying from one minute to an hour each.

Published herewith is a curve showing the precise number of separate and individually written items per annum appearing only in *The New York Times* from 1920 to date. It is a curve of many peaks and valleys. Altogether, it constitutes a wave pattern of ever-increasing magnitude. The cumulative record patterns into a ski-shaped curve—an initially long, almost horizontal pattern, with its nose finally rising ever more swiftly. It is an accelerating-acceleration curve.

The successive peaks relate to: my Navy days; my 1918 publication of *Transport* magazine; my 240 Stockade buildings of 1922–1927; the 4-D monograph and the Dymaxion House of 1927–28; my 1930–32 publication of *Shelter* magazine; the 1927–35 Dymaxion Car; the 1927–38 Dymaxion

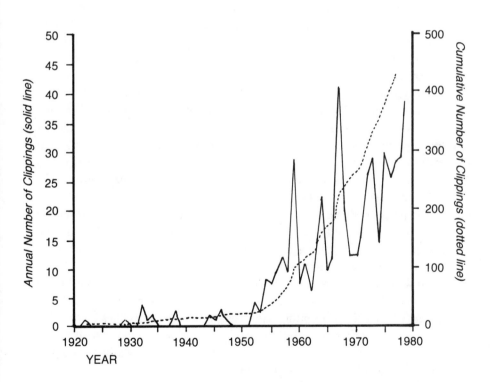

FIGURE 19. Dymaxion Clippings: The New York Times

Bathroom; my 1938 book *Nine Chains to the Moon;* the 1927 Industrial
Man's Ecological Transformation Charts; Lifelong Energetic/Synergetic
Geometry; the Dymaxion Deployment Unit produced by Butler Manufacturing Company of Kansas City in 1940; the 1930–Dymaxion Sky-Ocean
World Map, first published in multicolor in an eighteen-page section in *Life*
in March 1943; 1946 O-Volving-book-shelved, Underground Silo Library;
1947 Geodesic Domes; my world-around Geodesic Radomes for the Defense Early Warning system; my 1954 Marine Corps Air-Delivered Geodesic Domes; my U.S.A. Moscow Pavilion Dome; my U.S.A. pavilion for the
1967 Montreal World's Fair; my 1967 Triton (tetrahedronal) Floating City
for the U.S. Housing Authority; the 1965–1975 World Students' Design Science Decade; 1927 Inventory of World Resources, Human Trends and
Needs; my 1969 World Games—i.e., "How to Make the World Work," as
conducted that year at the New York Studio School, Yale University,
Southern Illinois University, University of Southern California, University
of Pennsylvania, University of Massachusetts, New York University; my
1970 two-and-a-half-mile-high (Mount Fuji–high) housing-sightseeing tower, completely engineered (but never built) for Matsutaro Shoriki, late owner of Nippon Television Network and the *Yomiuri Shimbun*—Japan's
largest-circulation daily newspaper; the 1960–73 "World Man Territory
Trusteeship" inaugurated on Cyprus under joint auspices of Archbishop
Makarios, Caress Crosby, the World Academy of Science and Art, and myself; my large-scale tensegrity projects; my eighteen books, especially *Synergetics*, volumes 1 and 2; scientific publications by others identifying my
work with discoveries at various levels of the microcosmic structuring of nature; and most latterly to a general admixture of editorial realizations that
my separately reported inventions and fundamental concepts all relate to a
total unified philosophy that now emerges as comprehensively pertinent to
unfolding historical reality.

The preponderance of later items by others relate clearly to my general
philosophy, to my fifty-year 1927 prognostications, and to my world-envi-
ronment-redesigning stratagems. There is a dawning awareness that I am
saying something realistic when I say we have been asking the politicians
to do what only we can do ourselves, technologically, by cooperative use of
our intellects and active initiatives plus our innate, politically transcendental
integrity and artifact-inventing and mass-producing capabilities.

I have been consistently faithful to my 1917 determination to treat myself
objectively as an historical guinea pig, and I assure any who may be interested that my files include as many unflattering items, such as notices from
the sheriff, letters from those who thought me to be a crank, crook, char-
latan, etc. I am glad that these negative charges are infrequent and to the

best of my knowledge untrue, though the record discloses the ease with which items taken out of context can be negatively interrelated and interpreted.

Because my Chronofile and archive's data constitute a faithfully comprehensive record, I am now able to comment objectively regarding my subjectively disclosed guinea-pig self (and I am usually more critically incisive with myself than I am with studies of other humans).

When my subject is being effective, I am glad, and when it is worriedly procrastinating, I am sad. When it makes mistakes, I learn the most and am elated. That is the extent of my prejudice.

I think the curves plottable from my data are acceptable as demonstrating the realization of the scientific marshaling of my guinea pig's case history, as deliberately and methodically undertaken a half-century ago. The curves document that my 1927 working assumptions are approximately congruent with the ensuing fifty-two-year unfoldment of evolutionary patternings in economics, technology, sociology, and mathematics. My 1927 assumptions being well published and now actively reviewed not only are proving valid, but many are also trending to further accredit my present prognosticating. My 1961 prognostications covering world educational developments to 1982—as contained in *Buckminster Fuller on Education,* now published by University of Massachusetts Press—are tending to be far more spontaneously accepted than were those of my 4-D monograph of 1928 (reissued as *4D Timelock* by the Lama Foundation in 1972).

Possibly a more telling trend regarding "Guinea Pig B" is the acceleration in the curve of the rate at which books by others refer to my work. Books usually represent a greater amount of research work, rumor filtering, and retrospective processing than do newspaper or magazine writing. The curve of books with reference to me or my work is accelerating even more swiftly than is the curve of news items published about my work.

It has been an expensive and often cumbersome task to keep the records and to hold together the archives that document the half-century history of this experimental undertaking, which had often to passage penniless times. However, that record-keeping has been accomplished. As a consequence it may serve to encourage others to commit themselves to nature's precessional principles.

* * *

Few who know me or of me—over and above friends familiar with my 1917 resolution to faithfully document the life of an individual and my 1927 resolution to conduct a lifelong experiment with that individual—are cognizant of the reasons governing adoption of several important stratagems within my personally conceived and adopted grand strategy of self-disciplines, though these have altogether governed the last half-century of my eighty-five years, and as yet continue to do so.

In 1927 I designed the experiment's strategies in a manner that seemed to me most probable to prove clearly that all the irreversible gains for all human individuals that I set about to produce could not be accomplished as conceived and initiated by business corporations, political states, academic, professional, labor, or any other social groups, no matter how powerfully rich, well-informed, well-intentioned, or well-armed they might be. I was concerned with the unique cerebral faculties, conceptual metaphysics, and physical articulatabilities integral to, and operative only within, the inventory of one single individual human's functioning.

As I initiated such a lifelong operation in 1927, it was evident to me that within the extant world-around, socioeconomic milieu, the physical resources essential to the reduction to physical realization and production of the individual's invented artifacts could only be legally acquired in three ways.

1. Within the U.S.S.R. only by first persuading the Communist party leaders that my concepts were either superior to or compatible with theirs, and thereafter waiting on their relative priority list for half a century until the first ten of their five-year plans had been completed.

In February 1933, five years after my strategic decision to rely on "socioeconomic precession"—which I will explain a few paragraphs later—an emissary of the U.S.S.R. planning authority (visiting the U.S.A. in connection with Henry Ford's Dearborn school for U.S.S.R. engineers) told me that the Soviets thought well of my industrially-to-be-produced, service-rented, air-deliverable, scientific dwelling machines—the Dymaxion houses. But popular knowledge of their potential, before the time when production of the resources essential to their manufacture had been adequately supplied to inherently prior tasks in the sound organization of their industrial economy, would (if known of in Russia) generate impatience for their realization. This would be a psychologically upsetting factor—ergo, Dymaxion houses would not be brought to public attention until after 1980; so, my 1927 decision to carry out their research and development in the U.S.A., where technological evolution permitted such an initiation, was valid.

2. Within one of the great dictatorships I might gain the physical means of realizing my technological artifacts by first persuading the dictator that his only militarily sustainable plans should be abandoned because they were diametrically opposed to my concepts (not pursued).

3. Within the remainder of the world I would acquire the means only in exchange for cash money or services. This brought me once more to the

FIGURE 20. Model of the Dymaxion 4-D House

number-one strategic question: how could the initially *moneyless, creditless,* physical-facilities-lacking individual succeed in realistically demonstrating that the invented artifacts not only could be practically realized but that their use would substantially increase the economic, technological, and social advantaging of all world-around humanity and not be inherently limited to advantaging only minorities.

I saw that twentieth-century money was an economic invention that could be manipulated, for instance, through the Federal Reserve Bank and its control of its member banks' rediscount rate—or again by the banks' loaning to already powerful organizations large blocks of the money of many small depositors to enhance the advantage only of the few through profitable exploitations of the many's needs. As mentioned in an earlier chapter, since Malthus (1810) it had been assumed by all the world's political ideologies—as it is even today—that there is a fundamental and lethal inadequacy of life support on our planet, wherefore, poverty and misery for vast millions of humans have been accepted as unavoidable. Wherefore, the also universally assumed law of "survival only of the fittest" had given historical rise to various political ideologies, as ways of coping with this fundamental inadequacy—each convinced that the ultimate proof of which ideological group is fittest to survive can be resolved only by periodic trial of arms.

Politicians' effectiveness is dependent on the degree of growth of their ongoing authority. Since there is no sustainable equilibrium in a 100-percent efficient, ever-regenerating physical Universe, the politician of the moment who has gained greatest effectiveness is the one whose gained authority is as yet increasing—i.e., the brightness of whose "star" is waxing. Once their authority becomes visibly less, they are "on the way out." The same is true of the money-making private-corporation executives. They must play company politics to ever progressively augment *personal authority.*

No matter how altruistic a public image they may attain and maintain, both the budding or full-bloom politicians and corporate executives must secretly have always on highest priority the increasing enhancement of their own public image as well as of their own financial credit. Whether public or private, professional or amateur, their own kudos-building or -maintenance requires that both the politicians and corporate executives forever be attempting to favorably reform the viewpoints of others regarding their particular organizations. To do so they are forever proposing to reform the organization commanded by those others whose prerogatives they hope to acquire.

Far different from the politicians', corporate executives', and religious leaders' strategies was the new noncompetitive course I took in 1927—i.e., that of reforming only the physical environment through artifacts, such as increasing safety and decreasing accidents by engineering improvements of motor vehicles while also providing overpasses and banked turns for the vehicles to drive on, instead of trying to reform the vehicle drivers' behaviors.

I planned to employ the ever-increasing and -improving scientific knowledge and technology to produce ever more effective human life-improving results with ever less investment of weight of materials, ergs of energy, seconds of time per each measurable level of improved artifact performance. I was hopeful of finally doing so much with so little as to implement comprehensive and economically sustainable physical success for all humanity, thereby to eliminate the need for lethally biased politics and their ultimate recourse to hot or cold warring.

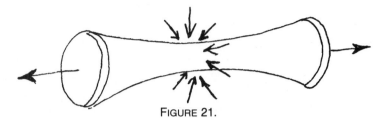

FIGURE 21.

The big question remained: How do you obtain the money to live with and to acquire the materials and tools with which to work?

The answer was "precession." What precession is, and why it was the answer, requires some explaining.

When we pull away from one another the opposite rigid-disc ends of a flexible, water-filled rubber cylinder, the middle part of the overall cylinder contracts in a concentric series of circular planes of diminishing radius perpendicular (at right angles) to the line of our pulling.

When we push toward one another on the two opposite ends of the same flexible, water-filled, rubber, rigid-disk-ended cylinder, the center of the cylinder swells maximally outward in a circular plane perpendicular (at right angles) to the line of our pushing together.

When we drop a stone in the water, a circular wave is generated that moves outwardly in a plane perpendicular (at right angles) to the line of stone-dropping—the outwardly expanding circular wave generates (at nine-

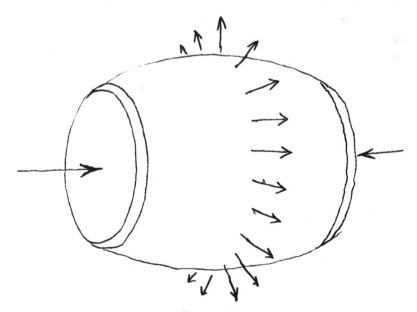

FIGURE 22.

ty degrees) a vertical wave that in turn generates an additional horizontally and outwardly expanding wave, and so on.

All these right-angle effects are processional effects. *Precession is the effect of bodies in motion on other bodies in motion.* The Sun and Earth are both in motion. Despite the 180-degree gravitational pull of the in-motion Sun upon the in-motion Earth, precession makes Earth orbit around the Sun in a direction that is at ninety degrees—i.e., at a right angle—to the direction of the Sun's gravitational pull upon Earth.

The successful regeneration of life growth on our planet Earth is ecologically accomplished always and only as the precessional—right-angled— "side effect" of the biological species' chromosomically programmed individual-survival preoccupations—the honeybees are chromosomically programmed to enter the flower blossoms in search of honey. Seemingly inadvertently (but realistically-precessionally) this occasions the bees' bumbling tail's becoming dusted with pollen (at ninety degrees to each bee's linear axis and flight path), whereafter the bees' further bumbling entries into other flowers inadvertently dusts off, pollenizes, and cross-fertilizes those flowers at right angles (precessionally) to the bees' operational axis—so, too, do all the mobile creatures of Earth cross-fertilize all the different rooted botanicals in one or another precessional (right-angled), inadvertent way.

Humans, as honey-money-seeking bees, do many of nature's required tasks only inadvertently. They initially produce swords with metal-forging-developed capability, which capability is later used to make steel into farm plows. Humans—in politically organized, group-fear-mandated acquisition of weaponry—have inadvertently developed so-much-more-performance-with-so-much-less material, effort, and time investment per each technological task accomplished as now inadvertently to have established a level of technological capability which, if applied exclusively to peaceful purposes,

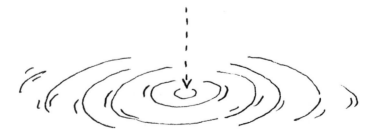

FIGURE 23.

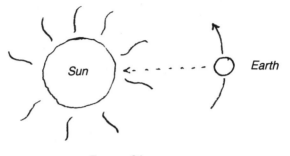

FIGURE 24.

can provide a sustainable high standard of living for all humanity, which accomplished fact makes war and all weaponry obsolete. Furthermore, all of this potential has happened only because of the at-ninety-degrees-realized generalized technology and science "side effects" or "fall-out" inadvertently discovered as special case manifest of the scientifically generalized principle of precession.

At the 1927 outset of project "Guinea Pig B" I assumed that *humanity was designed to perform an important function in Universe,* a function it would discover only after an initially innocent by-trial-and-error-discovered phase of capability development. During the initial phase humans, always born naked, helpless, and ignorant but with hunger, thirst, and curiosity to drive them, have been chromosomically programmed to operate successfully only by means of the general biological inadvertencies of bumbling "honey-seeking." Therefore, what humans called the side effects of their conscious drives in fact produced the main ecological effects of generalized technological regeneration. I therefore assumed that what humanity rated as "side effects" are nature's *main* effects. I adopted the precessional "side effects" as my prime objective.

So preoccupied with its honey-money bumbling has society been that the ninety-degree side effects of the century-old science of ecology remained long unnoticed by the populace. Ecology is the world-around complex intercomplementation of all the biological species' regenerative intercyclings with nature's geological and meteorological transformation recyclings. Society discovered ecology only when its economically sidewise discards of unprofitable substances became so prodigious as to pollutingly frustrate nature's regenerative mainstream intersupport. Society's surprise "discovery" of ecology in the 1960s constituted its as-yet-realistically-unresponded-to discovery of nature's main effects—ergo, of precession. It is a safe guess that not more than one human in 10 million is conceptually familiar with and sensorially comprehending of the principle of "precession."

In 1927 I reasoned that if humans' experiences gave them insights into what nature's main objectives might be, and if humans committed themselves, their lifetimes, and even their dependents and all their assets toward direct, efficient, and expeditious realization of any of nature's comprehensive evolutionary objectives, nature might realistically support such a main precessional commitment and all the ramifications of the individual's developmental needs, provided that no one else was trying to do what the precessionally committed saw needed to be done. Precession cannot be accomplished competitively. Precession cannot respond to angularly redundant forces. It can, however, respond to several angularly nonredundant forces at a given time.

Since nature was clearly intent on making humans successful in support of the integrity of eternally regenerative Universe, it seemed clear that if I undertook ever more humanly favorable physical-environment-producing artifact developments that in fact did improve the chances of all humanity's successful development, it was quite possible that nature would support my efforts, provided I were choosing the successively most efficient technical means of so doing. Nature was clearly supporting all her intercomplementary ecological regenerative tasks—ergo, I must so commit myself and must depend upon nature providing the physical means of realization of my invented environment-advantaging artifacts. I noted that nature did not require hydrogen to "earn a living" before allowing hydrogen to behave in the unique manner in which it does. Nature does not require that any of its intercomplementing members "earn a living."

Because I could see that this precessional principle of self-employment was a reasonably realistic possibility (though to the best of my knowledge never before consciously adopted and tested by others), I resolved to adopt such a course formally, realizing that there would be no human who could authorize my doing so nor any authority able to validate my decision so to do. I saw that there would be no humans to evaluate my work as it proceeded—nor to tell me what to do next.

I went on to reason that since economic machinery and logistics consist of bodies in motion, since precession governs the interbehaviors of all bodies in motion, and since human bodies are usually in motion, precession must govern all socioeconomic behaviors. Quite clearly humans do orbit at ninety degrees to the direction of their interattractions—orbiting elliptically around one another's most attractively dominant neighbors, as do also galaxies within supergalaxies and all the stars, moons, comets, asteroids, stardust particles, unattached molecules, atoms, and the electrons within the atoms. All orbit their respectively most interattractively dominant nuclei of the moment. I recognized that overall interproximities vary and that Newton's law of system interattractiveness varies inversely at a second-power rate of the mathematical distances intervening as well as in respect to the product of the masses of any two considered bodies. All of the foregoing evolutionary intertransformings I observed would occasion frequently changing interdominances.

I assumed that nature would "evaluate" my work as I went along. If I was doing what nature wanted done, and if I was doing it in promising ways, permitted by nature's principles, I would find my work being economically sustained—and vice versa, in which latter negative case I must quickly cease doing what I had been doing and seek logically alternative courses until I found the new course that nature signified her approval of by providing for its physical support.

Wherefore, I concluded that I would be informed by nature if I proceeded in the following manner:

(A) committed myself, my wife, and our infant daughter directly to the design, production, and demonstration of artifact accommodation of the most evident but as-yet-unattended-to human-environment-advantaging physical evolutionary tasks, and

(B) paid no attention to "earning a living" in humanity's established economic system, yet

(C) found my family's and my own life's needs being unsolicitedly provided for by seemingly pure happenstance and always only "in the nick of time," and

(D) being provided for "only coincidentally," yet found

(E) that this only "coincidentally," unbudgetable, yet realistic support persisted, and did so

(F) only so long as I continued spontaneously to commit myself unreservedly to the task of developing relevant artifacts, and if I

(G) never tried to persuade humanity to alter its customs and viewpoints and never asked anyone to listen to me and spoke informatively to others only when they asked me so to do, and if I

(H) never undertook competitively to produce artifacts others were developing, and attended only to that which no others attended

then I could tentatively conclude that my two assumptions were valid: (1) that nature might economically sustain human activity that served directly in the "mainstream" realization of essential cosmic regeneration, which had hitherto been accomplished only through seeming "right-angled" side effects of the chromosomically focused biological creatures; and (2) that the generalized physical law of precessional behaviors does govern socioeconomic behaviors as do also the generalized laws of acceleration and ephemeralization.

The 1927 precessional assumptions became ever-more-convincingly substantiated by experiences—only the "impossible" continued to happen. I became ever more convinced that I must go on developing artifacts that would make possible humanity's successful accomplishment of survival activities so much more logically and efficiently as to render the older, less efficient ways to be spontaneously abandoned by humanity. I resolved never to attack or oppose undesirable socioeconomic phenomena, but instead committed myself to evolving and cultivating tools that would accomplish humanity's necessitous tasks in so much easier, more pleasant, and more efficient ways that, without thinking about it, the undesirable ways would be abandoned by society. (I liked the popular 1944 song, "Accentuate the Positive, Eliminate the Negative.")

All the foregoing was, then, the precessional course I deliberately adopted in 1927. I had only the remaining days of my life to invest. It involved swift sorting out of the complex of design, production, testing, and demonstration tasks to be performed. What was the order of inherent priorities and successively overlapping interdependencies?

Socioeconomic precession by environment-controlling artifacts was a strategic course that obviously could be steered only by maximum reliance on our intuitive sensibilities, frequent position determination and course correcting, plus constant attendance upon the thoughts evolvingly generated by our commitment and its moment-to-moment, experience-produced new insights into the relative significance of the whole family of evolving events. It involved swift recognition and correction of all errors of judgment. It required being always "comprehensively considerate."

*　*　*

As navigational aids and "high-seas life-preserving devices" wisely to be employed in sailing such a course in heretofore-uncharted socioeconomic seas, I have patented every one of what seemed to me to be strategically important items amongst my inventions, and have done so as they occurred in all economically relevant countries around the world. This has cost threefold any and all royalties ever accruing to those patents. I did so for the following reasons:

Having no academically earned scientific degrees I could not qualify for membership in any scientific societies and could therefore not publish my discoveries officially in their journals. I found that filing of patent claims established an equally valid scientific record of my discoveries and inventions. The preamble texts of patent claims are often philosophically and historically enlightening. Of necessity they are meticulously specific in respect to the technological means of practical realizations of the inventions.

The worth of a patent, however, is not established by the merit of the invention but by the expertness with which its claims of invention are written. Almost anyone can obtain a patent from the patent office. What history has shown to be socioeconomically important is whether those claims can survive in the highest court trials of patent-infringement cases. Vast knowledge of the precedents in court-decision history and of the patent strategy of great corporations is essential in the writing of the claims.

While a U.S.A. patent can be obtained for less than $200, a patent that the great corporations' patent attorneys see no way of circumventing requires expensively expert professional services. Added to this is the cost of world-around major nations' patent coverage (which foreign patents must be applied for and obtained because every country can now air-deliver their inventions into any other country within less than a week, in contradistinction to a six-month water-delivery lag in 1900). This world-around patent coverage cost about $50,000 in 1975 (it was $30,000 in 1950) for obtaining each world-protected, probably court-sustainable, infringement-defying patent.

In every instance I sought the services of those lawyers most widely acknowledged to be *the* champion patent attorneys of that moment in the specific category of my type of inventions.

From time to time during the half-century since I first obtained a patent, the patent attorneys of more than 100 of the world's most powerful corporations have called upon my patent attorneys to obtain a license under one or more of my patents. In every one of these instances, phrasing his statement in varying ways, the visiting powerful corporation attorney has said to my attorney (usually as a flattering, but truthful, "one-professional-to-another," off-the-record remark), "Of course, the first thing my client asked me to do was to find a way of circumventing your client's patent, but you have written your claims so well that I was forced to advise my client to procure a license under your patent if indeed he wished to engage in the invention's manufacture without exposing himself to almost certainly devastating infringement expense."

That statement discloses two truths. The first is that big business, which now makes its major profits out of know-how, deliberately steals know-how wealth whenever possible; the second is that if I had not taken out patents, you would probably never have heard of me nor would you have learned that an independently operating little individual, starting penniless and creditless, had indeed succeeded in inventing what I, as the half-century "Guinea Pig B"—the test-case individual—have been able to accomplish.

My half-century experience also discovered the natural, unacceleratable lags existing between inventions and industrial uses in various technical categories, which occur as follows: in electronics—two years; aerodynamics—five years; automobiles—ten years; railroading—fifteen years; big-city buildings—twenty-five years; single-family dwellings—fifty years. Clearly these lags have consistently characterized the lengths of gestation periods in the different arts with which I was concerned. In the case of most of my inventions the gestation lags have been far greater than the seventeen-year lifespan of patents in those arts. Patents in the forty-five- to fifty-year invention-gestation-rated single-family-housing arts are financially worthless. I took out many patents in these arts, however, because it was in the field of human-life protection, support, and accommodation that the worst socioeconomic problems existed.

In 1927 the American Institute of Architects journal published a plan for a single-family dwelling they felt to be an optimum single-family dwelling under the improving technical circumstances of 1927—it included electric refrigeration instead of the old icebox, oil-burning furnaces instead of human-shovel-stoked coal furnaces, etc. Concerned with my accelerating ephemeralization, I inventoried all the design fixtures of that optimum single-family dwelling—its floor area, its volume, the number and placement of its windows, the number of lumens of light admitted, all of its plumbing and wired facilities, its insulation, etc.—and then I calculated its complete weight, including all of its pipes and wires out to the city mains. It weighed 150 tons.

Then, using the most advanced aircraft-engineering techniques and the highest-performance aluminum alloys, etc., I designed a dwell-in-able environment control of the same volume and floor area that in every way provided facilities and degrees of comfort equal to those of AIA's optimum 1927 single-family dwelling. My aeronautical-engineering-counterpart single-family dwelling weighed only three tons—a fact that I proved seventeen years later when, incorporating all logical interim technological improvements, we built that aircraft-engineering prototype in Beech Aircraft's plant in Wichita, Kansas.

This three-ton to 150-ton ($\frac{1}{50}$th) weight ratio of the difference between the technical capabilities of the aircraft versus the home-building arts clearly confirmed the reasonability of my working assumption that the accelerating ephemeralization of science and technology might someday accomplish so much with so little that we could sustainingly take care of all humanity at a higher standard of living than any have ever experienced, which would prove the Malthusian "only you or me" doctrine to be completely fallacious.

Having committed myself to precessional existence, I now focused all my effort for the rest of my life on applying the highest science and technology directly to the realization of human livingry.

Most of my inventions have come into public use long after my relevant patent rights have expired. Some of them have not yet come into public use but will do so fifty years after their 1927 invention and thirty-two years after the seventeen-year patents have expired. This has not mattered to me since I did not take out the patents to make money but only to document and demonstrate what the inventive little individual can accomplish, and to prove documentably the socioeconomic existence of such unique industrialization lags.

For instance, my mass-producible one-piece bathrooms that are now in mass production in West Germany and are fabricated as I planned, with glass-fiber-reinforced-polyester-resin, are almost exact visual-form replicas of the sheet-copper and aluminum prototypes I developed, installed, and thoroughly tested and proved at the United States Bureau of Standards, Hydraulic Division, in 1937–38, having first designed one in 1927—all of which, as designed, had to wait until the glass-reinforced-polyester-resins plastic industry had been developed, there being a half-century gestation period in the home-improvements art.

Paradoxically, the truly luxurious West German one-piece bathrooms are now about to be made obsolete by the combined effectiveness of my fog-gun self-cleaning device and my dry-packaged and hermetically sealed and mechanically-carried-away-and-packaged toilet device, which altogether eliminate all wet plumbing and do away with the need of piped-in-and-away water and water-borne wastes. The amount of water needed by the fog gun is less than a pint per day per family. All water for our advanced dwelling machine will be brought to the dwelling in quantities equal to milk and fruit juice consumption.

Now that I have proven that an individual can be world-effective while eschewing either money or political advantage-making, I do my best to discourage others from taking patents, which almost never "pay off" to the inventor. My patent taking was to effect a "bridgehead" accreditation to more effective employment of humanity's potentials.

My half-century experience in the foregoing experiment makes me feel certain that if I had developed any of the inventions to make money or to aggrandize self, I would have failed to do either, as have so many thousands failed when committed primarily to self-advantaging. I frequently hear from only-to-self-committed individuals who lament with pathetic self-conviction that others are trying to steal their inventions, wherefore they don't dare to disclose to anyone, while perversely yearning to profit by what to them is invention. Very often, unknown to them, prior disclosures of the same invention "idea" exist.

Ideas are easy to come by; reduction to practice is an arduous but inspirationally rewarding matter.

I have discovered that one of the important characteristics of most economic trends is that they are too slow in their motion to be visible to humans. We cannot see the motion of the stars, the atoms, a whirling airplane propellor, the growth of a tree, or the hour or minute hand of a clock. In the latter case we can see only the movement of the second hand. Humans do not get out of the way of that which they cannot see moving. As with the electromagnetic spectrum, most of the frequencies and motions of Universe are ultra or infra to man's sensorial tunability.

With a half-century of experience in prognosticating based on the rates of change of my ephemeralization and acceleration curves, I am firmly convinced that I can see clearly a number of coming events, and I am therefore vitally eager that people should not be hurt by the coming of these events, particularly when I can see ways in which it would be possible not only for them to avoid hurt but even to prosper by and enjoy what now seems to me to be inevitable.

Much that I see to be inevitable is unthinkingly opposed by various factions of society. Reflex-conditioned society, facing exclusively toward its past, backs up into its future, often bumping its rump painfully but uncomprehendingly against the "potential-wealth coffers" of its future years' vastly multiplying capability to favorably control its own ecological evolution and the latter's *freedom-multiplying* devices.

My recitation of self-disciplines may suggest that all I had to do was to conceive of the discipline and institute it, whereas the fact is that my previously conditioned reflexes frequently contradicted my intentions, while circumstances beyond my control converged so powerfully as to divert me from my intended self-disciplines. It has taken constant disciplining and redisciplining to get myself under control to a productively effective degree.

Throughout the first half of my last fifty-two years of severe reorientation of my life pattern—in which I determined to give up forever the idea of "earning a living" for my family and self while depending entirely on ecological precession to provide the critically needed material, tools, and monies to carry on the work—my friends and family and my wife's family and friends would say that I was being stubbornly treacherous to my wife and daughter in not attempting to "earn a living." Thus goaded, I would from time to time accept a job that was proffered me by some friend, and for the moment all these friends and family were relieved and delighted. In each instance, however, all my grand strategy would languish and things would go wrong until, for one reason or another, I jumped off the deep end again and recommitted myself to the unfunded comprehensive program of solving problems by environment-modifying artifacts produced with the most advanced scientific and technological means. Then everything would go smoothly again.

By and large I seem to have made more mistakes than any others of whom I know, but have learned thereby to make ever swifter acknowledgment of the errors and thereafter immediately set about to deal more effectively with the truths disclosed by the acknowledgment of erroneous assumptions.

I don't want a reader of this chronicle to think that I am anything other than what I am—an average healthy human being with all the attendant weaknesses and vulnerabilities. What is important is that the reorientation of my life and the criteria of its conduct did render such an average human being more effective than under conventional circumstances.

There is one, as-yet-unmentioned, comprehensively overriding commitment that I made before developing all my already-recounted disciplines and commitments, especially to the principle of precession, whereby I gained complete release from the concept of earning a living for my family and myself and gained, as well, the day-to-day practical physical implementation of all my artifact-inventing and reduction of the latter to physical demonstration.

I have deliberately kept this all-important commitment to the last. If it had not come first in my life pattern however, it is quite possible that I might not have had the insights that led to all the intercomplementary resolutions and self-discipline.

* * *

My definition of the word *believe* means to accept an explanation of physical phenomena without any experiential evidence. At the outset of my resolve not only to do my own thinking but to keep that thinking concerned only with directly experienced evidence, I resolved to abandon completely all that I ever had been taught to believe. Experience had demonstrated to me that most people had an authority-trusting sense that persuaded them to believingly accept the dogma and legends of one religious group or another and to join that group's formalized worship of God.

I asked myself whether I had any direct experiences in life that made me have to assume a greater intellect than that of humans to be operative in Universe. I immediately referred back to my good education in the sciences and my directly experienced learning of the operation of a plurality of physical laws—such as the interattraction of celestial bodies, varying inversely as the second power of the arithmetical distances intervening—which laws could only be expressed in the purely intellectual terms of mathematics, which plurality of laws always and only related to eternal relationships existing *between* and not *in* any one of the interrelated phenomena when considered only separately. None of the eternal and always concurrently operative laws had ever been found to contradict one another—ergo, they were all designedly interaccommodative like a train of gears. Many also were interaugmentative. I said that when we use the word *design* in contradistinction to *randomness,* we immediately infer an intellect that sorts out a complex of potentials and interarranges components in complementary ways—ergo, human mind in discovering a plurality of these only mathematically expressible eternal laws, all of which are interaccommodative, is also discovering the intellectually designed scenario Universe, whose designing requires the a priori eternal existence of an intellectual integrity of eternally self-regenerative Universe. I said to myself, I am o'erwhelmed by the only experientially discovered evidence of an a priori eternal, omnicomprehensive, infinitely and exquisitely concerned, intellectual integrity that we *may* call God, though knowing that in whatever way we humans refer to this integrity, it will always be an inadequate expression of its cosmic omniscience and omnipotence.

At the time I resolved to do only my own experientially based thinking, in 1927, the Russian Revolution, then ten years old, was beginning to cope with its survival problems by including industrialization as well as farming. In 1928 they brought into operation their five-year plans of successively most important tasks to be accomplished. Realizing from the outset that in order to organize the complete preoccupation of all their over 100 million people with the Communist party's specific planning, it would be disastrous to their efforts to tolerate the continuing presence of any other mystically higher authority than that of the Communist party—such, for instance, as any of the great organized religions—probably in pure expediency, the Communist party said that science, which is utterly pragmatic, proved that there is no God—ergo, Russia, committed to omniscientific technology, was also thenceforth committed to atheism. Many intellectuals around the world accepted this "party-line" doctrine.

In 1930 Einstein, "Mr. Science" himself, published his "Cosmic Religious Sense—the Nonanthropomorphic Concept of God." Einstein said that the great scientists such as Kepler and Galileo, whom the Roman Catholic Church had excommunicated as "heretics," were, because of their absolute faith in the orderliness of Universe, far more committed to the nonanthropomorphic cosmic God than were the individuals heading the formal religious organizations.

Since 1927, whenever I am going to sleep, I always concentrate my thinking on what I call "Ever Rethinking the Lord's Prayer." The Lord's Prayer had obviously been evolved by a plurality of deeply earnest and thoughtful individuals whose names we will never know. My latest rethinking of it follows.

I am confident, contrary to the Russian assumption that science invalidated all possibilities of the existence of God, that, as specifically argued, my following declaration constitutes a scientifically meticulous, direct-experience-based proof of God.

EVER RETHINKING THE LORD'S PRAYER
July 12, 1979

To be satisfactory to science
all definitions
must be stated
in terms of experience.

I define Universe as
all of humanity's
in-all-known-time
consciously apprehended
and communicated (to self or others)
experiences.

In using the word, God,
I am consciously employing
four clearly differentiated
from one another
experience-engendered thoughts.

Firstly I mean:—
   those experience-engendered thoughts
   which are predicated upon past successions
   of unexpected, human discoveries
   of mathematically incisive,
   physically demonstrable answers
   to what theretofore had been misassumed
   to be forever unanswerable
   cosmic magnitude questions

wherefore I now assume it to be
scientifically manifest,
and therefore experientially reasonable that

scientifically explainable answers
may and probably will
eventually be given
to all questions
as engendered in all human thoughts
by the sum total
of all human experiences;
wherefore my first meaning for God is:—

all the experientially explained
or explainable answers
to all questions
of all time—

Secondly I mean:—
The individual's memory
of many surprising moments
of dawning comprehensions
of an interrelated significance
to be existent
amongst a number
of what had previously seemed to be
entirely uninterrelated experiences
all of which remembered experiences
engender the reasonable assumption
of the possible existence
of a total comprehension
of the integrated significance—
the meaning—
of all experiences.

Thirdly, I mean:—
the only intellectually discoverable
a priori, intellectual integrity
indisputably manifest as
the only mathematically statable
family
of generalized principles—

cosmic laws—
thus far discovered and codified
and ever physically redemonstrable
by scientists
to be not only unfailingly operative
but to be in eternal,
omni-interconsiderate,
omni-interaccommodative governance
of the complex
of everyday, naked-eye experiences
as well as of the multi-millions-fold greater range
of only instrumentally explored
infra- and ultra-tunable
micro- and macro-Universe events.

Fourthly, I mean:—
All the mystery inherent
in all human experience,
which, as a lifetime ratioed to eternity,
is individually limited
to almost negligible
twixt sleepings, glimpses
of only a few local episodes
of one of the infinite myriads
of concurrently and overlappingly operative
sum-totally never-ending
cosmic scenario serials

With these four meanings I now directly
address God.
"Our God—
Since omni-experience is your identity
You have given us
overwhelming manifest:—
of Your complete knowledge
of Your complete comprehension
of Your complete concern
of Your complete coordination
of Your complete responsibility
of Your complete capability to cope
in absolute wisdom and effectiveness

with all problems and events
and of Your eternally unfailing reliability
so to do

Yours, Dear God,
is the only and complete glory.

By Glory *I mean*
the synergetic totality
of all physical and metaphysical radiation
and of all physical and metaphysical gravity
of finite
but nonunitarily conceptual
scenario Universe
in whose synergetic totality
the a priori energy potentials
of both radiation and gravity
are initially equal
but whose respective
behavioral patterns are such
that radiation's entropic, redundant disintegratings
is always less effective
than gravity's nonredundant
syntropic integrating

Radiation is plural and differentiable,
radiation is focusable, beamable, and self-sinusing,
is interceptible, separatist, and biasable—
ergo, has shadowed voids and vulnerabilities;

Gravity is unit and undifferentiable
Gravity is comprehensive
inclusively embracing and permeative
is non-focusable and shadowless,
and is omni-integrative;
all of which characteristics of gravity
are also the characteristics of love.
Love is metaphysical gravity.

You, Dear God,
are the totally loving intellect
ever designing
and ever daring to test

and thereby irrefutably proving
to the uncompromising satisfaction
of Your own comprehensive and incisive
knowledge of the absolute truth
that Your generalized principles
adequately accommodate any and all
special case developments,
involvements, and side effects;
wherefore Your absolutely courageous
omnirigorous and ruthless self-testing
alone can and does absolutely guarantee
total conservation
of the integrity
of eternally regenerative Universe

Your eternally regenerative scenario Universe
is the minimum complex
of totally intercomplementary
totally intertransforming
nonsimultaneous, differently frequenced
and differently enduring
feedback closures
of a finite
but nonunitarily
nonsimultaneously conceptual system
in which naught is created
and naught is lost
and all occurs
in optimum efficiency.

Total accountability and total feedback
constitute the minimum and only
perpetual motion system.
Universe is the one and only
eternally regenerative system.

To accomplish Your regenerative integrity
You give Yourself the responsibility
of eternal, absolutely continuous,
tirelessly vigilant wisdom.

Wherefore we have absolute faith and trust in You,
and we worship You

awe-inspiredly,
all-thankfully,
rejoicingly,
lovingly,
Amen.

                              *   *   *

In considering theology and science I think it is important to note their differences regarding familiar and not-so-familiar cosmic concepts.

It is the very essence of my thinking that, for a principle to qualify as generalizable in science, there must be no known exceptions to its reliability. Exceptionless means eternal. Principles can be only eternal.

Mathematics are eternal. Principles are mathematically demonstrable—as manifest, for instance, in synergy. Principles are truly independent of any additional special case, time-size aspects of their manifestation. There are principles governing covarying rates of relative size-time interrelationships. That principle is manifest in $E = mc^2$, c^2 being the utterly unimpeded rate of growth of an omnidirectionally expanding light wave's surface as demonstrated in vacuo.

This also involves the mathematical principle that a system's linear dimension grows at a first-power rate, while its surface grows at a second-power rate and its volume at a third-power rate. A steel needle with an initial length of six feet and a diameter of two inches, having a "slenderness" (L/R) ratio of 36/1, is reduced to a needle three inches long with a diameter of .08333 of an inch. The six-foot needle sinks in the water. The three-inch needle floats on the water: its volume—ergo, its weight—has become so negligible that its surface relates only to the surface tension of the water, its weight being much less than can be supported by the atomic interattractions producing the molecular membrane of the water surface.

To demonstrate frequency in pure principle I observe painfully that I cannot put my finger through the plane of revolution of a swiftly rotating airplane propellor and withdraw it before it gets hit. Yet machine guns can be timed to fire bullets between successively revolving propellor blades. My muscle and brain cannot reflex and act that fast. I might get my finger through once but can't get it back in time. Operationally speaking, "solid" means very high frequency present in pure principle. I can see through my glasses because light moving through only one way at 186,000 m.p.s. has ample time to avoid the frequency of interference events occurring locally in pure principle.

There are no solids. There are no things. There are only interfering and noninterfering patterns operative in pure principle, and principles are eternal. Principles never contradict principles. Principles can interaccommodate one another only in noninterfering frequency ways. Principles can interaugment one another if frequency is synchronizable.

Acknowledging the mathematically elegant intellectual integrity of eternally regenerative Universe is one way of identifying God.

Everything the brain deals with relates to high-frequency thingness. Mind, and mind alone, deals with understanding the interrelationships existing only *between* and not *in* any one principle, considered only by itself. Principles themselves are often subsets of interrelationships existing only between specific principles.

God may also be identified as the synergy of the interbehavioral relationships of all the principles unpredicted by the behaviors or characteristics of any of the principles considered only separately.

The synergetic integral of the totality of all principles is God, whose sum-total behavior in pure principle is beyond our comprehension and is utterly mysterious to us, because as humans—in pure principle—we do not and never will know all the principles.

Apparently the integrity of the synergy of all synergies of all principles is continually testing its own comprehensive adequacy to accommodate all challenges in pure principle to the maintenance in pure principle of the principle of nonsimultaneous, only-overlappingly-affected, complex unity's eternal regeneration.

Realization that the foregoing may be true tends to inform humans that the introduction into Universe of humans, in pure principle, with minds operating in pure principle, capable of apprehending and objectively employing in pure principle some of the eternal principles, was courageously undertaken by God to discover whether the principle of the eternally regenerative integrity of Universe can endure inviolate despite the dichotomy of knowledge brought about by introduction into the cosmic system of humans and their minds with access to and employment of some—but not all—of the eternal principles. This was an experiment in pure principle to test the adequacy of the synergy of synergies of principle to cope with the sometimes perverse, egotistical, selfish, and deceitful initiatives inherent in the concept of humans in pure principle without access to the wisdom accruing synergetically only to knowledge of all the principles—ergo, possibly capable of impairing the integrity of eternal regeneration. That may be what the integrity of God needs to know and needs to know by experimental evidence.

That is what I am thinking about in "Ever Rethinking the Lord's Prayer." It is also what I am thinking about in volume 2 of *Synergetics.* I think it is probably an intuitive awareness of the possible verity—of parts or of all—of the foregoing that makes the theologist disregard the scientist's brain-induced requirement of a cosmic beginning and ending.

All scientists have brains. Brains always and only coordinate the special case information progressively apprehended in pure principle by the separate senses operating in pure mathematical-frequency principle. Brain then sorts out the information to describe and identify special whole-system characteristics, storing them in the memory bank as system concepts for single or multiple recall for principle-seeking consideration and reconsideration as system integrities by searching and ever-reassessing mind.

Only minds have the capability to discover principles. Once in a very great while scientists' minds discover principles and put them to rigorous physical test before accepting them as principle. More often theologists or others discover principles but do not subject them to the rigorous physical-special-case testing before accepting and employing them as working-assumption principles.

Principles are eternal. Special case interactions of principles are temporal and brain-apprehensible because in pure principle we have time, which is simply the principle of potentially different relative frequencies and not of beginnings and endings.

CHAPTER 5

The Geoscope

ONE OF THE WORLD-AROUND's most immediately critical problems is that of how to facilitate the swift development of all human individuals' discovery of all we know about human life on board Spaceship Earth at this moment in Universe—and how so to learn in the shortest possible time.

We have already referred many times to the world's pro tem power-structure-wrought obstacles blocking the critical path to human understanding of the nature of reality.

In the Victorian era, into which I was born, *reality* was everything we could see, smell, hear, taste, and touch. That is what *reality* had always been.

When I was three years of age, the electron was discovered. Science said the electron was a nonconceptual phenomenon. Because it was invisible, it could not be photographed . . . and it didn't "make the news." The electron was very real, however, because it could give you a shock—could even electrocute you. The new reality being invisible, approximately 99.9 percent of twentieth-century science was leading industrial technology's everyday, working reality into the ultra- and infravisible—the macroastrophysical and the microatomic, electronic, metallurgically alloying, chemically reacting, microbiologically, astrophysically exploring ranges of the electromagnetic wave spectrum of Universe. And 99.9 percent of these very real activities are nondirectly apprehensible by the bare human senses and are practically discovered and coped with only through powerful macro-micro operative instruments.

At the dawning of the twentieth century, without warning to humanity, the physical technology of Earthians' affairs was shifted over from a brain-sensed reality into a reality apprehended only by instruments, comprehended only by scientifically trained brains, understood and coped with only by experience-educated mind, and employed usefully only through mind's discovery and objectification of special case realizations of the only mathematically expressible laws governing each of the omni-intercomplementary family of scientific generalizations.

We have also noted how the power structures successively dominant over human affairs had for aeons successfully imposed a "specialization" upon the intellectually bright and physically talented members of society as a reliable means of keeping them academically and professionally divided—ergo, "conquered," powerless. The separate individuals' special, expert glimpses of the separate, invisible reality increments became so infinitesimally fractionated and narrow that they gave no hint of the significant part their work played in the omni-integrating evolutionary front of total knowledge and its power-structure exploitability in contradistinction to its omni-humanity-advantaging potentials. Thus the few became uselessly overadvantaged instead of the many becoming regeneratively ever more universally advantaged.

Hyperspecialization also prevented popular comprehension of what the ongoing world power structure was doing—ergo, hyperspecialization kept society preoccupied in ways nondetrimental to the power structure's interests and practically dependent upon the power structure's media for information.

In addition to (A) the difficulties of popular comprehension imposed by the invisibility of the frontiers of everyday reality, and (B) specialization as an obstacle to popular apprehension and comprehension of "what life is about"—which obstacles A and B must be effectively vanquished within the 1980s if humanity is to continue on our planet—we now discover another formidable obstacle that must also be vanquished by 1990. That obstacle (C) is humanity's inability to see more than a very limited number of rates of motion. Humans cannot see humans growing either bodily or as local human tissue. Humans cannot see the motion of the hour and minute hands of the clock or of the physical growth of trees. Humans can realize only retrospectively that they have grown because their clothes no longer fit. Humans find that trees have grown because yesteryear's view has been cut off—99.9 percent of what humans can "see" comprehendingly is the belated aftereffects of what happened.

Most of the important trend patternings are invisible—ergo, their eventuations are unanticipated by society. Because of obstacles A, B, and C most of the significant evolutionary trendings of human affairs cannot be detected and tuned in by people's sense-coordinating brains. Few of their vital challenges are apprehended in time by human brains. When humans cannot see something approaching to destroy them, they do not get out of the way.

Question: Is there not an instrument that can inform humanity about its invisibly trending evolutionary challenges—and do so in time to allow them to satisfactorily anticipate and cope with inexorable events? Yes! There is the Geoscope, which can be swiftly realized both physically and metaphysically.

* * *

Only for six one-thousandths of its three and one-half million known years of presence on Earth has humanity sensed the shape, size, rotation, and Sun-orbiting rate of our planet in the solar system as well as our Earth's relationship to other micro-macro-Universe events. Only human mind's capability to discover the only-mathematically-definable-and-employable physical laws—of the everywhere and everywhen nonsimultaneously intertransforming, differently enduring, differently energized, independently episodic and overlapping, eternally regenerative, scenario Universe's laws such as those of leverage, electromagnetics, and optics—has made possible humanity's additional discovery and participatory use of macro-micro-Universe information.

"Oh wad some power the giftie gie us to see oursels as others see us." To facilitate humanity's comprehension of its present status in Universe, what is needed is a sensorially tune-in-able physical means of "seeing oursels as others see us." Poet Robert Burns's wish was partially fulfilled when, for the first time, Earthian humans standing on the Moon took colored moving pictures of our planet Earth exactly as seen from the Moon and electromagnetically dispatched the pictures back to us on Earth to be seen over anybody's and everybody's properly tuned-in television sets.

Most people will say that if you want to get the best map of the whole world, use a globe, the bigger the better. The trouble with a globe is that you cannot possibly see all the world displayed on it at any one time. The experimentally disclosed fact is that, without revolving the library Earth-globe, you cannot read the names identifying the geographical data of more than one-quarter of its surface at any one viewing.

You may say "the larger the globe, the more you can see of the world in any one viewing." If that were true, you could use the real Earth as your optimum globe. The fact is that the bigger the globe, the less of its surface data you can see and read at any one time. With a twelve- or sixteen-inch globe you can get the most information possible in any one viewing. This is approximately one-quarter of the Earth's surface.

Because humans want to see their *whole* Earth at once, cartographic projections of the Earth's surface were developed—Mercator, polyconic, polar azimuthal, etc. The Mercator became the most familiarly used. It is as yet found in 1980 to be the map most frequently used in schools around the world. On it Greenland will often be seen to be larger than South America, and North America larger than Africa; it has no Antarctic continent; and the land on the left end of the map is seemingly 24,000 miles away from the land area on the right end while in reality those areas are actually adjacent. With only one exception—the Fuller Dymaxion Projection—all of the well-known methods of cartographic projection either chop the world data into a number of separately viewed parts or produce badly distorted images and continental fractionations.

It was to provide a satisfactory means for humanity to see correctly the entire surface of the globe all at the same time that the Dymaxion Sky-Ocean Projection was designed. With it, for the first time in history, humans can see their whole planet Earth's geography displayed on one flat surface without any visible distortion in shape or relative size of any of its data and without any breaks in its continental contour—that is, the whole world surface is viewable simultaneously as one-world island of unbroken contour in one-world ocean.

The Dymaxion transformational projection system that produces the Sky-Ocean World Map divides the sphere into its maximum omnisymmetrical, twelve-vertexed, thirty-arc-edged subdivisions of twenty equi-central-angled arcs of 63° 26' and sixty surface angles of 72° each, spherical triangles. The thirty great circle arcs of 63° 26' act as constant peripheral integrity controls, preventing the breaking open and spilling out of the discrete data and distorting of the constant angular symmetry, both central and surface, during the transformation from spherical to planar display of the twenty triangles of the spherical and planar bound icosahedron.

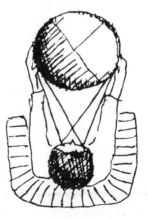

FIGURE 25.   Bird's-eye view of person looking at a sixteen-inch world globe.

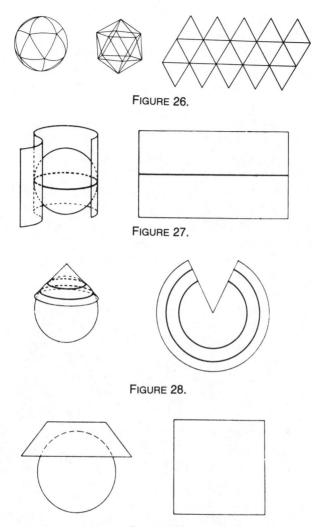

FIGURE 26.

FIGURE 27.

FIGURE 28.

FIGURE 29.

The more conventional projection systems that are widely used include the Mercator projection (Fig. 27), the conic projection (Fig. 28), and the polar azimuthal projection (Fig. 29). All three of these systems give rise to considerable visual distortion, which the Dymaxion projection avoids (see Fig. 30).

In 1964 the United States Information Agency asked me to consider the design of a building and an exhibition that might be adopted as the United States entry in the Montreal World's Fair of 1967, later known as "Expo '67."

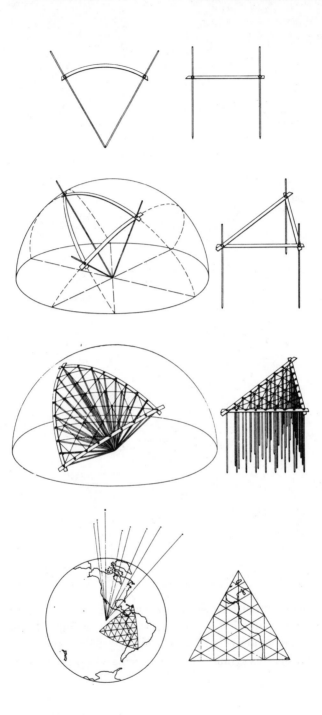

FIGURE 30.

I made a proposal, and the exhibition part of it was rejected. I was asked to continue, however, as the architect of the U.S.A. building to house an exhibition designed by others. Insofar as I know, I was the only one considered as architect of the building. I think this was because of the success the United States had experienced with my 1954 world-around, air-delivered, geodesic-dome trade fair pavilions and the U.S.A. Moscow Exhibit dome of 1959, which was purchased by the Russians as a permanent building after the United States exhibition was concluded.

Fortunately my U.S.A. geodesic dome for Expo '67 proved a success. Also, but more gradually, it is being realized by many that my rejected idea for the American exhibit is looming into ever greater prominence as a highly desirable social facility. I will therefore review the concept and development of my original idea.

I told the United States Information Agency in 1964 that by 1967 the regard of the rest of the world for the United States would be at its lowest ebb in many decades—if not in the total two centuries of the U.S.A.'s existence. Since each country's World's Fair exhibit would be well published all around Earth, I felt that it would be very important that the United States do something that would tend to regain the spontaneous admiration and confidence of the whole world. This could be done by inaugurating at Expo '67 a computerized exploration for the most universally creative and economically sound internal and external U.S.A. policy formulation.

What I proposed was based on my observation that world people had become extraordinarily confident in the fundamental reliability of the computer and its electronically controlled processes. I know that a great many people will contradict me, but I had predicated my conviction of society's subconsciously established confidence in the computer's reliability upon vital, therefore undeniable, behavior facts.

On the working assumption that humanity had established implicit confidence in the computers and automated instrumentation, I proposed in 1964 that the United States Expo '67 exhibition should have a 400-foot-diameter 5/8 sphere building similar in shape to the 250-foot-diameter building actually built for Expo '67. In the basement of this building would be housed an extraordinary computer facility. On entering the building by thirty-six external ramps and escalators leading in at every ten degrees of circumferential direction, the visitors would arrive upon a great balcony reaching completely around the building's interior quarter-mile perimeter. The visitors would see an excitingly detailed 100-foot-diameter world globe suspended high within the 400-foot-diameter 5/8 sphere main building. Cities such as New York, London, Tokyo, and Los Angeles would appear as flattened-out, basketball-sized blotches with the tallest buildings and radio towers only about one-sixteenth of an inch high.

Periodically the great spherical Earth would be seen to be transforming slowly into an icosahedron—a polyhedron with twenty (equilateral) triangular facets. The visitors would witness that in the processes of these transformations there are no visible changes in the relative size and shape of any of the land and water masses of the 100-foot-diameter miniature Earth. Slowly the 100-foot-diameter icosahedronal Earth's surface would be seen to be parting along some of its triangular edges, as the whole surface slowly opens mechanically as an orange's skin or an animal's skin might be peeled carefully in one piece. With slits introduced into its perimeter at various places it would be relaxed to subside into a flattened-out pattern as is a bearskin rug. The icosahedronal Earth's shell thus would be seen to gradually flatten out and be lowered to the floor of the building. The visitors would realize that they were now looking at the whole of the Earth's surface simultaneously without any visible distortion of the relative size and shape of the land and sea masses having occurred during the transformation from sphere to the flattened-out condition we call a map. My cartographic projection of the "Sky-Ocean World" functions in just such a manner as I have just now described.

This stretched-out, football-field-sized world map would disclose the continents arrayed as one world-island in one world-ocean with no breaks in the continental contours. Its scale would be 1/500,000th of reality. Three millimeters or one eighth of an inch would represent a mile. A big 1000-foot-long oil tanker would appear to be less than one millimeter or only one fiftieth of an inch in length. A major airport's runways would each be about three millimeters or one eighth of an inch long. A major football stadium would measure less than one millimeter or one fiftieth of an inch long at this scale.

The great map would be wired throughout so that minibulbs closely installed all over its surface could be lighted by the computer at appropriate points to show various, accurately positioned, proportional data regarding world conditions, events, and resources. World events would occur and transform on this live world map's ever-evoluting face. If we had 100,000 light bulbs for instance, each mini-light-bulb could represent 40,000 people—a medium-sized town. Mexico City, New York City, or Tokyo would be a cluster of 250 bulbs. The bulbs could be computer-distributed to represent the exact geographical distribution positioning of the people. Military movements of a million troops would be dramatically visible. The position of every airplane in the sky and every ship on the world ocean could be computer-control displayed. Weekend and holiday exoduses from cities into the country or travel to other cities would be vividly displayed by computer-controlled tallying instruments.

I proposed that on this stretched-out, reliably accurate, world map of our Spaceship Earth a great world logistics game be played by introducing into the computers all the known inventory and whereabouts of the various metaphysical and physical resources of the Earth. (This inventory, which took forty years to develop to high perfection, is now housed at my head-quarters.)

We would then enter into the computer all the inventory of human trends, known needs, and fundamental behavior characteristics.

I proposed that individuals and teams would undertake to play the World Game with those resources, behaviors, trends, vital needs, developmental desirables, and regenerative inspirations. The players as individuals or teams would each develop their own theory of how to make the total world work successfully for all of humanity. Each individual or team would play a the-ory through to the end of a predeclared program. It could be played with or without competitors.

The objective of the game would be to explore ways to make it possible for anybody and everybody in the human family to enjoy the total Earth without any human interfering with any other human and without any hu-man gaining advantage at the expense of another.

FIGURE 31. Dymaxion Sky-Ocean World Map

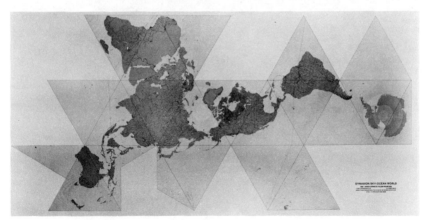

FIGURE 32.   Cornell Geoscope

170

To accomplish the game's objective the resources, pathways, and dwelling points around the surface of our 8000-mile-diameter, spherical Spaceship Earth must be fully employed by the players in such a way that the world's individual humans would each be able to exercise complete actional discretion and would have such freedom of decision regarding the investment of their time in their waking hours that they would be able to travel independently, or in groups, either to and fro locally or continuing intermittently on around the world, dwelling from time to time here or there, finding everywhere facilities to accommodate their needs in an uncompromising manner. The game would seek to use the world's resources, interprocesses, and evolutionary developments in such a way that all the foregoing would be possible.

*　　*　　*

It was to satisfy the same need of humanity—to comprehend the total planetary, all-evolutionary historical significance of each day's develop-

FIGURE 33.　Nottingham Geoscope

ments—that the 200-foot, or sixty-meter, -diameter Geoscope was developed. The Geoscope is a gossamer, open trusswork spherical structure wherewith humanity can see and read all the spherical data of the Earth's geography as seen from either its inside or its outside and in its proper interorientation within the theater of local Universe events.

When completely installed and ready for use, all Geoscopes are oriented so that their polar axes are always parallel to the real Earth's north-south polar axis, with the latitude and longitude of the installed Geoscope's zenith point always corresponding exactly with the latitude and longitude of the critically located point on our real planet Earth at which the Geoscope is installed. As a consequence of the polar axis and zenith correspondences of the Geoscope mini-Earths and the real Earth, it will be found that the miniature Earth Geoscope's real omnidirectional celestial-theater orientation always corresponds exactly with the real omnidirectional celestial-theater orientation of the real planet Earth.

Since the two spheres (mini-Earth and real Earth) are rigidly coupled together tangentially at the same latitude-longitude point on the real Earth as the latitude-longitude zenith point on the Geoscope sphere, the geographical-geometrical orientation attitudes brought about by their respective axial rotations and orbital travel around the Sun will be identical. The Geoscope has the same relationship to the Earth as has one of the relatively small lifeboats mounted fore and aft on the davits of an ocean cruise ship to the big ship herself. If the big ship changes its course from north to east, the lifeboat does likewise. If the bow rises and falls in a head-on sea, so too does the bow of the davits-mounted lifeboat .

The 4000-mile—1/46th light-second—distance existing between the center of the Earth sphere and that of the Geoscope sphere mounted on the Earth's surface is astronomically negligible when compared to any of the celestial distances. The distance from Earth to its nearest star—the Sun—is 92 million miles, or eight light-minutes, away. The next nearest star is 25 trillion miles away. Such celestially negligible distances as 4000 miles are canceled out as visibly unappreciable. Such negligible distances are called "parallax" by the astronomer or navigator.

Standing at night with your eyes at the center of such a Geoscope—miniature Earth—and viewing the stars outwardly through its fly-screen surface, on which are thinly outlined all the contours of all the world's continents, you will see the exact relationship of all the stars to the Earth's surface. Any star in zenith over any one geographical point on the Earth can be verified to be in zenith at that moment over that point on Earth by telephoning someone at that point. What you will see from the center of mini-Earth at any one time is exactly what you would see if you were safely stationed at the center of real planet Earth and had X-ray eyes and could look outwardly through 4000 miles of matter to see the stars viewable in zenith outwardly of any one given geographical point of our axially spinning, Sun-orbiting, sphere Earth at any one given moment. As viewed from its center, Geoscope becomes a true planetarium—no imitation stars and no imitation sky. In the Geoscope we have the real stars in their real sky in exact zenith position as seen through the Geoscope's spherical triangle windows outwardly and around our Earth sphere in all directions as of any given moment—as our Earth revolves and zooms along its Sun orbit within that vast starry environment.

Because the real planet Earth is revolving around its north-south polar axis, so, too, is mini-Earth. They are both thus revolving without effecting any change of the observed position of Polaris—the North Star—in respect to mini-Earth's north pole. Therefore, the observer at the center of the Geoscope feels spontaneously the celestial fixity not only of Polaris but also of all the other stars as seen outwardly through the Geoscope's triangular windows. Because outwardly of Geoscope's equator what we can see of the starry scene is changing most rapidly and ever less rapidly until, looking out along the polar axis, we observe no change, we get the same feeling as we do looking out the window of a railway car, automobile, or airplane. We see and feel the scene changing as a consequence of our vehicle's motion and not of the scenery's motion. For the first time in human experience Geoscope's mini-Earth spherical structure is clearly seen and felt to be revolving within the theater of Universe, and those holding steady their bodies, heads and their eyes and standing at the Geoscope's center, feel-see their Earth revolving within the vast theater of the starry sky.

With Geoscopes locally available around the world, all children experiencing its true celestial-event orientations will feel themselves being rotated around from west to east by the Earth to be shaded from the Sun's light by the rolling-around Earth's western horizon . . . which deep shadowing they will call night.

They will feel their western horizon to be rotating around with them and to be obscuring (or eclipsing) the Sun. They will spontaneously say "Sunclipse" instead of "Sunset." In the same way they will say spontaneously "Sunsight" in the morning as the Earth revolves the Sun into seeability, thus spontaneously acquiring two poetical, two-syllable, truly meaningful words to replace the two-syllable, misinformative, but poetical words of their ancestry—"Sunset" and "Sunrise."

The new educational technology of world man will of eventual, emergency-emerged, critical necessity come to produce and use the Geoscopes as basic educational tools for acquiring both cosmic and local Universe orientation. It will be universally used as the visual reference for all hourly news broadcasts everywhere around the Earth. Geoscope will spontaneously induce total-Earth, total-humanity viewing significance in regard to all our individual daily experiences. It will spontaneously eliminate nationalistic cerebrating.

The most usefully informative model of the Geoscope now under consideration is a 200-foot-diameter, structurally gossamer, look-into-able and look-out-able, geodesic sphere to be suspended with its bottom 100 feet above ground by approximately invisible cables strung tautly from the tops of three remotely erected 200-foot-high masts.

The vast number of computer-selected, colored, miniature electric light bulbs displayed on the spherical frame's surface of the 200-foot-diameter Geoscope, with their intensity and diminutive size as well as their minimum distance of 100 feet from viewing eyes (as seen from either the center of the sphere or from the ground outside and 100 feet below), will altogether produce a visually continuous-surface picture equal in detailed resolution to that of a fine-screen halftone print or that of an excellent, omnidirectionally-viewable, spherical television tube's picturing. It may well be that by the time the first 200-foot Geoscope is undertaken, we may be able to develop a spherical TV tube of that size or a complex of spherically coordinated TV tubes. This giant, 200-foot-diameter sphere will be a miniature Earth—the most accurate global representation of our planet ever to be realized.

I have produced several fully working, lesser-diameter models of such Geoscope (or mini-Earth) facilities. Most notable were the twenty-foot-diameter one at Cornell University in 1952; the semicompleted, 200-foot-diameter one at the University of Minnesota in 1954–56; the ten-foot-diameter one at Princeton University in 1955; and, in semidemonstrability, the 250-foot-diameter, 3/4 sphere, spherical structure used as the U.S.A. pavilion at Expo '67 in Montreal, Canada, in 1967; and the fifty-foot-diameter Geoscope permanently installed exactly astride the ninetieth meridian of our planet Earth as the Religious Center of Southern Illinois University's campus at Edwardsville, Illinois, in 1970.

To our 1953–55 University of Minnesota and Princeton University Geoscope development classes I suggested that our first 200-footer should serve as an everyday facility of the United Nations. I proposed that it be triangularly suspended from the top of five 300-foot-high tower masts to be erected from a group of rock ledges in New York City's East River—known on the government charts as Blackwell's ledges. These ledges are situated in the middle of the East River a quarter of a mile south of what was once called Blackwell's Island, then for thirty years Welfare Island, and in the 1970s was renamed Roosevelt Island. All the East River water traffic running between New York's Lower Harbor and Long Island Sound or the Harlem River passes to the west of Blackwell's ledges—that is, between the ledges and the United Nations buildings. The tallest UN building is 400 feet high. I proposed that the 200-foot Geoscope sphere be hung above the ledges with its bottom 200 feet above the water, which would locate its top at the same 400-foot height as that of the UN building and 100 feet higher than the tops of the supporting masts. I proposed that the intercabling of the mast tops and their tangentially triangling support of and tiedown of the sphere be done with high-tensile and small-diameter, high-carbon rod steel, so delicate that the dull-black-plated support system would be invisible— the geodesic-tensegrity sphere being of such low weight as to make this invisibility highly feasible.

This would result in the 200-foot sphere seeming to be floating in midair as though it were a small celestial body that had come in very close to Earth at just the right location to make it highly visible to occupants of the UN building as well as to all those in New York City in the vicinity of Fiftieth Street.

In designing the optimum public Geoscope in 1950 I chose the 200-foot-diameter, approximately transparent, gossamer-structured sphere because at that time the United States Air Force was, wherever possible, engaged in making radio-triangulated, geographically accurate photographic maps of the whole Earth's surface. The airplane's exact geographical position at the moment of photographing was determined by electromagnetics—geographical position fix by cross-triangulation from two known station points on Earth. This electromagnetic-beam-crossing triangulation, triggered by the camera, accurately identified the position of the airplane at the moment of its photographing of any one picture and as located on the latitude-longitude coordinate grid of our Earth's planetary sphere. The Air Force's geographical photography work was known as the aerial (photographic) mosaicking of the world.

With the U.S.A. entering into a third, but coldly conducted, ententingly competing, small-nation puppetry-manipulated world war with the U.S.S.R. and its allies, we can understand why it was that the U.S.A. was so intently flying those world-around, radio-triangulated photomosaic missions.

The mosaic grid was flown over all those countries of the world that permitted the U.S.A. to do so. Different series of the photographic mosaicking were flown at different altitudes. The lowest-flown altitude gave the greatest details. It was the communist countries' prohibition against the U.S.A.'s photographic mapping that caused the U.S.A. to develop the Russian-shot-down, ultra-high-flying U-2, hoping to accomplish the triangulation task.

The optimum Geoscope is designed to make practical an omnidirectional

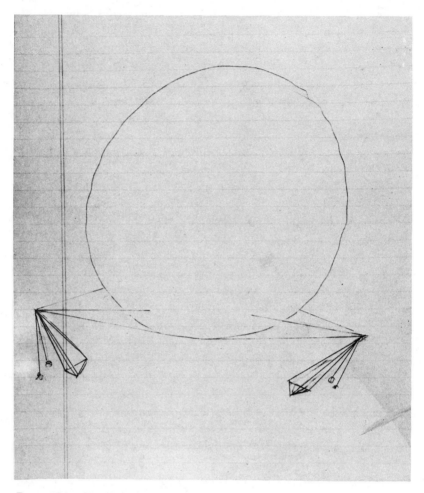

FIGURE 34.　Drawing for proposed United Nations 200-foot Geoscope

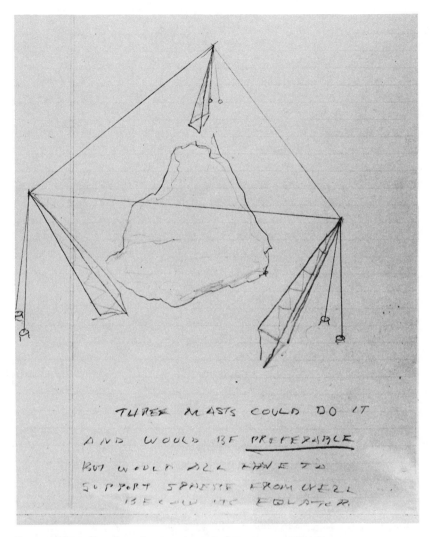

FIGURE 34a. Drawing of support masts for proposed UN Geoscope

Three masts could do it and would be preferable, but all would have to support the sphere from well below its equator.

FIGURE 34b.   Bird's-eye view of UN Geoscope

moving picture displayed on the surface of a large sphere for presenting all manner of information relevant to all human affairs as they occur around the whole of our planet, so that the whole world's population can learn for itself how to comprehend the significance of the world-around information as compounded with other powerfully relevant, long-known, and broadcast news and other Geoscope-mounted information.

The lowest level at which the Air Force radio-triangulation-fixing photo-mosaicking was flown obviously produced the greatest detail. The Air Force did all their photographing on the moving picture industry's thirty-five-millimeter film. In photo-industry lingo "contact" prints of the thirty-five-mm. frames means actual—unenlarged—film-frame size, black-and-white or colored prints, about 2¼ × 2¼-square-inch prints. Contacts of those 35-mm. frames as photographed by the Air Force's lowest-level mosaicking, when assembled like a picture puzzle and pasted onto a balloon of the right size, altogether produce one united, spherical surface picture of the whole world. The diameter of such a spherical picture "globe" made up of contact prints of the lowest-level mosaicing is about 200 feet. The higher the level of mosaic flying, the smaller the sphere produced.

Since I knew in 1950 that I could produce a 200-foot-diameter, adequately strong, but lightly trussed geodesic sphere, I determined to design a 200-foot Geoscope.

During World War II the largest clear-span, steel-trussed, quadrangularly based airplane hangars' narrowest horizontal dimension's truss spannings built were approximately 250 feet wide. To make them a foot wider would have doubled the weight of the steel trusses.

No clear-span, spherical structure of that size had ever been built anywhere in 1950. The structural engineering profession did not at that time assume that such a large, clear-span, *spherical* structure could be economically produced. As yet standing in prime condition, St. Peter's 150-foot-diameter marble dome built in Rome over 400 years ago and the Pantheon's equally excellent-condition 150-foot-diameter marble dome built in Rome about 1700 years ago were, in 1950, history's largest clear-span domes. In 1950 the largest-ever steel-framed, radial-arch dome of 150-foot diameter was built. Geodesic structures opened up the ability of humans to build unlimited-diameter clear-span spherical structures. (By 1958 I had built a clear-span geodesic hemispherical dome of 384-foot diameter. Since then they have gone to 700 feet in diameter, and they will keep on growing in clear-span size at an ever faster rate until we enclose whole cities.)

The thirty-five-millimeter pictures taken by the U.S. Air Force at their lowest level of mosaicking (which would produce a 200-foot-diameter sphere) were of such detail that you could, with your naked eye, identify your own home grounds and even your house, which would be a 1/100th-of-an-inch speck—the smallest speck seeable by human eye. You would not be able to see your car in front of the house, nor could you see humans or cows. But you could see clearly your 400-acre-or-greater farm.

This 200-foot-size Geoscope would make it possible for humans to identify the true scale of themselves and their activities on our planet. Humans could thus comprehend much more readily that their personal survival problems related intimately to all humanity's survival.

The 200-foot Geoscope's surface geography would be at a scale of one to 200,000. At this scale, on a 200-foot-diameter miniature "Earth," we set the following approximate equivalencies:

> 1 foot = 200,000 feet
> 1 foot = 38 miles
> 1 inch = 3 miles = 15,000 feet
> $\frac{1}{16}$ inch = 1040 feet
> $\frac{1}{16}$ inch = 3 football stadia
> $\frac{1}{16}$ inch = length of *Queen Elizabeth 2*
> $\frac{1}{16}$ inch = length of average oil tanker
> $\frac{1}{64}$ inch = edge of one acre

Since the size of the smallest line that can be seen separately from another line is 1/120th of an inch, the width of two lines of 1/120th of an inch would be 1/60th of an inch. A 1/120th-inch line enclosing a square 1/64th of an inch would not have a visible interior area, so for this reason an acre as shown on the 200-foot-diameter Geoscope would appear only as a square dot 1/64th of an inch along its outer edge. An average home-house would make a square speck of about 1/100th of an inch to the edge.

Speaking "approximately," the city of greater Los Angeles would make a circle one and one-half feet in diameter on the 200-foot-diameter Geoscope. A small town of 5000 people would make a circle one inch in diameter. Looking at the 200-foot-diameter Geoscope from 1000 feet away, you could say realistically to yourself, "I can't see it from here, but my house is a seeable speck on that world," and putting powerful binoculars to your eyes, you could see that speck.

The Geoscope's electronic computers will store all relevant inventories of world data arranged chronologically, in the order and spacing of discovery, as they have occurred throughout all known history.

Historical patterns too slow for the human eye and mind to comprehend, such as the multimillions-of-years-to-transpire changes in the geology of our planet—for instance, the picturing on the Geoscope Earth in two minutes of the drifting apart of the continental plates.

Or in another four-minute sequence picturing, the last four one-million-years-each ice ages, spaced 250,000 years apart, their transforming of the world's ocean waters into ice cappings, which water shift reveals peninsulas interconnecting what we now know of only as islands—for instance, the Malay Peninsula including all of Java, Sumatra, Borneo, Bali, Sulawesi, and the Philippines, as it did in the last ice age.

The geographically *varying population growths* of our Earth can be run off on the Geoscope at a rate of one second per century. This would show humanity first appearing on the coral atolls in the waters of Southeast Asia and the Indian Ocean, then coming up on the lands of China and India and East Africa, and spreading westward into Europe and thence westward to the Americas, with a small second-magnitude migration, rafting on the Japan Current and flowing the other way.

Another change to be illustrated is resource transpositioning, such as the shift in geographical location of the world's iron metal from mines of yesterday, much of which is now converted into world-around city buildings, railway tracks, and bridges, all of which latter are scrapped when the buildings or railways become obsolete. Yesterday's buildings and equipment have now become our "highest grade" iron mines. The data covering such epoch shifts may be comprehensively introduced into the computer's memory bank and acceleratingly displayed around the interior or exterior surface of the Geoscope "Earth," to be comprehended by any human of sound brain and mind.

The 200-foot Geoscope could present the cloud cover and weather history for all the known weather histories as recorded by ship captains around the world and in the recent century by world-around weather stations.

At Boulder, Colorado, the United States Meteorological Service has a large computer-equipped headquarters. They have two large world maps on the walls of the main lobby of their building; the first world map has displayed on it all the weather data just received seconds ago from stations all around the world. Throughout all the last thirty cold-warring years there has been no breakdown in the integrity of the hourly interweather reporting amongst all the nations around the Earth.

On the other identically sized and colored world map is shown the predicted world weather map emanating from the huge computer into which has been fed all the known weather data from each of the world-around weather stations for each year and day of the year for all the known years of weather record-keeping. Out of that ever-increasing data the computers figure the most probable weather conditions for each locality for each minute of the day for each day of the year. The computer map is becoming ever more identical to the actual world weather map.

This meteorological headquarters of the U.S.A. at Boulder, Colorado, sits high on the eastern slope of the Rocky Mountains, with Denver and the Great Plains stretched out far below. Walter Orr Roberts took moving picture footage of the vast area stretched out below Boulder. He had his moving picture camera take one picture per minute. There were all kinds of clouds in the sky down below Boulder. Much of the time you could see clearly between the clouds, at which time you could see the whole city of Denver with vast open land around it. He took such one-minute-apart pictures for many hours. He then projected the moving picture at the conventional twenty-four-frames-per-second rate and was astonished to see the cloud formation acting exactly like ocean waves rolling across the scene, with cresting-breaking waves having deep intervening troughs through which you could see the wave bottoms (on which Denver sat). It is very probable that the world history of weather for 200 years shown at high-speed acceleration on the Geoscope might display very great regularities of seasonal changing, with possible regularities of multiyear periods between dry and wet weather, etc.

The world history of earthquakes and volcanic eruptions could be shown on the 200-foot Geoscope and, if the world-around picturing is accelerated to contract time in important degree, it might readily disclose rhythms that would visually predict the coming quakes and eruptions.

Since the military intelligence of each of the world's military powers keeps careful track of their respective enemies' disposition of their armaments, troops, and navies, such strategic matters are not secret to the military of both sides and are only unknown to the world people. The 200-foot Geoscope installed outside the UN might display all that is known of those military dispositions around the Earth. All humanity would be able to see where all the world's submarines are located. This might greatly alter the dependency of people upon their political leaders and tend to induce an active democratic participation in world affairs. The UN delegates would obviously be greatly aided and stimulated by the 200-foot Geoscope disclosures to be viewed through all their east-facing windows.

Around-the-world evolutionary changes in transportation means, quantity, average miles per year, etc.—the number of people engaged in world travel and their average distancing, their convergencies in cities and deployments to remote places—would all be dramatically displayed on an accelerated rate of disclosure around the world. The present "real time" disposition of all aircraft operating around the world would be displayed, as well as their departure points and destinations. The accelerated pattern of world movement of population from farms and cities would be dramatic.

Juxtaposition and overlaying of seemingly unrelated information may produce unexpected and otherwise unimaginable pictures quickly and synergetically.

One of the most fantastic capabilities of the human brain is that of complex pattern recognition. If world-encompassing actions were accelerated, or a facsimile of the action presented within the velocity range of human comprehension, not only would the motion become clearly visible, but also some fundamental principles or heretofore unfamiliar forms of behavior probably would be exposed. The brain quickly correlates such new information with previously acquired data and insight gained from other experiences and adds understanding to the new phenomena being examined. Many of today's seemingly completely new and complex occurrences are in fact relatively simple and are clearly related to other phenomena with which we have learned to deal successfully.

With the Geoscope humanity would be able to recognize formerly invisible patterns and thereby to forecast and plan in vastly greater magnitude than heretofore.

The consequences of various world plans could be computed and projected, using the accumulated history-long inventory of economic, demographic, and sociologic data. All the world data would be dynamically viewable and picturable and relayable by radio to all the world, so that common consideration in a most educated manner of all world problems by all world people would become a practical everyday, -hour and -minute event.

From our usual local, only tangentially viewed, horizon-to-horizon observations—within which we see such a small fraction of the Earth that it seems to be horizontal—we conclude that in order to be a sphere, the Earth must indeed be very, very large. Other lands and other people seem very remote and strange. The interrelationship between their activities and ours is difficult to comprehend. When one realizes, on the other hand, that we all are in fact on the surface of a very tiny spherical spaceship on a long and seemingly inexplicably purposed journey, our proximity to each other becomes clear, and the absurdity of many of our conflicts becomes evident.

For the first time in all human history humanity's function as local Universe information-gatherer and local Universe problem-solver will be a practical reality, using the whole of Earth's comprehensive resources and data, and incisive, computer-augmented problem-solving capabilities with all humanity's spontaneous democratic participation, allowing humankind to use its intellect to the fullest in attempting to make our existence successful.

The proposed UN East River Blackwell's ledge installation of the 200-foot Geoscope was brought to the attention of U Thant when he was the Secretary General of the United Nations. It appealed to him so much that he gave a luncheon at New York City's Hotel Pierre for me and all the ambassadors to the UN from around the Earth. It was well attended, with more than half of the world's permanent ambassadors to the UN present. He had me give a thorough presentation speech describing the 200-footer. It met with great favor. Thereafter, on a number of prominent occasions, U Thant represented the concept. The estimated cost at that time was $10 million. Inflation would make it about $50 million today. There was no visible source of funding. The UN itself did not have any funds for such a purpose. The development of the popularity of World Game and the increasing need for the 200-foot Geoscope might suggest that its realization may not be far off.

The Geoscope will make possible communication of evolutionary phenomena not hitherto comprehendingly communicable via humans' conceptual faculties regarding their Spaceship Earth's orientation and course of travel amongst the other planets around the Sun, as well as of the comprehensive evolutionary developments occurring around the surface of our Spaceship Earth as already described. Many events about to take place will be dramatically evidenced, as will the avoidability of many events which, if unanticipated by humans, would tend to destroy us all—and on the other hand, if reliably anticipated, will make possible safe and happy continuance.

*   *   *

It is logical to consider at this point the continuingly important part played by the historically significant, omni-world-around, electromagnetically triangulated, aerial-photo-mapped, latitude-longitude-coordinated, geographical data—the triangular gridding of whose great sphere serves as the spherical scoreboard upon which to display the Geoscope's World Game "software."

In 1900—three years before the airplane, nine years before the discovery of the North Pole, eleven years before the discovery of the South Pole, and thirty-five years before radar—world-around geographical information had multiplied to such an extent that the major governments of the Earth agreed to have their geographers hold an omniworld meeting to adopt universal standards of cartography and geography. The world's cartographers agreed to adopt a one-million-to-one scale of producing their master world maps. At that same meeting of world geographers and cartographers it was noted by many of those professionals that the rectilinear, latitude-longitude, geographical coordinate system's angular-direction-and-linearly-measured-distances method of surveying of the world (at that time in universal use) had permitted much large-scale error to creep in. It was proving less and less satisfactory to go on trying to "square" the spherical surface of the Earth. Spherical trigonometry, for instance, showed that a spherical cubing of the

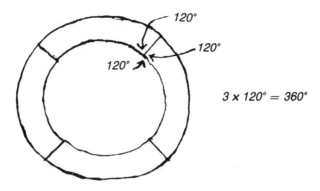

FIGURE 35.   Spherical cubing

Earth produced eight 120-degree corners of that cube, and not 90 degrees as it was popularly misconceived to be doing.

Most of the positioning of the geographical data had been done by explorers, often without the use of sextants and only from their estimates, as recorded in journals—for instance, "leaving the confluence of rivers X and Y, I traveled northwest for eight hours when I came upon a lake about a mile long." The explorer then made a drawing of these relationships from his pocket compass observations, pocket watch, and observations from high points of the direction of other high points and viewable features.

As a consequence the U.S. Navy, the U.S. Hydrographic Survey, and the U.S Geological Survey services determined to inaugurate a triangular surveying of the Earth's surface, starting at a point in North America whose position was obtained and frequently reverified by celestial observation and spherical trigonometry.

At that time the U.S. Navy had an astronomically fixed, triangularly surveyed and measured-off, meticulously buoy-marked, and multi-land-points-observed "official nautical mile," just eastward of Owl's Head lighthouse in the protected deep waters of Penobscot Bay in the state of Maine. Over this official mile all the ships built for the Navy had to be repeatedly run in reverse directions—with and against the tide, with and against the wind, etc.—to prove that they could maintain the top speed called for in their builders' contracts with the U.S. government. In that same Penobscot Bay there was one most conveniently sightable, uninhabited small island near the Navy's "measured mile." On this island—named "Compass Island"—

the U.S.A. surveyors built a high wooden pyramid whose apex position they carefully calculated by many-times-repeated sextant observations of the Sun and major stars. Other wooden "monumented" geographical points on other islands in Penobscot Bay were sharply located by their intertriangular relationships with Compass Island. This complex of intertriangulated islands became the base grid from which the whole U.S. continental intertriangulation grew. By the time of World War II's commencement most of the United States latitude-longitude mapping had been triangularly corrected and its geographical features accurately repositioned on government maps.

Churchill's grand strategy of coping with the Nazi-Germans' and Italians' occupancy of all Europe except the British Isles was to open the offensive against them from North Africa. This was called the "soft-underbelly" attack.

World War II introduced also the radio-triangulation control of bombing flights' navigational courses and bomb-drop points, which thus could be accomplished from above cloud cover. Such radio control was strictly dependent on whatever ground-mapping accuracy existed on the prior-to-radio-triangulated plotted maps.

Franklin Roosevelt's grand strategy agreement with Churchill called for the U.S.A.'s swift extension of its radio triangulation surveying from the already radio-triangulated U.S.A. southward into Mexico and thence through Central America into South America, thence from Brazil's easternmost capes to Ascension Island in the South Atlantic, and by triangulation of the latter with South America's other Atlantic islands to North Africa, and thence to North African positions opposite Italy on the south shores of the Mediterranean.

From their scientifically "known" North African geographical points the first U.S.A. bombing flight was carried out on Sicily—that flight's course being only "hopefully" coordinated with the first U.S.A. landing of its troops on Sicily. Because the geographical location of Sicily had never been radio-triangulated and coordinated with the latitude-longitude grid, the U.S.A. bombing had to rely on the non-triangulatedly-verified old latitude-longitude charts. The whereabouts of Sicily was so far off the triangularly radio-coordinated grid that the U.S. Air Force bombs let go above the clouds inadvertently landed in the midst of much of its own U.S.A. troops. With Sicily finally occupied, the world radio-triangulated grid was extended reliably all the way from the U.S.A. into successively radio-corrected mapping areas of Italy, as the U.S.A. forces worked slowly northward. Positioning errors in the old world mapping as great as fifteen or twenty miles were often discovered and corrected.

After the U.S.A.'s successful military penetration northward in Italy and the Normandy landing in France, the intercontinental radio triangulation became established all the way from the U.S.A. through Central America, South America, across the Atlantic into North Africa and thence into Italy—and was extended throughout all France as the military penetration of the Allies prevailed. Finally the world triangulation entered Germany and came to Berlin. The U.S.A. reached Berlin after Russia had already taken the portion of Germany in which Berlin was located.

By agreement of their general staffs the Russians and U.S.A. allies entered Berlin almost simultaneously. The U.S.A intelligence operatives rushed to seize as much as possible of the Germans' aerial-photo-coordinated radio-triangulated flight maps over Russia, hoping that this triangulation might have been carried deeply into Russia by the Germans. Apparently the Germans had not carried their radio-triangulated, photo-positional corrections deeply into Russia, or the Russians had found and removed the data before the U.S.A. got there—for none was found by the U.S.A. or its allies.

Though at the time the U.S.S.R. and U.S.A. were ostensibly allied, their behind-the-scenes transnational socialist and transnational free-enterprising interests were powerfully at work—each making one-sided, strategically anticipatory moves.

As a result of all the foregoing the Russians had all the long-ago-published, omnitriangularly corrected geographical data of America, while the U.S.A. had no such data of Russian geographical corrections—which, with errors as great as twenty miles in the latitude-longitude positioning of Russia's cities and other strategic points, meant that with the post–World War II inception of intercontinental atomic bomb warfare the Russians knew and as yet know exactly where all the U.S.A. targets are, but the U.S.A. did not know where Russian targets were—not within any strategically effective limits. To confuse the U.S.A. even more the U.S.S.R. built mock towns and cities at the incorrectly mapped points and put radio broadcasting stations where their cities were supposed to be—but weren't—as mispublished only by the pretriangulated gridding of the U.S.S.R.

Since the communist and capitalist worlds were organizing themselves for Armageddon and were committed to intercontinental atomic bombing, the exact location of targets was of highest importance. What the world public did not know and what both the U.S.S.R. and U.S.A. military leaders did know was that the U.S.A. had no radio-corrected triangulation map of the U.S.S.R. and that the U.S.S.R. did have radio-corrected triangulation maps of the U.S.A. and as well triangulation of all the U.S.A.'s allies—Russia knew exactly where the U.S.A. is, and the U.S.A. may not as yet know where much of the U.S.S.R. is.

It was this fact that caused the U.S.S.R. to resist any inspection-of-atomic-bomb-manufacturing agreements (or any other ground-level "inspection" by the U.S.A.) as regularly demanded by the U.S.A. and its allies whenever strategic inter-U.S.S.R.-and-U.S.A.-negotiated agreements were attempted. It probably was the U.S.A.-attempted cross-triangulation operation conducted from the Iran-Afghanistan border whose operation was curtailed with termination of Shahist Iran. It was the U.S.A.'s CIA's transfer of its electronic surveillance into other Afghanistan territory that gave the U.S.S.R. a valid cause for militarily entering Afghanistan, which the Russians have long wanted to do in order eventually to reach through to the Indian Ocean. Anticipating the ultimate development of a valid cause for moving into Afghanistan, the Russians had already made the Afghans "a present" of a modern high-tonnage-carrying highway system from Russia into Kabul.

The military policy of the U.S.A. deceiving its own public first became manifest during World War II, when the U.S.A. repeatedly denied in the press and radio that a U.S. Navy ship had been sunk by the enemy—though it had been so proclaimed by the enemy's broadcasting. Long after the facts the U.S.A. would publish the losses in a low-key manner. The adoption of the policy of self-deception was never announced by the U.S.A., but it was assumed tacitly to have been instituted to bolster U.S.A. morale. That the U.S.A. fighting forces and their supporting public were assumed by the U.S.A. leaders to be so stupid as not to realize what was happening when time after time it was learned only days later that the ships were indeed sunk was the beginning of the end of U.S.A. populace credit for the operational integrity of its representative government.

*   *   *

For several years I was a member of the "Dartmouth Conference." This was an arrangement made by Norman Cousins and two other Americans with the Russian Academy of Sciences to produce teams of U.S.S.R. and U.S.A. leaders in various fields—teams of approximately twenty-five on each side—to meet in such years as seemed expedient, first in the U.S.A. at Dartmouth College and next at Moscow-and-Leningrad, next at the Westchester Country Club in New York, etc. I was a member of the Moscow-Leningrad and Westchester, New York, conferences.

The conferees discussed every known point of contention existing between the two countries. The U.S.A. team on which I served consisted of John Kenneth Galbraith, Harvard economist; Paul Dudley White, Eisenhower's cardiologist; Norton Simon, financier; Leslie Paffrath, the director of the Johnson Foundation; two Harvard U.S.S.R.-specializing professors; a U.S. Navy admiral and a U.S. Army general. The latter four had been on many

U.S.S.R./U.S.A. arms-problem negotiating teams. The balance of the U.S.A. team consisted of Norman Cousins (team leader); Dr. Franklin Murphy, the chancellor of UCLA, now chairman of the board of the Los Angeles Times-Mirror Corporation; David Rockefeller; and myself.

The Russian team included the president of their Academy of Sciences, their leading astronomer (who was in charge of their space-vehicle guidance), their leading climatologist, others of their leading scientists, their most eminent writers, philosophers, economists, an admiral, a general—thirty in all. Present also were a dozen "simultaneous interpreters" loaned by the UN.

We all lived at the same hotel. The dining room had only four-place tables. As you entered, you chose quickly with which of the Russians you wished to sit. They were the first to reach the dining room. You tried to sit successively with each of the U.S.S.R. team members. The moment you sat down with a Russian, an interpreter moved in with you. To our U.S.A. surprise it turned out at the end of the conference that all the Russians could speak English, while amongst the U.S.A. representatives only the two Harvard professors could speak Russian.

Our meetings consisted of: (A) those lasting all day, every day, at which all the officially-to-be-considered points were discussed; and (B) the very small individual dining room and other casual meetings at dinner parties and receptions. At the latter it seemed as though all points of contention could be coped with in a manner satisfactory to both sides. At the formal all-day meetings, however, everyone seemed so intractable that nothing could be resolved.

For the last day of the first week-long conferences, some in Moscow, some in Leningrad, it was decided by the leaders of the two teams that instead of having summaries prepared of what had occurred, each side would select one of its members to give a speculative half-day-long prognostication regarding all prominent features of human life on planet Earth for the next half-century. Each prognosticator would have half a day in which to make his or her presentation. It was assumed that the prognosticators would indicate how much each side was accommodating the other side's conference issues. These presentations were expected to provide a clue as to what extent the respective sides would be yielding in the future to the opposing arguments presented during the previous formal sessions.

The Russians chose their leading meteorologist to give the U.S.S.R prognostication. He would have all of Saturday morning to present it.

I was chosen to present the U.S.A. prognostication. I had all Saturday afternoon to do so. In preparation I made a tensegrity sphere to demonstrate new human-use potentials of nature's fundamental structuring principles of discontinuous-compression-and-continuous-tension as employed in all geodesics and synergetics. I also calculated the weight of a great cathedral we passed each day on the walk to the grand palace in which we held our conferences. Employing tensegrity principles, I was able to show a 99-percent weight reduction for enclosing an equal amount of clear-span to that of the cathedral, including adequately engineered snow-loading, wind-loading, and earthquake-proofing.

I based my presentation on the twentieth century's unprecedented invisible revolution in chemistry, electronics, and metallurgy, by means of which we could now do so much more with so much less weight, volume, energy, and time per each accomplished function as to suggest that we humans would soon prove invalid Malthus's seemingly infallible scientific conclusion that economically on our planet Earth it had to be "only you or me—not enough for both." I then outlined the changes in patterning of life on Earth if there were ample high standard of living, life support for all. My discourse, its predictions, and the raisons d'êtres for those predictions were approximately the same as those of this book—*Critical Path.*

What I said pleased both the U.S.A. and U.S.S.R. delegates. On the walk home to our hotel each individual delegate from both sides hustled up beside me and told me how excitedly pleased he or she was over my statements. The Russians were unanimously enthusiastic about what I said. Fortunately, all the U.S.A. delegates *seemed* equally pleased. At the farewell banquet that night the president of the U.S.S.R. Academy of Sciences said in his closing speech, "From now on Buckminster Fuller will be ranked in the U.S.S.R. side-by-side with Franklin and Edison." I assumed that the Russians had so classified me because I was not only an inventor but dwelt in the lands of capitalism—despite the fact that I am apolitical and an ardent advocate of an omnihumanity-advantaging freedom of individual initiative, and not of private enterprise's only selfishly benefited freedoms.

In our second meeting, two years later at the Westchester Country Club, many of the American participants lived nearby and so went home each night. Together with the Johnson Foundation director I lived at the club with the Russians. I found that the young editor of *Pravda* was the only Russian amongst them who seemed free to explore and discuss spontaneously the world's future prospects. Though obviously a faithful communist, his speculative thoughts seemed not to be bound within popularly established party-line dogma.

What I learned from the Russians—regarding which I am certain they were seriously convinced—was that "the U.S.S.R. would never be willing to negotiate with the U.S.A. regarding any world-around, supreme-power matters when the U.S.S.R. was in a weaker military position than the U.S.A."

They said to me, "Every time we struggle to attain parity with the U.S.A. so that we can negotiate, the U.S.A. institutes an arms advancement before the meeting, wherefore we are deprived of tolerable negotiating conditions.

"Worse than that," they said, "this continually defeats turning our massive high-technology productivity toward realizing a life-style for our socialist economy equal to or better than that already enjoyed by capitalism—whose world-publicized high standard of living is a thorn in our side as we remain unable to do so—not because of technical or social inability but because of the preoccupation of technological resources with the cold warring."

Assuming that an atomic war would mean that both sides would lose*—ergo, it would not occur—the U.S.S.R. determined to outnumber and thus overpower the U.S.A. in the design and the production of conventional air and sea armaments and in the training and maintenance of a vastly greater standing army, whereafter they felt they could negotiate constructively for the establishment and maintenance of peaceful world-around conditions.

It must be remembered that, in their 1920s-formulated, successive-multistaged five-year industrial planning, the Russians had assumed a World War II to occur in the early 1940s, at which time it would be evident to the private-enterprise world that socialism could be successful—which private enterprise had always said would be impossible—ergo, the private-enterprise-dominated countries would start a war to destroy socialism but would do it in a highly deceptive manner by having a Nazi propaganda offensive launched against the German industrial cartels, which would suddenly be turned against the U.S.S.R. This is exactly what happened. The Germans first made the U.S.S.R. their ally. When well into Poland and at the Russian border, the Nazis turned treacherously against the U.S.S.R. The anti-U.S.S.R. strategy of the "Cliveden set" miscarried when, soon thereafter, the U.S.S.R. and the U.S.A. became allies.

No one in the U.S.A. can understand the bitterness as yet existent in the U.S.S.R. over the millions of U.S.S.R. troops and civilians killed by the Nazis. The U.S.S.R. could not understand the U.S.A. rearming of the Germans, with whom the U.S.S.R. was much more concerned as a World War IV enemy than with the U.S.A. as such an enemy.

The Russians had assumed in their five-year planning that when World War II terminated, they would be able to divert all their high industrial productivity toward advantaging all their people to prove that socialism could produce an economically desirable life-style equal to or better than that provided by capitalism. Again the Russian planning became thwarted when Western capitalism, which had been socialized by FDR's New Deal, real-

*See p. 117, "Legally Piggily" chapter, and page 192 of this chapter.

ized at the cessation of World War II that it could not carry on without the vast government procurement program which is occasioned only by war. To cope with this situation the capitalists invented World War III (which they called the cold war).

The Russians queried of the U.S., their supposed ally, "Who are you going to fight?" and the U.S.A. answered, "You."

This meant that the U.S.S.R. would have to focus all its high-science-and-technology productivity on producing armaments for decades of around-the-world cold warring, in the conduct of which both the Russians and the U.S.A. would have to avoid direct, all-out interconfrontation. With the joining of supreme-powers war by direct military confrontation, neither side could withdraw without all-out surrender. However, all-out intercontinental atomic war would mean the end of human life on Earth. Therefore, the U.S.A. and U.S.S.R., in testing their respective strengths, would have to operate indirectly against one another through their respective puppet nations, hopefully intent on drawing forth the "secret weapons" in the other's arsenals. Thus we have the North versus the South Koreans, the "Vietnamese" versus the Vietcong, the Israelis versus the Arabs, etc.

The Russians decided early on that atomic warheads would not be used because the rocket delivery times traveling at 14,000 miles per hour were such that with radar traveling at 700,000,000 miles per hour, both sides would know ten minutes before being struck that the enemy had fired their atomic warheads—ergo, both sides would have plenty of time to send off all their atomic warheads, and both sides would lose. So while deceptively continuing the atomic-warhead race with the U.S.A., the U.S.S.R. committed itself realistically to producing the strongest navy in history.

The U.S.A. politicans kept the U.S.A. populace feeling militarily secure because they could point out that the U.S.A. was developing far more atomic warheads than was the U.S.S.R. The U.S.A. was doing so because big oil money, which successfully lobbied Washington's Capitol Hill energy policies—knowing that petroleum would ultimately be exhausted—fostered atomic-warhead production in order to build up the atomic technology industry (in the development of which the U.S. people's government had spent over $200 billion) and its nuclear scientist personnel whom they, the world-power-structure organizations, would need to employ in operating the atomic-energy plants and the electrical-distribution network as world petroleum supplies dwindled. They would need the energy meters in order to continue exploiting the capitalist world's energy needs.

When *Jane's Annual World Inventory of Ships* showed that the U.S.S.R. Navy had reached parity with the U.S.A., the U.S. politicans laughed it off by saying the Russians did not even have aircraft carriers. This was true because the U.S.S.R. had seen that aircraft carriers are "highly vulnerable," so they built huge airplane-carrying submarines from which a plane would take off by "Vertol"—vertical flight to height, followed by horizontal flight—ergo, needing no runways. This Vertol-from-submarine launching was strongly advocated by some of the U.S. Navy's most astute officers, whose word was not heeded because the aircraft carriers were much more profitable business for private enterprise. The weapons industry's Washington lobbyists were more persuasive than the U.S. Navy's experts.

With its naval fleet supremacy established but lacking en route support bases, the U.S.S.R. then set about to develop disarmament talks with the U.S.A. from a superior conventional-warpower position—that of controlling the high-seas lines of supply.

Realizing that the U.S.A. senators had jurisdiction over all peace negotiating and that the U.S.A. Senate's Republican membership was intent to deprive the Democratic President of peace-making success, and that apparently the U.S.A. was not going to go along with ratification of the SALT treaty, the Russians decided to put the heat on the U.S.A. so that a global naval-line-of-supply confrontation incident such as the occupation of Afghanistan would demonstrate—as it has in Iran—that the U.S.A. can no longer control the Indian Ocean and Arabian Sea and therefore cannot take yesteryears' sure-to-win military steps against Iran.

The U.S.A.'s half-century dominance of world affairs is now terminating, just as did Great Britain's century and a third of dominance come to an end with the 1929 economic crash.

* * *

Sir Halford Mackinder was Britain's chief geographical advisor from the latter Victorian period to 1930. Mackinder pointed out that the British Empire was built on its mastery of the world's sea routes from the Orient to Europe. He also pointed out to the British, circa 1900, that what the world's seacoasts might really be was not what one saw when looking at the world maps. He showed the British that the railways were the large-tonnage-capacity, previously seagoing, cargo carriers going up onto the land. He further showed them that the Trans-Siberian Railway was being built by the Russians to short-circuit the Orient-to-Europe high-tonnage cargo routes. Mackinder pointed out that the Trans-Siberian Railway was strategically too far to the north. Its snow impediment was too great to be economical. The British kept the Russians bottled up by refusing them an Atlantic port—Russia had to go to Archangel in the Arctic Sea and, on the Pacific coast, to Vladivostok.

The Orient Express ran only from Paris to Constantinople in Asia Minor. The czar-backing Russian-power-structure interests, hoping to compete with the British, represented the inheritors of the before-the-water-route, overland-caravaning powers of the Old World. Mackinder showed the British that the only economically successful trans-Europe and Asia railroad route would have to be from France to Constantinople and thence via Turkey and Iran to Kabul, Afghanistan, and thence through the Khyber Pass, through Sinkiang and Inner Mongolia to Shanghai, China, cutting shipping times down very much as compared with the sea routes around Africa to the Orient. Mackinder's counsel was heeded by the British.

Mackinder showed the British that Russia could, by taking Afghanistan and Pakistan, reach the Persian Gulf and then come through the Indian Ocean to intercept British cargo ships en route to the Orient. Mackinder identified on the map what he called "the Heartland." The heart of Mackinder's Heartland was Afghanistan, with its Khyber Pass leading to the east and its ability to break through to the Arabian Sea and the Persian Gulf. Mackinder said, "Whoever controls the Heartland, rules the world." Afghanistan was (and as yet is) the heart of the world's heartland.

After World War I the British were so "tired" that they did not listen to Mackinder as they had before. In the 1920s he tried to make the British realize that the airplane altogether eliminated the world's shorelines as the limit of travel. The British did not see the airplane as a cargo carrier and believed that their world trading exclusively by ships of the sea would not be threatened by air traffic. No one had ever flown across an ocean, let alone set up air-cargo fleets capable of competing with their seagoing fleets. One of the factors that they failed to envision was that of the technology becoming ever lighter per unit of functional performance until it became feasibly and economically air-deliverable.

Mackinder developed a doctorate-level school in London in the 1920s. One of his students was a talented German named Haushofer, who listened to Mackinder pointing out that the armored tanks were, in effect, the navy destroyers coming out of the sea and running up on the land. Mackinder said to his students, "The French Maginot Line and all great fortresses around the world are obsolete." He continued, "The airplane raiders above and the armored tanks on the land could circumvent, overrun, and overfly the fortresses and overwhelm any troops or other defense." Haushofer graduated from Mackinder's school, returned to Germany, and went to work for Goering, Hitler's air minister. Haushofer described Mackinder's science in German as *Geopolitik*. From his description of Mackinder's concept, which the British were not heeding, Goering developed his *blitzkrieg*—lightning war—with the Luftwaffe commanding the sky and tanks and other armored vehicles commanding the land. Goering flew over and rolled over the Maginot Line and took all Europe.

Until the end of World War II the British had kept the Afghanistan heartland well under control. Then, after World War II, they let its militarily guaranteed isolation greatly deteriorate. Meanwhile the Russians were busy giving Afghanistan such "presents" as a first-class highway from Russia to Kabul. The U.S.A. gave them naught.

In 1954 the British Foreign Office advised the U.S. State Department that they had just learned from their ambassador in Kabul, Afghanistan, that Russia, East Germany, Czechoslovakia, and China had all installed impressive exhibition buildings in Kabul to take part in Afghanistan's most sacredly important holiday—the Geshin Fair. Neither the United Kingdom nor the U.S.A. nor any of their allies had an exhibit in Kabul.

I received an emergency call from Jack Masey of the U.S. State Department's U.S. Information Agency. He asked me how long it would take me to produce a 10,000-square-foot-floor-area geodesic dome so light and compactly shippable that it could be sent by one DC-4 airplane to Kabul. My Raleigh, North Carolina, shop had it produced in twenty-five days, complete with a high-tension, all-weather skin outwardly tensed to its geodesic, tubular aluminum frame. All the struts and hubs of the dome were color-coded. The 114-feet-in-diameter dome was test-assembled at the Raleigh airport and accepted by the U.S.A.

It was flown to Kabul with my one engineering representative to supervise its erection by the Afghans. It was assembled in one day just in time for the Geshin Fair opening. The U.S.A. show inside consisted of the Borden's "laughing cow," bouncing ball bearings, and Lionel trains. No one showed interest in the show inside, but all the Afghans, the Russians and East Germans, the Chinese and Czechs, were fascinated with the geodesic dome itself. The Russians asked permission to bring in their moving picture equipment to make a documentary of the dome construction. The then king of Afghanistan fell in love with the dome—it was a great modern-materials Afghan yurt—the Afghans' own architecture. The king asked the U.S.A. to give him the dome, but the U.S.A. refused and sent the dome off as an around-the-world traveling show.

The Russians, finding the Afghans making themselves working automobiles out of the most battered second-hand cars shipped into Kabul and then driving them around on very rough dirt roads, made the Afghans a present of macadam-surfaced, first-class roads, which delighted the Afghans because they provided some real distance driving—the Russians extended the highways all the way into the U.S.S.R. These roads recently (1979) provided the means for the U.S.S.R. to roll their armed forces into Afghanistan.

Having been a long-time student of Sir Halford Mackinder's work, I was fascinated through my dome experience to discover that the U.S. diplomacy apparently knew nothing of Mackinder's "Heartland" concept—or considered it to be no longer relevant.

When early in 1979 the U.S.S.R. took over Kabul, Afghanistan, it was because the balance of world power had shifted from U.S.A. to U.S.S.R. mastery.

As we have related, Mackinder had identified "The Heartland" on the maps. The heart of his Heartland was Kabul, Afghanistan. Also, the Russians with their now-great navy had access to the Atlantic Ocean only at Archangel and the Baltic ports and Vladivostok in the North Pacific. With Afghanistan under their control the Russians were able to control all the northern and eastern borders of Iran and the western borders of Pakistan.

Russia always uses the power structure's number-one strategy—"divide to conquer!"—and does so with psychological expertise. She often finds religious divisibility the most propitious. It was feasible in Iran, which could be divided religiously against the incumbent political power—ergo, the Muslims versus the Shahdom of Iran—with knowledge that after driving out the U.S.A.-supported Shahdom, it (the U.S.S.R.) could divide the Muslims into their subsects and militarily overwhelm Iran. The U.S.A.'s secretly supported Kurdish opposition to Russia in Afghanistan and to the Muslims in Iran would become the final obstacles to the Russians' century-held objective of gaining direct access to the Indian Ocean and therewith complete control of U.S.A. access to Arabian oil. The Russians' move into Afghanistan was not just a power-structure play. They were exercising their evolutionary ascendancy into the world's top power position. The Heartland—Afghanistan and its ultimate access to the Indian Ocean—is the historic prizes of the world's top power position.

Fortunately for the cross-breeding world citizens of North America and for the rest of the world, the U.S.S.R. is most probably intent on getting the world power structure under irreversible control as quickly as possible so that it can institute controlled demilitarization and thereby turn its immense productivity toward improving the standard of living for the socialist world and thus prove socialism's life-style to be equal to or better than the best of the life-styles produced by capitalism. I am confident that Russia does truly intend world disarmament. She will keep a powerful upper hand at each stage of disarmament but will seek to have the world's militarily scrapped metals reinvested in peacefully productive livingry advantage for all the world's peoples.

I have only *one* objection to the concept of comprehensive socialism: So far it has made no provision for effective development of the individual initiative of humans. Too long has such freedom of initiative been usurped either by the Communist party, representing only 1 percent of the U.S.S.R. population, or by the Western world's private enterprise's utterly selfish exploitation for money-making rather than for common sense–making. I have discussed this point with the Russians. They admit that a *party* dictatorship is not "democracy" and, at the same time, also admit that it is for *true* democracy to which the Russians, the Chinese, and most people of the world aspire. Possibly the electronically operative democracy and its ability to cope with complex problem-solving will also make safe the realization of individual initiative to be exercised on behalf of all humanity by any humans anywhere.

CHAPTER 6

World Game

I THINK YOU MAY FIND the physical design science revolution and its "software" outlined in my World Game thesis to be the most thorough, effective, and realistically feasible strategy for accomplishing sustainable physical and metaphysical success for all humanity, all to be realized within the shortest possible time.

In my book *Operating Manual for Spaceship Earth* (E. P. Dutton, 1963) you will find my identification of the phenomenon *wealth*. Wealth consists of physical energy (as matter or radiation) combined with metaphysical know-what and know-how. The scientists make it clear that no physical energy of Universe gets lost—ergo, the physical constituent of wealth is cosmically irreducible. Experience teaches us that every time we employ our metaphysical know-what and know-how wealth, we always learn more. Experience can only increase—ergo, the metaphysical component of wealth can only increase, and totally integrated wealth itself can only increase.

From the comprehensively informed World Game viewpoint, those who have learned how to make money with money—which money can never be anything but a medium of wealth exchanging—have now completely severed money from its constant functional identity with real wealth. With their game of making money with money the money-makers and their economists continue to exploit the general political and religious world's assumptions that a fundamental inadequacy of human life support exists around our planet.

These money interests are wrong. Because of (A) the constant increase in strength per pound of new metallic alloys, (B) the constant increase in horsepower per each pound and cubic inch of aircraft engines, and (C) the ever-increasing performance per pounds and cubic inches of new chemistries and electronics, in general we have the capability, which can be fully realized within ten years, of producing and sustaining a higher standard of living for all humanity than that ever heretofore experienced or dreamt of by any.

This is not an opinion or a hope—it is an engineeringly demonstrable fact. This can be done using only the already proven technology and with the already mined, refined, and in-recirculating physical resources.

This will be an inherently sustainable physical success for all humanity and all its generations to come. It can be accomplished not only within ten years but with the phasing out forever of all use of fossil fuels and atomic energy. Our technological strategy makes it incontrovertible that we can live luxuriously entirely on our daily Sun-radiation-and-gravity-produced income energy. The quantity of physical, cosmic energy wealth as radiation arriving aboard planet Earth each minute is greater than all the energy used annually by all humanity. World Game makes it eminently clear that we have four billion billionaires aboard our planet, as accounted by *real wealth,* which fact is obscured from public knowledge by the exclusively conceived and operated money game and its monopolized credit system accounting.

Wealth is, then, the already organized human capability and know-how to employ the fixed, inanimate, planetary assets and omnicosmically operative and only celestially emanating natural energy income in such a manner as to predictably cope with so many forward days of so many human lives by providing for their (1) protection, (2) comfort, and (3) nurturing, and for (4) the accommodation of the ongoing development by humans of their as-yet-untapped store of intellectual and aesthetic faculties, while (5) continually eliminating restraints and (6) increasing the range and depth of their information-accumulating experience.

The success of all humanity can be accomplished only by a terrestrially comprehensive, technologically competent, design revolution. This revolution must develop artifacts whose energy-use efficiency not only occasions the artifacts' spontaneous adoption by humanity, but therewith also occasions the inadvertent, unregretted abandonment and permanent obsolescence of socially and economically undesirable viewpoints, customs, and practices.

This design revolution must employ world-around, satellite-interlinked, data-banks-and-computer-accomplished conversion of present-day, exclusively geocentric, Spaceship Earth wealth accounting by synchronizing our planetary economic affairs with the cosmic, interstellar, intergalactic, complex family of physical, time-energy behavior laws, demonstrated by astrophysics to be synergetically in economic governance not only throughout our Milky Way's 100 billion stars, but also throughout the two billion additional such galaxies now discovered and observed by astrophysics within our phototelescopic range. Little planet Earth of our small star the Sun is not exempt from the inexorable, synergetic integration of the complex of time-energy, electromagnetic, chemical structuring and destructuring's inventory of the intertransformative laws that govern the generalized, regenerative economic-investment system of the physical and metaphysical assets of what physics now finds to be an eternally regenerative, 100-percent-efficient scenario Universe.

Simultaneous "shooting the works" of the biggest atomic explosions mutually deliverable by the most powerful long-range weapons systems of the most powerful political systems on planet Earth—designed to reinforce their exclusively politico-economic accounting concepts—can produce less than a visible twinkle in the galactic theater. Obviously Universe is not saying, "We cannot afford another galaxy—let alone another star—let alone another terrestrial crew of cosmically invisible human information-harvesting and -processing functionaries, whose problem-solving capabilities are being strangled by ignorant fears and selfishness aboard tiny planet Earth."

Scientifically faithful, synergetically integrated, time-energy, electrochemical process accounting shows that it costs energetic Universe more than a million dollars to produce each gallon of petroleum when the amount of energy as heat and pressure used for the length of time necessary to produce that gallon of petroleum is charged for at the New York Con Edison Company's retail kilowatt-hour rates for that much electricity.

About 90 percent of all U.S.A. employment is engaged in tasks producing no life-support wealth. These non-life-support-producing employees are spending three, four, and more gallons of gasoline daily to go to their non-wealth-producing jobs—ergo, we are completely wasting $3 trillion of cosmic wealth per day in the U.S.A.

In real, energy-time, know-how accounting of wealth the planet Earth's four billion billionaires have not yet been notified of their good fortune. Their heritage probating is being postponed by the lawyers for the now inherently obsolete power structures of all kinds—religious, political, financial, professional, and academic—all of which exploitative systems are organized only to take biased advantage of all scarcities, physical and metaphysical.

Evolution has now accelerated into revolution, which, if it goes bloody, will render all humanity extinct, but if it goes via the design revolution, all humanity will win. This is a new kind of revolution; it is one that, instead of revengefully pulling down the top fortunate few, will elevate all the heretofore unfortunates and the fortunates alike to new and sustainable heights of realized life far superior to those previously tenuously attained by the most privileged few.

World Game comprehensively details that which individual humans must do to realize total success for all and do so within the critical time limit, before humanity passes the point of no return en route to self-extinction.

* * *

Quickly reviewing the earliest large-scale wealth trading by humans, payments were made in "kind"—that is, with livestock that could be driven from here to there. Most valuable were cattle. When "money," or heads of cattle (known as capital, *capita* meaning "head" in Latin), was loaned to enterprisers, the latter's cattle were held by the lender as collateral until the enterprise venture was completed. The interim birth and growth of calves into cattle became the "interest" on the loan to be paid by the borrower to the lender of the venture's working capital. Much later, metal money replaced the cattle. The concept of interest due to the loaner persisted, but since metal does not breed more metal, the interest paid reduces the real-wealth value of the collateral when returned to the borrower.

As the scale of long-distance trading exceeded the distances to which the cattle could be driven, the trading shifted primarily into water-borne ships. Ships carry far greater loads than can humans or beasts of burden. In the earliest days of international trading by ships cattle were used as "money." This became increasingly impractical, and the Phoenicians invented iron money in the form of miniature bull horns. With metal as money there swiftly developed a world-around preference for gold, due to its scarcity and easily recognized weight per volume as well as its nontarnishability. World-trading ships carrying gold soon became prey to hijacking pirates. As mentioned in our "Legally Piggily" chapter, when the British Empire came into world-around and century-enduring supremacy in 1805, its administrators made trade treaties with countries from every region of the world. Thereafter both sides kept their trading on books of import-export accounts that were balanced annually, and the debtor nation paid the other by shifting their gold deposited in a London bank to the other's London bank, thus keeping the gold off the ships—ergo, out of reach of small-time pirates.

This is how what is known as the international "balance of trade" originated with the powerful industrializing countries of Europe; although rich in technical experience and inventive "know-how," they lacked an adequate supply of fundamental metallic and other resources with which to realize the industrial potentials for their inventions. They were motivated to establish military supremacy over nonindustrialized countries in Africa, South America, and the Far East, within which countries the European scientists found the metal ores essential to their industries.

Present-day Ghana provides a good example of the foregoing. Ghana is rich in bauxite—the ore from which aluminum is extracted by electrolytic refinement. Ghana also has the Volta River and its basin. The Ghanaians, however, did not know of the convertibility of bauxite into aluminum. Americans with vast capital came into Ghana, arranged to have all the inhabitants of the Volta River basin banished from that basin, then built one of the world's largest hydroelectric dams there. They used the electricity thus generated to convert the Ghanaian bauxite (which was just so much dirt to the Ghanaians) into aluminum ingots. These ingots were, and as yet are, shipped to America and Europe, where the aluminum is transformed into airplanes, cooking utensils, etc., and sold back to the Ghanaians and others around the world at such a markup in price that the Ghanaians' balance of import-export trading finds them ever deeper in debt to those countries that "developed" their natural resources. The societies in the manipulating countries call these source people "the underdeveloped countries" or "the Third World."

There can be no planetary equity until all the sovereign nations are abolished and we have but one accounting system—that of the one family of humans aboard Spaceship Earth.

Ample food and growing capacity exist on our planet to feed well every world human. But the sovereign nations and their international-trade-balancing system, and the individual hoarders of foods and other goods within the separate nations, prevent the distribution of the foods.*

World Gaming discloses that humanity will perish on this planet if the sovereignty of nations is not abandoned and if the World Game's world-around computerized time-energy accounting is not forthwith inaugurated. The *first* step in bringing about the desovereignization will be the closing of the gaps in the world electric power grid. The world-unifying electric power accounting will be the beginning of the omnienergy accounting for world economic management.

World Game is a continuing scientific research and physical-prototyping development. It is devoted to progressive discovery of how most efficiently and expeditiously to employ (1) the total world-around resources, (2) total accumulated knowledge, and (3) the total already-produced technological tooling of Spaceship Earth, all three to the ever-advancing equal advantage of all its present and future passengers.

World Game is the antithesis of World War Gaming as played by the joint chiefs of staff of the world's most powerful sovereign nations' respective military, air, and naval establishments. Predicated upon the British Empire's post-Magellan, historically first, spherical, world-around empire and its first

*See the World Game Laboratory publication, *Ho-Ping: Food for Everyone,* by Medard Gabel, Doubleday, 1979.

"inventory of vital statistics of the world," as assembled in 1805 by the East India Company College's professor of political economics, Thomas Malthus, and his findings therefrom which we have already described.

World War Gaming, in contradistinction to World Gaming, assumes Thomas Malthus's theory that there exists a lethal inadequacy of life support on our planet. World War Gaming also assumes Darwin's "survival only of the fittest" to be ruling evolution. As already mentioned in Chapter 3, this is why the United States and the U.S.S.R. have jointly spent over $200 billion annually for the last thirty years ($6 trillion total) to buy science's most effective means of destroying their respective "enemies." World War Gaming is the consequence. World War Gaming employs the ever-evolutingly-advancing, most comprehensive and incisive, scientifically and technologically feasible capabilities to develop and mass-produce weaponry systems that will ever more swiftly devastate all enemy life-support artifacts and kill ever more enemy people at ever greater ranges in ever shorter periods of time.

In contradistinction to the inherently vast wastage of World War Gaming's objectives, World Gaming takes advantage of ephemeralization—technology's ever-higher-strength-per-weight metallic alloys and chemistries and ever-more-comprehensively-incisive-and-inclusive electronic circuitry performances per volumes and weights of apparatus used—and employs ever-progressively-less weight and volume of materials, ergs of energy, and seconds of time per each technical function accomplished and employs those ever improving functions to produce ever more advanced *livingry artifacts* instead of the *killingry weapons* of World War gaming.

World Game assumes evolutionary stages of advancement of its successive systems of production, distribution, maintenance, design improvement, world-around integrating, precision tool-automating, and mass-producing of its ever-advancing livingry service. All these successive prototype stages of development are based on my fifty-two-year-maintained omnihistory inventory of world resources (both physical and metaphysical) and my inventory of technical trendings and progressively evolving human needs—both group and individual.

World Game's now clearly demonstrated capability to produce the higher-than-ever-before-experienced living standard means an ever-healthier, ever-less-environmentally-restrained, ever-better-informed and -comprehensively-educated, ever-more-thoughtfully, -spontaneously, and -cooperatively-productive total humanity operating as an ever-more-mutually-intertrusting and -interconsiderate world family, living in an ever-more-generous and less wasteful way, at an ever-more-foresighted and -comprehensively-anticipatory level; engaged in ever-more-constructive initiative-taking and cooperative intersupport of one another's initiatives and explorations; an ever-more-truly omniloving, classless, raceless, human family of Earth's planetarians—all engaged competently in local Universe information-harvesting and in local Universe problem-solving, in successful support of the 100-percent integrity of eternally regenerative Universe, that being the function in Universe that World Game assumes occasioned the inclusion of humans and their generalized-principles-discovering-minds in the design of Universe.

Technical artifacts, invented and produced by humans, employing generalized scientific principles of Universe—such as the principles of leverage, optics, magnetics, mass attraction, etc.—to cope successfully with life challenges varying among *lethal, difficult, tolerable,* or *benign* environmental conditions, constitute any and all differences existing between the life activities of originally naked humans in a few mid-ocean tropical "Gardens of Eden" on planet Earth three million years ago and the life-styles of humans today in skyscraper cities or in space suits exiting from their Moon-landed, space-rocketed capsule to bring back to Earth sample rocks from the Moon environment, all the while being intimately satellite-relay-televised in color to one billion people on a planet 320,000 miles away from the Moon-landed astronauts, the one billion viewers being situated in their environment-control homes around planet Earth, as those viewing Earthian billions and the Moon-landing astronauts alike are being vitally sustained by foods grown elsewhere than where they live, which foods are preserved and shipped in environment-controlling cans and packages or in artifact-produced frozen or dehydrated conditions.

World Game's design science employs all the known generalized principles and technical inventions and invents others where artifacts adequate for solving the newly emerging and foreseeably arising problems do not as yet exist. World Gaming, incorporating ever-more performance per function and higher energy efficiencies with ever-less pounds and volumes of resources, continually redesigns the artifacts and technical systems employing those ever-improving materials.

World Gaming recognizes that there are no unnatural materials. If nature permits their chemical-element associabilities, the materials and their functionings are natural. If nature does not permit or bring about their associability, they cannot exist. The substances permitted by nature may be unfamiliar to humans, but they are never unnatural—i.e., "synthetic." World Gaming notes that humans' fear of the unfamiliar often prevents realization of humanity's imminent acquisition of improved living conditions for everyone.

World Gaming takes advantage of the ever-changing world-resource patterns, such as that of steel and other metals scrapped from obsolete buildings and machinery as the latter's designs are made obsolete by the latest military-and-naval-produced hardware. Scrap of the discontinued hardware constitutes new high-grade ore mines existing entirely above ground. As an example: there are no tin mines in the United States. All tin came originally either from England, Malaysia, Bolivia, or Tanganyika. Tin was first used for making bronze, then pewter utensils, then for tinning bathtubs and cans, next for babbitting of machinery bearings, soldering. Outperformed by newer, more effective technologies all of these early tin uses became obsolete, and that tin was recovered. Since 1940 U.S. aeronautical production tooling has involved so much tin in its soft tooling phases that the inventory of ever-remelted tin of the U.S. aircraft industry and its swift-design-change-accomodating "soft-kirksite" toolings is now (1980) greater than that remaining in the world mines—ergo, the U.S. requires no further purchases of foreign tin. Having originally no tin mines, the U.S. has an above-ground source of tin that is now the world's largest tin "mine." World resource maps showing only the tin-in-the-ground mines are completely misinforming. World war gaming and those economic advisors of leading governments use only the in-the-ground-mine data.

As noted earlier, there are 100 dots on the Dymaxion Sky-Ocean Map, which is always used as the "playing field" in playing World Game. Each dot represents forty-four million people, that being 1 percent of the 4.4 billion humans now (1980) aboard Spaceship Earth.

Each dot is located at the geometrical center for the forty-four million people it represents. As the dots show, approximately 90 percent of humanity live north of the equator. The 10 percent who live south of the Equator live very close to it. Humanity is a "northern hemisphere" creature and is now about to integrate over the North Pole into a one-town world. We have entered a north-south, air-and-space-vehicle, world traffic pattern and are swiftly abandoning yesterday's east-west ship and railway pattern. As the doing-more-work-with-less-pounds-of-material invisible revolution keeps advancing, we have ever-more-powerful and greater-weight-and-capacity air vehicles to carry the ever-more-efficient and -lighter machinery and structures, which classes of goods were once so heavy as formerly to be shippable only by sea or rail.

As mentioned earlier, all the great rivers of the Earth are clearly shown on the world map. The source of these rivers' water supply to 54 percent of humanity comes from a vast frozen reservoir atop the Himalayas—only a small fraction of this potential waterpower has as yet been dammed for hydroelectric generation and irrigation system development. With such hydro development the 54 percent of humanity in China, Southeast Asia, and

India will all become physically prosperous in high degree. Likewise, the great, as-yet-undeveloped hydroelectric and irrigation systems of the other continents are clearly demonstrable as holding high standards of living to be realized for all humanity.

It is engineeringly demonstrable that there is no known way to deliver energy safely from one part of the world to another in larger quantities and in swifter manner than by high-voltage-conducted "electricity." For the first half of the twentieth century the limit-distance of technically practical deliverability of electricity was 350 miles. As a consequence of the post–World War II space program's employment and advancement of the invisible metallurgical, chemical, and electronics more-with-lessing technology, twenty-five years ago it became technically feasible and expedient to employ ultra-high-voltage and superconductivity, which can deliver electrical ener-within a radial range of 1500 miles from the system's dynamo generators.

To the World Game seminar of 1969 I presented my integrated, world-around, high-voltage electrical energy network concept. Employing the new 1500-mile transmission reach, this network made it technically feasible to span the Bering Straits to integrate the Alaskan U.S.A. and Canadian networks with Russia's grid, which had recently been extended eastward into northern Siberia and Kamchatka to harness with hydroelectric dams the several powerful northwardly flowing rivers of northeasternmost U.S.S.R. This proposed network would interlink the daylight half of the world with the nighttime half.

Electrical-energy integration of the night and day regions of the Earth will bring all the capacity into use at all times, thus overnight doubling the generating capacity of humanity because it will integrate all the most extreme night and day peaks and valleys. From the Bering Straits, Europe and Africa will be integrated westwardly through the U.S.S.R., and China, Southeast Asia; India will become network-integrated southwardly through the U.S.S.R. Central and South America will be integrated southwardly through Canada, the U.S.A., and Mexico.

Graphs of each of the world's 150 nations showing their twentieth-century histories of inanimate energy production per capita of their respective populations together with graphs of those countries' birthrates show without exception that the birthrates decrease at exactly the same rate that the per capita consumption of inanimate electrical energy increases. The world's population will stop increasing when and if the integrated world electrical energy grid is realized. This grid is the World Game's highest priority objective. (See Fig. 36.)

There is no single power source around Earth so great as that of the wind. But winds do not blow in synchronization with the time patterning of hu-

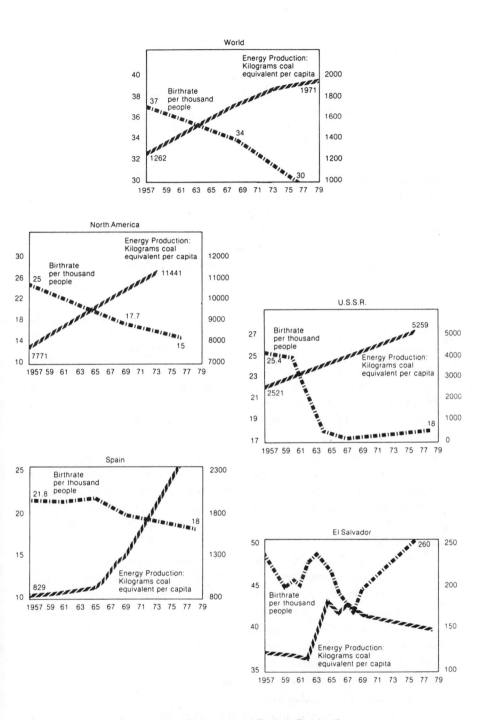

FIGURE 36.   Birthrate and Energy Production

man needs. Generating electricity when the wind blows and feeding it into batteries and withdrawing the charge when needed involves a 75-percent in-and-out loss of the electrical energy. Since 1975, when it was an efficient but new practice, all fifty U.S.A. states have been required by federal regulation to allow individual windmill owners to feed their windpower-generated electric current directly into the local utility power lines. The individuals get credited for their input on their monthly electricity bills. This practice was developed by Windworks of Wisconsin, which in turn was founded by a mid-1960s World Game prototyping operation. It has been found that within a 100-mile radius a wind is always blowing. Windmills installed around the world converting their direct current into alternating current and feeding the electric energy into the world network can harvest the planet Earth's prime daily energy income source—the wind—and adequately supply all the world's energy needs.

With the world's prime resources and its people and its potential integratabilities evidenced by World Game's world map, obvious design science inventions are called for, such as a "backbone" irrigation canal from the Himalayas leading south along the central highlands of the Indian continent, wherewith all the frequently devastating droughts would be eliminated for India's one-eighth of all humanity.

With such comprehensive viewability as is provided by World Game and its Sky-Ocean World Map, it is quickly realized that (with a few rare exceptions) humanity need do very little further mining. The metals already scrapped from obsolete machinery and structures, which recirculate on a sum-total-of-all-metals-average every twenty-two years, are now able to do so much more work with ever less weight per each given function with each recirculation as to make the present scrap resources of almost all metals adequate to take care of all humanity's forward needs.

While World Game discovers and identifies the world income energy sources,* it is also concerned with using the energy income in the most efficient technologies. In producing liquid-fuel-energy-powered engines, World Game's design science must pay attention to the fact that reciprocating engines such as are installed in all our automobiles are only 15-percent efficient, turbines are 30-percent efficient, jet propulsion engines are 65-percent efficient, and fuel cells are 80-percent efficient. Due to inefficiently designed technical equipment and building technology, the overall mechanical efficiency of the United States economy is in 1980 only 5 percent. This means that for every one hundred units of energy consumed, ninety-five units go unused—"down the drain."

---

*See World Game Laboratory's *Energy, Earth and Everyone* by Medard Gabel, Doubleday, rev. ed., 1980.

Using only proven and now-available technology, it is feasible to increase the overall efficiency to 15 percent. This alone would reduce our overall energy consumption by two-thirds.

There are two kinds of objective engineering designing: objects that consist of a plurality of intercomplementarily moving parts (machinery) and those that do not (structures). Mechanical efficiency denotes the percent of work effectiveness accomplished by the machine per units of energy consumed. Structural efficiency relates to the functions, strength, and durability accomplished per each unit of weight of material involved.

Humanly occupied environment-controlling structures have many energy-wasting features, all of which are highly correctable. In designing the environment-controlling structural enclosures, World Game's design science heeds the following facts:

(A) Spherical structures enclose the greatest volume with least surface.

(B) Geodesic spherical structures, which are inherently omnitriangularly framed entirely of great-circle chords, give the strongest structure per weight of materials employed.

(C) Amongst the geodesic great-circle spherical structures, those based on the discontinuous compression, continuous tension—"tensegrity"—icosahedra give the most environmental enclosure per pound and volume of material employed.

(D) Every time the linear dimension of a symmetrical structure is doubled (i.e. $1 \rightarrow 2$) the surface area of the enclosure increases at a two to the second-power rate (i.e., 2^2), while the environment-controlling structure's volume increases at a two to the third-power rate (i.e., 2^3). Wherefore, every time a geodesic dome's diameter is doubled, it has eight times as many contained molecules of atmosphere but only four times as much enclosing shell—ergo, each progressive doubling of dome diameters halves the amount of enclosing surface through which each molecule of interior atmosphere may either gain or lose energy as heat. (See "Old Man River's City" project, pp. 315–23.) Whole cities are most efficiently enclosed under one large dome.

(E) Every time we enclose a geodesic dome within a greater-diametered geodesic dome whose radially concentric interspacing is greater than the depth of the frost penetration of that area, while at the same time avoiding use of any metal interconnections between the inner and outer domes' structuring, the heat losses and gains of the innermost domes are halved in respect to those of non-domed-over domes of the same dimensions.

(F) If in producing the geodesic domes-within-domes we make them transparent or translucent on their sunny side and opaque and inwardly reflecting on the nonsunny side, they will entrap progressively greater amounts of Sun energy as heat for longer and greater periods of time as the diameters are increased.

(G) If growing vegetation—i.e., trees, vegetables, corn, sugar, ground cover, etc.—is planted within the dome, the photosynthetic conversion of Sun radiation into hydrocarbon molecules will chemically and simultaneously

   (1) convert the monoxide gases given off by human occupants into human-supporting (air) atmosphere, thus eliminating all necessity for windows or air conditioning apparatus, and

   (2) harvest hydrocarbon molecule-trapped energy as food or as fuel-alcohol energy.

(H) If the wind drag of buildings is employed to turbine-convert wind-power into tank-stored compressed air, the latter may be stored within the space between the inner and outer domes' skins as low-pressure atmosphere in quantities adequate to pneumatically and evenly distribute any concentrated outer cover loadings throughout all the tensional components of the geodesic-tensegrity structures.

(I) As the Sun's radiation is outwardly and diffusingly reflected by the

FIGURE 37. The dome housed the exhibit of the University of Science and Technology, Kumasi, at Ghana's first international trade fair.

FIGURE 38. Illustration depicts use of the Bernoulli effect as applied to a geodesic dome. Upward draft is caused by solar heating of outside surface which then heats nearby surrounding air. The warm air rises creating a thermal column. Air is sucked out of the large openings at the ground level causing reduced pressure inside the dome. Reduced pressure causes air near top vent to rush in through small opening. Increased flow of air through small opening cools the incoming air.

dome structure's convex outer surface, vertical thermal-column movements of the Sun-heated outside atmosphere develop, which spirally rising columns of heated atmosphere will draw air out from under the dome's large lower-edge summertime openings, which voluminous outward drafting in turn pulls air into the dome through the small cross-sectioned ventilators at the dome's apex. This pressure differential between the small air entry and large exhaust openings produces the Bernoulli chilling effect, which in hot weather will swiftly cool the dome's interior atmosphere. World Game has proven this in geodesic domes at the African equator.

(J) It is clearly demonstrable that the conversion of windpower by dome-within-dome, drag-operated air turbines will power the compressing and tank storage of air and will thus produce ample power to operate a pneumatic-tool system for all mechanical operating needs within the dome. Pneumatic tools avoid the human-electrocution perils of electrically operated domestic technology.

(K) Sum-totally it is now demonstrable that properly designed domes within domes become energy-harvesting machines that provide more energy than is needed for the high-standard life support of their human occupants, wherefore such dwelling machines may become exporters of energy in variously stored and controlled forms, such as alcohol.

(L) It has been satisfactorily demonstrated that the reflective, concave inner surface of the geodesic, dome-within-dome, environment-controlling shells will act as parabolic, Sun-radiation concentrators, focusing the Sun radiation income into heating of a circularly arced, liquid-containing pipe, whereby the Sun's heat may be stored liquidly in vacuum-enclosed subterranean tanks for subsequent use in a variety of ways. The by-product heat from the air compressing is used to heat water stored in the same reservoir.

(M) World Game's design science treats the tensegrity-structured, dome-within-dome geodesic environment controls as comprehensive energy-harvesting, -storing, and -exchanging devices. Typically, the vegetation most efficiently employed includes the growth of corn and the "winged bean" in the sunlight area and mushrooms in the hot, dark areas.

(N) Radiotelephones and income-energy generators render the dwelling machine semiautonomous.

(O) Two sanitary devices as described earlier render the environment controls independent of water-supply lines and sewage-carry-away systems:
  (1) the fog gun for cleaning the human skin and all other surfaces with a high-pressure air gun into whose airstream small amounts of atomized water are fed;
  (2) the carton packaging and mechanized, convey-away system of human wastes to be delivered to elsewhere-located fertilizer or gas-generating works or to anaerobic methane gas and dry fertilizer-generating equipment of the dwelling machines themselves.

These two devices eliminate all wet plumbing, which has been responsible for breeding most of all the infectious bacteria heretofore entering human abodes, while also eliminating the infectious splashback feature of water-filled bowls and their water-flushed toilets.

World Game finds that wealth measures the degree to which humans have used their minds to discover scientific principles and have used those principles to invent artifacts and environment-controlling and -implementing, complex-artifact systems which, as powered only by daily energy income, can be demonstrably shown to be able to take care of given numbers of people for given numbers of forward days. "Taking care" of humans means to provide them with "pleasingly," healthily, satisfactorily stabilized environmental conditions under all of nature's known potential variables while adequately feeding them, giving them medical care, increasing their degrees of freedom, and increasing their technological options (see *Operating Manual for Spaceship Earth*).

As already mentioned, World Game finds that the world's wealth and its medium of interchanges—i.e., the world's monetary accounting systems—have been divorced from one another. Those bankers and insurance-company managements that have learned how they may legally employ to their own exclusive advantage the vast magnitudes of savings of real wealth deposited with them by those who have produced the wealth and who are quite unaware that those deposits are taken out of the bank and loaned out at swiftly increasing interest rates to others in such quantities as to underwrite the magnitude of purchasing, production, and sale of products that can be produced only by the involvements of such vast magnitudes of real-wealth tokens, and may therefore overpower all wealth capabilities of any of the individual depositors of the savings-account deposits of the real-wealth products.

World Gaming requires progressive inventorying of condensed recalls of already introduced major concepts and their integration with one another, plus additional new concepts to produce newer and greater synergetic realization.

* * *

In the reality of physical-resource and knowledge potential we have four billion billionaires on our planet, the probating and delivery of whose legacy, as amassed by the more-with-lessing contributions and loving sacrifices of all humans in all history, has been postponed by the game of making money with money by those who as yet misinformedly operate on the 1810 Malthusian assumption that "humanity is multiplying its population at a geometric rate while increasing its life-support foods, etc., only at an arithmetic rate"—ergo, the money-makers assume that there is nowhere nearly enough life support for all. Malthus said the majority of humans are designed to suffer and die far short of their potential life-span. Darwin's "survival only of the fittest" dictum has combined with that of Malthus to persuade the "haves" to be intelligently selfish and to legally fortify their "haveness" position against the "have-nots."

With legal planning of their lawyer-advised banking leaders, the "haves" have now succeeded in cornering all the world's monetary gold as well as the preponderance of the world's petroleum sources—along with their refineries and world-around petro-delivery systems together also with acquisitions of all the atomic power-generating plants, originally paid for by the U.S. taxpayers—and thereafter in severing the *monetary system* from the *wealth system* while marking up the negotiable equity value of gold and petroleum tenfold. They also have contrived their own game of international monetary banking of international balances of trade and credit accounting, greatly aided by the priorly established existence of 150 "sovereign" nations around planet Earth.

The division of world political power into 150 sovereign nations is a consequence of thousands of years of successive and individually independent contriving of history's most powerful leaders. The number-one strategy of the successful leaders of history's successively established supreme socioeconomic control systems has always been to induce the spontaneous self-divisioning of those designed to be conquered and to keep them spontaneously self-dividing and their divisions lethally interarrayed against one another in order to keep them conquered. The longer the self-divisionings can be self-perpetuating, the more spontaneously are the divisions accepted institutionally by the successive generations as being "natural" divisions, seemingly as inherently and individually existent as are different hills, valleys, rivers, and biological species. The prime vulnerabilities of humanity, which make it subject to spontaneous self-dividing, are those of different speech patterns, skin color, religions, social customs, class or caste systems, political preferences, and all varieties of individually unique "troubles," suffering, and discontent.

The historical consequence of this aeons-ago-commenced employment of this grand strategy of "divide to conquer and keep divided to keep conquered" accounts for the "natural" acceptance today by world peoples of the seemingly "God-given" existence of 150 sovereign nations of the world and their respective geographical division of all the world's dry land (as well as for all the specialized categories of human activities). This prime strategy of supreme-power wielders accounts for all the many local political divisions within the sovereign nations as well as for all the religions and for the officially encouraged maintenance of the many languages and proud maintenance of local dialects. Above all that number-one strategy accounts for the emotionally enflamed maintenance of the concepts of different races and classes of human beings and their division into highly specialized categories as "culturally" maintained by the various systems and power structures over all the highly educated individuals and those intellectuals who, if not focused professionally on highly specialized subjects, might otherwise—as comprehensivists—seem potentially dangerous to the rulers.

It is highly relevant to the foregoing that in 1959 science had incontrovertibly demonstrated that all the known anthropological and biological case histories comprehensively and scientifically explored show that the extinctions of all human tribes and of all biological species have always been brought about by overspecializations resultant upon either willful or environment-induced inbreeding. If, for instance, we inbreed—by mating two fast-running horses—there is the mathematical probability of concentrating the fast-running genes but also of breeding in this special capability only by inadvertently breeding out the general adaptability to cope with the infrequent high-energy-concentrating events. For example, exquisitely designed birds' wings are a hindrance in walking, and the long bills of wading birds, which are perfect for marshland foraging, are relatively useless in other less specialized feeding. Generalized adaptability is needed to cope with large changes in the environment. Here lies the present chief peril of the human passengers on Spaceship Earth.

World Game makes it clear that the world electrical systems' energy-network integration and its comprehensive powering of automated, special case machinery would most effectively counter the peril of overspecialization of the humans and would introduce the omni-Universe-operative, time-energy, kilowatt-hours-per-year, commonwealth accounting system. This cosmic accounting will computer-establish the up-to-the-moment-realized cosmic-energy-income-harnessing thus far accomplished; and the technical-efficiency levels attained in the various energy-employing technologies operative around the world; and the resultant per capita individually employable world commonwealth facilities; and the per capita "consumable," "employable," and "enjoyable" "credits" in respect to any specific consumables, commodities, services, conveniences, or tools as manifest on the satellite-relay-integrated world computers and as individually called for and read out on each individual's electronic computer "credit card." The individually available information will govern the individual's design science choices of the highest relative-efficiency systems to be employed. It will also tell people whether they can do this or that, and if so, how they can go most swiftly—for instance, from New York to Australia—and will "book" a travel reservation and will prepay the bill for the travel accommodation. All such information is continually computer-integrated to produce the commonwealth evaluations and their read-out-ability on world-individual's pocket-computer "credit card." These will always register the world individual's share of the ever-increasingly-employable technological savings reserves and their respective technologically operative capabilities. With humanity employing such a world-around, satellite-relayed, and world-integrated computer accounting system, the world can, overnight, physically realize the "Omnibillionaire Commonwealth" of its humans.

Because (1) the interalloying of metals produces the invisible revolution of ever-higher-strength and -durability performance per pound of material employed, and because (2) the ever-higher performances produce new conditions of technological challenge, new alloys and new atomic circuits are progressively discovered and developed to provide ever-more-satisfactorily-advanced performances, and because (3) the structures and energy-operated machines using the ever-improving metal-alloy capabilities progressively make obsolete the older machines and structures, the latter become progressively scrapped and melted. It is World Game's concern to see that the progressively recovered metals are alloyed anew in ever-higher-performance atomic arrangements and are ever more promptly re-employed in new machinery and structures of ever-higher performance with ever-less weights and volumetric bulks. This progression is known in World Gaming as "Ever-Progressively-Accelerating Ephemeralization."

Wherefore: with every accelerated scrapping, recovery, and recirculation the same basic metals and the alloys of those metals progressively serve the needs of ever more people at ever-higher standards of performance. Thus we discover that the world's already-mined and -used, ever-recirculating metals become the technologically regenerative, universal "bloodstream" for realizing the ever-improving know-how of human advancement of its ever-increasing ability to cope with vital challenges. The metals, and chemistries in general, have thus become the recirculatable medium upon which is loaded the new, advanced design science inventions resultant upon progressively advancing experiences and knowledge of humanity regarding how to cope more effectively with life's evolutionarily successive challenges.

Within the twentieth century this invisible revolution of "continually learning how to do more with the same" or "more with less" resources (metallurgically, electronically, chemically, mechanically, structurally, aerodynamically, and hydrodynamically) has in only three quarters of the twentieth century brought 60 percent of humanity into enjoying a vastly more effective, healthier, and more realistically informative means of coping with life's challenges than was experienced by the most powerful monarch or financial or political potentate of 1900; furthermore, during this eighty years of time the world population has doubled, wherefore the gain has been 120-fold. During this same twentieth century's first eight decades life expectancy has been doubled for the 60 percent thus advantaged, and the range of their everyday travelability has twenty-folded. During those same eighty years that 60 percent of humanity has gone from 90-percent illiterate to 95-percent literate. They are no longer locally rooted peoples. They are on their way to becoming omni-world-around living humans preoccupied with local Universe's evolutionary affairs. In 1948 the average U.S. family moved "out of town" every five years. In 1978 they moved every three years.

In 1970 the percent of those unprecedentedly advantaged passed the 50-percent mark. Since 1970, and for the first time in history, the majority of humanity has become widely traveling "haves," in contrast to the previous multimillions of years of 99 percent of all humans being locally rooted "have-nots." The number of U.S.A. millionaires quintupled in eight years—from 110,000 in 1971 to 550,000 in 1979.

The plotted curve of the rate of gain for increasing proportions of all humanity being thus swiftly advantaged by the doing more for more people with less and less matter and energy per function—all accomplished with computers, satellites, alloys, etc.—indicates that 100 percent of *all humanity* will be thus advantaged before 2000 A.D. In less than twenty years (less than one generation) all humanity is scheduled by evolution (not by any world planning body) to become physically more successful and metaphysically more interestingly occupied than have any humans ever been in all known history—provided that humanity does not commit ignorance-, fear-, and-panic-induced total-species suicide.

Why might they panic? All the present bureaucracies of political governments, great religious organizations, and all big businesses find that physical success for all humanity would be devastating to the perpetuation of their ongoing activities. This is because all of them are founded on the premise of ameliorating individual cases while generally exploiting on behalf of their respective political, religious, or business organizations the condition of no-where-nearly-enough-life-support-for-all and its resultant great human suffering and discontent.

Reason number two for fear-wrought panic is because all of the 150 nations of our planet are about to be desovereignized by evolution; that is, they are about to become operatively obsolete—about to be given up altogether. There are millions in the U.S.A., for instance, who on discovery that their government was about to become bankrupt and defunct would become activist "patriots," and might get out their guns and start a Nazi movement, seeking dictatorially to reinstate the "good old days." If people in many of the 150 nations succeeded in re-establishing their sovereignties and all the customs-barrier, balance-of-trade shacklings, it would soon be discovered that the 150 nations represent 150 "blood clots" imperiling the free inter-flowing of the evolution-producing metals and products recirculation as well as of the popular technical know-how disseminating.

We have today, in fact, 150 supreme admirals and only one ship—Spaceship Earth. We have the 150 admirals in their 150 staterooms each trying to run their respective stateroom as if it were a separate ship. We have the starboard side admirals' league trying to sink the port side admirals' league. If either is successful in careening the ship to drown the "enemy" side, the whole ship will be lost.

Long ago the world's great religions learned how to become transnational or more effectively supranational. Next the world's great ideologies learned how to become supranational. Most recently the world's largest financial-enterprise corporations have become completely supranational in their operation. Big religion, ideologies, and businesses alike found it intolerable to operate only within 150 walled-in pens. Freeing themselves by graduating into supranational status, they have left all the people in the 150 pens to struggle with all the disadvantages of 150 mutually opposed economic policies. The European Economic Community is a local attempt to cope with this world problem.

The United States of America is not a nation. Nations are large tribes of humans that have been geographically isolated for millennia and have progressively inbred the physical types surviving under those unique geographical conditions. As mentioned, the U.S.S.R. had 146 naturally evolved "nations" to integrate, the physiognomies of each U.S.S.R. nation looking quite different from the others'. The United States of America is a cross-breeding integration of humans from all the nations of the planet Earth; though often speaking of itself as the United States of America, it is not America. Its population is only one-half that of North and South America. The North Americans, consisting of Canadians, the U.S. citizens, and Mexicans, are evolutionarily cross-breeding into a single hybrid family of world humans.

As a sequel to the foregoing scientific data (see Chapter 1, pp. 9–11), which proves the invalidity of humanity's assumption of a plurality of different races and classes of humans to exist on our planet, the computer will be able to help in discovering the swiftest course for humanity to pursue in order to free itself of such self-deception. The computer can also disclose the economic savings of humanity to be accomplished by elimination of race, class, and creed differentials. The computers can and will show the increases in commonwealth to be realized by such elimination of false premises in social judgments.

World Gaming produces truthful, ergo corresponding, insights that are popularly communicable by world-around, satellite-relayed television, the practical workings of which, and their demonstrably favorable results for all, may readily induce agreeing vision and courage on the part of all individuals of spontaneously and progressively intercooperative humanity.

It is the *invisibility* of the alloys and chemistries and of the electronic circuitry of the design science revolution which finds that revolution to be as yet uncomprehended and ignorantly opposed by humanity's reliance only on yesterday's politically visible means of problem-solving. It is both the invisibility and misinformedness that occasions the lack of spontaneous popular support of the invisible design science revolution by the most powerful political and money-making systems. Big government can see no way to collect taxes to run its bureaucracy if people are served directly and individually by daily cosmic-energy-wealth income. Money-makers cannot find a way of putting meters between people and the wind, Sun, waves, etc. Neither big government nor big business pays any serious attention to the fact that we can live on our energy income, rather than on nature's energy savings account (fossil fuels), or by burning our Spaceship Earth's physical hull, which consists entirely of atomic energy in the form of matter.

In 1969 I initiated, and students developed, what have since become annual World Game seminars, attended by university faculties, students, scientists, engineers, and government officials—for its first three years at Southern Illinois University, next at the University of Southern California, and thereafter for four years at the University of Pennsylvania, and for one year at the University of Massachusetts. In 1979 the seminar was conducted partially at New York University and partially at the University of Pennsylvania; in 1980, at the University of Pennsylvania.

Seven years ago the World Game's annual research activity culminated in a book written by Medard Gabel, *Energy, Earth, and Everyone* (Doubleday, rev. ed., 1980), which demonstrated beyond any argument that humanity can carry on handsomely and adequately when advantaged only by its daily energy income from the Sun-gravity system. World Game also published a second book by Medard Gabel, *Ho-Ping: Food for Everyone* (Doubleday, 1979)—this time on world food resources, which shows that we can take ample care of all human food needs. The 1979 World Game was participated in by many experts on world food matters.

World Game will become increasingly effective in its prognoses and programming when the world-around, satellite-interrelayed computer system and its omni-Universe-operative (time-energy) accounting system are established. This system will identify the kilowatt-hour-expressed world inventory of foods, raw and recirculating resources, and all the world's unique mechanical and structural capabilities and their operating capacities as well as the respective kilowatt-hours of available energy-income-derived operating power with which to put their facilities to work. All the foregoing information will become available in respect to all the world-around technology's environment-controlling, life-sustaining, travel- and communication-accommodating structures and machines.

All the sulphur coming annually out of all the chimneys around the world exactly equals the amount of new sulphur being mined and distributed annually to keep world industry going. The people who let the sulphur go into the air are not in the sulphur business.

World government will require all industries to install the already-successfully-proven technology and therewith precipitate and recover all their profitwise-unwanted chemical by-products. Underwriting all those costs of installation and operation, world government will give tax credits to all those industries complying with the order, so that those industries can compete with those in the industry who do not have such pollution problems. World government will then stockpile all the chemical substances recovered from all previous liquid, gaseous, or solid dumpings, fumings, or runnings-off—known ignorantly as "pollution." The value of the recovered resources will more than offset the tax rebates given by the government in order to enforce precipitation. All the chemical substances in all their states are essential to the maintenance of the integrity of eternally regenerative Universe. Nature has no "pollution." This is a word coined in human ignorance regarding the presence of the right chemicals being released in the wrong places by those who profit only through selfish preoccupation and nonconsideration of others. The hour-to-hour changes in the inventory of world-government stockpiling of all recirculatable substances will be constantly fed into the world-integrated computer together with locations and summaries of the total inventories available for new tasks. World government will replace altogether all the scrapmongers who, to increase prices, hold their products off the market until they become scarce.

World Game records make it clear that the big money-makers of early U.S.A. history, those who funded the Harvard Business School, the Wharton School of Finance, etc., may have made their money in ways that were legal but ruthlessly scheming. The students at today's business schools are not given courses on how to cheat your mother-in-law or how to sell your friends short. Because the business schools make it plausible that fortunes may be won in a legal manner, we have present-day business executives trying to find legal ways of getting the public's money.

World Gaming makes it eminently clear that the simplest way for top executives of the supercorporations to make profits and keep their own salaries rising is to make their corporation the first in its field to raise prices despite any government, public, or labor opposition. The second way is to cut down on personnel at the retailing level and to force customers to wait in lines. No single human waiting line seems too formidable by itself, but if we consider all those standing in all the lines at all the different airlines at all the world's airports—as the computer does—and all the people wanting to secure an airline ticket waiting for half an hour on the telephone after hearing the ticket clerk's "Please hold," and all the people waiting for twenty minutes to place their orders in all the restaurants around the world, we discover the billions of human hours sacrificed daily by people whose time is of high value. Those in lines are being legally robbed of billions of their life-hour dollars, which go to the corporate profit account as savings in labor costs.

All the banks and airlines are now placing in their foyers chrome metal standards suspending velvet ropes within which the queue of customers may be neatly snaked. Airplanes have been squeezing paying passengers closer and closer together in wider planes until as many as eleven people sit abreast today.

The World Game–maintained inventory of socially abundant *resources* breaks down into eight main categories:

1. Reliably operative and subconsciously sustaining, effectively available twenty-four hours a day, anywhere in the Universe: *gravity, love.*
2. Available only within ten miles of the surface of the Earth in sufficient quantity to conduct sound: i.e., the complex of atmospheric gases whose Sun-induced expansion on the sunny side and shadow-side-of-the-world-induced contraction together produce the world's *winds,* which in turn produce all the world's *waves.*
3. Available in sufficient quantity to sustain human life only within two miles above planet Earth's spherical surface: *oxygen.*
4. Available aboard our planet only during the day: *sunlight.*
5. Not everywhere or everywhen available: *water, food, clothing, shelter, vision, initiative, friendliness.*
6. Only partially available for individual human consumption, being also required for industrial production: e.g., *water.*
7. Not publicly available because used entirely by industry: e.g., *helium.*
8. Not available to industry because used entirely by scientific laboratories: e.g., *moon rocks.*

World Game's integrated world computer system will have the task of differentiating out the abundant resources and facilities from the scarce, and differentiating the scarce into degrees of scarcity as well as into the day-to-day fluctuations of the borderline cases. The computer will keep constant track of where the resources are geographically located or where they are traveling. That which is in constant abundance is 100-percent socializable. That which is scarce must be reserved for tasks that serve all society in general. The element oxygen in the atmosphere is in abundance at sea level and need not be distributed by artifacts. Oxygen at 11,000 feet and more above sea level is critically scarce and must be compressed into tanks and distributed for breathing through masks and tubes.

The gas helium is very scarce on planet Earth. It has very important, unique characteristics. Number one, it is not flammable, as is hydrogen, though it weighs almost as little as hydrogen. Helium, though the socially theoretical property of everyone, becomes useless to anyone if compressed into four billion separate bottles, each of which is distributed to each of our at-present four billion Earthians. There are a number of technical tasks that helium can perform to the advantage of all humanity, all of which can be programmed into the computer.

The relative abundance of the ninety-two regenerative chemical elements in the thus-far-known Universe is about the same as the inventory of their relative abundance on Earth. The relative abundance of the chemical elements is also approximately the same as that of their occurrence in the organisms of the human bodies. All this data and all the tasks that can be performed by each element to the greatest advantage of all humanity will be programmed into the world-integrated computers to make it evident to all humanity which eco-technological strategy at any given time will produce the highest advantage for all, against which information it can be determined what alternative advantages might attend implementing and supplying the essentials for realization of newly proposed invention initiatives of various humans.

It was World Game that asked, as described before, one of the world's greatest oil geologists, François de Chadenèdes, if he could write an accurate scenario of nature producing petroleum on planet Earth through the photosynthetic transformation-into-hydrocarbon of Sun radiation by the vegetation and algae and the succession of events following their transformation as the vegetation is consumed by other biologicals, or is transformed into various residues, all of which are blown by winds or washed by streams and gradually accumulate in various geographical locations and become progressively buried within the planet's outer crust. Thereafter there were various heats and pressures (caused by ice ages, etc.), earthquakes, or deep burial below water or soil until those chemical heats and pressure conditions occurred which are essential to the production of petroleum. De Chadenèdes said he could, and after a year he presented us with the scenario with all of its time increments and pressure conditions spelled out. We then asked him to figure how much it would cost nature per each gallon of petroleum for that much pressure and heat for that much time, were it calculated at the retail rate for that much energy for that length of time as charged us by the public utilities. The cost came to well over a million dollars per gallon.

Since World Game's accounting system is that of the Universe's own time-energy intertransforming requirements, we must accept as cosmically unquestionable this costing of petroleum, coal, and gas resources, which nature has been syntropically importing and accumulating on planet Earth in order, ten billion years hence, to turn the Earth into an energy-exporting (entropic) star.

For this reason World Game considers all fossil fuels to be nature's own savings account, deposited in our "Earth bank" and not to be stolen by exploiters. Everyone knows that we should live on our (energy) income and not our savings account. Nor should we burn our capital-account production equipment in order to produce meter-marketable energy, for there will soon be no further production capability. Atomic energy by fission or fusion constitutes burning our terrestrial production equipment.

As mentioned, World Game finds that 60 percent of all the jobs in the U.S.A. are not producing any real wealth—i.e., real life support. They are in fear-underwriting industries or are checking-on-other-checkers, etc. The majority of the jobs occasion the individuals using three to four gallons per day in their automobiles to go to and from work—at true cosmic costing this means four million dollars per worker per day. Obviously the computer finds that it would save the planet Earth's energy account $500 trillion a day to give all the non-wealth-producing workers their full pay to stay at home.

In the same way the World Game's world-around-integrated computers will show that it will save-pay handsomely to pay all professors and teachers in full to stay at home or in their laboratories and relinquish all teaching to video cassettes, whose selectable programs are to be called out by the individual students of all ages around the world to be shown on their home television sets. The old educational facilities and a small fraction of individual teachers who love most to teach will use the old educational facilities within which to produce the cassette programs.

The computer will prove to society that it will pay to introduce automation wherever feasible and to allow the machines to work twenty-four-hour days while paying yesterday's workers in full to stay home. Only those who love each particular technology will keep the world-around video education in operation. Those who pass the exams to qualify for such working will not be paid for it. They will act as does any amateur athlete—doing what they do for the love of it. This competing to qualify for all the production and service jobs will govern all work. The work will not be paid for. Everything the individual needs is already paid for. Rudyard Kipling's "L'Envois" tells the story.

> *When Earth's last picture is painted,*
> *And the tubes are all twisted and dried,*

The oldest of colors have faded
And the youngest of critics have died,
We shall rest
And well shall we need to
Lie down for an eon or two
'Til the master of all good workmen
Shall put us to work anew.

Then only the master shall praise us,
And only the master shall blame,
No one will work for money,
And no one will work for fame.
But all for the love of the working
And each in his separate star
Shall draw the thing as he sees it
For the God of things as they are.

World Game shows that we can discontinue newspapers and save the trees for fuel-alcohol production. World Game finds that all news can be disseminated by television and that computers can keep track of all the information that fills the advertising and want-advertisement pages, and any individual looking for any kind of opportunity can get the matching information from the computer in seconds. Individuals can go shopping by cable television.

Local Universe is the term used by World Game to identify the macrocosmic limits of human observation. These macro-limits are identified as the radius of the present maximum phototelescopic-and-radar-reached information (in 1980 the spherical sweepout of an approximately eleven-and-one-half-billion-light-year radius) around planet Earth in all directions.

World Game takes the inventory of relative abundance of all the chemical elements present within that radius as spectroscopically analyzed by the light received in all directions around us from all the stars of all the galaxies within that eleven-and-one-half-billion-light-year radial distance.

World Game takes the relative abundance of all the chemical elements thus far found on planet Earth. The local Universe inventories and the Earthian inventory of the relative abundance are somewhat similar, as is the relative abundance of the chemical elements present or acceptably present in human beings' bodies. The Earthian inventory includes all the isotopes of all the chemical elements and the relative abundance of the latter. In respect to the Earthian abundance, some of the elements are so relatively plenitudinous as to make them available for various universal technological uses; they are therefore socializable, but only when employed with other elements in instruments, machinery, structures, medicines, and nutriment.

World Game notes that gold is the most electrically conductive of all elements. It is also the most highly reflective of all metals, and therefore has many functional uses. New computer circuiting and such functions as the new laser energy beaming with rubies will occupy the majority of the rare metals and jewels.

Rubies function in producing laser beams, etc. Diamonds, being the hardest of all elements, have many cutting and other technical functions. All the rare stones and metals will have industry's unique industrial tasks to perform. The question then arises as to who will determine which technological initiatives should have prior access to the inherently scarce, high-advantage functionings of the scarce and rare inventories of chemical elements.

World Game finds that the computers fed with all the relevant energy-efficiency facts will be able to demonstrate which uses will produce the greatest long-term benefit for all humanity.

World Game foresees that the greatest problems for humanity to solve in the future will be how to accommodate the initiatives of millions of humans who, freed from muscle- and nerve-reflexing jobs, find their inventory of past experiences and their minds integrating synergetically to envision ever-greater advantages to be realized for humanity. We will realize this age of regenerative inventing which is rendering humans very effective in their cosmic functioning as local Universe information-gatherers and local Universe problem-solvers in support of the integrity of eternally regenerative Universe.

* * *

I consider it essential to pay all my bills in the swiftest possible manner. In whatever system I find myself I commit myself to "play the game," for I am not a political revolutionary; I am a design science revolutionary.

Responding to criticism by individuals who said that the reason Buckminster Fuller was not *trying* to "earn his living" was because he was incapable of doing so, I told one of my audiences in 1947 about *Obnoxico,* a theoretical enterprise I had invented through which I could make vast amounts of dollars in one year on an entirely legal basis—but one as typically undesirable to me as is all money-making.

I said, "You have to decide whether you want to make money or make sense, because the two are mutually exclusive."

I do not consider it to be money-making when I insist upon being refunded for the development and overhead cost of the services I perform annually for others, which performance I undertake only in response to the requests of others.

The private-enterprise corporation called Obnoxico was schematically designed only to serve as an object lesson. Obnoxico was designed to exploit the most sentimental weaknesses of humanity. In my theoretical Obnoxico's catalog the number-one item suggested that on the last day that your baby wears diapers you very carefully remove them, repin them empty, and stuff them full of tissue paper in just the shape in which they were when last occupied by your baby. You pack this assembly carefully into a strong corrugated-paperboard container and send it to Obnoxico, which will base-metallize the diapers, then gold- or silverplate them and send them back to you to be filled with ferns and hung in the back window of your car. The easily forecastable profits from this one item ran into millions of dollars per year.

Eagerly my friends of 1947 on being told of Obnoxico joined in the fun and began inventing items for its catalog. Next they began sending me Obnoxico items then beginning to come on the market in 1950 for the first time and as advertised in magazines: plastic pebbles for your garden walk and the now-prevalent, but then-new, plastic flowers.

I then showed how the contributors of the original items sent to me in fun—to keep the joke going—could be persuaded to accept shares in Obnoxico in exchange for their contributions. Then the Faustian aspect of the enterprise revealed itself, for it was clearly foreseeable that the stockholders would swiftly become so rich that they would tend to take the whole matter seriously. Overnight they would lose their sense of humor as their greed was stimulated and they became ruthlessly deliberate exploiters of humanity.

Somehow or other the theoretical Obnoxico concept has now twenty-five years later become a burgeoning reality. Private enterprise is now building airports with ever-longer walkways and hotels with ever-increasing numbers of levels of ground-floor and basement arcades to accommodate the ever-more-swiftly multiplying Obnoxico stores.

Human beings traveling away from home with cash in their pockets, thinking fondly of those left behind or soon-to-be-joined loved ones, are hooked by the realistic statuettes of four-year-old girls and boys with upturned faces saying in a cartoon "balloon," "What did you bring me, Daddy?"

As the banking system pleads for more savings-account deposits (so that they can loan your money out to others at interest plus costs) the Obnoxico industry bleeds off an ever-greater percentage of all the potential savings as they are sentimentally or jokingly spent for acrylic toilet seats with dollar bills cast in the transparent plastic material, two teddy bears hugging an alligator, etc.

World Game is Anti-Obnoxico and commits itself to making Obnoxico and allied activities obsolete rather than attacking it directly.

PART III

CHAPTER 7

Critical Path: Part One

I N SCIENTIFIC PROGNOSTICATION we have a condition analogous to a fact of archery—the farther back you are able to draw your longbow, the farther ahead you can shoot. For this reason we opened this book with our "Speculative Prehistory," taking us back five million years through four ice ages, and at least three and one-half million years of scientifically proven presence of humans on Earth. We are confident of the validity of our speculative prehistory because it is predicated on naked humans' physical limits of existence and on environmentally permitted and induced human behavior and on human artifact-altered environments and their progressive circumstance-delimiting and capability-increasing effects. It is also synergetically comprehensive.

In reviewing the full range of humans' presence on Earth we discover two main evolutionary trendings.

Class-two evolutionary trendings are all those events that seem to be resultant upon human initiative-taking or political reforms that adjust to the changes wrought by the progressive introduction of environment-altering artifacts. All the class-two evolutionary events tend to flatter human ego and persuade humanity to deceive itself by taking credit for favorable changes in circumstances while blaming other humans or "acts of God" for unfavorable changes. It therefore assumes that humanity is running the Universe wherefore, if its power-structure leaders decide that it is valid to cash in all of nature's available riches to further enrich the present rich or to protect them militarily from attacks by their assumed enemies—all at the cost of terminating human presence on planet Earth—that is the power-structure leaders' divine privilege.

All the class-one evolutionary trending is utterly transcendental to any human vision, planning, manipulation, and corruption. Class-one evolution accounts for humans' presence on Earth. It accounts for their having always been born naked, helpless for months, and inexperienced—ergo, ignorant, hungry, thirsty, curious, and therefore fated to learn how to survive only through trial-and-error-won, progressive accumulation of experience. Class-one evolution accounted for humanity's all-unexpected invention of verbal (aural, sound) communication, and thereby the integration of the experience-won information of the many, whereby the integrated information of the many increased the capability of humanity at large to cope with the exigencies of life. It is class-one evolution that led, after the progressive integration of the total experience-won information, to the unpredicted invention of writing or visual communication, by means of which the dead could speak to the living and within which total written information history human mind from time to time discovered repetitive patterns, which in turn sometimes led to the discovery of generalized scientific principles.

Class-one evolution had human fathers and mothers for multimillions of years serving as the memory-bank authority that showed children what they could safely eat and how to communicate. The parents told the children what they could or could not do to get along with the "system" into which they were born. The parents told the children what they should or should not believe. To history's children the parents were "the authority." The myriad esoteric, illiterate ways in which the parents communicated to their children were parroted by the children. Thus were esoteric dialects proliferated until their many progressive deviations multiplied the many initially different world languages.

It was class-one evolution that in the mid-1920s disclosed to the world's children and their parents that the voice coming over the radio had more up-to-the-minute information regarding many more subjects than had the parents. The parents did not tell the children that the radio people had more authoritative information—it was self-evident to the children, who witnessed their parents running next door to the neighbors to tell them what the radio people had just told them.

The people who were selected as broadcasters by the radio stations were selected for the *commonality of their diction* in contradistinction to the millions of *esoteric jargons* with which the parents had communicated. The radio people were also picked for the size and richness of their vocabularies and the facility with which they drew upon such conventionalized vocabularies.

Because it was self-evident to the children that the radio people were greater authorities than their parents, the children now emulated the diction and vocabularies of the radio people. Not to be belittled in their children's estimation, the parents learned the commonly accepted radio people's pronunciation of an ever-enlarging conventional vocabulary. Within half a century (two human generations) this completely altered and improved the world's languages.

The speed of sound is approximately 700 miles per hour. The speed of electromagnetic radiation is 700 *million* miles per hour. Sound can travel only in conducting mediums—for instance, in the Earth's atmosphere. Electromagnetic radiation can travel on indefinitely through Universe. The amount of information humans can acquire visually is a millionfold greater in range, speed, and meaning than is the information they acquire aurally.

* * *

The university and college students who became the first to make the world news as dissidents in 1965 and 1966 were born in the years TV came into the American home. The Class of '66ers were the first human beings to be reared by the "third parent," whose TV voice and TV presence were often heard and felt by the children much more than those of the two blood parents. TV daily briefed them visually—ergo, vividly—on the world-around news, regarding the world's continual aches, pains, disasters, Olympic triumphs, etc.

The young were saying, "I know that Dad and Mom love me to pieces, and I love them to pieces, but they don't know what it's all about. They come home from the office or golf links or hairdressers and sit down to beer and small talk or 'sitcoms.' They have nothing to do with our going into Vietnam. They have nothing to do with our going to the Moon. They have nothing to do with anything except earning a living—and spending it on TV-advertised goods. The whole world is in great trouble. My compassion is for all the people anywhere who are in trouble. Since the older people don't seem to know what is going on and are too preoccupied with irrelevancies, I and my contemporaries must do our own thinking and find out what needs to be done to make the world work."

As we wrote in the opening lines of our "Self-Disciplines," Chapter 4, up to the time of the radio the older people were always saying to the young, "Never mind what you think. Listen. We are trying to teach you." With the TV making it clear to the young that the parents did not know much about anything and were not "the authority," the young, responding to intuition, said to themselves, "I am going to have to do my own thinking and take my own actions." Nonetheless, they were utterly unskilled in world affairs, highly idealistic, and easily exploitable.

The abrupt, spontaneous historical events on the Berkeley campus of the University of California and elsewhere occasioned youth's discarding forev-

er the authority of their elders. The Class of 1966 shocked the world by saying that it felt no special loyalty to its families, its university, its state, or
its nation. The youth of the Class of 1966 were thought by the oldsters to
be shockingly immoral and lacking in idealism. Not so! They were as idealistic and full of compassion as any child has ever been, but their loyalty
was to *all humanity*. They were no longer the victims of local class or race
bias. Their idealism was at first skillfully exploited by the psycho-guerrilla
warfaring of the communist-capitalist secret operations. Soon the young realized that they were using their heads for punching bags and cudgel targets
instead of for thinking. Many of their numbers began to listen to my lectures
about solving problems by appropriate technology instead of by physical
struggling or political revolution. Informed by me, they began to say man-
kind can do anything it wants. "Why don't our officials and families stop
talking about their local biases and wasting wealth on warring—all because
they assume that 'war is necessary' simply because there does not seem to
be enough to take care of even one-half of humanity's needs."

The young ones asked, "Why not up the performances per units of invested resources and thus make enough to go around?" Their elders repeated, "Never mind what you think," so the young ones stopped asking.

Occurring after millions of years of the absolute unquestioned caring for
the young by the authority of the elders, this metaphysical cutoff—like its
physical counterpart, the cutting of the umbilical cord after the child is born
and has access to its own oxygen—occurred when humanity had acquired
enough relevantly critical information to be able to proceed on its own initiatives divested of the many misinterpretations by the elders as to the total
significance of the total information. This cut-off experience is typical of all
class-one evolution, which is always transcendental to all class-two evolution—to human planning, contriving, manipulation, or corruption.

Also typical of class-one evolution are the two trends we have mentioned
so many times in the previous chapters—the *invisible* chemical, metallurgical, and electronic production of ever-more-efficient and satisfyingly effective performance with the investment of ever-less weight and volume of
materials per unit function formed or performed—i.e., *ephemeralization*—
accomplished within ever-less increments of time—i.e., *acceleration*.

These coordinate class-one evolutionary trendings, which have been manifest for three quarters of a century, are as yet unrecognized by any world
economists, heads of state, or business leaders. Though there is a popular
intuition that acceleration may be in evidence, it is not officially heeded. Individuals amongst political and business leaders are often aware of changing
conditions, such as that which makes suddenly available a pocket calculator
or a quartz watch. They do not comprehend that these individual "goodies"

are parts of overall *ephemeralization* and *acceleration* trending that, within only three quarters of a century, has converted those enjoying an adequate and pleasing standard of living from less than 1 percent of all humanity in 1900 to 60 percent of all humanity in 1980, the latter enjoying an even higher standard of living than had been enjoyed before 1900 by any of the world's kings or financial potentates of all history. Class-one evolution alone accounts for the doubling within this century of the life "expectancy" of that 60 percent of all humanity which, by 1980, has had its standard of living so spectacularly advanced.

* * *

All technical evolution has a fundamental behavior pattern. First there is scientific discovery of a generalized principle, which occurs as a subjective realization by an experimentally probing individual. Next comes objective employment of that principle in a special case invention. Next the invention is reduced to practice. This gives humanity an increased technical advantage over the physical environment. If successful as a tool of society, the invention is used in bigger, swifter, and everyday ways. For instance, it goes progressively from a little steel steamship to ever-bigger fleets of constantly swifter, higher-powered ocean giants.

There comes a time, however, when we discover other ways of doing the same task more economically—as, for instance, when we discover that a 200-ton transoceanic jet airplane—considered on an annual round-trip-frequency basis—can outperform the passenger-carrying capability of the 85,000-ton *Queen Mary*.

All the technical curves rise in tonnage and volumetric size to reach a "giant" peak, after which progressive miniaturization sets in. After that, a new and more economical art takes over and then goes through the same cycle of doing progressively more with less, first by getting bigger and taking advantage, for instance, of the fact that doubling the length of a ship increases its wetted surface fourfold but increases its payload volume eightfold. Inasmuch as the cost of driving progressively bigger ships through the water at a given speed increases in direct proportion to the increase in friction of the wetted surface, the eightfolding of payload volume gained with each fourfolding of wetted surface means twice as much profit for the same effort each time the ship's length is doubled.

This principle of advantage gain through geometric size increase holds true for ships of both air and water. Eventually doubling of length of seagoing ships finally runs into trouble. For instance, an ocean liner made more than 1000 feet long would have to span between two giant waves and would have to be doubled in size to do so. If doubled in size once more, however, she could no longer be accommodated by the sizes of the great world canals, dry docks, or harbor depths.

At this point the miniaturization of doing more with less first ensues through substitution of an entirely new art—David's slingshot over Goliath's club operated from beyond reach of the giant.

This overall and inexorable trending to do more with less is known sum-totally as "progressive ephemeralization." Ephemeralization trends toward an ultimate doing of *everything* with *nothing at all,* which is a trend of the *omniweighable physical* to be mastered by the *omniweightless metaphysics of intellect.*

All the missile-hurling arts of man and men's warring or fighting to the death have followed this same fundamental evolutionary pattern of bigger, then smaller.

Assuming that there were not and never will be enough vital support resources to go around, we conclude that there must be repeating eventualities in wars to see which side could pursue its most favored theory of survival under fundamental inadequacies. Humanity has continually done more killing with less human effort at greater and greater distances and at ever-higher speeds and with ever-increasing accuracy.

The killing went from a thrown stone to a spear to a sling to a bow-and-arrow to a pistol, a musket, a cannon, and so on until man used the great weapons-carrying battleships. Suddenly a little two-ton, torpedo-carrying airplane sank a 45,000-ton battleship, and then the 2,000-miles-per-hour airplane was outperformed by the 16,000-miles-per hour, atom-bomb-carrying rocket of minuscule weight in comparison to the bomb-carrying plane. If world warring persists as a consequence of the concept of "survival only of the fittest minority," there will come the approximately weightless death rays operating at 700 million miles per hour.

At the present point of history the uranium bomb has been displaced by the hydrogen bomb, and then it was discovered that if either side used that new greatest weapon, both sides and the rest of humanity would perish, so the biggest weapon could not be used. Nor could the equally large and mutually destructive biological or chemical gas warfaring. Both sides then discovered that killing of the enemy's people was not their objective.

Killing the enemy's ideology *is* the objective. Killing the enemy's people brings sympathy and support for the enemy from the rest of the world, and "gaining the good opinion and support of the rest of the world" is one of the new world-warring's objectives.

At this point both sides have started to explore the waging of more war with lesser—more limited—killing but more politically and economically devastating techniques. Just as ephemeralization employed ever-more-minuscule instruments and thus took technology out of the limited ranges of the human senses into the vast and invisible ranges of the electromagnetic spectrum reality, so too has major warfaring almost disappeared from the visible contacts of human soldiery and entered into the realm of invisible psychology.

In the new invisible miniaturization phase of major world-warring both sides carry on an attention-focusing guerilla warfare (as was conducted in Vietnam) while making their most powerful attacks through subversion, vandalism, and skillful agitation of any and all possible areas of discontent within the formally assumed enemy's home economics.

In carrying on this new and unfamiliar world-warring they do not have to send ideological proselytizers to persuade the people of the other side to abandon their home country's political system and adopt that of their former enemies. Instead they can readily involve, induce, and persuade individuals of the other side to look for discontent wherever it manifests itself and thereafter to "amplify" that condition by whatever psychological means until the situation erupts in public confusion, demonstrations, terrorism, etc. The idea is to make a mess of the other's economy and customs and thus to discredit the other's political system in the eyes of the rest of the world and to destroy the enemy people's confidence in their own system.

Because the active operators are sometimes engaged on a basis of just gratifying their own personal discontent, they are often unaware that they are acting as agents. Because almost everyone has at least one discontent, a well-trained conscious agent can invoke the multiplyingly effective but unwitting agency of hundreds of other discontent promoters and joiners—in ever-larger, more amplified, masses.

As a consequence of this new invisible phase of world-war trending, a most paradoxical condition exists. The highly idealistic youth of college age who are convinced that they are demonstrating against war are, despite the most humane and compassionate motives, often in fact the front-line soldiers operating as unwitting "shock troops." Meanwhile the conventionally recognized soldiers engaged in visible "war-zone" warfare (either of ambush or open battle) are carrying on only a secondary—albeit often mortally fatal—decoy operation.

This invisible world-around warring to destroy the enemy's economy wherever it is operative, above all by demonstrating its homeland weaknesses and vulnerabilities to the rest of the world, and thus hoping to destroy the confidence of the enemy people in themselves, is far more devastating than could be a physical death ray, for it does everything with nothing. Furthermore it operates as "news," which moves around the Earth by electromagnetic waves operating at 700 million miles per hour.

At the moment the highly controlled political states have a great defensive advantage over the "open, freedom-nurturing" states by virtue of the former's controlled "news." For it is the omniexcitable news in the "free" countries that is primarily exploited to publish and spread and thus create a chain reaction of dismay throughout any and all of their organized-discontent actions.

With the United States and Russia jointly spending over $200 billion a year getting ready for an ultimate showdown between them, they each average about $20 billion a year waging psychoguerilla warfare. Both the U.S.S.R. and the U.S.A. were intent to break down the other one's economy before coming to the far more costly all-out war. The brilliantly trained individuals in Russia who came out to train other individuals in America did so in such a manner that those trained in America had no idea that what they were being excited into doing had anything to do with Russia. The American students' idealism was often brilliantly exploited by Russia to break down America's confidence in advanced education. Theretofore Americans had such blind confidence in education that they would elect any politicians promising to provide state-financed advanced-education facilities.

What the Russians' strategists knew was that the presidents of the U.S.A. universities, public or private, were "sitting ducks" for their psychological shooting. The university presidents of both private and state universities were primarily involved in the politics of raising funds for their institutions. The presidents had no internal "defenses" because they had never had need for them. They found that neither the faculty nor the students knew much about the presidents and that it would be very easy to attack their on-campus positions. They could effectively exaggerate any faults manifest by the presidents.

Within one year the presidents of 100 universities of America were "shot down." None of them were defended by their faculties, whose numbers were scared to death of losing their tenure. The determination of the students to do their own thinking was readily exploited in attacking the university presidents.

While all the foregoing curves of the rising and falling of the technical evolution of weaponry have taken place, there has also occurred, all unnoticed by all parties to the warfaring, a vast "fallout" from the "defense" technology into the domestic technology of ephemeralization's doing ever more with less. Within two-thirds of a century this unnoticed and inadvertent fallout has converted 40 percent of total humanity from have-not-ness to a high standard of living have-ness and makes clear that the only way all of humanity may be elevated to such advantage is by further acceleration of the technical invention revolution.

It becomes evident that all of youth's world-around clamor for peace can only be realized through technological revolution, which will do so much more with so much less per each function as ultimately to produce enough to support all of humanity. It is also clear that such a task can only be accomplished by the technical *design revolution*.

As those many who have become involved in the new invisible warfaring discover that their aims can be attained only through the design revolution, all the young world-around idealists will have to face up to the question of whether they prefer to keep on agitating simply because they have come to enjoy a sense of power and importance by so doing. All who are really dedicated to the earliest possible attainment of economic and physical success for all humanity—and thereby realistically to eliminate war—will have to shift their efforts from the political arena to participation in the design revolution. The latter course involves the development of ever-self-regenerating and improving scientific and technical competence. In turn this means that the individual must plunge earnestly and dedicatedly into initiating self-development, using the resources of the educational system.

* * *

All the aforementioned class-one evolutionary trending provides powerful long-distance prognostication data. Keeping track of the integrated *ephemeralization* and *acceleration* trends and their socioeconomic resultants, per each world human, made possible my 1938 *Nine Chains to the Moon* and my 1950 magazine-published Prognostication that by 2000 A.D. all humanity either would be enjoying a higher but generally unfamiliar standard of living than any humans had ever known—or would have altogether perished.

This book has already mentioned many of these class-one evolutionary trendings.

* * *

In naval science we have four scientifically developed prognosticating arts. In my own semantic formulating "prognosticating" is both subjective and objective: subjective—"if I don't do anything, such and such will happen"; objective—"if I do so and so, such and such will happen." *Pure science* means "setting in order the facts of experience and therefrom deducing generalized principles if and when they are manifest." *Applied science* means "the development of technological procedures for objective employment of a plurality of the generalized principles." *Art* means "the skillful realization of humanly satisfying or challenging special case applications of the theoretical schemes of applied science."

The number-one naval prognosticating science and art is that of designing and producing the generalized tools—machine tools—that, when housed and assembled in navy yards or floating dry docks, can produce both macro and micro special-case tools—with both the generalized and special-case tools operative at degrees of dimensional controls beyond that of human sight; at temperatures above and below humans' organic tolerance; at weights and sizes beyond human muscle-maneuverability; at electromagnetic frequencies beyond the range of human optical or tactile tunability or tolerance; at quantation determination and integration of metallurgical and chemical formulations, in temperature and pressure regions beyond humans' direct sensorially apprehending control.

The number-two naval prognosticating science and art is that in which, employing the number-one prognosticating science and art tools, we design fleets of ships and special case ships and other special case tools as a complex of intersupportive technology capable of coping with nature's conditions at the interface of sea and sky while traveling on, over, or under the seas to any part of the world reachable by the deep water's continuum— i.e., to three-quarters of all the surface of planet Earth; with the sea-transport capability of integrating the world's remotely occurring, unique, and intercomplementary physical resources; and with the ability to protect such sea commerce against any and all pirates or others hostile to class-two evolutionary phenomena.

The number-three naval prognosticating science and art is that of celestial navigation, which permits us to reliably prognosticate the arrival of our ship anywhere around the world at such and such an hour and on such and such a date.

The number-four naval prognosticating science and art is that of ballistics—"the art and science of controlling the trajectory of an explosively hurled missile." Ballistics is divided into two parts—interior and exterior. *Interior ballistics* deals with all the controllable variables governing the trajectory of the gun's explosively hurled missile, which controllable variables are operative *before* the gun is fired; *exterior ballistics* deals with all the controllable variables operative *after* the gun is fired. These controllable interior- and exterior-ballistics variables altogether govern the trajectory of the gun's explosively hurled missiles.

Interior-ballistics variables include the design of the gun, its bore, its length, its metallurgy, its expansion and contraction in changing temperatures, and similar factors. Interior ballistics is also concerned with the design of the missile itself, with the gunpowder to be used, and with the temperature of that powder. The interior variables are exhaustively studied, scientifically recorded and controlled.

The exterior-ballistics variables relate to the direction and velocity of the winds blowing between the firing ship and the target ship. The exterior-ballistics variables include all weather conditions. They are concerned with the course and speed of the gun-firing ship as well as of the target ship. The exterior-ballistics variables are numerous but not as numerous as the interior-ballistics variables. The exterior-ballistics variables include the information regarding the relative accuracy of the previously fired missile and the swiftly calculated corrections to bring the trajectory on to the target.

In the science of ballistics the variables entering into the problem of firing from a swiftly moving, steerable ship on a heaving sea at a variably steerable target ship moving at unannounced variable speeds on a heaving sea are much more numerous than the variables entering into the firing of a gun from a fixed position on the dry land toward another fixed-position target on the same dry land.

In naval gunnery in the precomputer days large charts, containing titles and spaces for all the known variable data of both interior and exterior ballistics, were printed. These charts were laid out and tacked to a great table in the "plotting room" in the most structurally protected positions within the bowels of the ship. All the interior-ballistics data was corrected when any of its data changed and was immediately entered onto the chart. There was no use entering any exterior-ballistics data until the enemy ship was located, after which all the up-to-the-minute-and-second changing data of the exterior ballistics were entered onto the charts. When all the data were in, complex mathematical integration of the data took place, and the proper angles of elevation and horizontal compass orientation of the guns themselves were arrived at. Guns were at first individually, then coordinatedly, aimed at the target ship by both horizontal and vertical angle controls, being separately and continuously human-eye-and-hand aimed at the target ship by easily spun hand-wheels geared to power-driven equipment that kept the big guns in constant adjustment to the rolling, pitching, and yawing of the firing ship. The rate of changing of interior-ballistics data was—and as yet is— very slow compared to the rate of change of the data of exterior ballistics.

As a naval officer I was once concerned with all these matters. I became gradually interested in the possibility that all the variables involved in naval ballistics might be identified with all the variables operative in the most complex problems of Universe. I intuited that the combined sciences of navigation and ballistics might embrace all the variables governing Universe-event prognostication. It could be that: (1) navy yard industrialization, (2) fleet operation and individual ship design, (3) astronavigation, and (4) ballistics constituted the four "special case" corner complexes of a generalized tetrahedral complex of variable design factors governing all human-mind-controllable participation in all cosmic, alternative-intertransforming potentials.

It was eminently clear that astronomy, enormously advantaged by Newton's mass-interattraction law, having acquired comprehensive data regarding the ever-changing interpositioning of celestial bodies, groups of bodies, and galaxies of bodies, was extremely successful in prognosticating for many years, centuries, and millennia ahead the relative interpositioning of all known celestial bodies to split-second accuracy almost anywhere within millions of light-years around and away from Earth. We could say that the more cosmically comprehensive the consideration, the more accurate the prognosticating.

I therefore decided to always include the most micro-macro cosmically inclusive data in all my prognosticating. Obviously this was not "crystal-balling" nonsense but a very elegantly inclusive and incisive integration of the four naval sciences and arts of prognosticating.

Quite clearly the four special case design systems of the naval sciences and arts can be generalized to accommodate the realization of all the objective initiatives of humanity. The four-cornered tetrahedron is the *minimum structural system* in Universe. It excludes all the irrelevant information of Universe and includes all the information relevant to the system. The tetrahedral structure system has six unique interrelationships existing among the system's four unique groups of system variables.

We have also mentioned elsewhere in this book and in other books the differentiation between craft and industrial tools—i.e., craft tools are all the tools that can be invented and produced by one individual alone in the wilderness, such as spears, bows and arrows, pottery, baskets, fire, etc., whereas the industrial tools are all the tools that cannot be produced by one human. Because it takes two humans to produce the need to communicate and to invent the means of that communication, we say that the spoken word was the first industrial tool. "In the beginning [of industrialization—i.e., technologically effective human cooperation] *was the word.*" The spoken and comprehended word greatly expedited the development of humanity's information on how to cope with life's challenges.

The four naval sciences and arts make it possible for us to sort out the human capabilities provided by class-one-evolution-developed industrialization as a human-cooperative-interadvantaging system—differentiated from all the illusory propaganda of industrialization's exploitation by exclusively monetary-profit-motivated business or personal-kudos-profit-motivated politics. Our "Legally Piggily" chapter clearly recounts the manner in which business took over industrialization for its own special-case self-advantaging. See this *Time* magazine item of August 6, 1979, to clarify the aptness of the word "Piggily."

Those Record Oil Company Profits

With memories of long gasoline lines still fresh, the earnings reported by many oil companies last week could hardly be expected to be greeted by cheers. All told, the industry had its best second quarter ever. Profits of the 23 biggest U.S. firms totaled $5.47 billion, a rise of 66% over the same period last year. Among the five large international companies, Texaco's earnings leaped by 132% to $365 million. Earnings of the others: Exxon, up 20% to $830 million; Mobil, up 38% to $404 million; Socal, up 61% to $412 million; and Gulf, up 65% to $291 million. These gains came on top of strong earnings in the first quarter. For the first half, the combined profits of the five giants came to $4.6 billion, or an increase of 49% over the same period last year.

See also p. 401 of Chronology in Appendix II.

The strictly government-operated NASA Apollo Project—its Cape Canaveral blast-off base in Florida; its Mission Control Center in Houston, Texas; its design- and theory-development base in Alabama; and its administration headquarters in Washington, D.C.—employed business's industrial facilities but was a human-endeavor cooperating project. It held at bay any importantly diverting manifests of selfishness, even amongst its dramatically publicized astronauts. Their individual names have faded into a dim admixture of identities—omnisublimated by the magnificent demonstration of humanity's industrially cooperative capability to accomplish history's most imaginatively "impossible," scientifically "possible" feat—rocket-ferrying of humans over to the Moon and returning them safely back on board our Spaceship Earth.

We now directly address the accomplishing by humanity of a less visually dramatic but far more difficult task—that of rendering comprehensively and eternally successful a failure-prone, competitively greedy, selfishly wasteful, fearful, and inferiority-conditioned humanity—and of doing so in a decade.

Starting in 1927 (fifty-three years ago) I developed an as-comprehensive-as-possible inventory of relevant scientific and industrial data and set about making systemically scientific prognostications regarding trends affecting our Spaceship Earth and all of its passengers. This attempted scientific prognosticating involved the comprehensive inventorying of resources aboard our Spaceship Earth. These resources broke down into all the energy associative as matter and all the energy dissociative as radiation. The metaphysical resources broke down into all the inventory of generalized principles and all the inventory of special case knowledge considerations.

To ensure that I was comprehensively adequate in dealing with cosmic-scale prognosticating, I undertook in 1927 and thereafter to discover and scientifically demonstrate nature's own mathematical coordinate system. I had intuitively initiated that search in 1899, at the age of four. This latter search and its successful discovery of that cosmic-coordination system is treated with both comprehensively and incisively in my two-volume *Synergetics* (Macmillan, 1975 and 1979)—each volume about 800 pages. All those who would like to understand the relatively high accuracy of my prognosticating science will find it necessary to become students of those two volumes of *Synergetics.* They make clear that I have found a method of guaranteeing that my prognostications include all relevant variables.

For those who do not have time to study *Synergetics* or my books such as *Nine Chains to the Moon,* I will point out such studies as my 760-year-long chart of the chemical element isolations by humans, which discloses the interrelationship of pure science with technological science as applied to world-encircling, human-protecting and -transporting, environment controls and the accelerating acceleration in human evolution that it undeniably discloses.

In 1942 I sought a means of discovering whether any regular rate of occurrence of scientific events existed. I, of course, discovered that the relative importance of a suitable cut and classification of the events into pure and not-so-pure scientific events had first to be accomplished.

As I started so to do, I immediately realized that there was one single pure-science set of events that belonged to one family—that is, the history of human scientists' progressive isolation of the family of ninety-two regenerative chemical elements—a family of exactly and successively numbered members whose membership qualifications could not be confused—one electron, one proton; two electrons and two protons. I decided to make a chart of the isolations plotted against time.

The first known isolation by a human—that of arsenic—occurred in Italy in 1250 A.D. So I designed my chart to be 760 years long, running from 1250 A.D. to 2010 A.D. I made my chart high enough to accommodate twenty posturanium isolations, should any occur. One year after I made and posted my chart, the first posturanium element was isolated. The last of the first ninety-two to be isolated—promethium, chemical element #61—was not discovered until 1954, twelve years after I designed and posted the chart. The preuranium element isolations did not occur without regularity.

I planned the designing of my 760-year-long chart in such a manner that vertical room was left for 112 horizontal steps, so that as each element became isolated, the position of it went one step higher. When history opens, humans had already at some earlier times isolated and put to use nine chemical elements. Nobody has any idea how, when, and where the isolations of carbon, lead, tin, mercury, silver, copper, sulphur, gold, and iron occurred. They were found already in use in different parts of the world when humans first made record of the fact long before 1250 A.D. Because nine isolations had already occurred, I started plotting my chart nine steps

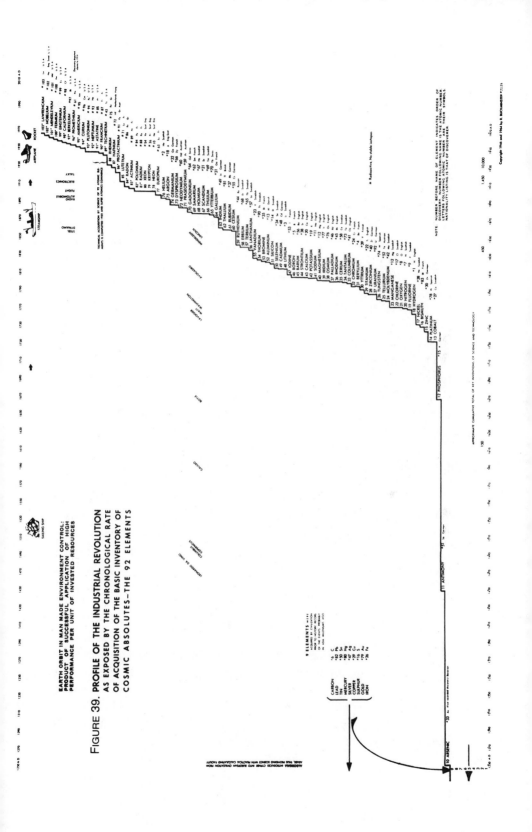

EARTH ORBIT IN MAN MADE ENVIRONMENT CONTROL:
PRODUCT OF SUCCESSFUL APPLICATION OF HIGH
PERFORMANCE PER UNIT OF INVESTED RESOURCES

FIGURE 39. PROFILE OF THE INDUSTRIAL REVOLUTION
AS EXPOSED BY THE CHRONOLOGICAL RATE
OF ACQUISITION OF THE BASIC INVENTORY OF
COSMIC ABSOLUTES—THE 92 ELEMENTS

Copyright 1946 and 1964 by R. BUCKMINSTER FULLER

high. I posted arsenic, chemical element #33, on the tenth step. The next isolation came 200 years later—chemical element #51, antimony. This was followed by a 220-year hiatus running to 1670, when science isolated chemical element #15, phosphorus. Another sixty-two-year lag brought us to the isolation of chemical element #27, cobalt, in 1732, and later in the same year element #78, platinum. Thereafter they arrived at an average rate of one every two years.

The rate accelerated markedly for the next forty years until element #5, boron, was isolated; during those forty years thirty-one other elements were isolated. Between boron, in 1810, and gallium, element #31, there is a slowing down in the rate, with seventeen more elements being isolated. Between gallium and europium, chemical element #63, another twelve were isolated. There is a very steady rate of acquisition by humans of the next five isolated chemical elements—from europium to polonium, element #84. Then there is a marked slowing down of the rate of isolation from actinium, #89, to rhenium, #75. In the isolation of the next five elements, technetium, #43, to plutonium, #94, there is an almost vertical rate of isolating, all five isolations taking place during 1930–1931 although not announced until years later. Between 1932 and 1969 ten elements were isolated, from curium, element #96, to lawrencium, element #103—the 103rd successive isolation. Not only is there a very steady rate of climb of these transuranium element isolations but all of them are successively isolated in the order of their successive atomic numbers, whereas none of the pre-uranium—before element #92—isolations occur by their successive numbers.

What we have been witnessing is a series of accelerations and slowdowns. The accelerations always occur in peacetime and the slowdowns in wartime. In wartime the military uses what the scientists developed in peacetime. Quite clearly the purest of pure science activity, chemical-element isolating, occurs under peaceful conditions.

This whole 760-year curve of pure-science isolations is altogether a curve of acceleration against calendar time.

I then recalled that what pure science does today does not get into the academic curricula for a few years. A few years later again applied science makes special case objective use of the pure-science finding as some invention. Use of the invention by industry begins to alter the environment of the everyday happenings. The altered environment calls for an evolutionary advancement of everyday human life.

I then said to myself that history makes it clear that environmental advancements alter life-styles and introduce new economic eras.

Because environmental-technology advancements embodying the technical advancements are clearly implemented by pure science's discoveries, and the altered environments introduce new eras in human experience, I asked myself to isolate out from all other inventing of history the unique stages of human-advantaging environment controls that made it possible for humans to thrive under conditions in which the humans would, but for the new environment control, perish and, from within the uniquely advanced life-style within the environment, accomplish control of energies operating outside the environment control, and therewith propel the environment-controlling device and its human occupants in one occupant-controlled complete circuit of the Earth.

Along the top of the chart, in 1520, we see how Magellan used a sailing vessel in which he went most of the way around the world before he was killed. His crew completed the circumnavigation, which took two years. Three hundred fifty years later, humans circumnavigated the globe in a steel steamship. Seventy-five years later, they circumnavigated in a special-alloy aluminum airplane. Thirty-five years later, they circumnavigated in an exotic metals rocket. The wooden sailing ship took two years to circumnavigate; the steel steamship, two months; the aluminum airplane took two weeks and the exotic metals rocket capsule took only a little over one hour to encircle the planet Earth.

In the successive circumnavigation arts no one at each successive stage could dream of the next stage of circumnavigation. We have on this chart the curve of the basic acceleration of science accomplishments as plotted against time.

We have on the chart a second-degree acceleration manifest in the contraction of the lags between the successive circumnavigation from 350 years to sixty-five to thirty years between four states of the art of circumnavigation and a third-degree acceleration manifest in the contraction of time taken to circumnavigate from two years ... to two months ... to two weeks ... to one hour. It is implicit in the rate of contraction between completely inconceivable later arts that by 1985 we should be able to transmit humans around the globe by radio scanning or an equivalently unexpected means.

*   *   *

For those who wish to gain only a cursory concept of my prognosticating I point to my fifty-three-year-maintained curves of ephemeralization as manifest in a number of charts—for instance, the one recording the annually decreasing pounds-per-delivered-horsepower of aircraft engines. The tenth-anniversary issue of *Fortune* magazine (February 1940) has an article I prepared on industrialization in which many charts of ephemeralization in various technologies are shown.

In such comprehensive surveying of human experiences and the lessons we have learned it became progressively clearer that humans were given their minds to discover generalized principles and to employ those principles objectively in special case technologies. That led me to assume that the class-two evolution was a designed-in but sometime-to-be-terminated phase of class-one evolution. It seemed logical, as humans progressed from absolute ignorance—learning only by trial-and-error—that they would go through a very long period of doing all the right things for all the wrong reasons. Quite clearly nature did not tell the honeybee to go out and cross-pollinate the vegetation. What nature did was to chromosomically program the honeybee to go after honey and inadvertently—at right angles—to cross-pollinate the vegetation. What nature told humanity chromosomically was, "I'm hungry, my kids are hungry; I'm cold, my kids are cold. Go after that food and that coat. They cost money—go after money. They say you have to earn it. OK, I'll earn it." Buzz, buzz, honey-money bee. No human chromosomes say make the world work for everybody—only mind can tell you that.

In support of the integrity of ecology's complex regeneration of life on planet Earth, class-one evolution first designed all the vegetation to photosynthetically (syntropically) convert the randomly occurring entropic Sun radiation into highly orderly molecular structures, which are consumed by other orderly molecule-proliferating biological organisms. That syntropic complex of ecological interactions not only made possible the gradual conduct of human society by mind instead of by cunning and muscle but also led to human minds' consciously acting as local-in-Universe information-harvesters and local-in-Universe problem-solvers, all in support of the integrity of eternally regenerative Universe.

It seemed that the time would come evolutionarily when humans might have acquired enough knowledge of generalized principles to permit a graduation from class-two (entropically selfish) evolution into class-one (syntropically cooperative) evolution, thereafter making all the right moves for all the right reasons.

This book should make it quite evident that I think humanity has now reached that critical moment of potential transformation of humans' affairs from class-two evolution into class-one evolution. Assuming that to be so, we look upon "Legally Piggily" (see Chapter 3) as the last and highest tide of doing all the wrong things for the unknown right reasons, just before reaching the condition of all of humanity having acquired enough of the right information to graduate from class-two evolutionary entropic nonsense into consciously competent syntropic participation in class one's eternally intertransforming evolution in support of the integrity of cosmic-scenario-Universe's eternal regeneration.

Prognostication is often a subjective science—it anticipates what is going to happen to us. Navigation and ballistics are always objective sciences, for they make possible prognostication of what will happen if we employ the full family of mathematically integratable factors governing local systemic intertransformabilities, as permitted by the generalized principles, which always provide six alternative moves with every turn to play in "the game of Universe." These permitted six moves for each turn to play are the six edges of the tetrahedral system and are clearly explained in *Synergetics,* vol. 2, § 537.40.

Class-one evolution has succeeded in ever increasing the range, frequency, and safe velocity of human travel, exploration, and information growth. Further, humans have developed environment-controlling vehicles and local environment-controlling habitats that permit their survival under conditions uncopable-with prior to the technological evolution. All these are resultant upon human mind's being given access to the generalized principles governing the design of the successfully operating, eternally regenerative, scenario Universe.

The space programs entered into by the Russians and the Americans, because of the military implications of possible containment of one by the other, were class-two evolutionary events; however, they opened the possibility for humanity to participate consciously in class-one evolution's continual increase in the range, speed, and frequency of humanity's travel and information-gathering in local Universe as well as its participation in ever-more local problem-solving within the ever-greater ranges of Universe thus reached.

The space program integrated the sciences of navigation, ballistics, astrophysics, metallurgy, chemistry, and bio-anthropology. Bio-anthropology is the positive class-one evolution's anticipatorily undertaken improvement of both subjective and objective, energetic, environmentally controllable events in order to keep already-healthy life even healthier, whether in safely penetrating environments theretofore lethally hostile to human life or in just improving the chances for the healthiest to continue their optimum health or in multiplying the numbers of humans who enjoy optimum health—working eventually toward avoiding any humans ever losing their optimum health.

Bio-anthropology is class-one evolution's takeover and expansion of class-two evolution's medicine, which copes essentially only with humans who have lost their good health.

The space program, as an integration of the plurality of projective-objective sciences, called for the employment of what is known as the "critical path" as the comprehensive design science's individual parts production, subassembly, general assembly, progressive full assembly testings, and launch scheduling.

A critical path develops an exhaustive list of all that has to be accomplished in order to arrive successfully at a given objective theretofore never reached. The Apollo Project was the official name of the undertaking that was to ferry humans over *to* and land them *on* the Moon and return them safely to mother—Spaceship Earth.

The critical-path organization of the Apollo Project disclosed some two million tasks that had to be successfully accomplished before the human astronauts were to be returned safely to Spaceship Earth. NASA's Apollo management then put a scientifically and technically competent control group to work to identify all the approximately two million tasks, a million of which required technological performances the design, production, and successful operation of which had never before been undertaken by humans.

In this book we have set down our prehistory, our techno-social history of "Humans in Universe," and then in the "Legally Piggily" chapter we have chronicled the overall pattern of class-two evolutionary events that have, during the last half-century, gone critical—bringing humanity to a moment of crisis adequate in magnitude to springboard humanity into oblivion or into a relatively utopian future.

Because automobiles were becoming ever-more popular in the 1920s and because they were using inherently exhaustible fossil fuels, such an approaching critical moment in human history as we are now experiencing was clearly visible to me and many others a half-century ago. I did not, however, know of any other humans who thought there was anything that they *personally* could do about this problem and any other such "too big" problems. Nonetheless, I committed my life to dealing only with *total* Spaceship Earth and *all* its passengers' regeneration. I have therefore included the chapter on the self-disciplines I adopted at thirty-two years of age at the 1927 outset (or soon thereafter) of my lifetime commitment. These disciplines were adopted in view of the physical magnitude and the metaphysical integrity involved in the balance-of-my-life commitment. Many of the disciplines are importantly relevant today in respect to the way in which unknown, economically insecure, individual humans may function effectively in this world crisis.

Soon after 1927 I developed the World Game as an especially important integration of the complex of self-adopted disciplines and tasks I found myself progressively adopting as the years passed and as my inventory of discovered errors and lessons thereby learned multiplied. Our chapters on the Geoscope and the World Game provide important frames of reference in the formulation of a critical-path chart of what humanity must accomplish within a decade—or probably perish.

This last section of the book focuses on the critical path itself and constitutes my own single human being's inherently limited, 1927-and-there-after, anticipatory formulations of the order of absolutely essential tasks to be successfully accomplished between 1927 and crossing of the epochal threshold into happy continuance of all humans in Universe. Others can and will vastly improve upon my critical path. What is now needed, however, is an "icebreaker" critical-path submission. Here it is, in the order of my spontaneous formulations of it.

In presenting it I need first to develop, if possible, some powerfully integrating generalizations of already-introduced concepts. For instance, we have developed the earlier concept of a system as dividing all the Universe into all the Universe outside the system—the presently tuned-out, irrelevant macrocosm—all the Universe inside the system—the presently untuned-in, irrelevant microcosm—and all the small remainder of the present, individually tuned-in Universe of which the Universe-dividing system consists, together with all of its presently integrated, common knowledge of tuned-in, omnirelevant considerations. Systems scientifically describe conceptual ramifications of thoughts and ideas. This omnicosmic, four-dimensional, geometrical conception of a system is a scientific generalization (see "System—400.00" in *Synergetics*, vols. 1 and 2).

Human organisms are systems. They are complex but very important systems of energetically operative, integral tools. Some of them are internally operative in manufacturing, maintaining, repairing, and replacing the whole inventory of specialized interior as well as generalized exterior tools. All of the integral exterior tools such as the human hand and eyes have highly generalized but circumstantially limited capabilities—for instance, they cannot work nakedly above or below a very small temperature range, but within their temperature limits their uses are myriad.

Human mind, discovering principles, devises special case, less frequently employed, nonintegral, from-self-detached, craft tools. In due course human mind, discovering more principles, uses the organically integral tools to operate the simple, detached craft tools such as the stone hammer and knife, to produce much more effective generalized industrial tools, such as a blacksmith's forge and anvil, metal hammers and tongs, with which the smith in turn produces even more specialized tools, such as metal horseshoes and forged metal carpenter's hammers, to outperform wooden mallets and stone hammers. Human mind, stimulated by the succession of experiences attendant upon hitching an ox, a water buffalo, a camel, or an elephant to an earth-working tool, came to the discovery of the windmill and the waterwheel, and then coupled the windmill or waterwheel with a grain-grinding stone milling wheel; then in time conceived of the principle of using energy other than human muscle to operate a class of tools known as the machine tools, consisting of lathes, drill presses, metal planers, milling machines, grinding machines, shapers, slotters, etc. Each such machine tool performs in far finer, more powerful degree the metallic-substance-forming and surface-finishing functions initially performed in principle but under much more limited conditions only by the human hands and other of the integral organic exterior tools.

All of the foregoing involves energy as work and as matter and a complex of energy interexchanging. All such complex internal and external energy intertransforming and exchanging can be spoken of as interior and exterior metabolics.

We are gradually working toward a complex integration of many of our already-introduced complex concepts into a generalization of interior and exterior ballistics, which as energy intertransforming and exchanging can be spoken of as interior and exterior metabolics.

How apt a name for the human organism is "an interior and exterior metabolic system." We find that in these interior and exterior metabolic systems, the interior tooling is highly generalized, while the exterior tools are highly specialized and able to cope with many variables, but that the data regarding the different toolings vary hardly at all, which is to say that the more nearly generalized the system, the less variable the inventory of its constituents, wherefore the great scientific generalizations are eternal and never vary. We find in the succession of naval science and arts that the navy yard machine tools varied hardly at all, being improved upon only slowly, and that the number-two science and art of designing fleets and ships and their integral interior ballistics varied more frequently than did the design of the navy yard machine tools, whereas the exterior ballistics and navigation dealt with swiftly changing sea and weather conditions, though the navigational mathematics of spherical trigonometry itself consisted of eternally invariant generalized principles.

We find our concept of industrialization to be an exterior-to-humans metabolic system.

We find our critical path to consist of a succession of omnirelevant, frequently varying, widely ranging, highly specialized exterior metabolic systems, being operated by humans, which humans themselves are limited-range, rarely variant, interior and exterior metabolic systems.

A.   In the "Self-Disciplines" chapter of this book, I recounted that the larger the number of humans I undertook to serve, the more effective I became, wherefore I concluded that if I committed myself to serving everyone, I would be optimally effective.

B.   I find the foregoing (A) to be sociologically akin to the hard-science fact that astronomy and astrophysics—dealing in total-known-Universe—enjoy humanity's farthest-ahead-in-time, reliable prognosticating record by a reliably proven prognosticated-events-margin of hundreds of years.

C. There seems to be a scientific generalization at work here that relates intimately to the phenomena synergy—behavior of whole systems unpredicted by the behavior or integral characteristics of any parts of the system when the parts are considered only separately. What is inferred here is that a competitive employment of the whole family of generalized principles employed to serve the successful human functioning in Universe renders one maximally effective.

All scientific generalizations are synergetic—that is, they describe scientifically discovered interrelationships of system parts that vary in respect to one another at only mathematically describable different rates of change, which interrelationships are in no way suggested by separate inspection of any one part of the system.

D. The generalization discovered to be commonly operative in the foregoing paragraphs A, B, and C says, "To be optimally effective, undertake at outset the most comprehensive task in the most comprehensive and incisively detailed manner."

In undertaking our critical-path development of a practically realizable means of bringing about all humanity's spontaneously realizable escape from fearfully ignorant self-destruction—and entrance into a design-science-artifacts-produced-and-induced, sustainable, and unprecedentedly high standard of living for all, to be accomplished within a generation—we are being taught by the foregoing paragraphs A, B, C, D, to immediately "undertake the greatest task with thorough commitment of attention to every detail."

We are being taught by all the foregoing to assume as closely as possible the viewpoint, the patience, and the competence of God.

CHAPTER 8

Critical Path: Part Two

IN THE PRECEDING CHAPTER, "Critical Path: Part One," I sought to forestall any hesitance on the part of humanity to go "for the works." It is to be everything for everybody or oblivion.

While it is fairly simple to write a list of socioeconomic conditions we consider to be fundamental to omnihumanity's sustainable physical and metaphysical success, we must remember that our grand strategy is based on producing the artifacts that will induce the right behaviors rather than depending on politically enacted and enforced reforms. What we count on is political reaction in its bipartisan tail-of-the-dragon function, now flappingly, now snappingly, yielding one way or the other to society's vivid realization of the arrival of historically unprecedented crises and dawning awareness of the availability of possibly effective but unfamiliar technophysical means of coping with the ever-more-frequently-occurring crises as are occasioned by the practical development and availability of hitherto-nonexistent artifacts. Much of the successive emergencies will prove to be caused by society's adoption of only a few of all the artifacts—development only of those artifacts that could be turned into the most immediate profits as fostered by the armaments appropriations.

The emergency-wrought political adjustment will go on until, in the stress of ever-greater emergency, society spontaneously adopts all of our critical path's artifacts. The great emergencies may finally force political society to "do the right things" for the right reasons. (I found my way into so doing, half a century ago, as occasioned, however, only by total crises in my own life—why should not others do so?) If political society does decide to do the right tasks for the right reasons, it will probably find our critical-path artifacts to be both cogently and specifically essential.

252

In contradistinction to the critical path of the Apollo Project—one-half of whose two million or so tasks to be accomplished involved the development of technology that was nonexistent at the outset of Apollo—our critical path's inventory of essential technologies consists of 100-percent-already-developed technologies (see Appendix I, "Chronology of Scientific Discoveries and Artifacts"). Most of these are in use but in the production of the wrong systems—in the "weaponry" systems or in the "money-making-for-the-few" systems instead of in "high-wealth-livingry-production-for-all" systems.

For the foregoing reasons most of the tasks that need to be attended to in such a manner as to make all humanity sustainingly successful involve only the right application of the already-developed technologies which have been funded and applied to the wrong tasks. It must be remembered that the overwhelming reason for their being applied to the wrong tasks is the assumption of those commanding the political and economic power structures that there is a fundamental inadequacy of life support on our planet—that it has to be "you or me," nowhere nearly enough for both.

Our 1927 and thenceforth developed critical path has no as-yet-to-be-accomplished technologies. It needs only the education of the world regarding the fact that invisible *ephemeralization* and *acceleration* now make what had previously seemed to be inadequate life support for all humanity to be rendered bounteously adequate.

The development of our *omni-world-integrating electrical-energy network grid,* which will realistically put all humanity on the same economic accounting system and will integrate the world's economic interests and value systems and lead most swiftly to the realistic elimination of the 150 sovereign-nation systems, needs only a relatively few geographical interlinking operations. It does not need the invention and development of new technologies.

Inasmuch as society's educational system's conditioned reflexes are half a millennium out of gear with the discovered facts of cosmic operation, a TV-accomplished, swift reorientation of humanity's reflexes to accord with the discovered facts is a high-priority critical path task. If humanity's reflexes were already updated and we were as yet behaving as ineptly as we are at present, then there would be no hope. You may recall that I have scientifically demonstrated the half-millennium-out-of-gearness with facts by demonstrating the misconditioned reflexes of humanity's leading scientists—I have tested many audiences of scientists, who all admit they are as yet seeing the Sun "go down," though science has known for 500 years that this is not what is happening. Remember the wind blowing from the northwest when a low pressure to the southeast of us is drafting the wind by us. Remember we have established that there is no "up" or "down" in Universe, no "wide-wide-world," no "four-corners of the Earth," etc., etc.

It was the fact that my 1927 fifty-year critical-path technological stages had already been acceleratingly completed that made it possible for me to make public announcement ten years ago that it was feasible within a ten-year design science revolution—while melting all weaponry and using those metals for livingry—to have all humanity living at a sustainably higher standard of living than any humans have ever experienced while simultaneously phasing out all further use of fossil fuels and atomic energy—because we can live comfortably and luxuriously on daily energy income from the Sun in its many derivative phases.

Because all the technology inventing and all the metals mining and other chemical materials necessary for developing sustainable, omniphysical, and increasingly metaphysical success for all humanity have already been accomplished, our critical path's overall strategy of realization differs greatly from that of the Apollo Project.

Our critical-path realization requirement is one of an omnihumanity TV and printed-media familiarization with the retrospective inventory, by dates and items, of history's totally known scientific discoveries and artifacts, all of which have been influential in such a manner as to induce the chain discovery of the relevant next-to-be-discovered-and-invented items, but also the social uses of them and the resultant reconditioning of human reflexes thereby brought about. The synergetic effect of all the discoveries and artifact inventions altogether plays a major part in implementing realization of the function of humans-in-Universe in support of the omni-self-regenerative scenario Universe. This whole history of already accomplished scientific discovery and technological invention is intimately relevant to our ten-year design science revolution wherein we divert all that accomplished technology from exclusively weaponry or money-making objectives to omnihumanity's omnisustainable physical success. Realization of this physical success is enabled by the now existence of the critical-path technologies needing only to be redirected from killingry to livingry purposes. What must be accomplished is the world-around TV and printed-media reorientation of humanity by the realistic scenarioing of the peaceful uses of the already-accomplished half-century accrual of the 1927-to-1979 critical-path-artifacts developments.

We discover, of course, that our half-century critical-path undertaking—designed and initiated in 1927—is a class-two (or humanly contrived) evolution, which by good fortune (or by God's guidance) has coincided, along almost all of the half-century-long way, with the Universe's class-one evolutionary development—possibly because we undertook at outset to design our human-contrived path as closely as possible to the way our mind told us "God" would design it.

I had, in 1927, little of the experience that people have today in critical-path designing. I did, however, think of it in exactly those same operational terms and stages as those employed by the Apollo Project's conceivers: "What are the first-things-first?"—the number-one, -two, -three, and so forth artifacts to be accomplished in order to develop the ultimate environmental controls whose artifacts would be so safely, obviously operable and economically favorable as spontaneously to persuade humanity how to behave in grave moments of emergency in order to make decisions leading expeditiously to economic and physically sustainable success for all humanity.

Here follows my critical-path program of realization as first inscribed in 1927 and many times revised thereafter as Part IV of what I call: "Comprehensively Anticipatory Design Science's Universal Requirements for Realizing Omnihumanity Advantaging Local Environment Controls, Which are Omniconsiderate of Both Cosmic Evolution Potentials and Terrestrial Ecology Integrities."

Phase I, Individual

CRITICAL PATH TO ULTIMATE

IV. *Realization*

The whole program of realization is to be considered in the following order, which breaks into two primary categories or phases: (A) the initial work to be undertaken by the individual prior to engagement of the aid of associates, and (B) original and initial work to be undertaken by the first group of associates. These two phases may be organized as follows:

A. Research and development by initiating individual—prior to inauguration of design action and development action involving full-time employment of others. Inauguration of a general work pattern as a natural pattern coinciding with best scientific procedure, to wit:

Preliminary
Initiation of diary and notebook
Initiation of photographic documentation
Initiation of tactical conferences

1. Comprehensive library study of accrued arts
   a. Past
   b. Contemporary

    c. Theory of design—pertinent arts to be studied by the initiating individual include:

      (1) Anthropological data

      (2) Energetic-synergetic geometry—the philosophy of mensuration and transformation, relative size

      (3) Theory of structural exploration

      (4) Theory of mechanical exploration

      (5) Theory of chemical exploration

      (6) Energy as structure

      (7) Dwelling process as an "energy exchange"

      (8) Dwelling process as an "energy balance sheet"

      (9) Theory of structural complex

      (10) Theory of service complex

      (11) Theory of process complex

      (12) Theory of structural and mechanical logistics

      (13) Theory of complex resolution

      (14) Tensioning by crystalline, pneumatic, hydraulic, magnetic means

      (15) Compressioning by crystalline, pneumatic, hydraulic, magnetic means

2. Listing therefrom of authorities available for further information:

    a. Local, personal contact

    b. Remote correspondence

3. Pursuant to information thus gained, calling at suggested local laboratories:

    a. University

    b. Industry

    c. Setting up of informative tests for firsthand knowledge in own laboratory

4. First phase of design assumption:

    a. Consideration of novel, complex interaction unique to project

    b. Preferred apparatus from competitive field

    c. Design of appropriate flowsheets

5. Flowsheets submitted to:

    a. Those competitive specialists who have proved helpful in steps 3b and 3c

b. Industrial producers of similar equipment and assemblies
c. Make informative tests for closure of gaps supporting assumed theory

6. Submit specifications and drawings of general assembly and unique component parts for informative bids by manufacturers:
   a. Second redesign of flowsheet based on available and suggested apparatus, price information, etc.

7. Prepare report consisting of diary of above, supported by photographic documentation and collected literature—with trial-balance conclusions in indicated economic advantage (which, if positive, will inaugurate Phase II)

Phase II, Collective

IV. B. Design and development undertaking—involving plural-authorship phase and specialization of full-time associates. Consideration of relationship of prototype to industrial complex by constant review of principles of solution initially selected as appropriate to assumptions. Adoption of assumptions for realization in design of pertinent principles and latest technology afforded.

1. Comprehensive survey of entire sequence of operations from original undertaking to clientele synchronization. Realization strategy number 1 by individual (Phase I). Realization strategy number 2 by associates (Phase II).
   a. Physical tests in principle of the design assumptions' unique inclusions not evidenced in available data
   b. General-assembly drawings (schematic) providing primary assembly drawing schedule reference
   c. General-assembly assumption, small-scale models, and mock-up full size
   d. Primary assembly, subassembly, and parts calculations (stress)
   e. Trial balance of probable parts weights, direct manufacturing costs (approximately three times material costs; includes labor, supervision, and inspection), forecast of overall cost magnitudes, and curve plotting—at various rates of production, ratioed to direct costs per part and "all other costs"—i.e., "overhead," tool and plant "amortization," "contingencies," "profit"
   f. "Freezing" of general assembly and its reference drawing

g. Drawing for first full-size production prototype commences in general assembly, primary assembly, subassembly, and parts

h. Budget of calculating and drawing time is set, with tactical deadlines for each

i. Parts drawing and full-size lofting and offset patterns

j. Prototype parts production on "soft tools" commences

k. Subassembly and primary assemblies replace mock-up parts

l. Physical tests of parts and subassemblies with obvious corrections and necessary replacements (not improvements or desirables, which must be deferred until second prototype is undertaken, after all-comprehensive physical tests have been applied)

m. Photography of all parts and assemblies

n. Full assembly completed and inspected—cost

o. Static load tests

p. Operation tests

q. Assembly and disassembly

r. Photography of all phases

s. Packaging and shipping tests

t. Estimates of savings to be effected by special powered field tools

u. Opinion testing

v. *Final* production *"clean-up"* prototype placed in formal calculation and drawing with engineering budgeted deadlines

w. Parts cost scheduled by class A tools and time

x. Production tool layout fixed

y. Production tools ordered

z. Production dates set

a-1 Lofting and offsets produced of full-size test "masters" and templates

b-1 Fabrication of special jigs and fixtures

c-1 Production materials ordered

d-1 Production tool-jig-fixture tune-up

e-1 Parts and assembly testing

f-1 Field operation scheduling

g-1 Field tools ordered

h-1 Distribution strategy in terms of initial logic limitations

i-1 Field tests with special tools

j-1 Field tools ordered or placed in special design and fabrication

k-1 Test target area selected for first production

l-1 Production commences

m-1 First field assemblies with power tools

n-1 Maintenance service instituted and complaints
  (1) Alleviated
  (2) Analyzed
  (3) Change orders of parts instituted

o-1 Plans for "new" yearly model improvement run through all or previous steps—for original production

p-1 Cycle repeated

2. Production and distribution velocity assumption

3. Plotting the assumed progressive mass-production curbs to determine basic velocities of new industry

4. Tensioning by crystalline, pneumatic, hydraulic, magnetic means

5. Compressioning by crystalline, pneumatic, hydraulic, magnetic means

6. Consideration of manufacturer's basic production forms—relative to proposed design components for determination of minimum steps, minimum tools, and minimum waste in realization

7. Establishment of priority hierarchies of effort

8. Time-and-energy cost budgeting

9. Assumption of industry responsibility for field practices, not only in mechanical and structural, but in economic design

10. Designing for specific longevity of design appropriate to anticipated cycles of progressive obsolescence and replacement ability as ascertained from comprehensive economic-trend curves

11. Designing with view to efficient screening of component chemicals for recirculated employment in later designs

12. Maxima and minima *stated and realized* performance requirements per unit of invested energy and experience, and capital advantage of tools and structures employed and devised

13. Logistics assumptions, compacted shipping considerations as original design requirement in
    (a) Nesting
    (b) Packaging
    (c) Compounded package weight
    (d) Relationship to carriers of all types
    (e) Field delivery
    (f) Field assembly
    (g) Field service and replacement

14. Consideration of tool techniques

15. Consideration of materials' availability

16. Consideration of materials' ratio per total design

17. Elimination of special operator technique forming

18. Elimination of novel soft-tool designing

19. Numbers of
    (a) Types
    (b) Repeat parts
    (c) Subassemblies
    (d) Primary assemblies

20. Number of forming operations

21. Number of manufacturing tools by types

22. Schedule of forming operations included on parts drawings

23. Decimal fraction man-hours per operation

24. Designed-in overall one-man-ability at every stage of operation

25. Schedule of design routines and disciplines

26. Establish a "parts" inventory of "active" and "obsolete" drawings—from beginning

27. Establish a "parts" budget of "required" designs of "parts" for assemblies and major assembly and general assembly and molds

28. Drawing dimension standards

29. Establish a numbering system of controlled parts

30. Establish purchasing techniques, jig-and-fixture, lofting techniques

C. Public relations—to run concurrently with all phases of IV (B)
  1. Education of public
     Rule 1: Never show half-finished work
     a. General magnitude of product, production, distribution. But no particulars that will compromise latitude of scientific design and production philosophy of IV (B)
     b. Publicize the "facts"— i.e., the number of steps before "consumer realization"
     c. Understate all advantage
     d. Never seek publicity
     e. Have prepared releases for publisher requests when "facts" are ripe

* * *

That my 1927 half-century critical path's realization is seemingly two years overdue is an illusion—it took two years to design it, so it did not become effectively operative until 1929—which is just over a half-century ago.

My 1927 path designing was deliberately undertaken with the following first-things-first objectives:

I must avoid setting too short an overall consummation period for my critical path. It was of prime importance that I adopt a target date so far in the future as to avoid making uneasy any of the power structures of 1927—which might feel that their interests were threatened by what I was proposing. It was necessary that I reach so far beyond the power structures' research-determined vision of their most forward development that my concepts would appear to be either a pleasant "pipe dream" or innocuous nonsense.

I was able to do exactly that. The most powerful people I knew found me utterly unaccreditable but "interesting"—and to some "fascinating." This induced them to invite me to their parties to entertain their guests with my "dreaming out loud." For this reason the power structure's press very frequently gave my projects prominent publicity—because they found my concepts popularly entertaining, they published them ever more frequently and prominently, hoping for advertisements-inducing, increased readership. In 1930 the author of "Buck Rogers" told me that he frequently used my concepts for his cartoons.

I will now discuss the probable order of livingry-reoriented realization of the socioeconomic results of our already-accomplished, half-century, critical-path-artifacts development. I will discuss the operationally introduced sequence of their realizations in terms of the many critical-path-relevant subjects that I also have introduced throughout this book.

For instance, we have pointed out that the geologist François de Chardenèdes wrote for me a scenario of the technology of nature's producing petroleum which disclosed that the amount of energy employed by nature as heat and pressure for the amount of time required to produce each gallon of petroleum, if paid for at the rate at which the public utilities now charge retail customers for electricity, must cost over a million dollars a gallon. Combine that information with the discovery that approximately 60 percent of the employed in U.S. America are working at tasks that are not producing any life support. Jobs of inspectors-of-inspectors; jobs with insurance companies that induce people to bet that their house is going to be destroyed by fire while the insurance company bets that it isn't. All these are negative preoccupations . . . jobs with the underwriting of insurance underwriters by other insurance underwriters—people checking up on one another in all the different departments of the Treasury, the Internal Revenue, FBI, CIA, and in counterespionage. About 60 percent of all human activity in America is not producing any physical life protection, life support, or development accommodation, which physical life support alone constitutes real wealth.

The majority of Americans reach their jobs by automobile, probably averaging four gallons a day—thereby, each is spending four million real cosmic-physical-Universe dollars a day without producing any physical Universe life-support wealth accredited in the energy-time—metabolic—accounting system eternally governing regenerative Universe. Humans are designed to learn how to survive only through trial-and-error-won knowledge. Long-known errors are, however, no longer cosmicly tolerated. The 350 trillion cosmic dollars a day wasted by the 60 percent of no-wealth-producing human job-holders in the U.S.A., together with the $19 quadrillion a day wasted by the no-wealth-producing human job-holders in all other automobiles-to-work countries, also can no longer be cosmicly tolerated.

Today we have computers that enable us to answer some very big questions if all the relevant data is fed into the computer and all the questions are properly asked. As for instance, "Which would cost society the least: to carry on as at present, trying politically to create more no-wealth-producing jobs, or paying everybody handsome fellowships to stay at home and save all those million-dollar-each gallons of petroleum?" Stated evermore succinctly the big question will be: "Which costs more—paying all present job-holders a billionaire's lifelong $400,000-a-day fellowship to stay at home, or having them each spend $4 million a day to commute to work?" Every computer will declare it to be much less expensive to pay people not to go to work. The same computers will also quickly reveal that there is no way in which each and every human could each day spend $400,000 staying at the most expensive hotels and doing equally expensive things; they could rarely spend 4000 of the 1980-deflated dollars a day, which is only 1 percent of a billionaire's daily income.

Why would all the people not continually buy all kinds of expensive things? Answer . . . because they will want to travel around the world, and they will quickly discover that while you can't take it with you into the next world, you also can't take it with you around this world. They will each discover for themselves that the greatest luxury in the world is to be able to live unencumbered while able to get any information you want in split seconds and any desirable environmental condition you want in a day.

The actuarial curve indicates an eighty-year life expectancy by 2000 A.D. This amounts to 700,800 hours per lifetime. I would like to make some assumptions regarding the future use by humans of those hours. I'm assuming the present average is a forty-hour work week and forty-nine work weeks per year. This amounts to 156,800 potential birth-to-death work hours per lifetime. If we spent only forty of our eighty years at work, that would be 78,400 lifetime work hours. As of our present life-style, we would be giving 11 percent of our lifetime to work in producing for self or for others.

For instance, a four-day work week of five hours per day with a three-day weekend would result in living in the same spot and clogging up the highways with local weekend to-and-froing. We now propose instead of chopping life into work-week increments that we consolidate our work service potential into a few years of continuous six-day-per-week, eight-hour-per-day service as in the military or medical internship.

Assuming that as a result of technological advances, the machines can produce adequate life-support in half the present time. Present-day custom would adopt a three-day, five-hour-per-day work week. This means twenty hours per week is all that is necessary to tend the machines that accomplish adequate life-support production. The internship service concept is composed of an eight-hour-per-day, six-day work week, a total of forty-eight hours per week. Because of mechanical advance, we are now assuming that the forty-hour week is reducible to a twenty-hour work week. This means that our originally required lifetime work service of 78,400 hours has through technical advance been reduced to 36,200 lifetime work hours. At the constant intern service rate of 48 hours per week, the 36,200 hours of lifetime production can be accomplished in 754 weeks or fourteen and a half years.

We are now going to assume a college- or university-level education available to all humans—probably to be effected through a stay-at-home, video call-up procedure involving six years in all. We assume that there is great advantage to the individual of having work-years' experience intervening between the bachelor degree and graduate work. We assume entry into bachelor work at eighteen years of age. This means that at twenty-one years of age the students can enter upon their internship production service consisting of forty-eight-hour work weeks. The students will then enter upon four years of this total fourteen and a half years of production service responsibility. This brings them to age twenty-five. They will then enter upon their three years of graduate work greatly informed by their production-work years. At twenty-eight the graduate students will enter upon their final ten years of production service. At thirty-eight they will have completed their service in direct production support of humanity. With their wisdom probably evolved, they will have more than half their lives still to live. They will be extremely well informed. They will be free to initiate their own mind-informed commitments to the improvement of human functioning in support of the eternally regenerative integrity of Universe.

It is very probable that the technological advances will be far greater than those of the foregoing assumptions.

At present all the great new city office buildings have fancy plumbing (with which only the typewriters sleep) while a majority of city people sleep in inferior quarters with poor plumbing. The moment we start giving everyone those handsome life fellowships, we will find almost all the great new business buildings in the cities being depopulated to such an extent that we shall, in quick order, be able to turn those buildings into great apartment houses and hotels to accommodate the free-will residential convergences of humanity in central cities. Although such skyscrapers are far less efficient than the "ultimate" city buildings, they will provide a satisfying step forward in accommodating humanity's successively occurring desires and needs to *deploy* into wilderness country or archeological research country or sports country or to converge to meet with other humans for conferences or other collateral developments of which there will be an ever-multiplying, exciting availability.

*   *   *

Along with making it economically feasible to permit a large majority of people to remain at home in country or city, to think fearlessly and unselfishly, we will permit all children to study at home, eliminating the school-house, schoolteachers, school janitors, and school-bus systems, which cost unnecessary trillions of dollars world-around each school year. At home we shall provide each child with a private room, television set, and video-education cassettes as well as world-satellite-interrelayed computer and controlled video-encyclopedia access. These will make it possible for any child anywhere to obtain lucidly, faithfully, and attractively presented authoritative information on any subject.

Students will be able to review the definitions and explanations of several authorities on any given subject, as there are different viewpoints of a number of great scholars on any given subject. The system will never get tired of answering the questions or even the same questions asked and answered until the child is sure that he or she has understood. To make children evermore confident of their understanding and useful enjoyment of their thoughts, each will be given access to basic tools and direct experiences in the purposeful use of the tools.

Children and grown people will be able to get their continuing intellectual education . . . at their home terminals. They will get their social experience and tool-handling education in locally organized neighborhood activities when humans wish to converge.

All those who have attained high scholarly capability assure us that the only real education is self-education. They also say that this self-disciplining is most often inspired by great teachers who make it seem apparent that it will be excitingly worthwhile to take the trouble to bring oneself to apprehend and then comprehend variously pertinent data, phenomena, and derived principles. The intimate manuscript records of all the great self-educated individuals show that they discern intuitively when and what it is that they want to learn. Thereafter they arrange to do so by four main strategies. The first is by self-conducted experiments, if they are scientists. The second is by going to those live humans who have educated themselves from direct experiences. The third is to contact through books those who have discovered and learned but are now dead. Fourth, they sometimes have recourse to the esoteric and often exquisitely valuable information contained within the word-of-mouth information system relayed almost exclusively from generation to generation by the craftsmen-artists.

At heart fearful of losing their jobs, the tenured professional educators of today and all those earning a living by teaching are relentlessly fighting video. Since it would damage their position to tell the truth regarding their motives, the tenured pedants rationalize, "What the children need is the personal equation." What I've long observed in the moving picture world is millions and millions of human beings falling in love with female heroines or male heroes, though knowing only their photographic images cast upon a blank wall. All "the personal equation" was, and as yet is, transmitted probably a little more poignantly by electronics than would ever be feasible in ordinary, personal-contact life.

After beginning to receive their home-research lifetime fellowships and trying the video educational system themselves, professors and researchers won't protest anymore about loss of the "personal equation" in education.

I am certain that none of the world's problems—which we are all perforce thinking about today—have any hope of solution except through total democratic society's becoming thoroughly and comprehensively self-educated. Only thereby will society be able to identify and intercommunicate the vital problems of total world society. Only thereafter may humanity effectively sort out and put those problems into order of importance for solution in respect to the most fundamental principles governing humanity's survival and enjoyment of life on Earth.

* * *

I find one result after another of the last half-century's critical path of now-fulfilled, relevant artifact-inventions and developments demonstrating unexpectedly intimate interrelatedness and unanticipated synergetic ecosocial productivity. Number one, we shall find that we do indeed have enough "good-life resources" to go around. The computer will continually direct us back to basics. The computer will call our attention to the many relevant new potentials of the synergetic integration of critical-path events. If we continue to use our resources—metaphysical and physical—properly, there will continue to be ample to take care of all humanity: food, energy, shelter, travel, research, cultural development, inventive initiative in all the technologies, etc.

Obviously the first step is to pay people the handsome fellowships to stay at home and say to themselves, "What was I thinking about before I was first told, convincingly, that I had to 'earn a living' by doing what someone else said I had to do?" Then let them discover that their fellowship income will permit them to travel objectively to search and research and engage in creative or productive endeavors anywhere around the world.

With complete freedom of choice, much of humanity will begin to discover that it loves to work at tasks of its own choosing—that it loves to discipline itself to demonstrate its competence to others—that it will compete with the many to demonstrate its competence to serve on one of the multitude of production teams. There would be no pay for the work. It would be like qualifying for the Olympic team to be allowed to do what you want to do. You would have to prove that you could do the job you wanted to do better than anyone else available to get onto the production teams. Permission to serve on the world's production teams will be the greatest privilege that humanity can bestow on an individual. There is no joy equal to that of being able to work for all humanity and doing what you're doing well. It is difficult to match the gratification of not just crudely crafting a plaything for one child (which indeed can be very rewarding), but of producing exquisite somethings for a billion children. Activities of this kind are reinspirational to a mystical degree.

As with all humanity there would be no life-support problems whatever for those on the production teams. There would be no attempt to block automation to keep human muscle and repetitive-selection jobs operative. If any individual wants to leave a team to have other experience or to serve elsewhere, a replacement would be found on the waiting list of others who want to take on the job. There would be the continual inspiration to invent more automation—to emancipate humans from performing only sterile muscle-and-sorting functions. Those who are real craftsmen and are good at developing the tools-that-make-tools and love their work will be the heart of the production teams. There will be no need to earn more because your fellowship will always get you more than you want. You won't be able to buy any nonconsumables—you will only be able to rent. If you are renting more than you can use, the system will call the excess back.

Those who love to teach and have something valuable to teach can discipline themselves to qualify for membership on the subject-scenario-writing teams or on the video-cassette or disc production teams. Great scholars will thrive—whatever their fields may be. They will be free to devote their entire time to their labors of love. Vast numbers will discover that they are earnest, capable independent-research scholars. What they have to say, if unique, can become the subject of a video-cassette, world-satellite-relayed encyclopedia entry.

In 1927 the only plastics we had were celluloid—a nitrocellulose development, by-product of explosive nitroglycerine. Celluloid was hygroscopic and highly flammable. Quite clearly plastic materials of many kinds were desirable substances, as transparent and waterproof as glass but not easily breakable and of much lighter weight. We had in 1927 hard rubber fountain pens and casein (milk-derived) poker chips but nothing larger. Wanting better materials and looking at one's own fingernails, one could say that such and such a material is ostensibly feasible, so it will be developed. You then made a comprehensive list of all the desirable materials, and you kept a dated list of the times of their actual accomplishment. With a list of all the desired technologies you also kept a chronological chart of their successive realizations. You then compounded the information these observations were providing with your list of all the successively advancing structural-strength and mechanical-workability properties of all the metals. You continually compared these development records with your list of desired materials—those that would make possible solutions of various livingry problems. Such scientific research and engineering development of prototyping technologies to ever profit the total life-support and accommodation facilities will be one of the most popular production-team tasks.

The critical path already accomplished in the last fifty years makes all this and much more immediately possible of development. It would not be possible to consider many of these strategies prior to the invention on this planet of certain artifacts: for example, the rocketry-accomplished satellites or recent decades' proliferation of computers would not have been possible without the discovery of transistors, which would not have been possible without the prior discovery and development of all the discovering and inventing of all history. (See Appendix I.)

It was, however, possible in 1927 to see that such only-now-in-1980-physically-possible capabilities were and would always be desirable for society. Without being able to predict the discovery of transistors, chips, optical fibers, etc., it was easily possible to dream in 1927 that anything we needed to do could be done—never mind how—and to say to oneself, "I want a device like a fairy wand, which I need only wave while stating audibly the results I wish," and that this would be accomplished by subvisible, atomic behaviors. Whether this was to be done at the push of a button was of no real consequence. It is what we need and want to do that is reasonable that counts. My fifty-three-year critical path has proven that. I did not just state what was desired. I saw that it was my responsibility to undertake to design the artifacts that would best produce the desired results. Then, as first presented with new discoveries and developments by others, I must redesign my artifacts to take advantage of the now-proven additional technical capabilities.

For a number of reasons I felt doors that would open automatically on a human's approach would be desirable, and so I specified such automatically opening doors in my 1927 Dymaxion House. I also specified that they should fold sidewise in accordion pleats, so that the opened door-edge would not intercept the approaching human and cause a collision. My brother was an engineer on the Pittsfield, Massachusetts, staff of General Electric. A year after I had incorporated the foregoing equipment in the design of my proposed Dymaxion House, my brother telegraphed me to let me know that a General Electric scientist had just invented the photoelectric cell which, upon interruption of a light beam focused upon it, would activate a door opening by a miniature electric motor. As a practical and very reliable engineer, my brother considered my serious inclusion, in my designing, of technology that had not as yet been invented to be "lying" to myself and others. The critical-path concept had not as yet been conceived and incorporated in engineering-school curricula, so his telegram read, "Thank God, the just-invented photoelectric cell has saved you from being a liar. You can get one from General Electric for seventy dollars." The accordionlike foldable door also had not yet been invented in 1927. It was invented ten years later, once more saving me from "being a liar." So it went with hundreds of my half-century-to-come critical-path artifact inclusions of 1927.

Therewith I made the working assumption that "wishes are reasonable," that wishes defined the functions of not-as-yet-invented but highly desirable technology. It is, in fact, the as-yet-ungratifiable everyday needs that always inspire inventors in general. What you want for yourself may never be gratified. What you want for everybody, because you can see the total benefits that can accrue, is usually reasonable and technologically gratifiable, and to be realized possibly within your own generation.

CHAPTER 9

Critical Path: Part Three

WITHOUT LOSING SIGHT of all the foregoing, to which I will return later, I'd like to turn our attention to soil and land conservation and its essential functioning in support of total ecological regeneration and the work of those who would like to be on the productivity teams for reforesting the world as well as those working on ways to hold onto and regenerate the fertile topsoils—the people who are concerned in a very major way with the planet Earth as a total crystalline, hydraulic, and pneumatic system.

We can harness great streams and let gravity pull water inward to the sea while returning and reducing the runoff of topsoil-carrying-water. We can dam areas to recover washed-away topsoil as yet resident in freshwater lakes and streams and, using off-peak wind-power generation, repump bottom silts to dry land to enrich the soil's surfaces.

The engineering and planning teams of our post-1980-1990 world crisis period will look at our whole planet only omniconsiderately, whether dealing with the conservation of the soil or with how to employ gravity hydraulically, in an omni-intelligent and omniconsiderate manner: for instance, to irrigate most effectively, never again thinking in terms of individual local economies or individual material advantage terms, but thinking only in terms of the integrity of eternally regenerative Universe as aided locally by total planetary ecology support and thereby omnihuman support. In respect to optimum omniecology conservation there are some immediate-past-history experiences to be considered.

As recounted in our "Legally Piggily" chapter, during the time of the 1926 "bad hog market," which led to the 1929 Great Crash, which led in turn to the 1933 New Deal, after all the farmers had been displaced by the banks foreclosing on their farm mortgages and their farm machinery, the no-longer-worked-and-irrigated land dried out, and the wind-storm "dust bowls" began to grow and to blow away the topsoils; this sequence, followed by heavy rains, brought about vast land erosion.

The 1933-inaugurated New Deal instituted a program to rebuild the soil and get the farmers back on the land. They erected what they called "shelterbelts," produced by high hedges initially produced with swiftly and thickly growing Osage orange trees augmented progressively with other varieties of slower- but higher-growing bushes and trees. These high hedges enclosed square "sections"—quarter square miles—of potentially rich farmland. These shelterbelts wrought miracles in recapturing the as-yet-wind-borne soils and new, daily, stardust receipts of our planet. Altogether they rebuilt the soil throughout the last flat plains and prairies of the United States.

Using the knowledge gained in producing the U.S.A. shelterbelts, the recovery of fertile land from desert in Israel, accomplished twenty years later, was an extraordinary vindication of the New Deal agricultural department's soil-building theory. The Israeli shelterbelts were started in deserts with the water-capturing eucalyptus trees—all of whose roots collect local ground water. In the shelterbelt growth there is a decade-long series of planting of different kinds of tree and bush growths, which growth finally forms huge, high, dense, linear barriers of trees and bushes.

As they put farmers back on the land, the New Deal discovered that the productivity in America was such that with only 7 percent of the world's population here in North America (including the people of Canada and Mexico), the North American farms greatly overproduced its people's needs. Had they been able to look realistically at the whole Earth in terms of total productivity of the planet and the needs of all its people, administered by one world government, it would have been a different story. It still can be a different story.

Until after World War II there was no mechanical refrigeration of railway or highway vehicle transport. From 1900 until 1950 we had progressively re-iced refrigerator freight cars for railway transport of fresh meat and fruit. So many of the artifacts that now make possible special-environment-maintaining container-car conditions were not available until after World War II. In 1933 the technology was not yet suitable for serving the rest of the world's food needs from America, so farm overproductivity became frequent. In the game of food marketing in America entrepreneurs gain as *money,* in minutes of market trading, the major portion of the real life-support *wealth* produced by the farmers' year-long labor. For instance, cattlemen produce the original cattle that are sold to feeding and fattening farms in a series of price markups before the food finally reaches the dining room table. Of the present price paid by you and me for beefsteak, the cattlemen receive only a small percentage. Incidentally, all the corn and other grains fed to the cattle to fatten them renders those grains and kernels saleable as fat for prices tenfold what they bring simply as grain. The fat is useless to the buyer, but the hoax-myth that it makes the meat more palatable makes it impossible to buy the beef without the fat. If all the corn and grain going into useless fat were converted into alcohol for driving our cars, it would take care of much of our energy fuel needs.

In the 1920s and 1930s overproduction in U.S.A. farming frequently drove the prices paid to the farmer substantially below his costs, let alone his unpaid-for labor and worry. So the New Deal established what it called "the ever-normal-grainery," which recognized the farmer as the one to be protected. In "the ever-normal-grainery" the U.S.A. government stockpiled against periodic crop shortfalls. Under this program local representatives of the government would seal the farmers' harvests in local grain bins and pay them a fixed price adequate to cover their operating costs. Keeping surplus grain off the market kept the prices up. The New Deal U.S.A. government was, in fact, engaging in across-the-board price-fixing of everything—metals, oils, rents, wages, bank loans, etc. The farmer was paid to keep much of his land out of production, thus fostering productive acreage crop rotation for rebuilding the soil and other sound cultivating practices. For instituting all of those periodically unproductive acreage practices the government awarded the farmer a generous annual per-acre bonus.

This is how the government came to pay farmers for keeping acreage out of production as well as fixing prices so that farmers would not be victimized by the greed of the middlemen. Now for the "Legally Piggily" side of the story.

During the half-century since 1926 another set of class-one evolution events occurred which often seemed to be only-humanly-planned-and-contrived class-two evolution. In the "Legally Piggily" chapter we noted how the farmers' machinery was seized by the banks when the banks foreclosed on the farms. When the New Deal arrived, the banks owned vast quantities of farm machinery. It was rarely sold back to the individual farmers. They had no money or income enough to warrant a loan to them. Private-enterprise mobile brigades for mechanically planting, cultivating, and harvesting were formed and bought much of the bank-replevined farm machinery, which they transported by trucks from state to state, town to town, and farm to farm. These mobile farm-operating brigades start in the Deep South in early spring, moving north with the spring and their truck-mounted farm machinery. They travel together in caravans, with human mechanics aboard to operate the machinery which they unload at their local stops. Their crews occupy all the motels in the small farm towns along the way. Plowing and sowing seeds all the way northward, they turn around at the northern borders of the U.S.A. and return to the South to progressively reap the now-ready harvest with their CB radiotelephone-interlinked reaping-machinery crews. The grain harvested is now stored in the former "ever-normal-grainery" bins. The mobile-harvesting teams' managers then go to the local banks and are given certificates of receipt, which they then forward to the offices of the no-longer-locally-resident owners of the farmlands. These owners are no longer "farmers" or even nonfarmer individual humans. They are great business conglomerates.

In most areas of the American economy huge conglomerate money-making businesses have swept together many smaller money-making acquisitions; no single product name can adequately describe the vast money-making characteristics of these new conglomerates. Only a unique collection of alphabetical letters now identifies them. These conglomerates had nothing to do anymore with the "personal equation" idea of history's originally locally-owned-and-managed businesses.

"Practical"-size farm acreages rapidly grew from a hundred to thousands of acres, serviced mechanically by the already-described roving teams of workers. When the great corporations bought these farmlands, they bought with them the U.S.A. government's agreements to pay annual per-acre bonuses to the owners to compensate them for their nonearning, soil-conserving, rotationally unused acres.

Sponge-sucking together of a plethora of profit-wise-successful small enterprises—both of the invisible, metallurgical, chemical, and electronic revolution and of the highly profitable, successful, older visible-product companies—has produced conglomerates so powerful as to overwhelm the credit and business-doing capabilities not only of approximately all small single-category-of-production corporations but of all the old individually owned general store businesses.

Just as humans' names at one time indicated their occupations—Smith was a blacksmith, though successive generations of his progeny Smiths no longer smote—in the same way today's corporations' names mean nothing. International Telephone and Telegraph (ITT) company now owns and operates book publishing companies, makes musical instruments, bakes bread, and engages in hundreds of other essentially unrelated businesses. For this reason these super-supermarket conglomerates are now adopting multi-initial names and logos without providing the public any means of knowing what the initials stand for.

Many of the great conglomerates have such power and size—as, for instance, Exxon, GM or IBM—that any one of their annual business acreages, values of machinery, numbers of employees, budgets, etc., dwarf the corresponding acreage, plants, structures, budgets, and population of many of the world's nations.

A man named Edward Higbee was the first ever to write an article on this subject for *Time* magazine (June 29, 1962, pp. 10–11). Everyone at that time assumed that the American farmer was on the land and was a great political power. As I've mentioned earlier, when I was young, 90 percent of humanity in America lived and worked on the farms. "There resided the great grass-roots votes." Today only 7 percent live and work on the farms. Higbee caught on long ago to the fact that the farmers were no longer living and working on the farmland, though all the politicians in Washington thought they were on the land. The politicians were misinformedly doing everything they could to curry the voting favor of those vast-majority-of-the-population "farmers" supposedly living and working "out there" on the land. There were, however, almost no real, live human farmers out there on the farms whose votes they could curry with their favors. In a magnificently well-written two-page article in *Time* Higbee suddenly brought some but not all of the politicians to the realization that their picture of the "farmer" was mistaken. Many of the politicans found it "worth their while" to maintain the old picture in the public's concept. It provided invisible latitude for their wheeling and dealing.

Because everybody was living in cities, thousands of miles away from the farms, the public illusion that all the farms were being lived on and were being worked by those farmers has persisted to this day. The illusion persists despite the fact that superhighways- and automobile-touring Americans drive and fly ever more frequently across the vast farmlands of the country. The illusion is sustained by the clusters of tree-surrounded farmhouses, barns, chicken houses, silos, and sometimes windmills, which always lie on the horizon because the farmers did not wish to live or have their livestock near the roads, and the superhighways have been led along the outer "section lines." The fact that they are unoccupied cannot be seen at remote distances. Once in a while one of those farms is occupied by a conglomerate superintendent. The smoke from his house implies that all the farms are occupied. Seen from airplanes, the same illusion exists.

The big corporations have been taking advantage of all the favorable-to-the-corporations' sentimental illusions of the presence of farmers, gaining along with their enormous uncultivated farmland acquisitions large subsidies paid out by the U.S. government for "farmers'" rotationally unused farmland acreage. Billions of dollars of government subsidies now go to the conglomerate farmland owners.

In the "Legally Piggily," lawyer-capitalism-controlled time of Eisenhower Assistant Secretary of Agriculture Butz said, "You conglomerates can cut out all the green belts. There is a tremendous amount of valuable bonus-earning unused acreage under those shelterbelts." Suddenly all the shelter-belts were bulldozed away, so the conglomerate farmland owners could now legally claim the bulldozed-into-existence unplanted land to be "withheld production acreage," upon which they could realize very sizeable government subsidies. In vain did the few Mennonite and other religious sect farmers of Kansas's—and other states'—corn and wheat lands complain about the returning dust bowl occasioned by the bulldozing away of those shelterbelts.

We've talked in this book about entropy and syntropy: The entropic stars exporting energy as radiation; and the syntropic loci in Universe where energy is being imported and converted from radiation to matter. We noted how, despite Boltzmann's brilliant reasoning, the *syntropic importing loci* of Universe have not been scientifically accreditable as existing because they are astronomically invisible. They are invisible because of not giving off any radiation. We noted that the planet Earth is one of those syntropic energy-importing places—the only one we know of—where the entropic Sun radiation is constantly being impounded by the syntropic photosynthesis of the vegetation and converted from random radiation receipts into beautiful, orderly molecular structures (matter), with other living creatures and organisms in turn consuming the vegetation-produced molecules and thereby syntropically "growing" physically by themselves, producing large numbers of chemically orderly molecules. We observe this great syntropic operation pattern to be manifest in the natural ecology of our planet.

Some of the businesspeople described in "Legally Piggily" and others in political bureaucracies are willfully entropic, arguing that "ends justify means." For instance, almost all businesspeople undertake to make all the money they can in as short a time as possible both for their stockholders and themselves. The money they make is not the medium of exchange—gold, silver, and copper coinage—but the entirely "abstract," matterless *numbers* of digit dollars entered into their respective, legally valid credit accounts in the bank ledgers, or as manifest in the stocks and bond portfolios of individuals certifiably owning the corporate shares. Such abstract dollar entropic "worth-making" is the antithesis of syntropic-energetic-wealth-making by producing more service function with ever-less weight and volume of material, or by vegetation-and-its-physical-growth by ever-multiplying and -regenerating molecular structuring. The business and political entropy occurs in many ways. For instance, to make the most money with least costs, corporations put fumes into the sky and other wastes into the sluiceways; they cut out the shelterbelts, letting the topsoil blow away; they cut out employees to save money, while making the customers stand in line for long periods of time, often wasting the valuable productive time of those in line. Furthermore, the banks loan your (real-life-support, wealth-representing) dollars to others at 10 percent or more interest, which 10 percent the bank keeps, wherefore the banks' transaction, having produced no additional physical life-support wealth itself, means that the banks simply took their legally attested 10 percent away from your real-wealth account.

By and large the function of life on the planet is designed to be syntropic—to impound the radiation, conserve it, and use it to produce further syntropic functioning in overall support of the syntropic integrity of eternally regenerative Universe. The tendencies of many human beings—wanting to cultivate the soil, to care for the animals, the drive of artists to create, of artisans to build, of inventors to invent and develop time- and trouble-savers for others—are all manifests of the designed-in syntropic propensities of humans. The generous, compassionate propensity of humans is primarily syntropic. The selfish are "entropic." In order to keep Universe regenerative nature has placed human beings on this planet for their syntropic functioning.

We may safely assume that class-one evolution is syntropic and that class two is often entropically diseased. The drive to make money is inherently entropic, for it seeks to monopolize order while leaving un-cope-with-able disorder to overwhelm others. We must remember that the majority of those convincedly committed to "making money" are motivated to do so primarily because of their mistaken conviction that there is a fundamental (external) inadequacy of human life support on our planet. That has been true until yesterday. They were right until the syntropic, class-one evolutionary accelerating ephemeralization reached a point of doing so much more work with so much less effort, because of the reduction in weights per strength ratios, that we came ten years ago to the point where we could, by proven design, take care of everyone at standards higher than any have ever known.

In the vast majority of humans there is an innate inclination, propensity—even drive—to make sense and to produce order in consonance with universal order. The assumption by many humans that there is only entropic disorder seemingly present in Universe is brought about by looking only at the phases of energy separating out from any one system and by not looking at the same disengaging energies always joining syntropically in the production of other systems.

We will now consider other ramifications of the about-to-be-realized synergetic integration of all the objectives of the great half-century critical path.

All the artifacts needed for its synergetic fulfillment have been accomplished. (See historical table of realized scientific and technical accomplishments, Appendix I.) The generalized principles calling for their inclusion in the critical-path conceptioning of fifty years ago have been realized objectively in special-case discoveries, inventions, or designs taking place only during the last half-century.

It is a fact that we can now technologically recover and sort out the valuable chemistries in all the chimney-escaping or sluiceway-escaping "wastes," which, though unwanted by the local manufacturers, are necessary chemical-element components in the overall syntropic success of eternal regeneration of Universe. Nature has no pollutions—it has very valuable chemistries that function only under special conditions, so the critical-path strategy is to get all the money-maker-unwanted chemistries shunted into all their syntropically functioning routes. Pollution is simply energy—in the form of unfamiliar matter—which the timing of the omniregenerative cosmic system cannot immediately use but must use later.

We will now seek for the causes and solution of smog as a special case syntropic problem—whose solution, however, leads to understanding of how many other such problems will be solved.

We have places on our planet, like Los Angeles, that are world-famous for what is called "smog."

With the Earth revolving from west to east, the morning Sun heats the eastern slopes of mountains. In the afternoon it heats the western slopes as the eastern slopes cool off. The Northern Hemisphere's prevailing winds are being sucked from the northwest highs by low-pressure areas of the tropics in a southeast direction for the Northern Hemisphere observer, which phenomena we misidentify as "northwest winds." They are in reality southeast drafts. These prevailing southeast drafts dominate the environmental conditions of the 90 percent of humanity living north of the Equator—the majority of our planet's moist, life-support land is also north of the Equator. From the vast expanses of the North Pacific cool airs of the evening impinge upon the warm western slopes of all the Pacific islands and upon the West Coast mountains of the United States.

In the 1950s physics discovered that temperature differentials are equivalent to electrical-potential differentials and that what we have been calling "condensation" into water of water vapor is, in fact, electrolytic formation of atoms into water molecules. We have heating on one side of the mountains and cooling on the other. This produces an electric-potential differential between the eastern and western slopes as well as between the warm western slopes and the cool Pacific Ocean air.

Since what we used to call "condensation of moisture" is in fact electrolytic fixation—the low-floating, West Coast mist clouds of California are produced by the cool airs impinging on the warm mountainside, bringing about electric-potential differential and electrolytic fixation, which produces those lovely mists riding the western mountain slopes, particularly of Southern California, but also of all the western slopes of all the mountained Pacific islands.

We next observe the great twentieth-century influx of industry onto the California coast. Overnight settlements became towns and towns became cities, each with its own chamber of commerce doing its best to attract ever more industry. In order to pay for town governments taxes are necessary. In order to pay political obligations the elected town administrations need money to hire people to carry on all the legislatively conceived tasks—some of them necessary, many of them unnecessary, but all requiring large sums of money.

The Los Angeles Chamber of Commerce and the Los Angeles government did everything they could to invite industry to move into their domain because industries produce the greatest amount of taxable money-making. Industries also produce jobs and thereby in turn wages that can be taxed. Los Angeles did everything it could to attract industries and businesses. Having many locally occurring petroleum wells, one of the most logical of industries brought into Los Angeles was that of oil drilling, pumping, refining, storage, and shipping, such as those of the concentrated operations of the oil fields and harbor area of Los Angeles's Long Beach. Los Angeles built a vast number of huge refineries in the southwest part of the city. On its southeastern side Los Angeles positioned its steel mills to satisfy the large demand for steel products in the building of the oil refineries, their storage tanks and pipelines.

The fumes from these industries then loaded the mist and the warm airs, and the Sun-exposed upper cloud surfaces and their shaded lower surfaces produced temperature differentials, which in turn produced layer inversion, with the fumes locked in on the underside, which then acted as a widespread lower atmospheric lid, holding the industrial gases and fumes close to the ground throughout the whole Los Angeles basin. Thus smog became an industrially produced phenomenon.

Los Angeles's citizens became politically articulate about this "air pollution" and went to their city government saying, "We mustn't have this in our city." The city government then went to the utilities, refineries, and steel manufacturers and said, "Stop putting your smog-producing fumes into our sky. We've looked into the situation and find there exists equipment that makes it possible to precipitate that fume. But you don't have that equipment." The companies responded, "If we put in that fume-precipitation equipment, it will cost us so much more to produce here in L.A. than it does companies producing in places that don't have such controls that we won't be able to compete in our industry. We'll be forced out of business. So we're either going to have to cut out this nonsense about fume precipitation or move out of your city." The municipal government said, "For Heaven's sake, don't leave. Your tax base is essential to our political survival. We're politicians, we'll fix it up in some other way."

Soon thereafter the L.A. city government made the following pronouncement: "People, the smog is your fault. It's your backyard incinerators that are producing this smog." The people said, "Sure enough, we are incinerating in Los Angeles. We are in the wrong. We must stop incinerating." So a law was passed saying that nobody could incinerate within the city limits. The people did stop incinerating, and the smog abated—but only in minor degree. The real offender was the industrial fumes. Along came World War II, and the issue was buried under more immediately pressing matters.

When World War II was over, great numbers of additional citizens moved into California. Suddenly the smog problem was back, and the whole act of pre–World War II was repeated. The people complained to the municipal government, and the omnichanged government personnel had entirely forgotten about what had happened twenty years earlier. They went after the big corporations, which threatened to leave town, and the city once again pleaded, "Don't leave town. We need you here."

Once more the city blamed the people: "It's the fumes from your automobiles that are producing the smog. We have taken samples, with scientific instruments, of the below-the-smog air, which samples when analyzed proved the obnoxious fumes to be those of your automobiles." With their greatest election-fund support coming from the oil men, and with the most powerful regulation lobbying being carried on also by the oil men, the politicians of America took up the cry, "It's the automobiles." The people said, "Why, sure enough. We'll have to do something about it. We'll pass laws to limit the level of fumes coming out of each car and require the manufacturers to produce and install special smog-control equipment in each car." The automobile companies loved that. It meant more accessories to be manufactured and sold and an obvious way to rationalize increasing the price of their cars.

Christmas and New Year's Days are celebrated everywhere in America, but Los Angeles, being a relatively new and gigantic social body, is able to alter its celebration customs. The L.A. refineries and heavy industries have learned that the people of California want to take a Christmas vacation. So the holiday becomes a ten-or-more-day vacation starting the weekend before Christmas and continuing through the weekend after New Year's Day. It pays all the refineries and other heavy industries to shut down their plants. As the holiday proceeds, the air gets clearer and clearer, until on New

Year's Day—the traditional Rose Bowl Day—you find throughout Los Angeles a dreamy-clear view of all the surrounding, often snow-capped mountains. If you went out with scientific devices to measure the fume-level from the cars, your instrument would read approximately zero. The only reason that auto fumes were previously measurable was that the industrial-fume-laden ceiling held the auto fumes down and locked them in at the level at which you and I are breathing. I have taken many New Year's Day pictures from the hills of Los Angeles showing it to be absolutely clear. Then, on back-to-work industrial Monday, you see a vast, molasses-brown cloud rolling in from the southwest gradually to obscure the whole of Los Angeles.

There is no question about it. It *is* the refineries, the steel and other mills, and the public utility fumes that produce the smog. But no municipal government anywhere in America is going to let its industry go away. Therefore, cities are always going to find political ways of absolving the industries while blaming the people. Air does not stay in any one place. There is a preposterously stubborn myth about "this being my or someone else's airspace. . . . This is my air." Air keeps moving right through the geometry of our environment to continually recircle the Earth. The air belongs only to everybody on our planet.

We're going to have to gradually recognize that whatever our central government be—whether it's our United States government or a world government—it is going to have to put in equipment to precipitate fumes—no matter what it costs. Companies must install the precipitators or be put out of business. No one will be allowed to put fumes into the sky or noxious chemistries into our waters ever again. We do have the well-proven physical equipment to deal with this problem today. At the end of the year, when we figure a company's taxes, we will rebate the company taxes by whatever the cost of the fume- or chemical-precipitating equipment and the cost of its operation may be. All companies will be able to compete on a fair basis despite the initial and operative cost of the equipment. But the valuable recovered chemistries must be turned over to the government by the companies. Society must become aware of the high value of these recovered chemistries. For example, the amount of sulphur coming out of all the chimneys around the world annually exactly equals the amount of sulphur mined from the ground and purchased annually by industry to keep its wheels turning. The computers will quickly show that the value of the recovered chemistries turned over to the government will more than pay back the cost of their rebates to the industrial companies. The computers will also show that the reduction in cost of respiratory ailments and other deleterious smog effects brought about by elimination of the smog constitutes an out-and-out profit to society.

The recirculation of metals and other chemistries is now being handled only by what we call "mongers." Before World War I society wrongly assumed that metals and chemicals traveled only a one-way street to the rusting dump heaps. A company that produced iron assumed it to be consumed like food or rusted away until it had entirely disappeared. All physical substances were assumed to be entropic—i.e., to waste away, never to return. It was not until the enormous amounts of metals produced in World War I began to come back again into the market in the 1930s that those concerned with such matters began to recognize the economic advantages existing in obsolete-form metals returning as scrap, which metals were more highly refined and concentrated than were the newly mined ores. Scrap became extremely important.

The scrapmongers are in business to make money. They sell their scrap metals only when they feel sure they are getting the highest possible prices. To increase prices the profit-motivated mongers held onto their scrap. As a consequence their yards get bigger and bigger as well as more and more unsightly. This constitutes a blockage in the world's metals-recirculatory system. This means that world government is going to have to take over altogether all the functions of recirculation.

Talking about scrap, which is more accurately to be called recirculation, is analogous to talking about the bloodstream or other circulatory systems of humans and other organisms. We are an integral stage in an omniregenerative cosmic system. The Universe is 100-percent regenerative. Terrestrial ecology has been but is no longer 100-percent regenerative. Recirculation is regenerative. Blockages in that recirculation occur when money-making people, seeking special economic advantage for themselves, hold back the flow of regenerative essentials to increase their prices.

Governments are going to have to take over the function of eliminating any and all stoppages in the recirculatory integrity of our planet. All corporations are going to have to turn over to the government all the chemicals they recover by fume precipitation or filtered sluiceway condensations. Hoarding of any kind must be banished from human affairs. Today, in the copper industry, the quantity of recirculating scrap copper is so great that it dwarfs the newly mined copper production, which provokes the world copper-mine-owning cartel into maintaining a powerful Washington lobby that seeks to increase government stockpiling of copper.

All special-interest lobbies are entropic. Class-one evolution is progressively eliminating all blockages to recirculation. Regenerative recirculation of metals has the unique function of realizing the twenty-two-and-one-half-year recirculation cycle. It is these cyclically produced technological gains that make it possible to take care of ever-more humans at ever-higher standards of living with ever-less pounds and volume of matter and ever-less ergs of energy and seconds of time per each technical-function performance.

I was able to arrive at that figure of a twenty-two-and-one-half-year metals-recirculating cycle in 1936. I was working for the Phelps Dodge Company, who had asked me to give them some prognostications about the uses of copper in the future of world industry.

Copper is the most plentiful of the most efficient electric-power-production and -conduction metals. World War I was a power-production war. And copper is the most plentiful of nonsparking metals and is therefore logically employed in connection with gunpowder-handling equipment such as the shells inserted into the gun breeches. Because of these facts, the demand for copper in 1917 was epochally great.

Not long before World War I and its huge demand for copper, copper-ore-to-pure-metal reduction by the vastly less expensive flotation process and the also much less expensive electrolytic refining brought the cost of mining and refining copper so low that the cash value of the average amounts of recoverable gold and silver co-occurring with the copper—which gold and silver are automatically purchased by the U.S. government mint—exactly paid for all the mining and refining of the copper itself. The whole price paid for copper was profit. The mineowners then decided to mine only when the prices bid for copper were at a peak. The prices bid always peaked in wartime. With World War I over the world copper cartel waited and worked for the start of World War II.

In the 1930s the big copper companies were badly bothered by the influx of copper scrap into the marketplace. Up to the time when I came to study the copper situation, the rates of evolutionary change were so slow that the mineowners had no idea that the copper they sold would ever come back on the market to disturb their price.

By 1936 the copper price controls were completely challenged by the scrap influx. Phelps Dodge asked me to do some research on the problem, so I reviewed all the known, published data of the metals world. In the metals world very accurate records are kept about how metals have been and are now being used. Very profitable publications are maintained by the affluent metals businesses. Very accurate inventories exist detailing, for instance, how much of any given metal is built into an automobile. In 1936 there was only about thirty pounds of copper in each American automobile. Copper is expensive, and the auto manufacturers try to keep the use of expensive metals to a minimum. However, considerable copper is used in a gas station—for instance, in all the gas-tank-filling nozzle equipment—because it is nonsparking. You couldn't possibly use a sparking metal such as steel around gasoline.

I was able to arrive at that previously undiscovered twenty-two-and-one-half-year recycling figure by very carefully integrating the total inventory of the in-use tonnages of metals in all the main categories of their use—for instance, the inventoried copper in all extant buildings, in old roofings, gutterings, and flashings, brass pipes, and so forth. The total inventory of copper in old buildings, both business and residential, is an inventory that becomes obsolete and is scrapped and recirculated on an overall average of once every fifty years. Within the building category copper comes out faster from big city buildings than from single-family country residences.

What makes obsolete any of the major categories of metals in use is the rate at which the new technologies occur that make obsolete the older technologies. In the electronics industry there exists only a two-year lag between the discovery or invention of new functions and improved techniques and their acceptance and employment by the electronics industry. This short lag is occasioned by the fact that the physical phenomena involved operate at subvisible-to-human-sight levels. This means that the behaviors are considered only on a basis of figures. If this one works better than the others to a sufficient, numerically expressible degree without lowering contiguous behavioral efficiencies, it can be reliably calculated that adoption of the newer facility will produce universal advantage. No human *opinions* on the merits or demerits of the discoveries and their invented technical realizations are involved.

In the aeronautical arts—airframe, power plant, instrumentation, airport facilities, and ground-controlled flight-pattern technologies—there is a five-year gestation period between invention and industry's adoption for use. The discoveries and technical inventions in the aeronautical arts are both visible and invisible. When invisible, the decisions to adopt are made scientifically through instrumentally derived numbers—where visible, the decisions are made on past experience and opinionated comparisons. Where there is room for opinion and personal prejudice, the decisions to reject or to adopt take longer. The more science and the less opinion is involved, the quicker the new technology is adopted. It is the rate at which new inventions are adopted that spells the rate of obsolescence of the technologies they are to replace.

By taking the invention-gestation rates in the different industries, which we've discussed elsewhere in this book (two years in electronics between invention and use, five years in aviation between invention and use, ten years in automobile manufacturing, fifteen in railroad, twenty-five years in big buildings, and fifty years in single-family dwellings), we integrate the amount of copper in each use-category and their respective number of years of use, and thus find the average rate at which copper (and all the metals) come back as scrap to be every twenty-two and one-half years.

The unprecedentedly great World War I copper production occurred primarily in America. In one year, 1917, humanity took more copper out of the ground, refined it, and put it to work than had been cumulatively produced in all the world throughout all previously recorded history's years.

This produced in 1917 a vertical cliff on the "all-history charts of world copper production." Adding twenty-two and one-half years to 1917 would bring the date of reappearance of the crest of that 1917 world-record production scrap to July 1939. So I told Phelps Dodge in 1936 that three years later, in July 1939, they were going to be overwhelmed by scrap. Meanwhile, I became the science and technology consultant on the editorial staff of *Fortune* magazine in 1938. In July 1939 the head of research for Phelps Dodge called me up on the telephone and said, "Bucky, your twenty-two-and-one-half-year scrap-return prediction is absolutely right. Go down to the New York docks and observe." I did so. Alongside all the great cargo ships were cargo barges filled with scrap metals, piled enormously high.

Copper is plentiful enough to be trustworthily used but scarce enough to be used only in the most efficient manner. Copper is a sensitive metal—the so-called bellwether of the metals. Whatever copper does indicates exactly what the other metals are going to do in the price and production markets; for instance, steel scrap was also coming back at exactly the same rate as copper—twenty-two-and-one-half years after production from newly mined ore. Hoping to protect their anticipated very high prices when World War II came along, and all unbeknownst to the general public, all the U.S.A. metals owners in 1939 were selling all their scrap metal to Germany and Japan to fire back at America two years later when World War II did come along. It was not a moral thing for the scrapmongers to do. The public in general had not the slightest idea what was going on—the American business public didn't catch on to the idea of metal-scrap recirculation until long after World War II was over. The American and world public at large have not as yet caught on to the significance of recirculating scrap metals making almost obsolete further mining of metallic ores in general. The authors of the Club of Rome's "Limits to Growth" had never heard of scrap-metals recirculation.

I now point out again that with *acceleration of ephemeralization*—doing more with less—came the acceleration of the rate of gaining information on how to do more with less in the invisible world of electronics, metallurgy, chemistry, and atomics. By the time the metals came around in their twenty-two-and-one-half-year cycles, we had learned so much more that we could take care of many more people at a much higher standard of living with the same amount of metals. Wherefore, as we have earlier pointed out, metals became the very bloodstream-of-realization of class-one evolution— which class-one evolution is nature's way of taking care of ever-more people at ever-higher standards of living accomplished with the same quantity of metal—until all are cared for, at ever-higher standards of living, without further thought of anyone having to earn that right to live. This coming realization of sustainable physical success for all humanity has been earned by all the lives of all people in all past time.

I am progressively reviewing the evolutionary integration of all these now-timely and available technologies that together produce a situation unlike any encountered ever before in this planet's multibillion-year history—that of all humans becoming economically sustainable at higher standards of living than ever known and doing so without consciously earning that living. Meanwhile the people have begun recirculating around the world, introducing their thoughts and experiences to all countries. All the great religions have become transnational, each operating in every country permitting them so to do. Backed by wealthy central headquarters, various of the most powerful religions of history were amongst the first to send their monks and missionaries around the world to build the strength of their parent organizations. Not only the religions but all the big ideologies have now become transnational. Neither "free enterprise" nor "socialism" recognize any geographical limits. Today, big business, as detailed in "Legally Piggily" (Chapter 3), is completely transnational.

Now only the world's people are left bound within their respective 150 national pens. The separate national pens were evolutionarily logical in former times, when nature deployed all people so that they could learn how to cope only under the special conditions occurring at specific loci around our planet Earth. But now the full family of different experiences and the therefrom-developed technological artifacts are being integrated by class-one evolution.

Something transcendental to any organized human planning happened in America in the early 1930s, something that exhibited the cosmic-scale qualities of class-one evolution. The record of consistently increasing annual immigration to America and the United States since the *Mayflower* landed in 1620 peaked in 1910 at over a million persons a year. In the early 1930s, however, for the first time the number emigrating began to exceed the number immigrating to America. A 300-year pattern had reversed. The people of the world had come in *to* the United States, had cross-bred, and had started to become outbound again, but this time as cross-bred and as yet further cross-breeding world people.

Overall class-one evolution, as manifest in Chapter 1 of this book, showed us how humanity first established itself in the southwestern Pacific Ocean (Austronesia) of planet Earth. It showed us how, having built rafts, Pacific Ocean humans drifted north and eastward on the Japan Current to Alaska and then southward along the west coast of North and South America, then westward again to where they had started. This drift pattern left small colonies vast millennia ago, whose progeny are now intermixed with much later arrivals.

Next came the westward, overland migration. Artifacts of history show us how people—pioneering ever westward and mildly northward—coped as successfully as they did. In due course the swords and later the guns of the ever-faster-westward-colonizing or gypsying human families and individuals offered protection against unfriendly intruders until the colonies gradually developed common defense on an ever-larger scale. Mobile tribal hordes eventually became settled farming nations, and then built up so-called national defenses. We have reached the class-one evolutionary point now in the last half of the twentieth century where the largest and most powerful abstract institutions—religious, financial, and political—have all become transnational. Humans, trapped in 150 nation-state pens, are being manipulated from outside the nations by big ideological, religious, or big-money interests. The power of lobbying imposed on local governments by big world money or big world ideological systems is incredibly corrupting. Preemption of the metals supply by the expanding arms industry plus the trade barriers prevent the free circulation and recirculation of metals. This means we have 150 sovereign blood clots interrupting our recirculating metals, which would otherwise serve as the industrial, productive lifeblood with which we might realize our class-one evolutionary gains.

Class-one evolution makes it clear that all 150 of the world's sovereignties must go. There was a time when the United States was incredibly powerful—right after World War II. Today most of the people in America still think of their nation as being the most powerful of world nations—ergo, free to make its own most constructive moves. Quite the opposite is now true; as we've shown in the "Legally Piggily" chapter, the United States is both internally and externally bankrupt—it is also overpowered by Russia's navy and conventional arms.

The Senate Foreign Relations Committee asked me to speak to them five years ago, as documented in the *Congressional Record* of May 22, 1975. They asked me where our country and its people were going, and I said, "Not only have all the big corporations become transnational and taken all the former U.S.A. gold and other negotiable assets with them, but they have also left all the world's people locked into their 150 national pens, with those 150 nations blocking the flow of lifeblood metals without which we cannot realize the increasing know-how of all humanity. Very soon the nation-state sovereignties will have to be eliminated," or humanity will perish.

A nation's dictator need not consult with his people at all. A dictator can make a deal with another dictator to give up their respective sovereignties. A dictatorial party, such as the Russian Communist party, which is composed of only 1 percent of the Russian people, can make a deal with other dictators or dictatorial parties to give up their respective sovereignties. In a quasi-democracy such as America the president or prime minister's first oath of office is to protect the nation's sovereignty against all foreign incursion.

If any president of the United States or prime minister of any other quasi democracy even so much as discussed possibilities of desovereignizing, he or she would be immediately impeached. In discarding its sovereignty the United States of America faces the most difficult of all situations. Therefore class-one evolution is about to put the U.S.A. out of business through international bankruptcy. This will be a powerful example of class-one evolution at work. The bankruptcy need not be the end. It is simply nature's way of ridding the planet of the most powerful of yesterday's sovereignties and thereby setting off a chain of 149 additional desovereignizations, altogether removing the most stubborn barrier to the free circulation of the Earth's world-around metals, foods, and income energy supplies and people.

We are now in a position to get rid of the 150 sovereignties and have a recirculatory, interaccommodative, world-around democratic system.

We now have the immediately realizable capability to exercise our often-repeated option to make all the Earth's people physically and economically successful within only a decade by virtue of the already-executed fifty-year critical path of artifacts development which has acquired all the right technology.

In support of that statement we will now examine a live case history of "critical path" planning that I engaged in thirty-eight years ago on behalf of Brazil, a plan whose full-scale realization was set for 1993. Because this plan is successfully gestating at a rate that indicates fulfillment by 1993, it should give high credence to the whole of this book.

* * *

We have already noted in Chapter 5, "The Geoscope" (p. 186), that at Churchill and Roosevelt's pre–World War II secret meeting in the Bay of Fundy, Roosevelt accepted Churchill's grand strategy, which called for the initial landing of the Allies' armed forces in Europe's "soft underbelly"—i.e., landing in Sicily from the North African coast.

As we have also noted, implementation of the "soft-underbelly" strategy called for the U.S.A.'s swift extension of its radio-triangulated surveying from the already radio-triangulated northeastern U.S.A. to be extended southwestward through Mexico, Central America, Venezuela, and Amazo-

nian Brazil to two of easternmost Brazil's South Atlantic coastal points—
Pernambuco (Recife) and Rio. Next, Pernambuco and Rio were radio-
direction-finder-triangulated with Ascension Island in the mid–South Atlantic. Ascension Island was next radio-triangulated northwardly with
Dakar on Africa's northwestern coastal bulge and northeastwardly with La-
gos on the coast of Africa's Equatorial Gulf of Guinea. These two adequate-
ly-far-apart African points were finally radio-intertriangled with two North
African Mediterranean coast points occupied by the U.S. armed forces.

What has not been recounted, which is of great relevance to this book,
is the story of the price Brazil's then-dictator President Vargas demanded
of U.S.A.'s President Franklin Roosevelt for permission to do all that comprehensive radio surveying over Brazil. What Vargas wanted in exchange
was a well-informed and far-forwardly-sighted plan for the industrialization
of Brazil.

Roosevelt's staff gave the planning task to the U.S. engineering company
that had organized many of J. P. Morgan's foreign, electric-power-generat-
ing, private enterprises. Vargas rejected their planning as prejudiced exclusively in favor of U.S.A. capitalism's exploitation of Brazil.

At this point the U.S.A. secondhand-machinery business heard through
the J. P. Morgan engineering firm that Brazil was considering a comprehensive industrialization. This seemed their opportunity to realize an enormous
profit on their gargantuan inventory of secondhand machinery of all kinds,
which the dealers had bought at superbargain rates as the U.S.A.'s industrial economy was swiftly modernized for its World War II needs. Vargas
saw through their scheming and would have none of it.

Vargas then told Roosevelt that he—and his Brazilian advisors—had
read all the known authoritative publications by the Russians and other experts regarding the Russians' successive five-year incremented planning of
comprehensive industrialization. Vargas and his experts were convinced
that much was omitted by those publications regarding the behind-the-po-
litical-scenes master strategy of conceptioning and realization of the successive planning stages under the special physical circumstances of Russia's
geography and its adjacency to capitalist economies controlled by those who
were hostile to communism.

As inspection of my Dymaxion Sky-Ocean World Map will disclose, the
whole northern periphery of Russia is in the Arctic and has no adjacent enemy lands. The length of this most-often-frozen northern border of the
U.S.S.R. constitutes more than half of all its periphery. The other half is
mostly in desert and mountain land. Consequently the U.S.S.R. had relatively few vulnerable, natural border entry points to guard. With a population in the 1920s of 150 million—95 percent illiterate, hungry farm
workers, whose lives were to be reimplemented and reorganized into a pri-

marily industrial economy—the U.S.S.R. required instant adoption of a schedule of "first things first" to be accomplished, followed by a logical sequence of successively most important acquisitions and functioning capabilities. During the first two of the U.S.S.R.'s five-year-plan realizations approximately eighteen million of their population had to die of starvation in order to obtain their final goal, which was to produce a thereafter-ongoing adequacy of life support for all. The price to be paid in human want and suffering, great as it was, seemed a pittance in comparison to continuance-to-eternity of the "life-grinding-to-death" agrarian serfdom.

Under the circumstances of millions dying and many millions more in want, enemies of the attempt by communism to demonstrate that it could produce a better life for its people than that enjoyed elsewhere—which would, however, take two whole generations to prove—obviously produced a highly subvertible social condition, provided only that enemies could readily penetrate and themselves subsist under the restricted life-support condition. Study of the world map shows that Russia's limited physical access gave their five-year planning the optimum chance of succeeding.

Such information as the foregoing discussion of the U.S.S.R. border-control conditions was typical of what Vargas found missing in all the then-published data regarding the U.S.S.R.'s undertaking.

Vargas reminded Roosevelt that, coincident with the 1929 economic Great Crash of the Western world, Russia's first five-year plan had discovered much gold and that the U.S.S.R. had been able to make gold pay for contracts with the theretofore leading but in 1929–33 idle primary production corporations of the U.S.A. These contracts sent proven-"know-how" engineering teams to Russia to supervise the building, equipping, and start-up of prototype factories in all categories of industrialization: hydro and steam electrical generating, mining, blast furnaces, steel and other metal producing, glassmaking, cotton and wool fabricating, petroleum producing and refining, etc. Vargas said to Roosevelt, "Almost all of those U.S.A. corporate executive engineers must as yet be alive. Being so expert, they must all be performing very responsible tasks in the U.S.A. today. What I would like you to do for Brazil is to have someone in the U.S.A. contact and interview all those U.S.A. engineers who took part in the across-the-board Russian five-year plans' technical initiations."

Vargas felt that those U.S.A. engineers must have learned a great deal more about the realities of the U.S.S.R. five-year planning than could be found in the literature.

The White House sent this task to the engineering department of the U.S.A.'s Board of Economic Warfare for action. As head mechanical engineer of the board, and in consideration of my background—as, for instance, in plotting the forward trends of world industrialization for the Phelps

Dodge Company (at the time the third largest copper producer in the world) or my experience as science and technology consultant on the staff of *Fortune* magazine—I was given the task prescribed by Vargas.

The first thing I did was to contact Loy Henderson of the U.S. State Department, who had occupied the U.S.A. "desk" in Moscow in 1929 before ambassadorial relationships were established with Russia by Roosevelt in 1934. Henderson located for me a member of his 1929 Moscow staff, a man named Habicht who had handled all the travel arrangements for all the U.S.A. engineers who went to Russia in fulfillment of those prototyping contracts. Through Habicht I learned who all those engineers were as well as which ones were most esteemed by the Russian engineers with whom they dealt. I was able to locate them all in the U.S.A. By 1943 most were heads or senior vice presidents of their original companies. All agreed to hold interviews with me, since I had U.S. presidential authority. Thirty-two individuals in twenty-one corporations were interviewed, all of whom had participated in the first three of the successive five-year plans of the U.S.S.R.

My commission was not only to seek nonpublished angles on the U.S.S.R. planning strategy, but also to interpolate the principles into a plan for Brazil, where the geographical conditions were exactly the opposite of Russia's. Anybody could enter Brazil from almost any direction. Since that was so, I had to develop use of the principles in an altogether different manner. I inverted the equation. If you couldn't keep exploiters out, you made it easy for them to come in, and if foreign interests wanted, for instance, to explore for and produce important metals for export, they would be permitted to do so provided they also produced for Brazil a stockpile quota, which would always provide Brazil with a quantity of that metallic element equivalent to 2 percent of the quantity of that element known to exist on planet Earth— since Brazil's population was 2 percent of the world's population.

To prepare myself for serious discussion of such comprehensive world industrial planning, before leaving Washington to visit these U.S.A. engineer executives I contacted the presidents of the four leading U.S.A. foreign-engineering-project corporations. All four of them had heard that Brazil was considering adoption of a plan for comprehensive industrialization.

I asked each to give me a statement of the primary tasks to be accomplished in the industrialization of Brazil, listed both in order of relative importance and in order of production inception. All four corporations, eager for such business, submitted cogent lists.

I then started on my succession of interviews. The following surprising experience occurred as each of my successive interviews commenced. The corporate engineering officer I was interviewing would say something like this: "When I was starting that factory in 1929, the Russian team with which I worked would keep reminding me that we were not only building a cotton mill (or whatever type of production unit they were the experts for), we were also building a fortress." My interviewee would say: "I thought they were crazy talking that way. But now, today, look at those headlines in today's paper. My factory is indeed serving as a fortress. It is under attack by Hitler right this minute! What else did they say to me of importance to which I tended to pay little or *no* attention?"

This startling retrospective realization on the part of all my interviewees greatly enlivened their memories, and their recalls were many and highly relevant.

On the day following my recording of these Russian experiences and re-called strategic principles, I would discuss the application of their recalled Russian planning-strategy principles to the industrialization of Brazil, a matter in which these corporation officers were also inherently interested.

I then returned to Washington and wrote a plan for Brazil based on all I had learned. I had my plan typed in a narrow vertical column on one side of legal-size paper, leaving plenty of room for readers' note-making. Copies were sent by registered mail to each of the thirty-two interviewees. Each re-turned their copies with many marginal pencil notes: "Good," or "I didn't say that," or "This is what I said about that . . ." I then rewrote the whole plan, throwing out any items that did not have a sponsor from amongst the U.S.A. corporations' leading engineering executives. I then sent the only-by-senior-engineering-executives-sponsored inventory of items of the plan to all thirty-two of the interviewees.

Their responses to the first draft were:

2 were unequivocally against it.
2 were cranky in their letters for extraneous reasons, but distinctly in favor of various items.
7 were without comment.
4 did not express themselves in their covering letters, but indicated approval by comments written on page margins of my texts.
17 were unequivocally for the document, as indicated both in their covering letters and in their itemized comments—proving that the outline did properly report and interpolate the "area of agreement" (17 of 21 firms or offices favored the outline). They itemized a total of 13 objections and gave 146 itemized approvals, covering 125 in-dividual paragraphs in the outline, and made 52 suggestions for ad-ditions or modifications.

Just as my plan was complete, Vargas was deposed as president of Brazil. Forwarding of it to Brazil's new political leader might well be construed as an affront. The president of one of the major U.S.A. corporations involved in my "Compendium" thought so well of it that he took it informally to leading industrialists and powers behind the political scenes of Brazil. From time to time in the subsequent thirty-seven years I have heard of features of my plan being manifest in Brazil's economy.

In March of 1980 I was invited to visit Brazil by the Chamber of Commerce of Sao Paulo, its leading commercial-industrial city. I thought of the "Compendium," which had been sitting in my files for thirty-seven years. I had Xerox copies made and took them with me to Brazil and gave copies to many of its economic leaders. It was their consensus that the plan is now appropriate to their needs in almost all ways. They felt it to have been significant that I had thirty-seven years ago recommended that they switch their energy fuel from petroleum to alcohol, which is exactly what they are now doing.

The "Compendium," as I called it in 1943, and the 1943 reaction to it on the part of leading U.S.A. corporations' engineering vice presidents, now follows. No alterations have been made. It is printed exactly as typed in 1943. Not included are approximately 100 pages of the developmental phases of the undertaking, which included letters from individuals, etc.

A COMPENDIUM
OF CERTAIN ENGINEERING PRINCIPLES
PERTINENT TO BRAZIL'S CONTROL OF
IMPENDING ACCELERATION IN ITS
INDUSTRIALIZATION

Accrued to Experience of U.S. Engineers and Firms
Who Participated in the First Three of Russia's
Graduated Program of 5-Year Plans

*

August 13, 1943
R. Buckminster Fuller
Chief, Mechanical Engineering Section
U.S. Board of Economic Warfare

As a digest of the investigation, thoroughly documented in the main body of this report, the following admonitions, listed in order of interdependent significance, may be forwarded to those Brazilians concerned with control of their future industrialization as truly representing the majority opinion of the U.S. engineers concerned and experienced in this field.

Number One, it was pointed out by all those interviewed that *Brazil must make its own plan.*

This must be realistic and not a matter of their being coerced into some foreign-designed role, wrapped up under a Brazilian label printed elsewhere. No matter how excellent the consultative advice they may obtain from experiences outside their economy, they must themselves insure the success of their own program by the inherent strength of their own authority, which in turn must derive from specific requirements of their own political trend and from a deep consciousness of the adequacies of their own declared purposes and sequitur decisions.

It was also the consensus of opinion of the interviewed engineers that: *in order to plan successfully, there must be more than a singleness of purpose; there must be a dramatically tangible objective.*

Determination to raise the standard of living or to "do good" in this world lends no specific design guidance, which latter is essential to effective economic planning. Obviously everyone must do a certain amount of eating and sleeping. They have been doing that for a long time and will continue to do so in some degree without any planning.

It is the conditions under which the planned-for lives are to be lived, *as determined by the tangible objectives,* that in turn determine the *set of physical principles most expediently to be employed.*

With a *dramatically tangible objective* or, better, a progressive series of tangible objectives to be reached and passed as milestones, *any sincere planning,* no matter how relatively immature, *so long as it springs from an educated base,* will provide successful survival in some measurable degree superior to any unplanned overall existence.

INTERPOLATED CONCLUSIONS:

1. A workable, overall objective of air-minded Brazil upon which to pyramid its successive stages of plan would be:

(a) *To make Brazil the leading skyport of the world.* This, of course, means in effect a network of airports, which, in the world integration trends, are functionally called for by the fact that Brazil will represent the increasing air switchyard for (A) all the tropical air traffic which will be advantageously west-bound on the tradewinds from the Near East, Europe, and Africa to the Americas, and (B) north- and south-bound Pan-American traffic.

(b) That all highway systems shall radiate from the air and water ports of Brazil to its natural resources. That the initiative of individuals tending to explore for resources may thus be expedited.

(c) That Brazil, because it is unfeasible to maintain closure of its borders, employ that fact to advantage, instead of opposing it ineffectively, and therefore plan *to make Brazil the easiest country in the world to come to or leave*—in effect a nation-wide, ever-renewing world's fair. This should help keep their external purchasing power high. Since Brazil's boundaries touch those of every other South American country except two, community of interest, specifically pertaining to modernization, must be stimulated throughout all South American countries to prevent border animosities—no trade barriers, etc., as with Canada and the U.S.

(d) That they should subdivide the whole geographical area of Brazil into approximately 300 small resources-exploration areas of approximately 10,000 square miles each, efficiently interconnected and balanced for interdependence, so that they may never become politically disunited, i.e., Silver, Cotton States, etc., in U.S.

(d.2) Each area should contain its own super airport center or city. These would be centered approximately 100 miles from each other in all directions. This distance is chosen as representing the practical horizon relay distance for an eventual electronics, television, and power network. The means to create this transit system should be established and the Brazilians should apply their surplus human energy to the procurement thereof or there will be no appreciation nor understanding of how or why they became so blessed.

(d.3) That each area not already searched be explored radiantly from the airports.

(d.4) That in choosing the appropriate locations of the decentralized industries, and in determining the *methods of original development, stockpiling, and production* of discovered resources, that the decisions *always be predicated on "work" surveys which will determine approximately the most efficient overall expenditure of energy to the total economy.*

(e) That by virtue of the manifold, super airport network development, amplifying Brazil's already established 500 airports, the population will be decentralized from the southeastern coastal area throughout the whole of the country in such a manner that the center of the population will trend towards its geographical center, an essential to stabilization of the economy and to its economic security and its most efficient development energywise.

2. That Brazil must, without vacillation, determine upon the specific mathematical language of its industrialization.

(a) It was the consensus of opinion that they should standardize on the metric system, to which U.S. producer (but not consumer) industries are already adjusted.

(b) That they nominate immediately 60-cycle generation of power. (This choice in power standards will coincide mathematically with requirements of the decimal system of 12, should the latter continue, as indicated by present trend, to be scientifically desirable in Brazil.)

3. That in order to take advantage of the present state of industrial and scientific advance throughout the world, Brazil rent out to appropriate, skilled U.S. engineering firms the development of all its resources to the raw or stockpile stage. This should in no way be construed to refer to their production organizations for domestic consumption. The contracts will be kept in force by virtue of guaranteed schedules of performances; they shall be subject to strict regulation in the matter of labor conditions, interchangeable standards adopted by Brazil, monetary exchange rates, etc., the profits of export of natural resources to be retained in Brazil and "plowed back" into further development of resources.

(a) That all equipment brought in by these concerns shall, if the development leases are terminated, remain in Brazil as part of the nation's accruing resources; that equipment be admitted duty free.

(b) That the rental for these concessions shall be paid to Brazil not only in (A) United States dollar credits, but also in (B) *increments in kind of the respective resources thus developed.*

(c) *That the schedule of increments shall be such that Brazil's approximate proportion of world population* (i.e., 2%) shall be protected and instrumented in such a manner that the known world quantity of each resource element involved shall never be reduced to less than 2% remaining available above grade in concentrated storage within Brazil. This increment must be provided to Brazil before any product may be taken out of Brazil. Thus, as Brazil's industrialization develops, no matter what the design configuration may be, its proportion of the world's chemical element resources naturally occurring within its borders will remain such that its population may enjoy no less than the average standard towards which the whole world trends, i.e., towards equilibrious per capita distribution of the chemical elements serving in industrial functions enjoyed by an increasing proportion of all population:—therefore, towards dynamic equity of all elements per world person in mutually enjoyed services.

(d) That the choice of optimum overall sizes of equipment and choice of process methods, etc., be left entirely to the discretion of the licensees. This will eliminate this always inadequate phase of detail planning from government officials, leaving technical expediency to private initiative.

4. That Brazil recognize:

(a) That at present the best world source for industrial tools, power, and prime movers is the U.S., by virtue of the most recently overhauled and integrated standards attained by the U.S. economy for war purposes, and to the superior interchangeability of parts developed by the U.S.

(b) The highly developed psychological relationship of the worker and the segregated mass functions of each industrial operation designed into U.S. tools and at present providing the highest overall rate of service or product output per worker, and percentage of overall horsepower effectively distributed per unit operation in the world.

(c) That this initial outfitting at the hands of unit economies shall not be an exclusive, long-time policy, but merely an initial efficiency.

5. That the number one natural advantages to be thus developed will be those of energy sources of all categories. Increments from these energy developments are to be considered in terms of a continuing energy income, to be rapidly amplified by a concept of energy reinvestments for the whole economy. That the power of the Amazon watershed be harnessed and considered by designers as an integrated, moving assembly line for finally carrying forward whatever its major heavy products may be as a feeder gravity assembly line, possibly for mass-production house-assembly line.

6. That the number one immediately available *physical resource to be developed* (over and above those already functioning) is that of Brazil's hardwoods.

That complementary to the hardwood product developments, phenolic resins and other appropriate plastics and adhesives essential to fabrication of compound curvature plywoods be domestically developed to satisfy the manifold *structural* and container and vehicular body functions hitherto satisfied essentially by the materials used by expediency in much earlier industrial economies.

That the weight-strength factor of such compound curvature hardwood plywood be recognized as providing an advantage over any of the production steels or aluminum alloys yet developed, while at the same time embodying superior rigidity and other successful features relative to proofness against fire, insects, moisture, corrosion, distortion by heat, etc. Speaking by and large, "equivalent" design solutions in compound plywood weigh 1/6 those of solutions in steel; 1/3 those in aluminum alloys.

7. That insofar as possible, all domestic requirements be solved through the most modern or even new designs for the employment of these integrated, lightweight plastic products—plywood being in effect a plastic material reinforced by wood-fiber.

8. That Brazil, being by natural geography the beneficiary of vast annual vegetable increment, determine upon a national fuel policy developed from alcohols derived from vegetable sources, and that vigorous continuing research be maintained in the direction of new vegetable alcohol sources and products.

9. That a national policy of accelerated universal education be incepted, augmented throughout by the latest moving picture techniques developed for war instruction, particularly relating to translation of theoretical knowledge to technical application.
   (a) That individual moving pictures be developed relative to each and every external mechanical function of man: (1) a picture for the best use of all simple tools, then (2) their extension into the machine tools, (3) always compounding the use of the machine tools with the inherent mathematics.
   (b) The conversion of all principles of physics and theoretical chemistry into moving picture demonstrations and their further integration through pictures into pilot plant and mass production tool-up processes.
   (c) *That all primary school work be completely integrated with the vestibule schooling of decentralized local industries,* the present war trend be amplified to include their concomitant industrial nurseries, and the whole industrial activity be considered in effect an extension of the old household life, or its subsequent pre-industrial guild life. In effect, that the industrial world and home world are to be realistically integrated to provide improved conditions for both.
   (d) That Brazil recognize that the standards of industry are now advanced by prosaic efficiency requirements of the war to realistically include physical conditions so complementary to the human as to make these industries in effect as pleasant if not pleasanter work than hitherto characterizing work organized solely within the home.

(e) International exchange of students in advanced education. Government must subsidize building and equipping technical schools—even subsidizing students if necessary at first.

Brazil should consider the leased development services of U.S. engineering firms or any consulting services rendered by the latter to Brazil's planning authorities to constitute not an admission of weakness on the part of Brazil, but, on the contrary, to represent the availment of a *natural scientific principle* often employed but never before clearly comprehended as such; i.e., that the function, for instance, of U.S. engineers in Russia was not so much the well-advertised service of providing the original "know-how," which knowledge Russians could in time have as well gained by traveling abroad, but one of functioning as an *unprejudiced third party concerned only with operation of physical laws,* who, not even comprehending the local tongue, could unconcernedly *break* the ice jams of political theory or expediency in an *unorthodox manner,* thus providing gains that might otherwise be greatly delayed or never attained, because the stranger could break the rules with impunity.

As a corollary to this "relentless robot" sort of function—"jamming ahead with the work, irrespective of personal feelings or local precedence"—there was also available to Russia in the U.S. services the incalculable advantage of a scientific perspective upon their plans, *developed from outside the framework of reference,* the number one essential of all scientifically determined progress.

This perspective ability, gained by foreigners upon any economy, has been well known; for instance, to classical students of government and history. At the turn of the present century, English scholars considered Professor Lowell of U.S.'s Harvard University the greatest living authority on English government and legal precedent. At the same time U.S. authorities recognized Lord Brice of England as the greatest authority on U.S. political history and government.

We here in the United States are today receiving, from Japan in particular, a mortally expensive lesson on the subject of the advantage gained by international perspective. Japan's keen appraisal and selection of the essences of our industrial advantages, from out their settings of concomitant disadvantages—the latter bred out of local cultural habits—provided the means for Japan's accelerated advance into a challenging position of our economic prerogatives, despite inferior original position in natural resources.

In other words, Brazil should confidently expect the U.S. engineers to do in many ways a better job for them than those same engineers in many instances did for Russia. Under the outlined circumstances, Brazil may expect from U.S. an even more up-to-date industrial bill of fare than has ever before been concocted, even for the latest war effort, if they will leave the decisions on *technical organization of resources development* to those American engineers, reserving for Brazilians themselves the philosophy of consumer utilization of their resources, i.e., complete determination of the design of domestic services and products.

BIG "DON'T":

Number one error in "plan" principle discovered by U.S. engineers in Russia was that of their "economic planning." The Russians divided their whole program into "economic" and "technical" categories. The economic was supposed to come first. The economic planners made the mistake of assuming that the configuration of the latest worldwide industries as discovered at that moment would never change. The economists supposed that by analyzing each industry by materials employed that they could deduce the final technical requirements. Theirs was a static viewpoint. They never got to first base.

To comprehend their failure in this division one must inspect our own important errors. Many ill-advised public relations councilors in the United Nations [i.e. Allied nations] thought that their great productive machine could be valved over to production of any product at a moment's notice, like a soda fountain. Thinking themselves wiser than their engineers, they failed to understand that each product must be tooled from the bottom up; that none of the production set-up, even including its buildings, would be subject to conversion to production of other products. It was those non-mechanical-minded political economists who brought us into the costly mess of non-preparedness.

It was economic planning of political economists in Russia, completely unversed in theoretical, let alone practical mechanics, that almost lost their cause before it was started. The latter decided, for instance, to mass produce tractors, simply because these fitted the political propaganda need of wild promises to farm labor whose support they wooed. They gave priorities to tractor production materials and great tractor factory buildings before considering acquisition of production tools, and the machine tools which must come ahead of them, and the steel which must come ahead of the latter, etc. The plant went tractorless for years after building completion and finally functioned best as a fortress at Stalingrad. Some said this was because the Russians had slyly planned for it. This was not so. It was just thoroughly over-built on paper, which made it a good fortress. Russia got the tractors all right, in the end, but only after introduction of proper engineering methods at U.S. urging which comprehended the completeness of tooling-up problems.

This kind of "economic planning" would, if incepted in 1500 A.D., have assumed that the power utensil industry was the final word of the Almighty on how to solve all equipment problems. It would have started all economic analysis with inspection of the type and content of materials in coaches, sedan chairs, doublets, and have then attempted to say that cumulative totals of lead and tin equivalents represented the desirable priority stockpiling out of which to evolve their forward economy. This accountant type of economist, unfamiliar with mechanics as a dynamic experience, but glib with the classifications, always fails as a planner. Such men were essentially responsible for the progressive failure of the U.S. banking system to anticipate the needs of science-borne industrial evolution. They did not recognize it as a continuing process. They looked upon it as a fixed or finite investment.

Amongst the very real accomplishments of U.S. engineers in Russia was their hard-won success in converting the Russians from European professional engineering practices, which conveyed university science and engineering graduates *directly to responsible positions.* It was unheard of that such graduates should soil their hands.

Now, as a result of American engineering intercession, all Russian science, engineering, and technical students must after graduation spend two complete years in out-and-out shop and field jobs as laborers and mechanics' helpers. As a result of the lessons of error in the five-year plans, U.S. engineers say that if anything the Russians have now carried this practical side of all education too far.

In this connection a measured drawing replica prepared by technical accountants and draftsmen for Brazil of U.S. industry as is would be as lifeless an affair as was accomplished by the U.S. architectural profession for three-quarters of a century following the Civil War. Their measured copying of the classical "orders" of European architecture was not only inappropriate, wasteful, and useless, but it had the deleterious effect upon U.S. culture of adopting false standards and an inferiority complex regarding its own innate character and ability. The effect of this was to obscure from public recognition the fact that the "unarchitecturalized" engineering forms and buildings springing up to house a new industrial society were the unpresuming and unique architectural form of their own—grander than any before conceived in history. It took the perspective of clever designers in the very Europe from which U.S. professional architects were copying the "orders," upon the U.S. industrial engineer's forms, to discern the birth of a healthy new modern architecture. They adopted its form, superficially called it international architecture, and the U.S., still not realizing that they were responsible for the creation, asked these European designers to come over and command their architectural schools.

It is necessary that Brazil comprehend distinctly that much of the present industrial configuration of the U.S. economy is that of the nineteenth-century scaffolding work, so to speak, surrounding the net final twentieth-century structure just emerging.

In this connection the railroads, for instance, represented a *horizontal scaffolding* for temporary delivery services to set up an economy that could then graduate to a modern trackless and wireless economy.

Brazil can now adopt these emerged features because they are now developed to a prefabricated, know-how-degree as a finished phenomenon, eliminating the necessity of re-enactment of the many errors and experiences developed prior to the present state of overall advance.

In this connection it must be remembered that the railroads were first conceived as means to a nationwide real estate development. Because they were so wastefully heavy, they could not pay for their own development except in the terms of the land value increments accruing to the rights of way. They were therefore bonded for half centuries ahead to be financed out of the wealth they would indirectly open up. This expediency, however, served to get the people distributed over the land that they might further explore and develop the resources whose raw or unconcentrated products were then carried great distances to highly centralized and relatively inefficient cramped plants of the industrial east. If technology had been sufficiently advanced, the automobile would have done this much more thoroughly and quickly.

By the railroad means of *primary* decentralization of national personnel, the American center of population was moved westward approximately 500 miles in the course of a century-and-a-half. Russia, with a relatively minor percentage of the per capita railroad development of the trackless land and air transports, moved its center of population one thousand miles eastward in twenty-five years, while at the same time producing in accelerating volume for the present severe war.

This proved that the deployment of the people to the maximum of land area development does not spring from an initial transportation advantage provided exclusively by railroads. A modern railroad coach with one passenger weighs 140,000 pounds per passenger. The weight per passenger fully loaded is 3400 pounds. This is greater than the weight per passenger when a 1942 automobile carries only one person; i.e., 3000 pounds. Fully loaded, the average prewar auto weighs only 600 pounds per passenger. Postwar cars promise to reduce that average to under 300 pounds. Overall, door-to-door weight per passenger mile-per-minute of postwar air transport will provide advantage over the auto or railroad in ratio of better than ten to one.

It must be remembered that the railroads were developed to a design level, in the course of a century, competent to carry the structural and mechanical equipment and maintaining consumables of a civilization *averaging many times as heavy and several times as bulky per unit of function as that comprising our present-day mechanical environment, and hundreds of times the weight and bulk per unit of function of the now increasingly complete equipment of air-borne armies.*

Houses and buildings, man's largest and heaviest category of per capita controlled environment, so far but meagerly developed industrially, have averaged, throughout the 75 years between the Civil War and the beginning of present hostilities, a hundred tons per capita, whereas environment control design now well-developed for airplanes, whose stresses in the air or in landing are many times those to which houses may ever be subjected by hurricane or earthquake, nonetheless make possible man's comfortable ascent in minutes from tropic heats in the area of 150° F. to stratosphere temperatures of minus 65° F. This new range of environment control built lightly and sinuously into airplane enclosures indicates postwar housing solutions distinctly advanced in every standard of performance, yet weighing only a few hundred pounds per capita. Thus postwar human container weights of possibly one-quarter ton per occupant are to be compared with the lightest wallboard prefabricated structure of 1942, which weighed twenty-five tons (not including foundations), or better than five tons per capita, while the so-called permanent housing structures of 1942, including their foundations, still averaged in excess of 100 tons per capita and will be obsolete in ten years.

In order to comprehend the overall foot-poundage significance of transition from a rail-borne to an air-borne economy, it is necessary to envisage this vast change in tonnage per capita inherent in the changing design throughout all services which will be automatically propagated by the mass production industry of such lightweight housing. This industry is certain to take up the slack in world industrial production capacities and know-how created not only by the negative factor of war's end but by the most positive and dire necessity of rehousing the multi-millions of world's people, a rehousing whose standards progression will go on to rehouse the better than two billion population. This will be the greatest industry in all history. Brazil, with its Amazonian watershed, its hardwoods, its aluminum, its superior paper-making potentials (for paper will play a major role in the new houses), is in a unique position of advantage to initiate this industry on the scale required. Its network of jungle airport, scientific, tropic stations and exploration centers, and mechanical-chemical prototyping laboratories should divide up the problem.

It is further pointed out, to bring this prognostication home, that the highest building rate ever attained in the U.S. provided only 280,000 single family dwellings in one year; 1/4 the number required by annual marriages; 1/6 that required to offset annual disaster losses and complete obsolescence—a rate inadequate to total emergency. Such methods, which failed miserably to keep pace with civilization from 1913 on, obviously could not cope with a totalized world housing problem.

Realistic planning on the part of Brazil means taking advantage in advance of this vast accrual of overall foot-poundage saving per unit of designed environment control. If so, it is simply indicated that air transport can be relied upon by Brazil as the major category of direct physical communication. Air communication may be appropriately augmented in descending order of importance by roadways, waterways, cableways, and only in instance of highly specialized requirements, by railways.

Emerging from an era of steel surplus, shut-down, and scrap-dumping, in which millions were spent to find out how many things could be built of steel, such business being secured on our "substitute" basis by price and service advantages, we came sharply into the war-caused shortage of steel. It became our job to supply half the world's inherently wasteful, though efficiently energy designed, steel requirements of war. Despite the strong need, it is only within recent months that steel has been importantly reduced in building, so strong were designing habits and so difficult to change were labor and building codes.

In the course of abandoning all-steel buildings, and then steel structural buildings, for reinforced concrete and brick, first steps in real steel economy were taken by the engineer designer, Albert Kahn. These were effected through continuously welded steel reinforcing rods for large spans. Further steel reductions were effected by others through stressed steel wire reinforcement.

Opening just this month is the first steel-less bomber production plant of the Douglas Aircraft, designed and erected by Austin Company at Des Plaines, Illinois. Despite increasing spans unknown to prewar industrial requirements of 150 and 200 feet, with straightaways of several thousands of feet, the Austin Company provided a superior truss construction of laminated wood members not only for the roof but for all structural columns. Steel was eliminated even in the flooring, concrete aprons, and footings, without deleterious effect.

This was not a compromise. It was better building. The equivalent insurance rates indicated equal fire safety to that of a steel building because the structure was completely equipped with sprinklers linked up by plastic conduit. Practically the only steel used in the plant was for tools and equipment.

The tremendous advantage to Brazil, with its hardwoods so eminently suitable for building, as determined by the Ford Company in its Brazilian operations, that is implied in this change of affairs, freeing their industrial growth from any limitation by steel except for use in tools, is evident. It is even indicated that the bases, arbors, and frames of the machine tools themselves, etc., which were formerly made of heavy steel casting and in recent war years were increasingly fabricated out of welded steel sections, could now be expeditiously supplanted in many instances by compound curvature, conical or cylindrical form, phenolic resin laminated hardwood structures. This would eliminate another important category of heavy steel tonnage.

STANDARDS:

While a great deal of additional information was received from the interviews in connection with "optimum" versus "elephantine" or "insectine" sizes of equipment, to be amplified in production capacity by batteries of such optimum units—such as a thousand-ton blast furnace; 50,000 k.v.a. horizontal generator; grain storage in progressively decentralized 30,000 bushel silos, country-town elevators of half a million bushels and central market elevators of 1, 2, and 3 million bushels, etc.—these are, of course, only dramatic items amongst millions of optimum standards developed to high degree by the war effort.

Whether determined by guesswork or hard research, for Brazil to depend solely on the efforts of U.S. engineering concerns themselves, whose whole organization is given to maintenance of the latest stage of advance in such matters, is, in any event, inappropriate. This is the consensus of the interviews.

It is worth noting that there has been a long-time trend to increasing decentralization of such industrial operations into the foreign countries by the specialists in such fields, in lieu of the constantly decreasing foreign investment of dollars in uncontrolled operations.

SAFETY FACTOR:

In spite of a clearly defined trend of the major opinion cited in this report, it is worth noting that Russia's first five-year plan was characterized also by complete modernization of their existing industrial plant structure. Their 1914 industrial status was approximately that of Brazil's present stage of industrialization. A broad picture, with ample safety factor for present emergencies and future development, was demonstrated by the Russians, who renovated many old plants and augmented them with much new equipment in European Russia west of the Urals. East of the Urals Russia built its brand-new economy, literally growing its towns out of scientific exploration stations. To this new Russia they shifted their new tools from the European theatre when the enemy advanced and allowed their renovated old industry to take the gaff, essentially liquidating their "foothold" plants of the first five-year operation.

In the same way plans for realistically improving Brazil's present industrial plant may be considered as the stepping-stone of the moment, which Brazil can well afford to scrap when its brand-new scientific industry of the hinterland has gained youthful strength.

USE FORCES—DON'T FIGHT THEM:

Most urgent scientific admonition towards successfully realizing *any* plan is to *take advantage* of each of the trends and to develop them, no matter that it may be in a novel manner, *towards* the advantage of the populace concerned.

There is no reason, for instance, why Brazil should not develop from the start a completely smokeless industrialization providing a high standard of living. The smoke characterizing early industrialization of the North is now a mark of unattended inefficiency to northern engineers—important by-products are being wasted, environment frictions are being increased.

The area of dense jungleland of Brazil is greater than half of the U.S. It has been penetrated by few of the Brazilians, who, living in the cooler southeast, speak of it as the "green hell of the North." Ford officials say that most Brazilians inquire of them with as much wonder regarding the vast reaches of Brazilian jungles as do New Yorkers regarding the North Pole. Certain it is that the jungle in no way lends itself to the easy, speculative wanderings of homesteaders and prospectors.

An entirely different means for deploying the Brazilian population over the whole of their land for purposes of its development must be devised from those which augmented the pioneering of the U.S., Canadian, and Russian hinterlands.

Almost so simple that it will be shunned by those who prefer to plan the hard way, in order to take advantage of their hard-earned specialized experience of the past, is the technique now provided by modern warfare that would approach this whole Brazilian jungleland from above, bombing it open, then parachuting in with well-planned hand equipment and personal protective devices to carve out a complete polka-dot pattern of island airports over the whole country, into which pattern mechanical devices would be fed progressively as parachute deliveries graduate to plane-landed deliveries, etc. Each area would receive its quota of machine tools, drafting equipment, air conditioning, etc., and then its engineering and designing personnel would amplify the hold on the jungle. This "island" network of "tropical research and development stations" should form the nuclear structure for the new Brazil.

Dramatically emphasized by its absence was any discussion on the part of American engineers of aid to Russia in establishment of communications services, beyond Russian consultations in New York with the Radio Corporation of America. The wireless had supplanted almost completely the wired technique of early American communication. Russia was able to adopt an electronic stage of wireless communication without re-exploring the arduous step-by-step advances in communication by wired means. In the same way it is quite as practical for Brazil to consider accelerated development of its lands by an essentially trackless scheme. They will be able to buy, postwar, if not later manufacture for their own account, thousands of helicopters, which would make this form of functional exploration highly effective and easy to integrate.

INEXHAUSTIBLE WEALTH OF SCIENTIFIC PRINCIPLE:

Distinguishing characteristic of this digest is that it takes heed of the war's number one lesson, i.e., the advantage of employing science to satisfy *needs stated as functions.* Any economy, irrespective of the relative quantities of traditionally esteemed elements in its physical resources inventory, can outperform, per capita, any other economy in direct proportion to *the degree of the initial control in planning* conceded to science by politics—that is, "outperform" as measured in terms of services and satisfactions produced per potential consumer.

That Germany will probably be smothered by the Allied war effort should not be allowed to obliterate this lesson. The United Nations' already developed fuel and hydraulic generation flow and potential manpower, as well as its physical resources in most of the traditionally important economic categories, outranked Germany's initial inventory by one hundred to many hundreds percent. Advancing the physical odds constantly, which is what the continued war effort adds up to, does not change the fact that Germany's operational set-up of overall scientific ingenuity forced the world race committee (in order to maintain its prerogative) into repeatedly calling for new run-offs, at the same time rearranging the handicap until, in a finally "recognized heat," at last won by the United Nations, the handicap ratio was equivalent to starting Germany's horse at scratch in a one-mile mark. And because in the end sheer preponderance of physical advantage volumetrically smothers the scientifically engineered combustion, that blanketing must never be allowed to blind the world to the technical significance inherent in the demonstration. This is it: by discovering the sources of energy available (and every major economy has a scientifically potential superabundance); by decentralizing and enmobilizing parts fabrication and arranging a shifting foci of assembly to adjust to expediency, production may start with any one of a number of alternative raw sources of the atmosphere, vegetation, water, metallic ores, woods, etc. Concentrated energy in stabilized potentials, in the form of coal and oil, are great conveniences and represent a head start, but no more than that, to science. Thus is independence of immobile structure, tracked, wired, localized, frozen investment accomplished. Thus the economy divests itself of slavery to obsolescence. Thus is energy constantly remounted to provide the human intellect with the greatest hitting power, or an over-alert morphology.

Scrap elements everywhere, even in the form of bombed equipment and fired munitions, only represent an increased abundance of highly concentrated raws, ever more widely distributed. Scrap, *actual* or *potential,* i.e., in junkyard or in obsolete building, machine, or fixtures, it must be realized, is a "mine above ground" in highly concentrated forms of the original chemical elements which had been "reworked" by nature many times before man "worked" them. The ninety-two "elements" are never "secondhand." They are primary "electrical behavior" patterns. Energy to rework them is plentiful. They should always be rearranged in their most efficiently useful condition to the service of man. This is pure mathematics. Any evolutionary outcropping of the newer, more efficient arrangement can never be long suppressed.

CHAPTER 10

Critical Path: Part Four

HAVING COMMITTED OURSELVES to solving humanity's problems with artifacts, we can use the Geoscope and World Gaming strategies as a "test-bed," and can now sort out which comes first of various artifacts—all of which are going to be needed to get Spaceship Earth operating omnicooperatively on behalf of all.

Not only may we begin to make the whole world work for all humanity but incidentally to actualize the human functioning in Universe as local information-gatherers and local problem-solvers in support of the eternal regeneration of Universe itself.

No single move can bring us more swiftly in the direction of complete overall desovereignization, unblocking the free flow of technologies and resources, than that of instituting the world-around integrated electrical-energy network fully described in the Introduction to this book and the "World Game" chapter.

Next in artifact design priority to the integrated world electrical energy network comes the physical-environment-controlling equipment of world-around humanity's momentarily geographically fixed activities—fixed in contradistinction to humanity's swiftly mobile environment-controlling artifacts such as automobiles, buses, trains, airplanes, and satellites. So seemingly stationary are city skyscrapers that few think about the fact that all their parts have been transported from far away and that many of those parts and materials have been intertransported many times in the course of their production and assembling. As of 1980 the average U.S.A. family moved out of town to a new location every three years. They do so primarily in readjusting human production functions to relocated factories and offices and to new airport and shopping centers' living-local convenience. When I speak of mobile dwellings, I do not refer to camping trailers or tents, I speak of those dwellings which will stay geographically fixed for many months or years but which are readily and economically transportable and reinstallable over wide ranges of distance.

As I have mentioned before and now repeat in a more comprehensive manner, in 1800 the average human being was walking an annually cumulative distance of 1100 miles and riding ten additional annual miles. By 1900 the average human being was yet walking a total of yearly distance of 1100 miles but the average U.S.A. citizen's annual vehicle-ridden miles had increased to 400. All humanity is as yet in 1980 walking an annual average of 1100 miles but in the U.S.A., Europe, and parts of the Near East, Asia, Africa, and Australia, all men, women, and youngsters free to travel, are averaging over 20,000 annual miles of vehicular travel.

Class-one evolution has all humanity progressively cross-breeding to produce an integrated world human race. If we pass our present cosmic examination to continue aboard planet Earth in Universe, the to-and-froing of humanity will increase rapidly. The motion patterns of humanity, as also mentioned earlier, are pulsating between ever more widely convergent and divergent to-and-froing. Two main types of environment controls are required: a whole city under one dome for convergent phases of human living and single-family or small group air-deliverable domes for remote deployment for skiers, geologists, artists, and others.

*   *   *

Since 1927 I have been deeply involved with the issue of making high-performance shelter available to all humanity. By high performance I mean such environment-controlling shells—and their survival equipment—as can be produced only by the most advanced aircraft and space technology and the latter's level of technical problem-solving. In 1927 I anticipated a fifty-year-long gestation period for a new building industry. Since 1977 was the fifty-year target date, I began the prototyping of my Fly's Eye dome, which embodied design attention to all that I had learned not only throughout that fifty-year development period but in all my thirty-two earlier years. They will not be sold. Like telephones, they will be rentable.

The Fly's Eye uses a very few types of nestable, mass-produced fiberglass, sheet aluminum of thin gauge, or polyester-coated sheet steel components that, when assembled, produce a 5/8 sphere of the "Hex-Pent" geodesic configuration. As with the ports and pores of all organic systems, the size and shape of these openings sort, sieve and classify the in-bound and out-bound physical-component traffic of metabolic regeneration which the Fly's Eye domes embody.

The Fly's Eye domes' "pores" are all seven-foot-diameter circular openings. These circular openings serve alternately as doors, vents, solar-energy-cell mounts, etc. The circular openings constitute three-fourths of the surface area of the domes, while the manufactured shell-structure components constitute only one-fourth of the structures' surface. Since the circles have rigid rims, the closure of the circles can be accomplished by two, spread-apart drumheads of tensed, thin film or fabric materials—ergo, at low relative cost.

The structural shell components constitute a comprehensive leakproof, watershedding system that, with the circular openings covered, leads all rain and melting snow into the shell's watercourse cisterning system. The cylindrically rimmed circular openings will be tensilely covered with opaque, translucent, or transparent glass, plastic film, metal glazing or screening, or some combination thereof. They will serve as energy harvesters in the operation of the dwelling by parabolically collecting incoming energy in sunlight foci, liquid-heating cells and by circular-opening-mounted, wind-drag-driven, air turbines.

FIGURE 41.   26-foot-diameter Fly's Eye dome prototype

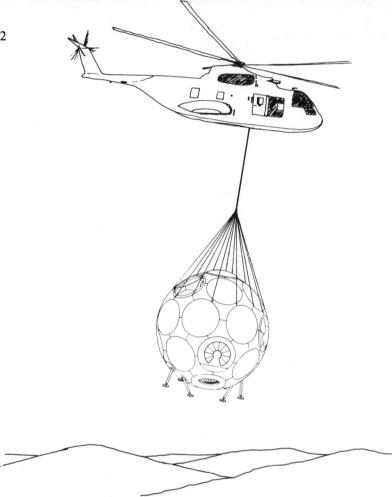

FIGURE 41. Fly's Eye dome transported by helicopter

Fly's Eye domes are of two sizes. The smaller twenty-six-foot-diameter
one is constructed of only one type of mass-produced, strong, lightweight,
hyperbolic-saddle-form component; the larger fifty-foot-diameter one is
comprised of only two types of mass-produced structural shell and water-
shed-constituting components, which are also of the hyperbolic-saddle type.

Both twenty-six- and fifty-foot-diameter domes can consist of two concentric identical domes with a space of six inches between and no metallic
interconnectors—this spacing produces highly effective insulation as well as
an excellent hot- and cold-air ducting system. The concentric domes' inter-
connection is accomplished with a seven-foot-diameter outside circle and
six-inch-deep conic tubes made fast at the seven-foot outside end of the circular openings of the spheres.

The smaller Fly's Eye provides the optimally workable fundamentals for
comfortable, efficient living in a two-story shelter. It is small compared to

a conventional house, but huge next to a van, camper, or almost any of the thousands of yachts enthusiastically occupied while tied up at the marina slips. Optimum use of space will be important.

The larger Fly's Eye is fifty feet in diameter, capable of enclosing three or more stories (each of 2000-square-foot floor area), a garden, trees, and a pool. While also equipped with all the living essentials at different levels, its space utilization will be quite different from the smaller Fly's Eye—the fifty-footer accommodates what we call the Garden of Eden living—living in a garden.

The Fly's Eye domes are designed as components of a "livingry" service.

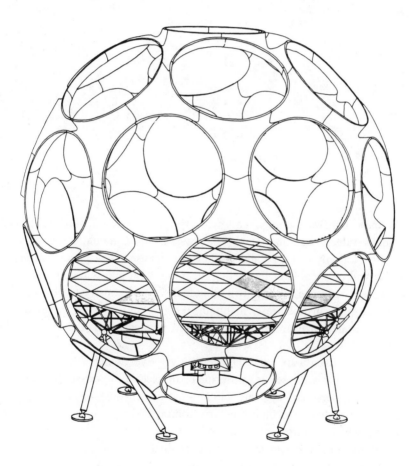

FIGURE 42. Fly's Eye dome with trussed flooring

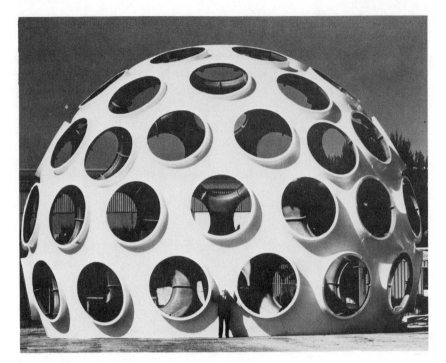

FIGURE 43. 50-foot-diameter Fly's Eye dome prototype

The basic hardware components will produce a beautiful, fully equipped, air-deliverable house that weighs and costs about as much as a good automobile. Not only will it be highly efficient in its use of energy and materials, it also will be capable of harvesting incoming light and wind energies. The software part of the product will include a service industry to air- or highway-transport, install, lease, maintain, remove, and relocate the domes or their separate hardware components. And as mentioned, they will not be sold.

Both the twenty-six- and fifty-foot Fly's Eye domes are semiautonomous—i.e., have no sewer, water-pipe, or electric-power-supply connections. The personal hygiene, clothes-and-utensil-washing functions are accomplished with the high-pressure, compressed air and atomized water fog gun which requires only a pint of water per hour.

The human excrement is sittingly deposited in the dry-packaging toilet. The human sits on fresh, plastic-film-covered, fore-and-aft seat halves. The excrement falls into the top-open plastic tube as it is formed by the two converging edges of the two plastic sheets, which are then electrosealed together from the originally separate two plastic film rolls, whose filmstrips first covered the two seat-sides. The hermetically sealed-off tubular section containing the excrement is then mechanically detached and conveyed away as litter to be neatly packed in a corrugated carton clearly marked for pickup and dispatch to the methane-gas-producing plant and the dry-powder fertilizer manufacturer or to be processed into methane gas and fertilizer powder by accessory equipment of the dome home itself.

* * *

Having undertaken the solution by artifacts of the world's great housing crisis, I came to regard the history of cities. Cities developed entirely before the thought of electricity or automobiles or before any of the millions of inventions registered in the United States Patent Office. For eminently mobile man, cities have become obsolete in terms of yesterday's functions—warehousing both new and formerly manufactured goods and housing immigrant factory workers. Rebuilding them to accommodate the new needs of world man requires demolition of the old buildings and their replacement of the new and now obsolete real estate, streets, water and sewer lines, and yesterday's no longer logical overall planning geometries. I sought to take on this challenge and developed plans for an entirely feasible and practical new way for humans to live together economically. Old Man River's City is one such design.

Old Man River's City, undertaken for East St. Louis, Illinois, takes its name from the song first sung by Paul Robeson fifty years ago, which dramatized the life of Afro-American blacks who lived along the south-of-St. Louis banks of the Mississippi River in the days of heavy north-south river traffic in cotton. Cessation of the traffic occurred when the east-west railway network outperformed the north-south Mississippi, Mexican Gulf, and Atlantic water routes, which left many of its riverbank communities, such as East St. Louis, marooned in economic dead spots. East St. Louis is an American city overwhelmed by poverty. Its population of 70,000 is 70 percent black.

I originally came to East St. Louis to discuss the design and possible realization of the Old Man River's City, having been asked to do so by East St. Louis community leaders themselves, being first approached by my friend Katherine Dunham, the famous black dancer. At the community leaders' request I presented a design that would help solve their problem. It is moon-crater-shaped: the crater's truncated cone top opening is a half-mile in diameter, rim-to-rim, while the truncated mountain itself is a mile in diameter at its base ring. The city has a one-mile-diameter geodesic, quarter-sphere, transparent umbrella mounted high above it to permit full, all-around viewing below the umbrella's bottom perimeter. The top of the dome roof is 1000 feet high. The bottom rim of the umbrella dome is 500 feet above the surrounding terrain, while the crater-top esplanade, looks 250 feet radially inward from the umbrella's bottom, is at the same 500-foot height. From the esplanade the truncated mountain cone slopes downwardly, inward and outward, to ground level 500 feet below.

The moon crater's inward and outward, exterior-surface slopes each consist of fifty terraces—the terrace floors are tiered vertically ten feet above or below one another. All the inwardly, downwardly sloping sides of the moon crater's terraced cone are used for communal life; its outward-sloping, tree-planted terraces are entirely for private life dwelling.

The private-home terraces on the outward circular bank are subdivided by trees and bushes to isolate them one from the other. This garden-divided exterior terracing hides the individual private-home terraces from one another while permitting each an unobstructed view outward to the faraway landscape. Thus landscape-partitioned from one another, the individual homes beneath the umbrella dome do not need their own separate weather roofs. The experience will be that of living outdoors in the garden, without any chance of rain and out of sight and sound of other humans, yet being subconsciously aware that your own advantage is not at the expense of others' zonal advantage.

The floors of the individual homes on the outward terraced slopes penetrate inwardly of the "mountainside" to provide an 85-percent-enclosed family apartment set back into the "mountain's" surface. Each family's apartment floor area totals 2500 feet, being 100 feet inwardly extended and twenty-five feet, one inch, wide at its outside terrace front line and twenty-five feet at its innermost chord line. Each apartment occupies only one six-hundredth of the circle's 360 degrees of arc. In addition there will be 1300 square feet of public space for each of the 25,000 families that Old Man River's City will accommodate on the fifty interior, communal, terraced slopes of the crater city.

The geodesic-sky parasol-umbrella protects the whole of Old Man River's City from rain or snow. The sky dome is transparent. Its aluminum-and-stainless-steel-trussed structure will be covered in two alternate ways: (1) glazed with wire-reinforced glass—ergo, fireproof; (2) with a pneumatically filled, glass-cloth-pillowed umbrella. The dome will admit all biological, life-supporting Sun radiation. The great umbrella is a watershed whose runoff is collected in a dome-level reservoir for a high-pressure fire sprinkler and service purification system, after which the reservoir's overflow is piped downwardly to a dome-surrounding "moat" reservoir.

The interiormost, circular diameter ground level of Old Man River's City is twice the size of the playing-ground area of any of the world's large athletic stadia. This means that it has about four times the interior horizontal area of a regulation football stadium's oval ground area.

The terraced (angle of repose) slopes of Old Man River's City, both outside and inside, are very gradual slopes and are thus unlike the steeply tiered athletic stadium's seating slopes. The angular difference is like that of a reclining chair versus an upright chair.

Many of the lower tiers of Old Man River's City's interior terraces have enough horizontal surface to accommodate groups of tennis courts, whole school and playground areas, supermarkets, outdoor theaters, etc. The terraces are of graduated widths. With the narrowest at the top, they become progressively wider at each lower level.

Inside—that is, below the moon crater's three-and-a-half-mile-circumferenced, surface-terraced mountain mass—are all the communal services not requiring daylight: for instance, all the multilevel circumferential trolleyways, interlevel ramps, roadways, and parking lots, with numerous radial crosswalks and local elevators. There are radial crosswalk bridges at every four terrace levels. These provide bridges—never more than two decks up or down—for walking homeward, outwardly from the interior community bowl, to one's individual, terraced, tree-hidden dwelling area. In addition to the foregoing interior structuring and facilities, the factory, office and parking space within the crater mountain is colossal—about ten million square feet. The city is as complete a living, working, studying, and playing complex as is a great ocean passenger ship—but without the space limitations imposed by the ship's streamlined forming to accommodate swift passage through the seas.

Because its life-style will be so vastly improved over present-day living, Old Man River's City has been designed to accommodate 25,000 families— i.e., 125,000 humans—though East St. Louis has now only 70,000 humans grouped in 14,000 families.

There are many exciting consequences of Old Man River's City community life being introverted and its private life extroverted.

Within the interior community bowl everyone can see what all the rest of the community is doing, as do the 125,000-member audiences of our present-day great "bowl" games see all the other humans present, though indistinctly at the farthest distances. The difference in Old Man River's City experience will be that each of its 125,000 individuals will have an average of 260 square feet of communal-terrace roaming space versus the six square feet of seating space of the football stadium fan—i.e., the OMR citizen will average forty-three times as much free space as does the football fan.

From the individual, external home terrace on the crater's outer slopes one can see no humans other than those within one's own family's home-terrace domain. People can look outwardly, however, from Old Man River's City as far as the eye can see at the interesting Mississippi River scenery outside the moon crater's umbrella limits. The Old Man River City's home

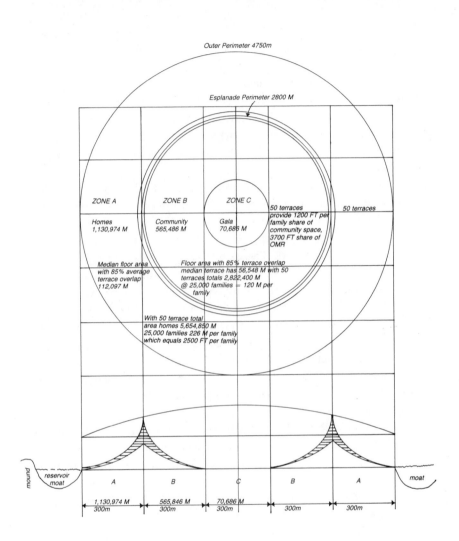

Figure 44. *Total Undercover Area 1,767,146 M*

318

FIGURE 45.   Model of Old Man River's City (elevation)

FIGURE 45a.   Model of Old Man River's City (aerial view)

FIGURE 46.   Plan view of Old Man River's City, East St. Louis, Illinois

views are analogous to those of individuals living in dwellings on mountain-sides, such as those of residents on the hills of Hong Kong Island or those above Berkeley, California. Such hillside dwellers overlook vast, mysterious-ly inspiring scenic areas, ever-changing with the nights, days, and weather.

The total roof surface area of the one-mile-diameter, quarter-sphere dome is only 2 percent that of the total roof and exterior skin surface area of all the buildings standing on an equal ground area in any large conventional city. The amount of external shell surface through which each interior mol-ecule of atmosphere can gain or lose heat is thus reduced by 98 percent. An-other energy-conservation factor is operative, for every time we double the sphere's diameter, we increase its surface by four and its volume by eight. Therefore, the energy efficiency doubles each time we double the dome size. This means that the structural efficiency, useful volume, and energy conser-vation are all at optimum in the Old Man River's City project. Throughout the year Old Man River's City will have a naturally mild climate. With a large, aerodynamically articulated, wind-and-weather-controlled ventilator system atop and round the dome, together with the 500-foot-high vertical opening that runs entirely around the city below the umbrella, the atmo-spheric controllability will guarantee fresh air as well as energy conserva-tion. The umbrella will jut out above and beyond all the outer-slope residential terrace areas as does a grandstand roof, so that neither rain nor snow will drift horizontally inwardly, being blocked from doing so by the mass inertia of the vast quantity of atmosphere embraced by the umbrella as well as by the vertical mass of the crater's cone within the dome.

Optimum efficiency also characterizes the way in which Old Man River's City is to be produced. The three-and-a-half-mile circumferential moon crater and its terracing will be developed entirely with modern, high-speed, highway-building equipment and earth-moving techniques as well as with suspension-bridge-building and air-space technologies. Construction will begin with installation of a set of concentrically interswitching railway tracks, with tangential shunting bypass tracks, on which great cranes and other machinery will travel. The mammoth, 500-feet-high and 2000-feet-wide-based, A-frame-shaped, circumferential segments of the crater become highly repetitive and economically producible. There will be 100 columns rising from the A-frame tops at the crater's top-rim esplanade. These 100 columns will be 500 feet high and will be spaced forty meters apart, mounted above the A-frames. The tops of the 100 columns will be 1000 feet high and will be capped by a circumferential ring.

The whole terraced crater structure, inside and out, will be of thin-wall reinforced concrete. This terraced shell will be cast-mounted upon, and will thus encase, an inverted, kitchen-sieve-like, domical basket, consisting of an omnitriangulated, quarter-sphere geodesic, basket-bowl, suspension web of fine-diameter, high-tensile steel rods and wires. The spider-fine steel web basket will be suspended from the A-frame tops at the base of the 100 columns. The whole structure is, in effect, a circular, triangularly self-stabilizing, "suspension bridge"-principled, terraced, ferroconcrete bowl with the human occupants and their goods constituting only a small fraction of the stress loads of equimagnitude highway traffic bridges.

The 1500-meter- (one-mile) diameter dome itself will be a horizontal wire wheel suspension consisting of an octahedral-tensegrity-trussed, one-quarter sphere geodesic dome suspended horizontally from the 100 circumferential columns. This method means mounting the dome one-quarter of a mile inwardly from the one-mile-diameter parasol dome's outer rim. This results in an inner clear span of only one-half mile, a distance comparable to that of the Golden Gate Bridge's central clear span between its two masts.

I said to the East St. Louisans at the outset that our first resolve must be *not* to compromise our design solution in order to qualify for any private foundation or government subsidy funds. Three-quarters of the United States national debt of almost $1 trillion and much of the private debt, which altogether transfers $25 billion a year "interest" from our nation's pocketbooks to the banks and insurance companies, has been amassed through government building subsidies that were designed strictly as "money-makers" for bankers, real estate operators, and handcraft building-industry interests. The funds were not amassed in the interest of the individuals and the community. I advised the East St. Louisans that we must develop our design and its production and assembly logistics strictly in terms of the individual and the community's best interests. I said that if we solve the human problem and do so in the most economical and satisfactory manner, independent of building codes, zoning restrictions, etc., while employing airspace technology, effectiveness, and safety, we will do that which no subsidized housing thus far has done. I pointed out that, with increasing socioeconomic emergencies, the economic support will ultimately materialize simply because we have what world-around humanity is looking for and needs. The money-making solutions of housing are exactly what humanity is not looking for but has had to accept, lacking any alternatives.

The East St. Louis schoolchildren are soon to be provided with a fifty-foot-diameter miniature OMR moon-crater city with which (and on which) to play, simulating actual living conditions. The children will furnish its terraces with miniaturized, scale-model equipment, landscape material, athletic facilities, interior transportation equipment, factories, and similar materials they will design and make. As the political leader of East St. Louis, who was formerly principal of its largest high school, says, "By the time Old Man River's City gets completed, our present high school students will be its grown occupants, and they might just as well start right now using their imaginations in play living in and operating it." Fabricating and assembling the model itself will be in strict conformity with the full-scale operation.

At the outset meeting of our OMR's City's development, I told the East St. Louisans that I would develop the design and models at my own expense and do so without fee. I said that what I would design must be so "right" that the entire community would fall in love with it . . . or it would be dropped. I said that if they did fall in love with it, I would carry on with all the development expense and that they must not allow the project to become a political football. It was fortunate that the East St. Louis community did fall spontaneously in love with the design. This held the project together through many critical moments of preliminary challenges of its validity and practicability. There were many critical meetings wherein skeptics, some of them powerful political activists, declared that this design, with its domed-over interior community and exterior private-dwelling terraces, might be part of its social enemy's conspiracy to entrap them. Fortunately the design gradually explained itself, until all the leaders of the community's diverse factions—political, ethnic, and economic, as well as the city's engineer—all agreed on its desirability.

I have been greatly aided in the Old Man River's City development by a group of volunteer architectural students from Washington University in St. Louis and, above all, by Professor James Fitzgibbon, head of Washington University's architectural school. As I am absent a great deal due to my world traveling, Jim, who is one of my best, lifelong friends, has been locally in command of the development. Most powerful support of the East St. Louisans has been provided by Wyvetter Younge, Carl Utchmann, and Bob Ahart.

Both the East St. Louis and St. Louis newspapers and radio and television stations have given good and favorable reception to the project. Now world-around interest in the Old Man River project is beginning to be manifest. As interest grows, more and more articles are being published about it, despite its having no public relations or advertising promotion. Quite to the contrary, I have asked the community to let the project gestate at a natural rate. Answer questions faithfully when they are asked, but otherwise be silently at work.

As the first favorable publicity occurred, it was inevitable that Illinois's political representatives would quickly offer the East St. Louisans their aid in securing government funds, which funds, however, would involve so many restrictions and compromises as to utterly emasculate the OMR City's design rationale. Thus it was a second victory for the project when I was able to dissuade the community from being tempted by the "millions" of dollars tendered them.

I have never engaged in a development that I have felt to have such promise for all humanity, while being, at the same time, so certain of realization, because its time is imminently at hand.

* * *

In 1951, at North Carolina State University at Raleigh, I designed an automated cotton mill.

Situated upon the banks of many New England rivers and employing the latter's waterpower, all the great cotton mills of the nineteenth-century U.S.A. were built four stories high. They used giant pulley wheels mounted on the hubs of their great main waterwheels to drive leather belts which led slantingly upward into the mills' top floors and thence to the ceiling-hung, pulley-driven shafting mounted under the ceilings of each of the mills' four floors. There were many pairs of pulleys, their axes hung in parallel. Each driving wheel had its own idler wheel. When the belts were shifted over from the idler to the driving wheel, they drove the wheels of their respective machines of the various types of cotton mill machinery, which was positioned just below the ceiling-hung shafts. To operate those early-in-the-nineteenth-century mills the owners imported whole town-size armies of immigrants, who settled into the companies' houses. Having no other sources available, the millworkers bought all their supplies from the company stores. Their wages were minimal. After one-half a century the organized-labor movement forced wage increases for them.

In the early twentieth century the cotton-manufacturing business owners abandoned their New England mills and moved their machinery into the Southern states, where homes need not be heated and where they could reach a low-cost labor market. Instead of the belting, overhead shafting, and pulleys, they used the World-War-I-developed electric motor drives for each separate machine. This freedom from a shafting-and-waterpower-driven system economizedly (which is not always most *economically*) called for single-story factories with large roof areas. The latter's black tar and gravel roofs impounded vast quantities of Sun heat, which in turn produced many internal environment-control problems.

Before that southward cotton-milling migration my earliest job before World War I had been as an apprentice cotton millwright (cotton machine fitter). The new mill we were equipping with machinery was located in Sherbrooke, Quebec. Most of the machinery was manufactured in Lancashire, England, some in France. Working first as a helper to the Lancashire master machine fitters, I learned how to put together by myself every one of the various kinds of cotton mill machines. These began with the cotton bail "openers" at railroad track level and the blowing of the cotton to the top (fourth) floor of the mill, after which the cotton went through the pickers, combers' cards, and slubbers, all of which gradually cleaned and formed the cotton into a continuous single strand of cotton, which strands then ran through the twisters, into thread-spinning machines, and thereafter into cotton cloth weaving machines.

Eventually, together with other fitters, I taught the cotton mill workers how to operate their machines. It was a powerful and valuable experience. It was synergetic—behavior of a whole system unpredicted by the behavior of any one of its parts only separately considered.

Fifty years later, with much other experience including the development of large geodesic domes, I found I could build a large spherical environment control for much less expense in materials and labor than was required to produce the traditional one-story-high Southern cotton mill. Inside the great column-free space of the clear-span geodesic sphere, an octet-truss mast structure would support many levels of surrounding, outwardly cantilevered, octet-truss platforms.

In the great steamships of yesterday the engine room area occupied a very large part of the ship's interior space. This was occupied by large equipment, such as three-decks-high engines and boilers. In place of decks these engine rooms had open-grating platforms, walkways, and stairways, all open for seeing through and for free circulation of the air.

In 1952, at the university in Raleigh, North Carolina, I was asked to lead a full-term design problem in their department of architecture. I proposed the designing and detailed scale-modeling of a large spherical cotton mill within which—and not touching the sphere—would be open-frame grating platforms supported by octahedron-tetrahedron trusses cantilevered outwardly around the central mast at many levels, with the octet-trussed platforms occurring only where the machinery was to be situated. In the conventional Southern one-story cotton factory all the machines are on one single floor, requiring the horizontal transfer of the semiprocessed cotton products of one machine to the next machine in the manufacturing sequence. In mill terms this carry-across-of-product is called "doffing." In my vertical mill proposal all "doffing" was eliminated. The first processing machinery would be situated on a cantilevered open truss at the highest point around the mast, inside the dome, and the products would start a continuous downward flow from one machine to another accomplished exclusively by gravity. No doffing would be required.

I designed this factory in conjunction with North Carolina State University's top cotton mill professors as well as with the operating superintendents and other industry experts from neighboring mills. All the cotton mill machinery companies' sales engineers participated in the project, which was being run for the senior class in architecture of North Carolina State University. (North Carolina State University happens to be the leading university in the cotton manufacturing area of the South, and has more engineers in that trade than can be found anywhere else.) We designed this factory to be completely automated. Inadvertently it became extraordinarily beautiful. (See Figs. 47, 47a and 47b.)

When the cotton mill owners moved their mills from New England into the Southland, they did not move their own homes. They remained deliberately remote from any labor hassling. When I developed this new mill, which all the professionals considered to be a great improvement, the ownership of the cotton mills was so far away from where the mills are located that the owners heard nothing of our new cotton mill development. The people who managed the mills for the remote owners were economists and statisticians, seeking only to squeeze every cent out of costs. They had no engineering-design analytical capability. They sought only to reduce labor costs. Nobody was then considering new cotton-manufacturing technology. It was assumed that all possibilities of improving the manufacturing processes had been exhausted long ago. As a consequence the cotton mill owners paid no attention whatsoever to the mill I designed; the North Carolina State cotton-manufacturing engineering scientists who participated in the project agreed that my spherical, gravity-serviced mill was optimally efficient and highly desirable. The design exists. We probably will see it adopt-

FIGURE 47.   Model of automated cotton mill, Raleigh, North Carolina

FIGURE 47a.   Model of automated cotton mill, Raleigh, North Carolina
(interior detail)

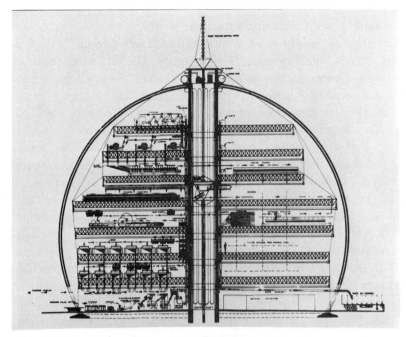

FIGURE 47b.   Cross-section of Raleigh cotton mill

ed one of these days. That is the way with critical-path items. They come into use only when class-one evolutïon needs them.

* * *

In the following year, 1952, at North Carolina State University I introduced the idea of what I called the mechanical Growth House. At that time I knew how to construct—and had already constructed—many geodesic domes. Some were enormous, spherical environment controls. As mentioned before, ever-larger spheres have ever-less surface area per unit of enclosed volume. Doubling a dome's diameter increases its surface fourfold while increasing its volume eightfold. Large domes can be completely transparent, allowing ultraviolet radiation to enter wherever necessary to support the growth of vegetation and the latter's impoundment of Sun energy through photosynthesis. Transparent domes can also be opaquely shuttered or mirrored where desired. It is highly feasible to produce two concentric, translucent spheres, the outer one being, for instance, 100 meters in diameter, and the inner one being four meters less in diameter than the outer one and having no metal conductors running between their two plastic and fiberglass intertrussed surfaces and with top and bottom, remotely controlled openings in both domes.

The southeastern United States has more of what we think of as *individual farmers* than anywhere else in this country. North Carolina State University, Cornell, and Iowa State University, are the leading agricultural-engineering-sciences schools in America. It was at North Carolina State that, in conjunction with the Growth House, I conducted comparative studies into (1) the economics of individually operated versus business-corporation-operated farms and (2) the critical-limit size and other conditions of individually owned and personally operated farms versus those same questions for corporation-operated farms. I also made comparative studies of farms operated by the very rich as tax write-offs versus the few little subsistence farms, such as those owned by the small tobacco farmers in North Carolina, which are worked entirely by the resident owner-farmers. These latter are very personal types of operation, in which the farmers carefully watch their crops, even to each tobacco leaf, to get the best out of their investment in the land. These little tobacco farms and certain subsistence farms were quite a different type of eco-technical game than that of the huge conglomerate-owned multithousands-of-acres farm operations. The small, individual farmers soon learned all the ways in which the government could help them run their farms.

For instance, the U.S. government at the time of the New Deal helped the small farmers by underwriting the cost of constructing little local dams on their land, which produced small ponds and lakes that the government stocked with fish. These new energy sources greatly increased the farmers' crop yields and earnings.

From that time on the farms began to hold the water that fell on them. People like myself who were light-plane flyers began to notice as we flew westward cross-country that, late in the afternoon with the Sun in the west, its brilliance began to reflect from the myriads of these little newly dammed farm ponds. Soon the glare of these farm ponds became almost blinding to the airplane pilot; before that period the farmland had been a dark carpet at dusk.

Overnight the New Deal had captured all that water for all those farms and had stocked them with highly reproductive fish.

I found that North Carolina State University at Raleigh was a great place to discuss the idea of a Growth House because the plant physiologists there were some of the best agricultural scientists I could find in America.

These scientists agreed with me about the desirability of producing a Growth House—an enormous clear-span sphere with no interior bearing walls or columns. It would have a great central mast around which, one above the other, would be cantilevered octahedron-tetrahedron arms, like branches of a tree extended at successive levels. The horizontally rotatable arms would carry the growing plants, with their roots hung in trays. The Growth House would be a multitiered-tray agriculture. Tray agriculture had already been studied a great deal in North Carolina and had been successfully developed. (We had some very satisfactory tray-growing experiments.) We then went on to find that inside the great sphere we could atomize the water, atomize all the chemical fertilization, and immerse the plants in a Sun-and-nutriment-filled atmosphere that would produce the greatest growth in a given time. The growth-supporting, rotatable arms could be separately rotated for cultivation. All the resultant food grown would gradually work downwardly by gravity, finally to be packaged or canned automatically and delivered in cases out through the bottom. This Growth House is completely designed and ready to be produced. If it were to be used to produce the new "winged bean," the life-support worth of its product would be enormous.

Referring back to my designing of the Dymaxion House of 1927—that of producing an environment most favorable to a living organism's growth and to its dynamic process, and doing so in the most economically pleasing and safe manner—we found that in designing our North Carolina Growth House we had used the same principles for inventorying its essential functions as those we had employed in designing the 1950–1956 North Carolina cotton mill and subsequent projects. Considering in some detail how such a most favorable environment can be arrived at, we see that, in the first place, we wished to have clear space wherever possible. Needing no interior bearing columns or walls, we would interrupt our enclosed space only when we had some service that we needed at that point. There would be no walls or partitions that arbitrarily stopped you from passing through. Space would be broken up only by devices that served you at preferred locations— for instance, by a bathroom or a clothes-storage device.

* * *

I saw in 1927 that all storage may be divided into two classes—things we rest on shelves, held in horizontal display by gravity, and things we hang vertically, with gravity always maintaining the economy of individual display. The horizontal storage we developed in the Dymaxion House is very different from the drawers of a conventional bedroom bureau. I developed what I called O-Volving shelves and storage walls. The storage walls had two parts: a hemicircular revolving coat closet and shoe rack structured with aluminum tubing (see Fig. 48). This hemicircular hanger tube hemi-revolved around a center axle with an ample amount of room for vertically hanging all clothing, short or long; and with a hemicircular shoe rack, rigged horizontally below the bottom of hung dresses, coats, etc. The revolv-

FIGURE 48.   Storage walls

ing coat closet had also the advantage of coming out into a room so you could pick things out very neatly instead of having to reach back blindly into a closet.

The horizontal O-Volving shelves operated like a paternoster, using vertically rotated circular chains (similar to a bicycle chain but more powerful) with geared wheels at top, vertically rotating the bicycle-chain-supported hanging shelves. The shelves were suspended in such a way that they would never tilt, yet were strong enough to support great weights. On pressing a button, electric motors rotated the two top sprocket wheels, from both of which, mounted at both ends of the rig, the bicycle-type chain loops were suspended. Each shelf in turn would appear swiftly at a single horizontal opening in the storage wall, positioned at a height safe from the reach of children. With these shelves children would never have to be told, "Don't!"

I was designing an environment that in every way could accommodate children learning what they have to learn in order to conduct themselves physically and safely, without getting into trouble with the operations of the environment, so an adult would never have to "don't" the children or discourage their curiosity-initiating—i.e., experiments—for fear that a child might get hurt.

*   *   *

 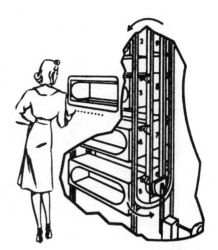

FIGURE 49.   O-Volving shelves

I then decided my O-Volving shelves would be very logical for use in a library. I designed a proposed library project for Princeton University which, although not built at that time, would be very practical if used in the future. It had a deep, fifty-meter-in-diameter, circular silo well going far below into the ground, with walls that were thoroughly waterproofed on their outside. Above this deep circular well I mounted two levels of Octe-truss floors, and above them a hemispherical geodesic dome sixty meters in diameter. I designed a radial arrangement of many consoles on the library's ground floor, each within a library book category. Instead of taking eleva-tors to the right floor and walking to the shelves, the O-Volving shelves would bring the one-meter-long shelves of books to you—ovolving vertically before your eyes, fast or slowly, until the right shelf arrives and you locate your book.

All the vertical bookshelves' ovolving was actuated by an electric push button and high-speed motor. It could be run by you at a speed suitable for your adequate inspection of the contiguous titles. Any book-seeker who wants to can dial for the book by computer-entered title or description, and it will ovolve to the seeker's window at high speed. When the book arrives at the console, it is practical to have it pneumatically and mechanically opened behind the console window for the reader's intimate viewing. The

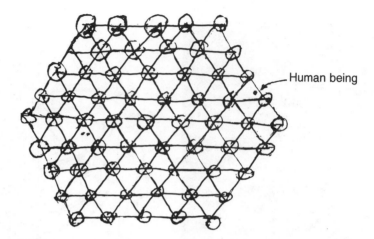

FIGURE 50.   O-Volving console floor placement patterning, Princeton University
Library project

reader cannot put hands on it, possibly to damage it. By push button the
viewer at the console can also order a Xerox copy of any or all of the book's
pages. Also by push buttons the viewer can order a copy of the book for
purchase. At the exit door of the library the Xeroxed pages or the purchased
book will be waiting for credit-card purchase.

In the Princeton University design there were two decks of consoles. One
was for the book-untouching, general library visitor; the other deck, twenty
feet above the ground level entrance, would be accessible only to research-
accredited visitors, who could remove the books from the shelves and open
them after they ovolved into place. The O-Volving consoles on both decks
would be triangularly arrayed all around the library's circular decks in a
pattern of as-close-to-one-another-packing as possible without making the
viewer feel crowded. The many perpendicularly book-loaded, O-Volving
shelves would be parallelly suspended within the vast and deep underground
air-conditioned silos. In terms of overall initial and operating costs compared to those of a multilevel, searchingly walk-around, fixed-steel-book-
stacks library, my design solution costs are extremely favorable.

The O-Volving shelf technology was perfected operationally to everyone's
satisfaction at Beech Aircraft thirty-five years ago. The principle is now
completely sound, only awaiting application.

*   *   *

In the early 1960s I was commissioned by a Japanese patron to design
one of my tetrahedronal floating cities for Tokyo Bay.

Three-quarters of our planet Earth is covered with water, most of which may float organic cities.

Floating cities pay no rent to landlords. They are situated on the water, which they desalinate and recirculate in many useful and nonpolluting ways. They are ships with all an ocean ship's technical autonomy, but they are also ships that will always be anchored. They don't have to go anywhere. Their shape and its human-life accommodations are not compromised, as must be the shape of the living quarters of ships whose hull shapes are constructed so that they may slip, fishlike, at high speed through the water and high seas with maximum economy.

Floating cities are designed with the most buoyantly stable conformation of deep-sea bell-buoys. Their omni-surface-terraced, slope-faced, tetrahedronal structuring is employed to avoid the lethal threat of precipitous falls by humans from vertically sheer high-rising buildings.

The tetrahedron has the most surface with the least volume of all polyhedra. As such it provides the most possible "outside" living. Its sloping external surface is adequate for all its occupants to enjoy their own private, outside, tiered-terracing, garden homes. These are most economically serviced from the common, omni-nearest-possible center of volume of all polyhedra.

All the mechanical organics of a floating city are situated low in its hull for maximum stability. All the shopping centers and other communal service facilities are inside the structure; tennis courts and other athletic facilities are on the top deck. When suitable, the floating cities are equipped with "alongside" or interiorly lagooned marinas for the safe mooring of the sail- and powerboats of the floating-city occupants. When moored in protected waters, the floating cities may be connected to the land by bridgeways.

In 1966 my Japanese patron died, and the United States Department of Housing and Urban Development commissioned me to carry out full design and economic analysis of the floating tetrahedronal city for potential U.S.A. use. With my associates I completed the design and study as well as a scaled-down model. The studies showed that the fabricating and operating costs were such that a floating city could sustain a high standard of living, yet be economically occupiable at a rental so low as to be just above that rated as the "poverty" level by HUD authorities. The secretary of HUD sent the drawings, engineering studies, and economic analysis to the Secretary of the Navy, who ordered the Navy's Bureau of Ships to analyze the project for its "water-worthiness," stability, and organic capability. The Bureau of Ships verified all our calculations and found the design to be practical and "water-worthy." The Secretary of the Navy then sent the project to the U.S. Navy's Bureau of Yards and Docks, where its fabrication and assembly procedures and cost were analyzed on a basis of the "floating city" being built in a shipyard as are aircraft carriers and other vessels. The cost analysis of the Navy Department came out within 10 percent of our cost—which bore out its occupiability at rental just above the poverty class.

At this point the city of Baltimore became interested in acquiring the first such floating city for anchorage just offshore in Chesapeake Bay, adjacent to Baltimore's waterfront. At this time President Lyndon Johnson's Democratic party went out of power. President Johnson took the model with him and installed it in his LBJ Texas library. The city of Baltimore's politicians went out of favor with the Nixon administration, and the whole project languished. The city of Toronto, Ontario, Canada, and other cities of the U.S.A. are interested in the possibility of acquiring such floating cities. Chances of one being inaugurated are now improving.

In relation to such floating cities it is to be noted that they are completely designed under one authority, and when they become obsolete, they are scrapped and melted and the materials go into subsequent production of a greatly advanced model whose improvements are based on earlier experiences as well as the general interim advances of all technology.

There are three types of floating cities: There is one for protected harbor waters, one for semiprotected waters, and one for unprotected deep-sea installations. The deep-sea type is supported by submarine pontoons posi-

FIGURE 51.   Triton Floating City

tioned under the turbulence, with their centers of buoyancy 100 feet below the ocean's surface. Structural columns rise from the submarine pontoons outwardly through the water to support the floating city high above the crests of the greatest waves, which thus pass innocuously below the city's lowest flooring, as rivers flow under great bridges. The deep-sea, deeply pontooned floating cities will be as motionless in respect to our planet as are islanded or land-based cities.

There are also deep-sea spherical and cylindrical geodesic floating cities whose hulls are positioned entirely below the ocean surface turbulence. Only their vertical entrance towers penetrate outwardly through the disturbed surface waters. The occupants of submarine cities with their vertical towers penetrating outwardly above water can be serviced by helicopters landing on the tower-top platforms. Such pontooned or hulled submarine cities also can provide safe mid-ocean docking for atomic-powered cargo- and passenger-carrying submarine transports. With their submarine hulls locked together below the turbulence, a safe passageway can be opened between them.

Even in mild weather docking cannot be done on the open water surface of the ocean. Even the mildest "old-sea" or ground swells would roll any two ocean ships' great tonnages into disastrous hull-smashing clashes. Relative mass attraction is proportional to the product of the masses of the interattracted pair multiplied by the second power of the relative proximity changes. When any two oceangoing steel vessels come within "critical proximity," their interattraction increases as the second power of their relative distance. Their interattraction is fourfolded every time the distance between them is halved. This chain-attraction-increasing force pulls them sideways toward one another, ultimately to touch and chew up one another's skins— that is, unless one is maneuvered in time backward or forward away from the other. Land harbors are essential for surface docking or inter-tie-up of ships of any size. There are relatively few big-ship harbors in the world. This fact, and the world-around scarcity of such good harbors as Athens' Piraeus, France's Cherbourg, Italy's Venice, the U.S.A.'s New York, or Tokyo's Yokohama, have greatly affected the geographical patterning of world history. The new ability to transfer cargoes at sea could completely alter world economic balances and could bring ships once more into economic competition with airplanes. The recent decades' development of seventy-knot submerged speed of the great atomic submarines, complemented by floating cities, could herald the beginning of a new era of subsurface oceanic traffic.

In due time small cruising yachts also will be able to sail or power around the world in safe, one-day runs from one protected floating city's harbor to the next.

*   *   *

In 1958 I saw clearly the progression of technical events altering all old engineering concepts regarding the relative increase in the overall weights of structures—and designed my sky-floating tensegrity structures, which I call "Cloud Nines."

A 100-foot-diameter, tensegrity-trussed, geodesic sphere weighing three tons encloses seven tons of air. The air-to-structural-weight ratio is two to one. When we double the size so that the geodesic sphere is 200 feet in diameter, the weight of the structure increases to seven tons while the weight of the air increases to fifty-six tons—the air-to-structure ratio changes as eight to one. When we double the size again to a 400-foot geodesic sphere— the size of several geodesic domes now operating—the weight of the air inside increases to about 500 tons while the weight of the structure increases to fifteen tons. The air-weight-to-structure-weight ratio is now thirty-three to one. When we get to a geodesic sphere one-half mile in diameter, the weight of the structure itself becomes of relatively negligible magnitude, for the ratio is approximately a thousand to one.

When the Sun shines on an open-frame aluminum geodesic sphere of one-half-mile diameter, the Sun penetrating through the frame and reflected from the aluminum members of the concave far side bounces back into the sphere and gradually heats the interior atmosphere to a mild degree. When the interior temperature of the sphere rises only one degree Fahrenheit, the weight of the air pushed out of the sphere is greater than the weight of the spherical-frame geodesic structure. This means that the total weight of the interior air plus the weight of the structure is much less than the surrounding atmosphere. This means that the total assemblage of the geodesic sphere and its contained air will have to float outwardly, into the sky, being displaced by the heavy atmosphere around it.

When a great bank of mist lies in a valley in the morning and the Sun shines upon it, the Sun heats the air inside the bank of mist. The heated air expands and therefore pushes some of itself outside the mist bank. The total assembly of the mist bank weighs less than the atmosphere surrounding it, and the mist bank floats aloft into the sky. Thus are clouds manufactured. As geodesic spheres get larger than one-half mile in diameter, they become floatable cloud structures.

If their surfaces were draped with outwardly hung polyethelene curtains to retard the rate at which air would come back in at night, the sphere and its internal atmosphere would continue to be so light as to remain aloft.

Such sky-floating geodesic/tensegrity spheres may be designed to float at preferred altitudes of thousands of feet. The weight of human beings added to such prefabricated "Cloud Nines" would be relatively negligible. Many thousands of passengers could be housed aboard one-mile-diameter and larger cloud structures. The passengers could come and go from cloud to cloud, or cloud to ground, as the clouds float around the Earth or are anchored to mountaintops.

While the building of such floating clouds is some years in the future, we may foresee that, with the floating tetrahedronal cities; air-deliverable skyscrapers; submarine islands; sub-dry-surface dwellings; domed-over cities; flyable dwelling machines; and rentable, autonomous-living, black boxes, man may be able to converge and deploy around Earth without its depletion.

*   *   *

In the 1920s Frank Lloyd Wright made a drawing of a mile-high tower building. Engineering feasibility studies were never made.

In 1966 I was contracted by a Japanese patron—Matsutaro Shoriki, owner of the Nippon Television Network Corporation—to undertake a design feasibility study for a 12,250-foot-high observation tower, which was to overtop the height of Mount Fuji on the island of Honshu. In view of the fact that at that time the world's tallest building was the Empire State Building at 1472 feet, including TV towers, and the tallest man-made structure was a 2000-foot TV transmission tower a mere one-sixth the proposed tower's height, totally-new-for-humanity considerations necessarily came into play. Our tightly phrased, detailed engineering report contained 10,000 words.

The patron's given budgetable limit for the project was $300 million. The

FIGURE 52. Cloud Nine Floating Tensegrity Spheres

feasibility study showed that a 12,250-foot tower that performed all the functions desired by the tower's patrons could be met by present technology, but not at the $300-million figure. The study, therefore, also included critical details covering the construction of an engineering- and function-satisfying tower of 8000 feet, which could be produced for $300 million.

The studies showed that there was nothing that presently operative technology could not cope with even at the 12,250-foot Mount Fuji height. Almost all objectionable features of the 12,250-foot tower were eliminated at the 8000-foot height.

Such formidable safe working assumptions had to be adopted as that of icing one foot thick covering the tower's entire surface; wind loadings of 250-mile-per-hour winds; allowance for ice dropping into protected areas; and unitary five-story-high, air compression and decompression elevators in order to accommodate pay-for-itself observatory traffic, etc. A section of the report even covered helicopter rescue operations from the observation section at the top should the elevator fail.

*   *   *

With all human beings furnished with their personal, automatic, computer-programming, "chips"-containing credit cards, the computers will be making it clear that all humanity will be able to employ their along-the-streetside-controlled, slot-machine-like, travel-program-and-ticket dispensers to get themselves from any part of the world to any other part of the world in the shortest possible time.

The world computers will keep track of all available air-travel passenger spaces in all directions. The airlines will operate on a load-shuffle-and-shuttle, special-destination-pallet basis. When each eight-seat-or-bed-capacity pallet is full, it will be hang-loaded by local cranes onto overhead monorails and electric-trolleyed into an en-route-to-destination plane. The destination-programmed, eight-place pallets will be overhead-monorail, electric-trolley loaded aboard through each plane's tail. The planes can carry many pallets with many different ultimate destinations.

For example, there will be a pallet for Sydney, Australia, being loaded in New York City's Waldorf-Astoria Hotel lobby. When it is full, the computer will have it overhead-monorailed to the first overseas plane going most directly toward Sydney—say to Mexico City. At Mexico City it will be computer-overhead-trolley-transferred to a plane for Papeete, Tahiti, in the Society Islands, and thence into another plane leaving in a short space of time from Papeete directly to Sydney.

At each world airport the computers will re-sort the variously destined pallets, sending them forward in the most efficient manner. The pallets will

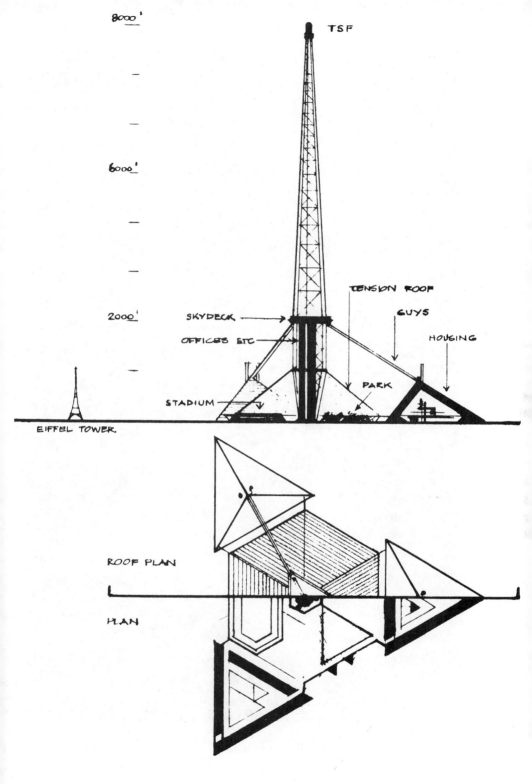

FIGURE 53. Tokyo Tower

339

Figure 54. Tokyo Tower

340

be computer-shuttle-sorted in and out of the planes through the planes' hinged-open tails and continually rerouted to their ultimate destination in the computer-determined swiftest manner.

The pallets themselves will accommodate all the passengers' luggage inside the floor-truss space below the passengers' seats. Passengers will never be separated from their luggage. On arrival at destination their pallet will take them "downtown" to their destination hotel.

There will be a variety of pallet designs. All the pallets for long-distance, multihoured flights will have all their seats convertible by elevation into comfortable full-length beds.

Travelers can even start their trips in a pallet in the lobby of their hotel. The pallet will be overhead-trolleyed into a truck thus to produce in effect a small bus. Pallets will be loaded into trucks through their tails by overhead trolley rails.

Because the world-around computer system is continually rerouting its pallets to adjust for unexpected delays, there will be no way of planning to hijack a plane from within a pallet.

* * *

We now find that every human being generates a self-surrounding, ultra-ultra-ultra-high-frequency electromagnetic field—exquisitely ephemeral but exquisitely real. Each individual's field alternates between positive and negative. When an individual is feeling predominantly negative mentally, the field is negative, and vice versa.

The sensitivity of the satellite-mounted, electronic, spy-sensing equipment developed by both Russia and the United States is such that satellites, dynamically space-stationed around the world, can take continual readings of the sum-total proportions of positive and negative electromagnetic field reactions of all humanity in respect to world-numbered "proposals"—to be broadcast at given times all around the world—regarding computer-discovered solutions to each and every world-human-affecting problem.

The computer will make it quite possible to continually confront humanity via the electronic media with its own world's nonpolitical, professionally trained, and examination-qualified management's successively evolved human-problem-solution proposals.

With adequate time to get the world informed of each of the nonpolitical, professional world-management committee's specific computer-derived problem-solution proposals, at specific world-around times readouts will be broadcast reporting the world majority's disposition toward any one proposed solution. All humanity can keep track of the changing disposition of the majority of all humanity and of how many are positive or negative in respect to any world-around, simultaneous, periodical presentation of any given proposition. After a proposition has been exposed for a given period of days and a 75-percent majority is attained, the professional-management world committee will be authorized to put the proposition into the world-around industrial production and service.

Thus will begin the world's first real tamper- and corruption-proof democracy. Humanity will make mistakes, but the minority, knowing that this is the first true democracy, will often go along spontaneously with the majority, knowing that if it develops that the majority has made a bad judgment, negative readings will swiftly occur as society discovers that it has chosen the wrong course.

Norbert Wiener's and Claude Shannon's cybernetic "feedbacks," which implement their "information theory," will swiftly and progressively correct the decisions and thereby the historical course of world-around citizenry evolution. Very swiftly all humanity will learn to think about total Earth, total humanity, and total accumulated knowledge, total resources, etc., and will begin to make some powerful omnihumanity, omni-Universe-considerate decisions.

When a 51-percent majority shows that humanity now regrets the previous decision, the world management committee will propose a means of correcting the course, and the foregoing processes will be repeated.

* * *

Refer to my 760-year "Pure Science Acceleration Chart" and the accompanying text in my book *Earth, Inc.* (Doubleday, 1973, pp. 3–26). In that piece and its chart, first published by me in 1959, I predicted that by 1985 we humans would be doing something as presently incredible as sending ourselves around the world by radio. Whatever this presently incredible form of circumnavigation may be, it will be right on schedule.

We have gradually been learning how to substitute various inanimate mechanical parts in our total human organic assembly. We have also been learning how to synthesize more and more of the atomic and molecular ingredients of our organic assembly. We have also been learning from the virologists' DNA-RNA about all the unique biological-design programming of various biological species. We have also been learning that you and I and "life" are not the physical equipment that we use. "Life" itself is entirely metaphysical—a pattern integrity.

Of timely relevance to nature's progressive disclosure that "life" is not physical, in early 1980 it was reported in science journals that a seventy-kilogram baby mammoth had been found preserved for 44,000 years in a chunk of hitherto-never-defrosted Siberian ice. Some of the animal's molecules were still "alive" when the beast was found, occasioning the observation that biochemists are trending to grow organisms—perhaps as complex as the woolly mammoth—from a single molecule of DNA or any part of the physical organism. But "life" is not the physical molecule or a morsel of flesh or a blood corpuscle—as we have been progressively discovering. These are all minor complexes of inanimate atoms.

Now, in July 1980, at eighty-five years of age, I have consumed over 1000 tons of food, water, and air, which progressively, atom by atom, has been chemically and electromagnetically converted into all the physical components of my organism and gradually displaced by other income atoms and molecules. Now all but 146 pounds of that 1000 tons have been progressively discarded. In 1895 I weighed in at seven pounds—at 146 pounds in 1980 my organism is the same slightly evolved and aged "personality" pattern being manifest in pure principle by the total complex of unique behaviors of the only-in-pure-principle-existent inanimate "atoms."

Each one of us is a unique behavioral pattern integrity. The metaphysical you and I are not the coarsely identified "cornflakes" and "prunes" that we ate in the days before yesterdays—some of which became constituents of what are identified momentarily as our "flesh" and "hair" functions.

Our human organisms were designed to initially operate only nakedly and only within the tropical-island areas of the Earthian biosphere. However, our metaphysical minds were given the capability progressively to discover and comprehend many of the principles governing various complex environment formulations as well as the principles that must be employed in order to permit human presence under those various intolerable-to-naked-human conditions. Excursions to the Moon require an additional special set of environment-suitable, external sensing-and-manipulating equipment.

We have already operative the equipment to accommodate abstract, metaphysical you or I observing various Moonscapes, which does not require our donning space suits. It requires only our subscribing to the *National Geographic.* We have now achieved exactly the right physical-information-gathering-and-problem-solving artifacts for the weightless, invisible, metaphysical you and I to employ our instrumental extensions to occupy, explore, and operate in scientific depth on the Moon, Mars, Venus, and the other celestial bodies of our solar system.

In thinking about what I've just said, remember that no human has ever seen or sensed outside of self. All our sensing is nerve-relayed inward to be directly sensed only in our brain. We have become so accustomed to the reliability of the information-relaying-inward to our brain that we now misassume that we are seeing things directly outside ourselves.

Let us consider an athlete—a hockey player who has played for a number of years on his city's professional team in his city's principal rink. He is injured and is hospitalized for months. He tunes his hospital-room television to his team's hockey games in their regular rink. He tends to see what is going on and groans and grins as though he were really present, on the rink. That is the way our sight system works, seemingly to see things transpire outside ourselves.

We noted earlier that all living organisms other than humans have special, integral organic equipment that gives them special advantage in special terrestrial environments—the seaweed that lives exposed to air at low tide and is submerged at high tide, the penguins that live and flourish only at water's edge in the Antarctic. Within a larger cosmic scheme humans are given the special physical equipment to flourish initially only within the planet Earth's biosphere. But humans are also given the metaphysical equipment with which to discover the principles governing metaphysical information-gathering and physical action-taking within extreme macro-micro ranges of physical Universe unreachable directly with the naked organism's primary equipment as initially implemented. It is possible for humans to design, produce, and enclose themselves within such awkward equipment as that which permits their effective coping with nakedly lethal environmental conditions such as those on the Moon. But having visited the Moon to prove our capability thus to cope, we discover that computer-controlled mechanical equipment can be rocketed to the Moon or elsewhere and can do an even better job of exploring and visually recording macro- and micro-remote environments, as well as their respective invisible physical, chemical, and electromagnetic phenomena. While the data that can be thus instrumentally attained are inherently fascinating, their real value consists of what may be discovered and comprehended thereby of the generalized scientific principles demonstrated to be operative in these remote-from-everyday-experience environments.

Eventually we realize that what is transpiring is that the metaphysical weightless mind of humans—the real you and I—is spontaneously preoccupied with hitherto-unharvested local Universe information and therefrom is gleaning omni-Universe-operative principles and therewith is solving local Universe problems in the comprehensively responsible maintenance of the local integrity of eternally regenerative Universe—which we have heretofore hypothesized as the reason humans are included in the cosmic scheme.

Our most prominent present local Universe problem is how to wean humanity from metabolic sustenance only by exploiting nature's local Universe energy savings account—energy being locally imported by cosmic evolution design to produce a new star ten billion years hence. How can we convince those in power the world around that we can live handsomely as supplied only by our daily income of cosmic energy? The answer is *we* can't convince *them*. Only the cosmic wisdom manifest in inexorable evolution can cope with such matters.

When I was twenty-seven years of age, Earthian humanity knew of only one galaxy—our own Milky (Latin: *Galactic*) Way. A year later astronomer Hubble discovered another galaxy. During the subsequent fifty-seven years human astronomers and astrophysicists have discovered two billion more galaxies, all doing their galactic acts within the eleven-and-one-half-billion-light-year-radiused sphere of humanity's present limit of omnidirectional observing.

The average star population of each of these two billion known galaxies is 100 billion. This is to say that the thus-far-discovered star population is two times 10^{20}—that is the integer two followed by twenty zeroes. Within this 200-quintillion star group our star Sun ranks among the pygmies. Each one of the 200 quintillion known stars is an atomic-energy plant. There is nothing new or cosmically illogical about atomic-energy plants. Nature—the intellectual integrity designer of eternally regenerative scenario Universe—designed human organisms to serve metaphysically weightless mind as the physical instruments of exploration and of development—first of the planet Earth's biosphere, and thereafter of that planet's local Universe operating planetary companions, and possibly later other whole star systems, thus to fulfill their cosmic functions as local Universe information-gatherers and local-Universe problem-solvers. As we have also discovered early in this book, nature's design of the human mind's complex organic instrument of exploration and information-gathering—known as the human body—solved all the structural compression problems of these exploratory organisms with water, which boils and freezes within very limited thermal range in respect to the vast range of cosmic temperatures. We also discovered that all the biological organisms—botanical or zoological—which altogether comprise the terrestrially regenerative system ecology (no ecology . . . no humans). Radiance from a candle diminishes rapidly as we recede from the candle. The intensity of all radiation from all radiant sources diminishes as the distance from the source increases. As Einstein's formula anticipated and physical experiments have proved, the sum-total energy content of all the radiation distributed radially outwardly in all directions from the source remains the same but the amount of energy concentrated at any one spherical surface point decreases as the distance from the source increases. Draw a picture of concentric circles, each circle divided into identical arc lengths. The further out we go more arcs of the same length are required to constitute the greater circles. Nature—the impeccable designer that knew exactly how to design and produce what we do not know how to design and produce—our human brain, out optical systems, etc., let alone all the complex interplays of all the organisms, visible and subvisible, of all ecology—has discovered and heeded its own designing laws which state that Sun energy—the atomic energy plant called Sun—is essential to life on planet Earth but that its radiation is too intense for direct exposure by many of the constituent members of the total ecological regeneration team. Such too-radiation-sensitive ecological constituents are designed to operate only within the Earth's earth or at its sea bottoms.

We have also learned earlier that in order to produce these limited-temperature-range organisms nature has designed them to be evolved and incubated only within the very special environmental conditions of planet Earth's biosphere. Nature as the omni-informed and omniconcerned, omniconsiderate cosmic designer discovered and heeded the fact that human organisms and their absolutely essential ecological support complex could not operate safely at a distance of less than ninety-two million miles away from their nearest atomic-energy plant—the Sun—and all the latter's lethal radiation involvements. The would-be exploiters of atomic energy on board our planet Earth will in due course discover there is no way for them to solve atomic-energy-radiation waste-disposal problems save by rocketing it all back into the Sun, where it belongs. Humans will then have to learn how to keep all humans and their ecological support system operating successfully on our vastly adequate daily income of solar atomic energy.

Cosmically acceptable and effective decisions of humanity regarding such matters will not be made by leaders single or plural, political or religious, military or mystic, by coercion or mob psychology.

The effective decisions can only be made by the independently thinking and adequately informed human individuals and their telepathetically intercommunicated wisdom—the wisdom of the majority of all such human individuals—qualifying for continuance in Universe as local cosmic problem-solvers—in love with the truth and in individually spontaneous self-commitment to absolute faith in the wisdom, integrity, and love of God, who seems to wish Earthian humans to survive.

APPENDIX I

Chronology of Scientific Discoveries and Artifacts

W HEN I PUBLISHED *Nine Chains to the Moon,* I was doing research for Phelps Dodge Company. As a copper company, they were eager to have a history of scientific inventions in relation to copper. I was given a team of fifth-year engineering students from Columbia University to compile a history of inventions. This team, consisting of metallurgical, electrical, civil, and mechanical engineers, did their research for me in 1936.

Heretofore all such listings of inventions and discoveries had been warped in favor of this country or that in regards to the place or date of origin of each of the listed inventions.

Using their information of their branches of science, and as typical New Yorkers with forebears from around the world, they were able to select the true origins of inventions. This list was published in *Nine Chains to the Moon* in 1938.

In the intervening forty-four years an enormous amount of inventing and discovering has taken place. In the last decade an accelerating increase in the number of inventions and scientific discoveries has occurred.

For example, during the intervening forty-four years our knowledge of humans in Universe has been extended from 50,000 years of existence to over three and one-half million. Our knowledge of the number of galaxies has increased from two to over two billion!

Earlier in *Critical Path* I pointed out that in order for humans to get to the Moon and safely back, a very large number of technological developments had to be accomplished. None of them would have been accomplished had not there been the previous artifact developments of all human history.

We felt it appropriate to again review the number, dates, and origins of the sources on which our latest technological critical-path developments had been predicated.

I feel it appropriate to compile our own latest chronology because the many published chronologies of scientific and engineering history have lacked many of the items we consider critical and have included many we have not considered critical.

ANCIENT	Stone Age tools for at least three million years
4000 B.C	Picto-linguistic writing, Tartaria
3500 B.C.	Bronze in Thailand
3500 B.C.	Sumerian picto-graphic writing (evolves later into cuneiform)
pre-3480 B.C.	Grain, domesticated animals, pictograms, copper, silver, gold, tin, lead, zinc, iron, carbon, sulphur, mercury; levers; wheels and wheeled vehicles; sledges (Scandinavia); stone wall structures; coal known, but its potentials unrecognized
3400 B.C.	Mesopotamian evidence that number language preceded written language by thousands of years
3400 B.C.	Irrigation system in Egypt
3100 B.C.	Egyptian hieroglyphics
3000 B.C.	Chinese ideograms, complex generalized concepts
	Drainage and sewage system in India
	Dams, canals, pyramids, heavy stone statues constructed using inclined plane and lever—Sumeria
	Pyramids in Egypt
2200 B.C.	Clay maps, Babylon
2100 B.C.	Babylonian calendar modified to include movement of stars
	True astonomical observation, Mesopotamia
	Spherical geometry in Babylon (120 L.C.D. triangles)
2000 B.C.	Cretan writing (led to Hittite writing in Anatolia several centuries later)
1800 B.C.	Babylonian cuneiform (Hammurabi's Code)
1700 B.C.	Network of roads, Babylon
	Linear A—development of Cretan writing with largest corpus from Hagia Triada
1500 B.C.	Phonetic spelling developed by Phoenicians
1400 B.C.	Linear B, Greek adaptation of Cretan writing either on mainland or at Knossus
1500–	
1100 B.C.	Cypro-Minoan, distant offshoot of Cretan writing
1000 B.C.	Phonetics transmitted by Phoenicians to Greeks

900 B.C.	Rustproof iron in India
640 B.C.	Beginning with Thales, the Ionian Greeks were the first of the Grecian natural philosophers.
600 B.C.	Discovery of "irrationals"
	Laws of right-angle triangle—Pythagoras
460 B.C.	Thinking microcosmically, Democritus was the first known human to conceive of a smallest cosmic entity, which he named the "atom."
600–400 B.C.	Thinking macrocosmically, the Greek Pythagorean scientists (situated to the north of Athens) were the first humans known and recorded to think of our world as a spherical entity.
410 B.C.	The Pythagorean Philolaus was the first to conceive of the Earth as a spherical body in motion around a central cosmic fire. He also conceived of the stars, Sun, Moon, and five planets—Venus, Mercury, Mars, Jupiter, and Saturn—as spherical bodies. His Sun was not at the center.
350 B.C.	All the Greek states adopt a 24-letter alphabet enabling Greek philosopher-scientists to record and transmit their ideas.
	A latter-day Pythagorean, Heraclides, was the first to conceive of the Earth sphere as spinning west to east. But Heraclides' cosmos was as yet geocentric. His Earth spun at the center of the fixed-stars Universe.
300 B.C.	Geometry—Euclid
	Most of Greek culture—poetry, science, and philosophy—and its written records are moved to Alexandria, Egypt, which was part of Alexander the Great's Greek Empire.
220 B.C.	Archimedes—law of displacement of floating bodies and specific gravity, hydraulic screw pump, much mathematics, many polyhedra; first formulation of concept of limit
200 B.C.	Phoenicians circumnavigate the Earth
	Aristarchus, the Greek, conceived of the Sun as at center of planetary revolutions. For him all the stars were fixed, and the Moon revolved around the Earth. He was almost killed for his unprecedented thoughts.
	Eratosthenes measuringly calculates circumference of Earth within 1.5-percent accuracy. Also, makes map of world from England on the northwest to mouth of Ganges in the east and all of Africa on the south.
	Hipparchus calculates distance of Earth to Moon, calculates solar year to within six minutes.

150 B.C.   Crates, Stoic philosopher, develops first terrestrial globe; celestial globes preceded it.

It is clear that a special chain of Greek scientist-philosopher-cosmologists consisting of Philolaus (410 B.C.), Heraclides (350 B.C.), and Aristarchus (200 B.C.) had successively evolved a concept of the solar system that was in fair agreement with Copernicus (1543 A.D.) and even with our late-twentieth-century conceptioning.

It is also clear that beginning with Plato's pupil, Aristotle (384 B.C.–322 B.C.), and his practical philosophy that the geocentric concept of the celestial system, despite its difficulty rationalized complexity, was after 200 B.C. becoming more and more formally adopted by the "authorities."

It seems almost equally clear that between 200 B.C. and 200 A.D. a deliberately planned policy of the combined political and religious powers undertook the conditioning of the human reflexes to misconceive, mis-see, or mostly not see at all the macro-micro systems in which we live. Their success drew the curtains on science for 1700 years—until 1500 A.D.

100 B.C.   Alexandrian library reputed to have reached 700,000 manuscript volumes, or rolls. Fortunately, volumes in Alexandria copiously copied and distributed to libraries all around civilized world of that time.

47 B.C.   40,000 volumes of Alexandrian library burned during siege in war between Caesar and Pompey.

200 A.D.   Ptolemy's conic, latitude-and-longitude world map reading from British Isles on west to China on east involved North Africa, Arabia, India. His *Almagest* publication containing storehouse of navigational data—catalog of over 1000 stars.

272 A.D.   Second burning of Alexandrian library by Roman emperor

300 A.D.   Compass, China

391 A.D.   Third burning of Alexandrian library by another Roman emperor

529 A.D.   Closing of all universities

642 A.D.   Final complete burning of library of Alexandria by Muslims

700 A.D.   Moorish invasion of Spain, introducing Arabic numerals and algebra

720–813 A.D.   Principal salts of arsenic, sulphur, and mercury are discovered.

875–925 A.D.   Persian Rhases applies chemical knowledge to preparation of medicines.

800 A.D.	Al-Khwarizmi, in Baghdad, writes treatise in Arabic explaining function of ciphra and positioning of numbers.
1000 A.D.	Leif Erikson reaches America
	Gunpowder in China
	First real lenses—Alhozen
	Avicenna's medical *Canon* and alchemical *De Anima*
1100	Bologna University established
1105	First recorded windmill in Europe
1118	Cannon used by Moors
1144	Paper used in Japan
	Alchemy introduced to Europe through translation of Arabic texts
1147	Use of woodcuts for capital letters
1180	Fixed steering rudder
1190	Paper mills at Herault, France
1200	Al-Khwarizmi's 780 A.D. "Treatise on Cipher" translated into Latin, published in Carthage, North Africa
1230	Hot-air balloons in China
1250	Discovery of arsenic
1260	Pivoted magnetic compass
1270	Treatise on lenses—Vitellio
	Compound lenses—Roger Bacon
	Silk-reeling machine
1280	Compendium of agricultural practice
	Spectacles
1290	Marco Polo returns to Europe from Far East with data.
	Spinning wheel
1300	Ship's compass
1310	Dissection of human body—De Luzzi
1320	Water-driven blast furnace
	Sawmill at Augsburg
1330	Crane at Luneberg
	Wool manufacture established at York
1346	Battle at Crécy, guns used in battle
	Division of hours and minutes into sixtieths
1350	Wire-pulling machines at Nürnberg
1390	Metal types, Korea
1400	Diving suit
	First book in movable type, Korea
1410	Street lights in London
1420	Velocipede—Fontana
	First European woodcut

1430	Scientific cartography
1440	Azores discovered
	Laws of perspective—Alberti
	Modern printing with movable type in Europe
	Copperplate engraving
1450	Printing established a universal symbolism for algebraic numerals
	Discovery of antimony
	Wagon springs
1460	Trigonometry—Regiomontanus
	Printing introduced in England—Caxton
1480	Canal lock
	Arquebus introduced
	Copper etching
1482	Leonardo da Vinci career begins: perspective frame, wheelbarrow, speaking tube. Also plans for: centrifugal pump, canal dredge, polygonal fort and outworks, breech-loading cannon, rifled firearms, antifriction roller bearings, lens grinder and polisher, universal joint, conical screw, rope and belt drive, link chain, submarine, bevel and spiral gear, proportional and paraboloid compasses, lathe, silk doubling, winding apparatus, flying machine, parachute, lamp chimney, helicopter, ship's log, double-deck streets, standardized mass-production house, perfect whorehouse.
1492	Moors driven from Spain
	Positioning of numbers was popularly established; first post–Dark Ages globe was made.
	Columbus discovers America.
1497	Cabot lands in North America
	Vasco da Gama reaches India
1500	First portable watch with iron mainspring
	Mechanical farming drill
1508	Multicolored woodcut
1511	Pneumatic beds
1513	Porcelain introduced in England
	Balboa discovers Pacific
1515	Camera obscura
1521	Discovery of potato by European population
1522	Magellan's voyage around the world is completed.
	First arithmetic book is published in England.
1524	Fodder-cutting machine

1535	Diving bell
	First English Bible is printed.
1539	First astronomical map
	Printing introduced to America (Mexico)—Pablos
1540	Padlock invented
	Invention of mathematical symbols—Vieta
	First handbook of dyeing
1541	Tartaglia finds general third-degree equation solution.
1543	Copernican system published
1544	Elaboration of algebraic symbols—Stifel
1545	Paré—surgical instruments
1548	Water-pumping works in Augsburg
1550	First known suspension bridge in Europe
1552	Iron-rolling machine—Brulier
1561	Copper mines discovered in England
1564	Coaches first made in England
1565	Lead pencil
1568	Mercator projection of world map
1576	Discovery of magnetic dip
1579	Automatic ribbon loom
1582	Tide mill pump, London
	Gregorian calendar revision
1585	Decimal system—Stevin
1589	Knitting frame
1590	Compound microscope—Jansen
1594	Use of clock to determine longitude
1600	Treatise on terrestrial magnetism and electricity—Gilbert
	Pendulum—Galileo
1605	Stevin revives study of statics.
	Theorems on inclined planes, pulleys and equilibrium—Galileo
1606	Discovery of Australia
1608	Telescope—Lippershay
1609	First laws of motion—Galileo
	Kepler's laws (first and second laws)
1612	Bituminous coal smelting—Sturtevant
1613	Gunpowder in mine blasting
1614	Logarithms—Napier
1615	Triangulation in surveying
1617	Log tables
	Adding machine—Napier
1620	Spirit thermometer

	Slide rule—Oughtred
	Bacon's *Novum Organum*
1624	First patent law in England
1628	Worcester's engine
	Harvey's discovery of circulation of blood
1629	Explanation of negative roots
	Branca's engine
1631	Invention of mathematical symbols x and :
1635	Discovery of microscopic organisms
	Infinitesimal calculus—Fermat
	Threshing machine
1637	Laws of refraction
	Periscope
1638	Formulation of infinite aggregate—Galileo
1639	Rain gauge
	Invention of coordinate geometry—Descartes
1640	Cotton manufacture in England
1642	Calculating machine—Pascal
1647	Calculation of foci of all lenses
1650	First bread made with yeast—England
	Magic lantern—Kircher
1650	Air pump—Von Guericke
1654	Mathematical induction—Pascal
	Laws of probability—Pascal
1657	Pendulum clock—Huygens
1658	Balance spring for clocks
	Red corpuscles discovered in blood
1661	Boyle's "skeptical chemist"
1662	Boyle's law
1666	Discovery of diffraction
	Newton discovers light dispersion by prism
	Reflecting telescope—Newton
1667	Paris observatory
	Cellular structure of plants
1669	Double refraction discovered
1670	Discovery of phosphorus
	Sulphur ball electric machine
1675	Greenwich observatory
	Determination of speed of light—Roemer
1677	Infinite series
	Calculus—Newton and Leibnitz

1680	Discovery of chlorophyll
1685	Foundation of scientific obstetrics
1687	Newton's *Principia,* laws of gravitation and motion
1688	Distillation of gas from coal
1690	Huygens's wave theory
1695	Plate glass
	Papin's engine
1698	Isogonic charts
	Savery's engine
1700	Explanation of beats, overtones, and sympathetic vibrations
1702	First daily newspaper, London
1704	Newton's *Optics*
1705	Newcomen's engine
1707	Physician's pulse watch in seconds
1708	Wet sand iron casting
1709	Coke used in blast furnace
1714	Mercury thermometer—Fahrenheit
1717	Iron-covered wooden railways
1720	Three-color copperplate printing
1727	First exact measurement of blood pressure
	Invention of stereotype
	Light images with silver nitrate
1732	Discovery of cobalt
	Discovery of platinum
1733	Roller spinning
	Flying shuttle—Kay
1736	Commercial sulfuric acid
1737	Centigrade thermometer
1738	Kinetic Theory of Gas—Bernoulli
1745	First technical school separate from military engineering
	Leyden jar
1746	Sulfuric acid by lead chamber process
	Discovery of zinc
1747	Beet sugar
1749	Scientific calculation of water resistance to ships—Euler
1751	Lightning jar
	Discovery of nickel
1753	Discovery of bismuth
1756	Latent heat—Black
1758	Achromatic telescope
1760	Steam blast—Smeaton

1761	Modern type chronometer
1763	Spinning jenny
1765	Steam engine
1766	Discovery of hydrogen
1767	Cast-iron rails
	History of Electricity (including phlogiston theory)—Priestley
1769	Steam carriage
	Lightning conductors on high buildings
1770	Caterpillar tread
	Screw-cutting lathe—Ramsden
1771	Discovery of fluorine
	Encyclopaedia Britannica, first edition
	Discovery of electric nature of nervous impulse—Galvani
1772	Vitamin cure for scurvy
	Discovery of nitrogen
1774	Boring machine—Wilkinson
	Lighting in Boston streets
	Discovery of chlorine
	Discovery of manganese
1775	Reciprocating engine with flywheel
1776	Reverberatory furnace
	Machine plane
	Chemical nomenclature "element," "compound"—Lavoisier
	Scientific explanation of combustion—Lavoisier
	Discovery of oxygen by Priestley—named by Lavoisier
1777	Torsion balance
	Torpedo—Bushnell
	Circular wood saw
	Steam hammer—Wilkinson
1778	Discovery of molybdenum
	Modern water closet—Bramah
1779	Cast-iron bridge sections
1780	Mass-produced cast-iron farm implements
1781	Drill plow
	Siberian highway begun
	Synthesis of water
1782	Discovery of tellurium
1783	Argand lamp
	Free hydrogen-balloon flight
	Discovery of tungsten

1784	Power loom
	Puddling process in manufacture of wrought iron—Cort
	Patent lock—Bramah
1785	Balloon flight across Channel
	Interchangeable musket parts
	First steam spinning mill
	Chlorine used as a bleach
1786	Gold leaf electroscope
1787	Steamboat
	Nail-making machine
1788	Galvanic electricity
1789	Discovery of uranium
	Discovery of zirconium
	Modern classification of plants—Jussieu
1790	Gas lighting
	Ultraviolet rays discovered
	Soda from sodium chloride
1791	Gas engine
	Discovery of titanium
1793	Cotton gin—Whitney
	First U.S. balloon flight
	First sulfuric acid made in U.S.
	Planer
1794	Discovery of yttrium
	École Polytechnique
1795	Food canning
	Hydraulic press—Bramah
1796	Lithography
	Natural cement
	Hydraulic cement
	Discovery of photosynthesis
1797	Cast-iron plow
	Carding machine
	Discovery of geometric interpretation of complex numbers
	Improved screw-cutting, and slide rest lathe—Maudsley
1798	Vaccination introduced
	Discovery of chromium
	Cavendish weighs Earth
	Discovery of beryllium
1799	High-pressure steam engine
	Laughing gas as anesthetic

	Manufactured bleaching powder
	Conservatoire National des Arts et Métiers
1800	Voltaic cells
	Infrared rays discovered
	Macadam roads—McAdam
	First experimental electrolysis
1801	Discovery of interference of light waves
	First asteroid discovered
	Discovery of columbium
	First practical submarine
1802	Machine dresser for cotton warps
	Planing machine
	Discovery of tantalum
1803	Atomic theory—Dalton
	Discovery of palladium
	Discovery of rhodium
	Discovery of cerium
	Boat propelled by steam power
1804	Jacquard loom
	Discovery of iridium
	Discovery of osmium
	Bottling factory
1807	Voyage of steamboat *S. C. Clermont* from New York to Albany
	Kymography-revolving cylinder, recording continuous motion
	Discovery of sodium
	Discovery of potassium
1808	Discovery of polarization of light
	Gay-Lussac's law of combining volumes of gases
	Discovery of strontium
	Discovery of barium
	Discovery of calcium
	Discovery of magnesium
1810	Discovery of boron
1811	Modern chemical notation
	Discovery of iodine
	Avogadro's hypothesis on composition of gases
1814	Steam printing press
	Steam locomotive
	Discovery of Fraunhofer black lines in Sun's light spectrum
1815	Stethoscope

	Macadam roads officially adopted in Britain
	Miner's safety lamp—Davy
1817	Discovery of lithium
	Discovery of cadmium
	Discovery of selenium
1818	Milling machine—Whitney
1819	Steamship *Savannah* crosses Atlantic
	Dulong and Petit's law
	Isomorphism of chemical elements discovered—Mitscherlich
1820	Modern wood planer
	Formulation of power of an aggregate—Bolzano
	Discovery of catalysis
1823	Faraday—laws of electromagnetism
	Calculating machine—Babbage
	Waterproof fabric
	Discovery of silicon
1824	Mechanical equivalent of heat—thermodynamics
1825	Algebraic numbers not expressed by radicals discovered
1826	Discovery of bromine
1827	Niepce—first photograph
	Practical ship's screw
	Brownian movement discovered
	Discovery of aluminum
	Ohm's Law—current equals pressure/resistance in given electric circuit
1828	Electromagnet
	Hot blast in iron production
	Wohler synthesis of urea
	Discovery of thorium
1829	Paper matrix stereotype
	Water-filtration plant, London
1830	Sewing machine
	Compressed air for underwater tunnels
	Discovery of vanadium
1831	Steam railway passenger train
	Mowing machine
	Phosphorus match
	Chloroform
1832	Magnetic telegraph
	Principles of induction—Faraday
	Magneto—Pixii

1833	Reaper—McCormick
	Laws of electrolysis—Faraday
	Principles of geology—Lyell
1834	Law of substitution in organic chemistry
1835	Revolver-type pistol
	Commutator
1836	Pin machine
	Harvester
	Type-casting machine
1837	First metal ship
	Electric motor—Davenport
	Discovery of nature of fermentation
	Screw propellor
	Shorthand—Pitman
1838	Rubber vulcanizing
	Photography—Daguerre
	Power-driven rope-making machine
	Use of single wire and ground circuit
	Steam drop hammer
1839	Penny postage in England
	Brick-making machinery
	Electrotype
	Discovery of lanthanum
1840	Corrugated iron roofing
	Microphotography
	First iron-link suspension bridge
	Liebig shows need for artificial fertilizer
1841	Principle of conservation of energy—Mayer
1842	Doppler effect discovered
	Mechanical equivalent of heat
	Superphosphate fertilizers
1843	Chemical spectrum analysis
	Gutta-percha
	Discovery of terbium
	Discovery of erbium
1844	First telegraph line, Washington to Baltimore
	Practical wood pulp paper
1845	Portland cement
	Turret lathe—Fitch
	Pneumatic tire (bicycle type)
	Sewing machine—Howe
	Mechanical boiler stoker

	Discovery of ruthenium
1846	Rotary printing press
	Ether—Warren and Morton
	Nitroglycerine and guncotton
	Prediction and discovery of Neptune
1847	Penny postage in U.S.
	Second law of thermodynamics
1848	Rotary fan
	Corliss engine
1849	Hydraulic turbine
	Steam power rock drill
1850	Law of mass action
1851	Wire rope for power transmission
	Vernier caliper
	Sewing machine—Singer
	Foucault pendulum
	Cast-iron-frame building
1852	Elevator with brake
	Gyroscope
	Hydraulic mining
	Theory of valence
1853	Mechanical ship's log
	Mass-production watches
	Gear-cutting machine
1854	Riemann's geometry
1855	Gas-stove burner
	Lathe safety lock
	Powdered milk
1856	Steel—Bessemer
	Perkin's aniline dye
1857	Kinetic theory of gases
	Passenger elevator—Otis
	Discovery of sols, theory of colloids
1858	Steel—Kelly
	Structure of organic compounds—Kekulé
1859	Storage cell—Planté
	Electric accumulator—Planté
	Absorption spectra
	First oil well
	On the Origin of Species by Natural Selection—Darwin
	Steamroller
1860	Dynamo, Italy

Ammonia refrigerator
Discovery of cesium
Asphalt paving
Laws of radiation, emission, and absorption
1861   Electric furnace in Siemens, England
Discovery of rubidium
Discovery of thallium
Germ theory of disease—Pasteur
Milling machine
1862   Machine gun—Gatling
Pasteurization
Monitor battleship
Synthesis of acetylene
1863   Solvay process for making soda
Argelander catalogs 324,000 stars
Discovery of indium
Cell theory—Schultze
1864   Electromagnetic theory—Maxwell
Cylindrical grinders
1865   Multiple-cell electrolytic copper
Law of heredity—Mendel
Modern ore stamp mill
Newland's octaves
Ring theory of the structure of benzene—Kekulé
Antiseptic surgery—Lister
1866   Bunsen burner
Underwater torpedo—Whitehead
First successful transatlantic telegraph cable
Dynamite—Nobel
1867   Railroad block signals
Elevated railroad in N.Y.C.
Micrometer caliper
1868   Railroad refrigerator car
Tungsten steel—Musket
First metallography of iron—Tscherroff
1869   Transcontinental railroad in U.S.
Air brake
Shield tunneling
Suez Canal
Science of eugenics—Galton
Periodic table—Mendeleyev

	"Angstrom" (wave length of light measurement)
1870	Celluloid
	Discovery of invertase
1871	Welt machine
1873	Automatic railroad coupler
	Typewriter
	Discovery of chromosomes
1874	Audruplex telegraph
	Atomic theory of electricity—Stoney
	Pressure-cooking method for canning food
1875	Telephone
	Discovery of gallium
1876	Gas engine—Otto four-cycle
	Toxins discovered
	Gibbs's phase rule
1877	Microphone
	Automatic gear cutters
	Anthrax cure
	Osmotic pressure
	Electric welding
	Reinforced-concrete beams
	Phonograph
1878	Incandescent lamp
	Synthesis of indigo
	Discovery of ytterbium
	Cathode ray—Crookes
	Basic removal phosphorus iron products
1879	Arc lamp
	Synthesis of saccharin
	Discovery of samarium
	Discovery of scandium
	Discovery of holmium
	Discovery of thulium
	First electrified railroad
1880	Centrifuge
	Discovery of gadolinium
	Ball bearings (cup and cone)
1881	Depressing freezing point solutions
1882	Tuberculosis bacillus isolated
	First central electric power station
	Hydroelectric plant

1883   Rayon
              Steam turbine
              Brooklyn Bridge
1884   Trolley car
              Fountain pen—Waterman
              Roll film—Eastman
              Manganese steel
              Skyscraper with steel frame
              Cocaine
              Micro-organisms responsible for cholera, tetanus,
              and diphtheria discovered
              Gasoline motor—Daimler
1885   Drinell's laws of metallography
              Linotype patented—Mergenthaler
              Transformer
              Hydrophobia cure—Pasteur
              Discovery of praseodymium
              Discovery of neodymium
              Van't Hoff's laws
1886   Aluminum commercially produced—Hall
              Electrolytic copper (series cell)
              Electric fan
              Fluorine isolated
              Discovery of dysprosium
              Discovery of germanium
1887   Split-phase induction motor
              Rotary converter
              Automatic telephone
              Esperanto—attempt at artificial universal language
              Ionization—Arhennius
              Fructose synthesized
              Monotype machine—Lanston
              Electromagnetic waves—Hertz
              Michelson–Morley experiment
              Voltaic cell explanation
1888   Allotrophy in heat treatment
              Adding machine (recording)
              Box camera
              Calcium carbide (acetylene)
              Nitrogen-fixing bacteria discovered
1889   Pneumatic tire inner tube

	Electric-induction motor
	Color film
1890	Electrolytic alkali
	Mantle gas burner
	Silicon carbide
	Synchronous converter
	Clincher tire
	Gold and silver refining (cyanide)
1891	Thermoelectric pyrometer
	Morrison electric auto
	Electric cooking
1892	A.C. motor—Tesla
	Automatic telephone switchboard
1893	Motion picture machine
	Zip fastener—Judson
	By-product coke oven
	Railroad car dumpers
	Artificial diamonds
1894	Submarine—Lake
	Dry-air blast furnace
	Liquid oxygen
	Experimental embryology
	Discovery of argon
	Andean railway
1895	Automobile
	Diesel oil engine
	Wireless telegraphy
	X ray—Roentgen
	Automatic screw machine
	Discovery of helium
1896	Disc plow
	Zeeman effect
	Ore unloader
	Discovery of europium
1897	Steel hopper cars
	Electric trip-hammer drill
	Cure beri-beri with vitamins
	Electron discovered
	Chromium
	Radio tuning—Lodge
1898	Discovery of krypton

Discovery of neon
Discovery of xenon
Discovery of polonium—Curies
Discovery of radium—Curies
Coil-and-condenser tuning system for radio—Lodge
X-ray diagnosis
1899   Discovery of actinium
Oil flotation of ore
Aspirin
1900   Nernst lamp
Mercury lamp
Quantum theory—Planck
Arrhenius discovers the pressure of radiation
Electric steelmaking
Induction furnace
Escalator
Revolver—Browning
Discovery of radon
Automatic stereotype plate process
Caterpillar tractor
Dirigible balloon—Zeppelin
1901   High-speed alloy steel
Gas welding
Wright glider
Transatlantic radio telegraph
Trans-Siberian Railroad completed
Discovery of yellow fever transmission
Isolation of adrenaline
DeVries theory of mutation
1902   Catalytic hydrogenation
Radio telegram
Discovery of heaviside layer
Photos by wire
1903   Edison cell
Oil-burning steamer
Ultramicroscope
Theory of colloids
Tantalum lamp
First successful turbogenerator at Chicago
Pacific cable—around-world message in 12 minutes
Ford Motor Company founded—beginning of mass-
production autos

Motor taxis in London
Bottlemaking machine
Wright brothers' gas engine–propelled airplane flight
1904   Fleury tube
Electrostatic fume precipitation—Cottrell
SAE founded
Safety razor blades
Reinforced concrete
Electric subway trains—N.Y.C.
1905   Mercury pump—Goede
Process-nitrogen fixation (cyanamide)
Synthetic ammonia
Power plant at Niagara
Special Theory of Relativity—Einstein
Fleming valve
1906   Turbine drive on *Lusitania* and *Mauretania*
Crystal detector (radio)
Gyrocompass
Deflocculated graphite
Nickel refining
Vacuum radio tube
1907   Automatic bottle-blowing machine
Phosphorus rustproofing (Parkerizing)
First Ford Model T and assembly-line production
Removable auto tire
Discovery of lutetium
Bakelite (phenolic resin plastic)
1908   Oil cracking
Electronic valence
Thermit process of welding railroad rails
East and Hudson river railroad tubes
Electron—Millikan
1909   Maxim silencer
Blériot flies English Channel
Duraluminum
North Pole reached—Peary
1910   Haber process
Poulson continuous-wave radio transmission
Roller bearings
1911   Pulmotor
Recognition of protons
South Pole discovered

X-ray study of metals
Kinemacolor movies
Hydroplane
First use of gyrocompass—Sperry
First cloud chamber

1912   First self-starter exhibited—Bendix
X-ray spectra, X-ray crystallography
Cellophane
Vitamins—Hopkins
Atomic numbers—Moseley
Successful diesel installation on ship
Diesel-engine submarines capable of transatlantic crossings
Copper from low-grade ore (electrowinning)

1913   Tungsten-filament lamp
Research on radiation—Geiger
Atom model—Bohr
Metal spray plating machine
100-kilocycle generator—Alexanderson
Nitrogen fixation from air

1914   Military tank
Regenerative circuit—Armstrong
Chrome-nickel-steel (in lab only)
Panama Canal
World War begun
Selenium photometer

1915   Chrome vanadium steel
Transcontinental phone service
Magnesium industry started
Theory of continental drift—Wegener
High vacuum radio tube—Langmuir
Tuned radio frequency reception—Alexanderson
First chlorine gas attack in World War I
General Relativity Theory—Einstein
Neon lamp—Claude
Radiotelephone
Introduction of chloropicrin, mustard gas

1916   Development of gas mask
Ajax Wyatt furnace
Helicopter
Depth bomb
Stainless steel (secret of World War I, first commercial use in 1928)

1917   Submarine detector
Sperry rangekeeper
Aerial photography
Discovery of protactinium
Optical glass industry in U.S.
Commercial cadmium
Vitamin B

1918   Electron employed
Examination by X ray of brain
Lewisite
Toaster
Sonar

1919   NC-4 flight across Atlantic via Bermuda and Azores
First wireless phone two-way conversation across Atlantic, from Brest, France, to Arlington, Virginia
Alcock and Brown nonstop flight across Atlantic
R-34 Atlantic flight
Lewis Langmuir theory of atomic structure
First man-made transmutation—Rutherford

1920   Neutron discovered—Harkens
Sodium from salt
Electric furnace production of phosphoric acid
Commercial radio broadcast of voice

1921   Compound gas engine
Electrical prospecting devices
Rubber plated on metal

1922   Thermocouple for interplanetary sensing
Fundamental complementarity in physical Universe
A.C. radio tube
Autogyro
Clear-fused quartz
Air conditioning
Practical automobile self-starter—Bendix
Push-button elevator
Insulin
Vitamin D
Radar

1923   Nitriding process
Discovery of hafnium
First chromium plating—Fink
Mercury steam boiler—Emmet
Chemical physiology of muscle contraction

Bulldozer
Hubble discovers another galaxy
1924   Flettner rotor ship
Spectrohelioscope
Atomic hydrogen welding
Insulin fattening
Liver for anemia
Wave mechanics—De Broglie
First dynamic loudspeakers on radio sets
First intercity bus lines
Air mail, from New York to San Francisco
1925   Beryllium copper
Electrochemical restoration of corrosion—Fink
Transmutation of mercury to gold
Discovery of rhenium
First commercial airline on regular schedule
Phototelegraphy
Methanol
Science and the Modern World—Whitehead
1926   Movies (talking)
Electric refrigerator
Dirigible to North Pole
Airplane to North Pole
Liquid-fuel rocket—Goddard
Conditioned Reflexes—Pavlov
1927   German lightweight streamline railcar, beginning of stream-
lining
Television (laboratory only)
Photoelectric cell
Lindbergh flies airplane nonstop across Atlantic from New
York to Paris
Heisenberg's indeterminacy
Dirac predicts existence of antiparticles
Holland Tunnel from New York to New Jersey
Dymaxion House—Buckminster Fuller
Energetic/Synergetic Geometry—B. Fuller
Michaelson's final, most accurate measurement of speed of
light in vacuo (accredited by world science in 1970)
Transatlantic telephone service inaugurated
1928   Teletype
Dirigible *Graf Zeppelin* flown across Atlantic by Dr. Eckner

	Sir Charles Kingsford-Smith flies Pacific, California to Australia
	Ford Model A
	Penicillin discovered—Fleming
	Tungsten and tantalum carbide
	Coalescence from brittle copper cathode
1929	Coaxial cables
	Rocket engine successful—Goddard
	Automatic airplane pilot
	"Paper bottles" first used for frozen juices and vegetables
	Closest packing effect—Aston
1930	Cyclotron (atom smasher)
	Electrolytic sheet copper
	Electrolytic powdered metal
	Spectra photography
	First air-conditioned passenger train
1931	Stratosphere balloon flight—Piccard
	Neoprene rubber developed
	Empire State Building completed (world's tallest at 1250 feet)
	Around-world airplane flight—Post and Gatty
	George Washington Bridge opened (3500-foot span)
	Ford Trimotor Stout aluminum airplane
	Pauli postulates neutrino (25 years before first observed)
	Godel's proof, hallmark of modern mathematics
	Heavy water—Urey
	A1 Williams sets seaplane speed record, 407 mph
1932	Boeing and Douglas DC-3 all-metal passenger airplanes
	Cosmic ray camera
	Inauguration of transcontinental U.S.A. airline service
	92nd isolation of a chemical element
	X-ray diffraction
	Neutron discovered
	Dymaxion House prototype
	First use of sulfa drugs
	South Atlantic transoceanic zeppelin service
1933	Dymaxion car successfully demonstrated (invented 1927, B. Fuller)
	FM broadcasting
	Positron—Anderson and Millikan
1934	Sulfanilamide discovered

	Casting of 200-inch mirror for Mount Palomar telescope
	High-intensity mercury arc lamp
	Perfection of sodium lamp
1935	Cortisone
	First trans-Pacific airplane passenger service (Pan Am)
	Flying boat
	Ion-exchange resins
	Public TV begins in England
	GE portable shortwave beam radio transceiver
1936	Rust cotton picker
	Micrometer
1937	Atomic fission theoretically envisaged by Hahn and Stresemann in Germany
	Discovery of technetium
	Jet engine, England—Whittle
	Nylon produced
1938	Ballpoint pen
1939	Sikorsky helicopter invented
	DDT
	Development of A-bomb funded (dubbed Manhattan Project in 1942)
	Discovery of francium
	Electron microscope
	Synthetic rubber
1940	First radio map of Milky Way published
	Discovery of astatine
	Discovery of plutonium
	Plutonium fission
	Meningitis cure
	Discovery of neptunium
	Rh factor discovered in blood
1941	Dacron
1942	Magnetic tape
	First sustained uranium fission reaction—Fermi
	V-2 rocket
1943	Sikorsky helicopter successfully flown
	Dymaxion projection Sky-Ocean World Map published—B. Fuller
	LSD-25—Hoffman
1944	DNA discovered
	Discovery of curium

First jet airplane (fighter), England

Prototype Dymaxion Houses constructed by Beech Aircraft, Wichita, Kansas

1945   World's first atomic bomb, Alamogordo, New Mexico

Streptomycin developed

Phototypesetting machine

Discovery of americium

1946   First regular transatlantic airplane (DC-4) passenger service

First all-electronic general-purpose digital computer

Pilotless radio-controlled rocket missile

1947   Geodesic dome—B. Fuller

"Atomic time clock" developed using carbon-14

Discovery of promethium

World's largest reflector telescope, 200-inch mirror (Mount Palomar)

Reflecting microscope developed

Commercial television broadcasting—U.S.

Speed of radio waves in vacuo—Essen

Supersonic air flight

Theory that all massive rotating bodies are magnetic—Blackett

1948   Aureomycin developed

Bathyscaphe

Xerography—Carlson (first envisioned in 1938)

Holograph—Gabor

Long-playing record—Goldmark

Polaroid Land camera marketed

Transistor invented—Bardeen, Brattain, Shockley

1949   Giant electronic computers introduced to implement complex stockpiling and anticipatory arming and preparation for World War III under title "cold war," invisible psychological warfare.

U.S.S.R. explodes A-bomb, ending U.S. monopoly

ACTH

General industrial automation emerging

Neomycin

1950   DC-6 airplane passenger service

1950s consumer goods "fall-out" from emergent technology: frost-free refrigerator, dishwasher, self-cleaning oven, etc.

Discovery of berkelium

Discovery of californium

1951   DC-7 propellor-drive airplane introduced
            Peat-fired gas turbine
            DNA helical structure discovered by Wilkins, Watson, Crick
            "Flying spot" microscope

1952   First hydrogen bomb explosion, Eniwetok Island, South Pacific
            Artificial lung-heart machine used in surgery
            Radioisotopes come into scientific, medical, industrial use

1953   Ford Motor Company 93-foot geodesic dome successfully installed
            Polio vaccine developed by Jonas Salk
            Cryosurgery—Swan
            Cosmic-ray observatory in Alaska

1954   *Nautilus,* first atomic-powered submarine, launched
            Solar battery capable of converting Sun's radiation into electricity
            Vertical-takeoff aircraft

1955   Discovery of radio emissions from Jupiter—Burke
            Maser invented by Towne
            Compatible color TV receiver (widespread use in U.S. in 10 years, and 40 million worldwide by early '70s)
            Open-heart surgery
            Discovery of molecular structure of insulin
            Artificial diamonds—gem-quality by early '70s
            Salk polio vaccine effective
            First glass with regular crystalline molecular pattern discovered

1956   Neutrino first detected
            Transcontinental helicopter flight, 37 hours
            First transatlantic telephone cable
            Mullard image-dissector camera
            Ion microscope

1957   International Geophysical Year
            First civilian nuclear-power station
            History's largest clear-span structural enclosure at Baton Rouge, Louisiana (384 feet in diameter)—B. Fuller
            Sputnik, first satellite launched by Earthians
            First containerized cargo ships
            First monorail—Cologne, Germany
            Discovery of nobelium

1958	Nuclear-powered ice-breaker ship
	First U.S. satellite orbits Earth
	Stereophonic phonograph recordings
	Geodesic domes at North and South Poles to house research
	Invisible high-energy Van Allen radiation belts discovered
	Discovery of mendelevium
	Law of Conservation of Parity does not hold for weak inter-actions—Lee, Yang
	Atomic submarine crosses Arctic Ocean and North Pole from Pacific Ocean to Atlantic submerged below ice cap.
1959	World-around air jet passenger service network established
	Unmanned rocket Luna 2 crash-lands on Moon (U.S.S.R.)
	Luna 3 circles Moon and sends first radiophoto of "far side" back to Earth
	First nuclear-powered passenger-cargo ship launched
	Luna 1 orbits Sun as first man-made planet (U.S.S.R.)
	St. Lawrence Seaway opens mid-America to ocean traffic
1960	Laser demonstrated—Maiman
	Chlorophyll is synthesized from man-made materials
	Structure of protein myoglobin elucidated—Kendrew, Perutz
	Birth control pills
	Pacemaker for human heart
	Bathyscaphe navigates seven miles inward to bottom of Pacific Ocean
	Nuclear submarine *Triton* circumnavigates Earth submerged the whole way—84 days
	First weather satellite, Tiros I (U.S.A.)
	U.S.S.R. recovers dogs after 17 orbits of Earth in satellite
1961	DNA genetic code deciphered—design control for all life
	Gagarin orbits Earth as first human spaceman
	Russians orbit Earth in hourly cycles in co-rocketing vehicles
	Discovery of lawrencium
	National electric ultra-high-voltage grids of France and Britain are connected by cable and superconductivity
	Methane used to supplement coal-gas in Britain
1962	Telstar, half-ton communication-relay satellite
	Satellite studies of cosmic radiation and Venus
	Advances in molecular biology—Perutz
	Four ice ages established from soil core diggings

1963   Friction welding
                Discovery of anti-xi-zeno, fundamental atomic particle of
                antimatter
                Measles vaccine perfected
                Syncom satellite holds position over spinning Earth
                Belt of copper needles orbited to test a secure global radio
                communications system
                Quasars discovered
1964   Verrazano Narrows Bridge, New York, world's longest sus-
                pension bridge
                Close-up photos of Moon's surface
                Divers live in underwater Sealab for nine days
1965   First space walks (U.S.A. and U.S.S.R.)
                Mars photos from 7000-mile fly-by
                First use of satellites in TV transmission
1966   Luna 9 instrument package makes soft landing on Moon
                Bubble memories for computers
1967   Docking of two unmanned spacecraft
                2.5-million-year-old human bone fragments
                DNA virus synthesized
                Human heart transplant
                B. Fuller's tetrahedral floating-city project
                Mendelevium 258, heaviest element yet known, discovered
                Chromium dioxide magnetic tape, doubling information-
                storage capacity
1968   First men orbit Moon
                Pulsars first detected
                Integrated circuits
                Ribonuclease molecule synthesized
1969   First humans on Moon
                First remote sensing satellite
                Single gene isolated
                Enzyme synthesized
                Structure of gamma globulin deciphered
                Fiber optics, microwaves, fluidics
1970   Venera 7 spacecraft makes soft landing on Venus
                Boeing 747 jumbo jet
                Completion of gene synthesis
                Largest fully steerable dish radio telescope
1971   First synthesis of hormone responsible for human growth
                First man-made object to orbit another planet—Mars

Moon soil brought back

1972   Jupiter fly-by launched

Computer-programmed subway train

1974   Orbiting space station

Astronauts spend 85 days aboard Skylab space station

"Close-in" pictures of Venus, Mercury, and Jupiter

1975   B. Fuller's *Synergetics* published

Particles with "charm" discovered

Venus soft landing with surface pictures

Satellite brings educational TV to 2400 villages in India

U.S.-Soviet satellite link-up

Marketing of home video recorders, home TV projection systems, and home personal computers

1976   Mars unmanned landing

Progress in unification of general relativity, quantum mechanics, and thermodynamics leads to prediction that miniature black holes (10^{15} grams) created early in history of Universe are exploding now, yielding burst of gamma rays that should be observable.

World's largest solar furnace, France

1977   Many moons discovered around Uranus

Gene-splitting technique to attack human disease

Cruise missile, neutron bomb, and charged particle beam weapons secretly researched

First explicit demonstration of a burn within the target core in fusion reaction

Fiber optics for telephone transmission using gallium arsenide lasers

Instant-motion-picture system marketed

Chinese claim to predict three of six major earthquakes

1978   World's first test tube baby

Smallpox completely eliminated from planet

All-microwave Seasat satellite launched to study ocean surface

Insulin production using recombinant DNA techniques

First transatlantic balloon flight

1979   Gossamer Albatross, human-powered England-to-France flight

Jupiter fly-by photographs

Fly's Eye dwelling-machine prototype completed

Interferon studied by cancer researchers

Chronological Inventory of Prominent Scientific, Technological, Economic, and Political World Events: 1895 to Date

U PON WHICH HAS BEEN SUPERIMPOSED the utterly personal chronology of Buckminster Fuller (RBF), his family, his discoveries and his inventions, both philosophic and technological.

The integration of the prime world history events with those of one individual and his family at first exaggerates the infinitesimal stature of the individual in respect to humanity's integrated, news-processed, and arbitrarily classified experience.

But this exaggerated relationship of the minute individual in respect to the whole is nonetheless the only possible common direct experience of each and every human being. All else is hearsay.

The inventions of the single individual at first seem irrelevant and preposterous as associated with the great legends of the publicly accredited historical accounting. Gradually, however, the relevancy of the philosophy of the individual to the comprehensive evolution may become visible, and his inventions may gradually appear feasible, even logical, if he persists and learns how to perfect them both by inclusions and refinements.

If the individual were not moved by the seeming significance of his undertakings, as exaggeratingly disclosed in this *chronological juxtaposition of all humans and one human,* he would not have an adequately sustaining drive to reduce his inventing to commonly assimilable practice and possible common advantage.

Taken out of the context of scientific search for data apparently governing and motivating the individual inventor in the era of the massive corporation and the massive state and the latter's apparently staggering economic and political starting advantage over the prime design initiative of the individual, the following record could only be classified as egotistical. However, it was compiled and is submitted in scientific earnest by its only possible *direct* observer. Because the lag between the dates of invention and common public use averages twenty-two years, the dates of the inventions listed must be considered only as harbingers, with their effective industrial realizations and public advantaging variously postponed.

1895   Automobile (first U.S.A. gasoline engine) designed under Charles Duryea's U.S. patent; wireless telegraph, automatic screw machine invented; X rays discovered; photoelectric cell; First diesel engine; RBF born July 12, Columbine Road, Milton, Mass.; Cleveland, President. At this time the Flatiron Building, 23rd Street and Broadway (at Fifth Avenue), New York City, was the tallest occupied building in the world, and the Eiffel Tower, built in 1889 and 984 feet high was the tallest man-made structure in the world and remained the tallest until Empire State Building of 1250 feet erected in 1930; psychoanalysis (Sigmund Freud).

1896   Steam turbine, disc plow; Anne Hewlett (RBF's future wife) born, January 9, Columbia Heights, Brooklyn, N.Y.; discovery of radioactivity in uranium.

1897   Electric trip-hammer drill; William McKinley inaugurated President; Electron discovered.

1898   Spanish-American War begins; U.S. annexes Hawaii; Curies discover radium.

1899   Flotation of ore (oil); RBF enters kindergarten, makes octet-truss.

1900   Escalator; Caterpillar tractor; dirigible balloon (Zeppelin); electric steelmaking; mercury lamp; quantum theory, by Max Planck; President McKinley re-elected; U.S. "Open Door" policy toward China; Boxer Rebellion.

1901   Wright brothers' glider; gas welding; Marconi's transatlantic radio telegraph; yellow fever vanquished; RBF enters elementary school; President McKinley assassinated; Theodore Roosevelt becomes President.

1902   Mt. Pelée erupts on the island of Martinique, destroying 30,000 people, powerful impression on RBF; RBF's father and mother travel to Buenos Aires via London and Rio and via White Star liner *Oceanic* and the steamers *Don* and *Magdalene*.

1903   Around-the-world telegram, 12 minutes; Wright brothers' gas-engine-propelled airplane flight, Kitty Hawk, N.C.; ultramicroscope; arc light; bottlemaking machine; oil-burning steamship; Ford Motor Company founded, beginning of mass-production automobiles.

1904   Theodore Roosevelt elected President, proposes "Corollary" to Monroe Doctrine; reinforced concrete; Russo-Japanese War; N.Y.C. electric rapid transit "subway" opens 42nd to 14th streets. (RBF's Uncle Waldo Fuller, a chief engineer of project. Uncle Waldo Fuller, a Harvard football great of 1883 who had gone to Klondike in the gold rush, was RBF's greatest living boyhood hero.) RBF enters Milton Academy, lower school; RBF's Grandmother Matilda Wolcott Andrews and all her grand family of Kings and Fullers go for summer to John Quinn's on Eagle Island in Penobscot Bay, Me., buy Bear, Compass, and Little Sprucehead Islands.

1905   Einstein's relativity; RBF's family occupy Bear Island, Me., as summer home; Russo-Japanese peace treaty signed at Portsmouth, N.H., with Teddy Roosevelt as mediator.

1906   Sperry gyrocompass; radio vacuum tube; crystal radio detector; RBF enters Milton Academy, upper school; San Francisco earthquake and fire; RBF has one of first appendectomies by Dr. Dan Jones of Massachusetts General Hospital.

1907   Ford's Model T automobile inaugurates major world mass-production industry, demountable tires, Bakelite (phenolic resin plastic); RBF's father has stroke, brain clot.

1908   East River (L.I.R.R.) and Hudson railroad tunnels; President William Howard Taft elected; fire destroys Chelsea, Mass., witnessed clearly by RBF from Milton Hill as RBF's mother and Grandmother Andrews described their witnessing of the Chicago fire from the cupola of their "Sweet Briar" farmhouse just north of Chicago.

1909   Blériot flies English Channel; North Pole discovered by Admiral Peary, April 6; typhus vaccine discovered.

1910   Salvarsan discovered; Albany-to-New-York Curtis flying-boat flight; RBF's father dies; cosmic rays identified.

1911   South Pole discovered by Amundsen, December 14; atomic nucleus proton discovered; hydroplane; pulmotor; first use, gyrocompass servos (Sperry); first cloud chamber.

1912   President Woodrow Wilson elected; vitamins; S.S. *Titanic* sunk in collision with iceberg; first S.O.S.; New Orleans music—"Alexander's Ragtime Band," Turkey Trot becomes popular; U.S.A.-type music and dance, displacement of classical and European dances.

1913   Tungsten incandescent lamp; gasoline "cracking" process; concept of atomic number (Moseley); RBF graduates from Milton Academy and enters Harvard University in Class of 1917. Although U.S. currency fully convertible to gold until 1933, U.S.A. internal monetary system goes off gold standard. Federal Reserve System established (as private bankers' gold becomes inadequate to implement new industrial mass-production magnitudes of trade). Although under many constraints Federal Reserve as yet in private banker management, as the Alexander Hamilton U.S. constitutional interpretation of the dogma persists that U.S. government had no fundamental wealth initiative and must borrow all wealth from private bankers and repay them through collection of taxes, tariffs, and excises. RBF's Milton home sold; U.S. intervention in Mexican Revolution.

1914   Military tank; Armstrong's regenerative radio circuit; chrome-nickel-steel (in-lab-only); Panama Canal; World War I begins as industrialized powers compete for world-around resources for their new technology; RBF expelled from Harvard College, then reinstated, after intensive experience as apprentice and millwright in cotton mill at Sherbrooke, Quebec, Canada.

1915   Transcontinental telephone; gas warfare; neon lamp; radiotelephone; RBF expelled from Harvard second time, employed in New York City by Armour & Co., worked in 28 branch houses throughout greater New York City, working 3 A.M. to 5 P.M. daily; Woolworth Building, N.Y.C., 792 feet high, 60 stories, succeeded Singer as world's tallest occupied building and remained tallest until exceeded by Empire State Building fifteen years later (1930).

1916   Stainless steel (secret World War I accomplishment), does not get into commercial use until 1928; depth bomb; President Wilson re-elected; S.S. *Lusitania* sunk by German submarine; RBF and AHF engaged; RBF corporal at U.S. military training camp, Plattsburg, N.Y.

1917   U.S. into World War I (April 6); Russian Revolution, U.S.S.R. born; Vitamin B; RBF enters U.S.N.R., March; AHF and RBF married July 12 at Rock Hall, the Hewlett family homestead at Lawrence, Long Island, N.Y., for 130 years (Rock Hall was built by Josiah Martin, British governor of Antigua, and his son Josiah Martin, British colonial governor of North Carolina, as their joint summer mansion about 1750, and was used by the English as Tory headquarters in Battle of New York during American Revolution).

1918   RBF assigned to short special course at U.S. Naval Academy, Annapolis. Over one million American troops safely deployed in Europe by July. World War I Armistice, November 11; electron employed and development of mass spectroscopy; toaster; RBF and Anne Fuller's first child, Alexandra Willets Fuller, born December 12; sonar.

1919 U.S. Navy flying boat NC-4 flies Atlantic in three jumps, Newfoundland, to Azores, to Lisbon, to Spain, May 16–27; transatlantic two-way radio telephone conversation, U.S.S. *George Washington* in Brest Harbor, France, to Arlington Tower, Washington, D.C. (U.S.S. *George Washington* was transport that carried President Wilson to France for Versailles Treaty and inauguration of League of Nations); Ensign RBF assigned temporarily to U.S.S. *George Washington*, then to U.S. Naval Academy, Annapolis, on a special course. Alcock and Brown fly Atlantic in airplane nonstop, Newfoundland to Ireland, June 14–16; British dirigible R-34 crosses Atlantic, England–U.S.A., July 2; RBF promoted to Lt. (j.g.) U.S.N. Then to active war zone Atlantic troop transport duty as personal aide for secret information to Admiral Albert Gleaves, who commanded cruiser and transport forces U.S. Atlantic Fleet. Service in U.S.S. *Great Northern*, U.S.S. *Seattle*; November 1—RBF resigns from U.S. Navy, as his admiral is assigned to commander-in-chief of Asiatic Fleet, and his daughter, Alexandra, successively contracts infantile paralysis and spinal meningitis in N.Y.C.; RBF becomes assistant export manager of Armour & Co. in their N.Y.C. headquarters in new Equitable Building at 120 Broadway; RBF, Anne, and Alexandra live in house on Pearsal Place, Lawrence, Long Island, N.Y.; alcoholic beverage prohibition begins in U.S.A.

1920 Neutron discovered; commercial radio broadcast of voice; Harding elected President; League of Nations, Geneva, Switzerland (minus U.S.A.); women get the vote, U.S.A., August 26.

1921 RBF resigns from Armour & Co. to become National Account Sales Manager of Kelley-Springfield Truck Co. with office in Equitable Building, N.Y.C.

1922 Practical automobile self-starter (Bendix); air conditioning; push-button elevator; insulin; vitamin D. RBF resigns Kelley-Springfield Truck Co. and starts career as independent enterpriser. Stockade Blocks invented by RBF's father-in-law, J. M. Hewlett, and manufactured by RBF; RBF and Anne's only child, Alexandra Willets Fuller, dies November 14, just before her fourth birthday. AHF's mother dies, and her brother, Willets, killed in auto accident; radar invented (Taylor and Young); *Reader's Digest* founded.

1923 House oil burners; RBF and Anne live in apartment, East 95th St., N.Y.C.; Hubble discovers another galaxy in addition to our own "Milky Way" galaxy. (In the half-century since Hubble's discovery of another galaxy other than our own "Milky Way," two billion galaxies each averaging 100 billion stars have been discovered and photographed—trying to record these precessional discoveries from

1923 onward would overwhelm this chronicling.) Bulldozer; sound-on-sound motion pictures.

1924   Coolidge elected President; first dynamic loudspeakers on radio sets, using Major Armstrong's regenerative circuits; first intercity bus lines established—Chicago to Detroit; Fageol twin coach—Greyhound buses; RBF and Anne have apartment, East 94th St., N.Y.C.; Soldiers' Bonus Act compensated soldiers for overseas duty—a million Americans had served overseas in World War I; transcontinental airmail carried by cloth-covered-wing biplanes.

1925   First commercial airline—Detroit to Chicago; phototelegraphy; methanol; Alfred North Whitehead's *Science and the Modern World* discloses separation of science and humanities with rise of scientific materialism.

1926   Electric refrigerator—adapted for domestic use from oceangoing technology; talking, moving pictures; Amundsen, Ellsworth, and Nobile fly to North Pole in Italian dirigible; Richard Byrd and Floyd Bennett fly Norway to North Pole and return, May 9, in airplane; Air Commerce Act provides federal aid to airlines and airports; RBF's five Stockade Building System companies have their blocks and building system employed in total of 240 homes and commercial buildings between 1922 and 1927; RBF fails to make money with Stockade, loses all the money his friends had ventured in support of his enterprise; RBF resigns as president of Stockade Company as company is acquired by Celotex Company; Firestone leases million acres in Liberia, Africa, for rubber plantations, provides medical/educational services to Liberians; Goddard launches first liquid-fuel rocket; Pavlov's *Conditioned Reflexes* published, U.S.S.R.

1927   Television (laboratory only, not in popular use in U.S.A. until 1947); photoelectric cell; Lindbergh flies airplane, *Spirit of St. Louis,* across Atlantic, New York to Paris, nonstop, May 20–21; Heisenberg's indeterminism; Holland Tunnel under Hudson River, New York to New Jersey; RBF's and AHF's second child, Allegra Fuller, born August 28, Chicago, Ill.; RBF and family live on Belmont Ave., Chicago; RBF writes book, *4D,* privately published; RBF founds "4D" company for research, development, and patent protection of his Dymaxion House and Car; Energetic/Synergetic geometry discovered by RBF; Dymaxion House invented as part of his concept of air-deliverable, mass-producible, world-around, dwelling machine based on anticipatory design science.

1928   Teletype; Hoover elected President; dirigible *Graf Zeppelin* flown across Atlantic by Dr. Eckner; Amelia Earhart flies Atlantic, June 17; Sir Charles Kingsford-Smith flies Pacific, Oakland, Calif., to

Brisbane, Australia, in airplane *Southern Cross,* May 31; both Amelia Earhart and Sir Charles Kingsford-Smith became warm friends
of RBF in 1934; Ford introduces Model A, with stainless steel head-
light trim; Kellogg-Briand Pact outlawing war signed by U.S.; Stalin
initiates five-year-plan for rapid industrialization of U.S.S.R.; penicillin discovered (Fleming).

1929   Aston's closest-packing-effect; RBF and family move from Chicago
to N.Y.C.; World Stock Market Crash, October 29; "Great Depression" begins; night airmail inaugurated out of Chicago in cloth-cov-
ered biplanes; RBF and family take house Woodmere, Long Island,
N.Y.; coaxial cables; rocket engine successful (Goddard); automatic
airplane pilot. "St. Valentine's Day Massacre" in Chicago. RBF fre-
quents Romany Marie's Tavern, Greenwich Village, N.Y.C.; "paper
bottles" first used for frozen juices and vegetables.

1930   Cyclotron (atom smasher); *Fortune* magazine, conceived in pre-1929
boom days to service the boom's millionaires, then frustrated by the
Crash, comes inadvertently into being as a protagonist of the (it is
hoped) re-emergent enterprise concept of a self-perpetuating
industrial-management capitalism, surprisingly escaped from Finance Capitalism's 1929 shipwreck and death, by "drowning," of international banking as the world's economic master; RBF and family
have house, Johnson Place, Woodmere; RBF also has apartment on
the roof, Lehigh-Starret Building, N.Y.C.; Empire State Building
(1250 feet) under construction—to become the world's tallest building; RBF sells Navy life insurance policy to finance taking over *T-
Square* magazine in Philadelphia and renames it *Shelter* magazine;
Einstein's "Cosmic Religious Sense—the Nonanthropomorphic Concept of God," published by the *New York Times* Sunday magazine.

1931   Piccard's stratosphere balloon flight; Post and Gatty fly around
world by airplane in succession of refueling short hops; George
Washington Bridge (New York) opens, 3500-foot span; Ford Trimo-
tor Stout aluminum airplane flown; Pauli postulates neutrino 25
years before observed directly (1955); Godel's proof—hallmark of
modern mathematics; neoprene rubber developed.

1932   Economic depression depth in U.S.A.; FDR elected President;
Boeing and Douglas DC-3 all-metal passenger airplane; inauguration
of transcontinental U.S.A. airline service; 92nd isolation of a chemical element; X-ray diffraction; neutron discovered; RBF closes *Shelter* magazine after November election of FDR and inauguration of
New Deal, hoping that economic ills *Shelter* cited might be corrected; *Fortune* magazine publishes "The Industry that Industry

Missed," citing RBF Dymaxion House as prototype of new mass-production house industry; first use of sulfa drugs.

1933 Dymaxion Car (invented 1927), built and successfully demonstrated by RBF in old plant of Locomobile Co. at Bridgeport, Conn., as first-stage experimental vehicle leading to eventual omnimedium wingless transport, propelled and maneuverably controlled by twin, orientable, rocket and jet-stilts; FM broadcasting; alcoholic beverage prohibition ends in U.S.A.; Adolf Hitler becomes chancellor of Germany, January 30; U.S. banks failing finally at peak rate of 5000 in one day, bank moratorium declared by FDR, March 6–9; Congress gives President power to control money (law upheld by U.S. Supreme Court, February 18, 1935); FDR begins "Fireside Chats," radio; approximately all of world's monetary gold paid over to U.S. government and put into Kentucky hill vaults; world completely off gold standard of exchange; RBF, Anne, and Allegra live in house in Darien, Conn.; "Dust Bowl" droughts begin to ravage Great Plains.

1934 NRA (U.S. National Relief Administration), WPA (U.S. Works Progress Administration), RFC (U.S. Reconstruction Finance Corporation, world's largest capital), REA (U.S. Rural Electric Administration), TVA (U.S. Tennessee Valley Authority), SEC (U.S. Securities and Exchange Commission), and HOLC (U.S. Home Owners Loan Corporation); RBF's mother dies; sulfanilamide discovered.

1935 RBF completes Dymaxion Transport #3—displayed at Chicago's "Century of Progress" World's Fair; cortisone; first trans-Pacific airplane passenger service, in Pan Am flying boats.

1936 RBF joins Phelps Dodge Corporation, Research Department, as assistant to its director; RBF, Anne, and Allegra have apartment, East 87th St., N.Y.C., between Park and Madison avenues; RBF as guest performer of director Gilbert Seldes in frequent experimental broadcasts of CBS television from Grand Central Station office building studio to 100 experimental sets of CBS executives; Allegra Fuller also guest on first TV shows; public television broadcasts begin in England; micrometer.

1937 Atomic fission theoretically envisaged by Hahn and Stresemann in Germany; jet engine, Whittle, England; nylon produced; RBF, Anne, and Allegra move to apartment, 105 East 88th St., N.Y.C.; Allegra to Dalton School, 100 E. 89th St., N.Y.C.; auto and steel industry labor unions win first big labor contracts.

1938 RBF book, *Nine Chains to the Moon,* published; RBF travels much of U.S. with Christopher Morley; RBF joins *Fortune* magazine staff as its science and technology consultant; Munich; Hitler.

1939   World War II begins; Sikorsky helicopter invented; Einstein and others warn FDR of possibilities of developing atomic bomb; FDR immediately funds the research, eventually to become the Manhattan Project; electron microscope; synthetic rubber.

1940   First radio map of Milky Way published, U.S.A.—invisible world emerging; plutonium fission; meningitis cure; RBF leaves *Fortune* magazine; backed by Robert Colgate, RBF inaugurates Dymaxion Deployment Unit of Butler Manufacturing Company, Kansas City; units used as first radar shacks and as air-conditioned dormitories of U.S. flyers and mechanics making fly-away delivery of war planes to Russians at head of Persian Gulf; FDR's Four Freedoms—freedom from fear, freedom from want, freedom of religion, freedom of speech; Rh factor discovered in blood.

1941   Penicillin comes into use to fight pneumonia; Lend-Lease Act; Atlantic Charter; Japanese attack Pearl Harbor, December 7; U.S.A. enters World War II, December 8; commercial TV inaugurated in U.S.A., but held up until war's end; aerosol spray.

1942   RBF joins U.S.A. Board of Economic Warfare, Washington, D.C., as its head mechanical engineer; first sustained uranium fission reaction achieved at University of Chicago; RBF, Anne, and Allegra move to 2222 Decatur Place, N.W., Washington, D.C.; magnetic tape.

1943   Sikorsky helicopter successfully flown; RBF's Dymaxion Projection Sky-Ocean World Map published in *Life* magazine, March 1; Hoffman discovers LSD-25.

1944   DNA discovered; first jet airplane (fighter), English; RBF becomes Special Assistant to Deputy Director, U.S. Foreign Economic Administration; prototype Dymaxion House manufactured by aircraft industry, Wichita, Kans., under joint auspices AFL-CIO Labor, War Production Board, War Manpower Commission, Aircraft Industry Production Board, Beech Aircraft's Executive Administration, with RBF as chief design engineer; RBF, Anne, and Allegra move to 6 Burns St., Forest Hills, N.Y.C., apartment, as RBF goes to live in Wichita, Kans., '44, '45, '46; "D-Day," Normandy invasion, June 6; FDR elected to fourth term.

1945   FDR dies April 12, Warm Springs, Ga.; Truman succeeds him as President; Mussolini executed April 28; Hitler commits suicide, April 29; Nuremburg War Crimes Tribunal; United Nations meets in San Francisco, April 25, chartered June 26; world's first atomic bomb exploded secretly near Alamogordo, N. M., July 16; Hiroshima, August 6—Nagasaki, August 9; VE Day, May 8—VJ Day, September 2—World War II ends; streptomycin developed; phototypesetting machine.

1946 Regular transatlantic airplane passenger service begins with prop-driven Douglas DC-4, secret transoceanic "workhorse" of World War II; League of Nations dissolved; RBF awarded first cartographic projection patent ever granted by U.S.A. Patent Office for Dymaxion Map (January 29); Eniac—first all-electronic general-purpose digital computer.

1947 Geodesic dome invented by RBF; "atomic time clock" developed using carbon-14; Marshall Plan aids European countries; Taft-Hartley Act limits power of labor; world's largest reflector telescope (Mount Palomar, Calif.), 200-inch, 14-ton mirror, remains largest until U.S.S.R.'s 236-incher constructed in early '70s; commercial television broadcasting gets underway in U.S.A.; RBF professor at Black Mountain College, N.C.; Nehru becomes prime minister of newly established independent India; new postwar automobile designs begin to emerge.

1948 President Truman wins close election over Dewey; aureomycin developed; RBF to Massachusetts Institute of Technology; RBF teaching, summer session, Black Mountain College; State of Israel established; Gandhi assassinated in India, January 30; xerography (Carlson); long-playing record (Goldmark); holography (Gabor) first proposed; Polaroid Land camera first marketed (invented before World War II, a million sold by 1956); Rock Hall given by Hewletts to the people of Nassau County, N.Y., as a museum.

1949 Giant electronic computers introduced to implement complex stockpiling and anticipatory arming and preparation for World War III under title "cold war"—invisible and psychological warfare; U.S.S.R. explodes first atomic bomb, ending U.S. monopoly; ACTH; general industrial automation emerging; Mao Tse-tung establishes People's Republic of China, October 1; RBF, dean at Black Mountain College, summer session; RBF to Chicago Institute of Design and to M.I.T. as visiting lecturer.

1950 DC-6 airplane passenger service inaugurated; Joseph "Witch Hunt" McCarthy; Brink's robbery of million dollars, Boston; RBF in heavy schedule of invited university appointments and lectures—M.I.T., North Carolina State University, University of Michigan; AHF and RBF's daughter Allegra Fuller graduates from Bennington College and marries Robert Snyder; Diner's Club introduces universal credit

card; 1950s consumer goods "fall-out" from emergent technology—
dishwasher, frost-free refrigerator, self-cleaning oven, etc.; Korean
War begins.

1951   DC-7 propellor-driven airplane introduced; DNA helical structure
discovered by Wilkins, Watson, Crick; RBF later points out similar-
ities of DNA helix to his tetrahelix model; rise of African national-
ism.

1952   U.S. detonates world's first hydrogen bomb, Eniwetok Island, South
Pacific; Geodesic Dome project started, in contract with RBF, for
Ford Motor Co., River Rouge headquarters; Eisenhower elected
President (in first step of Wall Street lawyers' strategy to overturn
New Deal controls of big business); Queen Elizabeth II crowned;
first commercial jetliner service, British DeHavilland Comet.

1953   Ford Motor Company's 50th anniversary, Dearborn, Mich.; 93-foot-
diameter geodesic Rotunda Dome installed as first successful industrial acceptance of RBF's concepts a quarter of a century after his
1927 prediction that first realization would be in 1952; Mount Everest climbed by Edmund Hillary and Tenzing Norkay, May 29; 50-
foot-diameter tensegrity sphere constructed under RBF's direction at
Princeton University; Alexandra Fuller Snyder born November 1
(RBF and Anne Fuller's first grandchild). Polio vaccine developed
by Jonas Salk; cryosurgery (Swan).

1954   *Nautilus,* first atomic-powered submarine launched; vertical-takeoff
aircraft; U.S.A.; RBF granted U.S. Patent No. 2,682,235 for geodesic
dome; U.S. Marine Corps' family-house-size geodesic dome helicopter air-lifted and delivered at 60 knots, front-page picture feature of
New York Times; geodesic domes adopted by U.S. Marines for all ad-
vanced-base enclosures; Supreme Court orders school desegregation;
compatible color TV receiver introduced, with widespread purchase
in U.S. within 10 years and 40 million worldwide by early '70s; open-
heart surgery; artificial diamonds—gem-quality by early '70s; Walter
O'Malley, owner of Brooklyn Dodgers, comes to RBF to develop
geodesic dome to be installed over Dodgers' Brooklyn baseball stadium.

1955   "DEW Line" geodesic radomes installed in Arctic; Warsaw Pact;
maser invented; Salk polio vaccine effective; Jaime Lawrence Snyder
born April 28 (RBF and Anne Fuller's first grandson); RBF conducted development at Princeton University Architecture School of
Brooklyn Dodger Stadium geodesic dome (Walter O'Malley and
Robert Oppenheimer both served as critics of the problem—much
newspaper note of the event); Eisenhower and Khrushchev meet at
Geneva, with their atomic scientists, followed by UN Food and Ag-

riculture Organization, at which time it became publicly known that scientists conceded that Malthus was wrong and there could be enough food for 100 percent of humanity *but* for time being obviously frustrated from realization by world political sovereignties.

1956   Transistor developed for consumer use; first transcontinental helicopter flight, 37 hours; first transatlantic telephone cable; U.S.A. International Trade Fairs adopt RBF's geodesic domes as main pavilions (first geodesic 100-foot-diameter trade fair dome flown to Kabul, Afghanistan, in one DC-4; dome erected in 48 hours by Afghans led by one U.S. engineer). RBF's first appointment as visiting lecturer, Southern Illinois University.

1957   International Geophysical Year; European Economic Community established; first civilian nuclear power station; history's largest clear-span structural enclosure, 384-foot-diameter RBF-designed geodesic dome in Baton Rouge, La. (until RBF's geodesic dome, the largest clear-span domes in the history of the world were the 150-foot-diameter St. Peter's dome in Rome and the 150-foot-diameter dome of the Pantheon, also in Rome); first satellite (Sputnik) launched by Earthians—orbits Earth every 90 minutes as humanity initiates the Space Age; first containerized cargo ships; Walter O'Malley moves his Dodgers baseball team from Brooklyn, N.Y., to Los Angeles, Calif., obviating his further need for geodesic dome.

1958   RBF makes first of his subsequently multiannual circuits of Earth in course of fulfilling his regular university appointments in South Africa, India, Japan, England, etc.; Boeing 707 commercial transport inaugurated; laser invented—patented with working model in 1960 (Maiman); geodesic domes go to Arctic and Antarctic and all around Earth; first U.S. satellite orbits Earth; invisible high-energy radiation Van Allen belts first observed around Earth; U.S. nuclear submarine *Nautilus,* under Commander William R. Anderson, crosses Arctic Ocean and North Pole from Pacific Ocean to Atlantic Ocean submerged below ice cap; RBF's Energetic/Synergetic Geometry discovered by nuclear physicists and molecular biologists to mathematically explain nature's fundamental structuring at the atomic nucleus and virus levels (see Dow Chemical Company's chief physicist, John Grebe, in paper to New York Academy of Sciences, and Dr. Klug, Birbeck College, London University); RBF awarded Gold Medal, Scarab, National Architectural Society.

1959   World-around air-jet passenger-service network established; Luna 2, Russian unmanned rocket, crash-lands on Moon; Luna 3 circles Moon and sends radiophotos of "far side" back to Earth; first nuclear-powered commercial ship launched; Luna 1, Russian rocket, into orbit around Sun as first man-made planet; 200-foot-diameter RBF-Kaiser gold-anodized aluminum geodesic dome is U.S.A.'s International Exhibit, Moscow, Russia—acclaimed by Khrushchev and after fair purchased (at full cost) by Russia from U.S.A. (dome now permanent structure in Moscow's Sokolniki Park); Alaska and Hawaii admitted as 49th and 50th states to U.S.A.; year-long outdoor garden exhibit of RBF's geodesic domes, Octetruss, and tensegrity mast at Museum of Modern Art, N.Y.C.; RBF appointed by State Department to visit Russia as representative of engineering in protocol exchange—Russians, in giving dinner for RBF, stated they had been following his work for 29 years; St. Lawrence Seaway opens mid-America to ocean traffic; Major Rogers, U.S.A.F., flies airplane 2455 m.p.h.; RBF appointed as University Professor (Research) at Southern Illinois University where he is awarded honorary Doctor of Arts degree; RBF and Anne erect geodesic dome home, 407 S. Forest, Carbondale, Ill., moving there from Forest Hills, N.Y.; 200-foot-diameter aluminum geodesic dome constructed as Palais des Sports, Paris, France; treaty reserving Antarctica for scientific research accepted by 12 nations. Judge Hofheinz of Houston comes to Walter O'Malley in Los Angeles to gain his aid in securing a National Baseball League membership for a team Hofheinz proposed forming in Houston, Texas—O'Malley told Hofheinz that he would need a domed-over stadium due to the weather pattern in Houston, O'Malley told Hofheinz to get in touch with RBF as the only one capable of designing such a dome, a matter that O'Malley assured Hofheinz he had studied deeply. Hofheinz contacts RBF and asks him to work on the design of such a dome; he had RBF meet with all his financial associates and explain why dome was possible despite no engineering anticipation that such might be possible.

1960   John F. Kennedy elected President; Peace Corps established; 114-foot-diameter, 10,000-square-foot-floor-space geodesic dome of Ford Motor Co. delivered by helicopter, fully erected; in 1960s oral birth control pills come into widespread use despite possible and unknown dangers; bathyscaphe navigates seven miles (35,810 feet) inward to bottom of Pacific Ocean, Marianas trench; U.S. nuclear submarine *Triton* circumnavigates Earth, submerged the whole way, in 84 days; Russia aids Egypt in beginning construction of Aswan High Dam on Nile; *Dymaxion World of Buckminster Fuller,* written with Robert W. Marks, published by Doubleday; U-2 photo-reconnaissance spy plane shot "in" by Russians—Americans agree to suspend flights; civil war breaks out in new Republic of Congo; Cyprus gains independence, with Archbishop Makarios as president; RBF awarded

Frank P. Brown Medal of Philadelphia's Franklin Institute and Gold Medal, American Institute of Architects (Philadelphia chapter); RBF continues intensive development of Houston stadium dome for Hofheinz.

1961   Dag Hammarskjöld, UN Secretary General, dies in plane crash, Congo; DNA genetic code deciphered—design control for all life; Russian Gagarin orbits Earth as first human spaceman; men (Russians) orbit Earth in hourly cycles in co-rocketing vehicles; over 2000 geodesic domes produced by over 100 industrial corporations, licensees of RBF, primarily air-delivered and speed-installed in 40 countries around Earth and in North and South Polar zones, 1951–1961. RBF proposes to 2000 architects of International Union of Architects at Fifth World Congress, London, England, to officially initiate Phase I of Design Science Decade—1965–75, which will put world on notice that making world work is an invention initiative and not a political responsibility and is only solvable by a world design revolution, which is the only revolution universally tolerable to diverse political interests of the world; and that the design revolution must be conducted by world-around students under university auspices and supported by professional-degree accrediting boards and visiting committees of all the architectural-engineering and scientist professions and officially underwritten by their professional societies. RBF granted patent for Octetruss; Bay of Pigs invasion of Cuba turned back by Fidel Castro; RBF continues Houston stadium dome design in aluminum for Judge Hofheinz.

1962   RBF appointed by Harvard University as Charles Eliot Norton Professor of Poetry—one-year appointment; a year of transition of comprehensive technology from dry land into sea and into sky, from visible to invisible, because more-with-lessing, through transistors, metallurgy, chemistry, electronics, and atomics transfers all basic controls to invisible ranges; one Telstar communications-relay satellite weighing only a quarter-ton replaces transatlantic cables weighing 75,000 tons in equivalent function; first American to orbit Earth—John Glenn; RBF established "Inventory of World Resources, Human Trends, and Needs" at Southern Illinois University with John McHale as executive director; John McHale's *R. Buckminster Fuller* published by Braziller; RBF exhibit at American Embassy in London, England; RBF awarded U.S. patent for tensegrity; U.S.A.–U.S.S.R. Cuban missile crisis confrontation. On eve of Hofheinz signing contract for aluminum dome with RBF company, Synergetics of Raleigh, N. C., which had engineered Union Tank Car Domes, U.S. Steel, intent that first such large structure—642-foot-diameter clear span, 208 feet high—should not be built in aluminum, subsidized a company, Roof Structures of St. Louis, Mo., which had long been attempting to invade RBF's patented geodesic field. Roof Structures took a license from RBF under his patent and entered a far lower bid on a steel geodesic with Hofheinz, who forsook RBF and gave contract to Roof Structures, who then proceeded to redesign their plans by using RBF's omnitriangulated truss, but by making the pattern of triangulating so asymmetrical as not to tread on RBF's allowed patent claims. They saved a small royalty fee at an enormous increase in cost of their structure which would work because of the omnitriangulation of RBF—but with greatly increased weight of structure. When Houston Astrodome opened in 1965, Judge Hofheinz's son was in charge of its public relations. He always explained to its sightseeing parties that the dome was in reality designed by RBF. (Ten years later the Judge's son became mayor of Houston.)

1963   Telstar communications satellite; Syncom communications satellite put into 24-hour orbit, holding flight position over one point of spinning Earth as predicted by Arthur C. Clarke in the 1940s; quasars first detected; World Congress of Virologists meeting Cold Spring Harbor, Long Island, N. Y., announce comprehensive discovery of protein shells of viruses, which they publicly acknowledge (featured, front page, *New York Herald-Tribune*) as having been anticipated by RBF's formula of frequency to the second power times 10 plus 2; publication of RBF's *Operating Manual for Spaceship Earth* (E. P. Dutton), *No More Secondhand God* (Doubleday, paperback), *Ideas and Integrities* (Prentice-Hall), and *Education Automation* (Doubleday, paperback) are published; Limited Atomic Test Ban Treaty, U.S.S.R.–U.S.A; President John F. Kennedy assassinated November 22—Lyndon Johnson succeeds him; RBF is member of Doxiadis' Delos Symposium #1; RBF delivers world student discourse on Design Science Decade as International Union of Architects convene their Sixth World Congress at Mexico City; RBF awarded American Institute of Architects Allied Professions Gold Medal, Plomado de Oro Award of the Mexican Society of Architects, and RBF Recognition Day commemorated by University of Colorado; seven-million-dollar railway train robbery, Cheddington, England; Federation of Malaysia established; ZIP (Zone Improvement Plan) Code introduced to deal with increasing volumes of mail, U.S.A.; RBF subject of five half-hour television broadcasts on National Educational Television Network on national hook-up—broadcasts concentrate on

Synergetics. Southern Illinois University's dean of their new School of Engineering asks the National Astronautical and Space Administration (NASA) for an advanced-structures research grant. NASA's director replies that the grant would be forthcoming provided RBF (a professor at Southern Illinois) would be willing to serve on NASA's "advanced structures" team and that the research grant to S.I.U. School of Engineering would be for a science master's development of a complete computerization of the mathematics of all types of geodesic structuring (which project went to a student, Joe Clinton). RBF agreed and served on the team until the Nixon government downgraded the NASA operation in 1968. The team adopted RBF's Octetruss and geodesic dome and studied the centrifugal spinning-into-sphericity of RBF's "Cloud Nine" tensegrity geodesic for assembly in space—its self-cooling ephemerality making it feasible to be decelerated on re-entry for self-positioning at outer atmosphere level.

1964   January 8—RBF "cover story," *Time* magazine; U.S. Civil Rights Act, July 2; antipoverty programs; Khrushchev ousted; Johnson elected President. RBF subject of BBC's first science program on their new wide-range Channel Two network on recommendation of scientists at Cavendish Laboratory of Cambridge University, because TV is visual and RBF had discovered the conceptually modelable mathematical-coordinate system of nature, which conceptual coordinate system bridged the gap of popular incomprehension existing between science and the humanities. RBF's serial articles, "Prospects of Humanity," appear in *Saturday Review*; RBF is Gold Key Laureate, Delta Phi Delta, National Fine Arts Honor Society; RBF commissioned as the architect of U.S.A. pavilion for Montreal's 1967 World's Fair, "Expo '67"; RBF is a member of U.S.A. team in Dartmouth (Leningrad) meeting of "Leading Citizens of U.S.S.R.–U.S.A.," assembled by U.S.S.R.'s Academy of Sciences with U.S.A.'s Norman Cousins, Arthur Larson, etc., to discuss all known points of contention between U.S.S.R. and U.S.; Berkeley Free Speech Movement; Mississippi Summer, civil rights project; RBF on Delos Symposium #2; four volumes of RBF's *Design Science Decade: "World Resources Inventory, Human Trends and Needs,"* published by Southern Illinois University; RBF member of Cancer Research Institute, N.Y.C.; China explodes her first atomic bomb; Verrazano Narrows Bridge, New York, constructed—world's longest suspension bridge (spans 4260 feet; 60 feet longer than Golden Gate, completed in 1937).

1965   World's longest tunnel, 7½ miles, complete through Mount Blanc, Switzerland; Churchill dies; civil rights voter registration protests at their height, U.S.A.—Selma-Montgomery federal-troop-protected march; first commercial satellite put in orbit to relay intercontinental electromagnetic wave programs as telephone, television, etc.; first space walks by both Russian and U.S.A. astronauts; U.S.A. space-ship photos of Mars from 7000-mile passing distance sent back to Earth; westward mobility of population evident as California becomes most populous state (New York now number two); massive electric power failure blacks out most of northeastern U.S. and two provinces of Canada, November 9–10; national origins quota system of immigration abolished, U.S.A.; U.S. forces in South Vietnam reach 184,000; Watts riots in Los Angeles black ghetto, August 11–16, $200 million property damage; RBF is member of Doxiadis' Delos Symposium #3; RBF given Creative Achievement Award of Brandeis University; U.S. begins bombing North Vietnam; U.S. Marines land in Dominican Republic.

1966   January—Russians make first successful instrument-package soft landing on Moon, followed in few months by U.S.A.'s successful duplication of feat as both send radio pictures of Moon's terrain back to Earth; July—RBF persuades Archbishop Makarios to cede token land of 200 acres at Kyrenia from Cyprus sovereignty to *World Man* under 50-year trusteeship of World Academy of Art and Science, a supranational organization; RBF is a member of Doxiadis' Delos Symposium #4; November—RBF's U.S.A. Pavilion, a 250-foot-diameter geodesic sphere, completed at Montreal, to open in April 1967; plasma-propulsion and ion-propulsion engines for space travel and ultra-high-speed, claimed first flown by Russians—no U.S.A. confirmation; RBF receives First Award of Excellence from Industrial Designers Society of America; RBF inaugurates computer game at Southern Illinois University, called World Game, how to make world work in such a manner that all of humanity can become physical and economic success and can enjoy all of Earth without one interfering with the other and without any one advantaged at expense of other; RBF asked to give lecture to scientists, engineers at Cape Kennedy to explain how fallout from space technology into domestic economy would bring first scientific house in history to world man on Earth, which would catalyze physical success on Earth for all humanity; *Time* runs "God Is Dead" cover story on decline of churches; bubble memories for computers.

1967   Cultural Revolution rocks China; China explodes her first hydrogen bomb; Arab-Israeli (U.S.S.R.–U.S.A.) Six-Day War; RBF appears on cover of *Saturday Review*, April 1; Soviets achieve first docking of two unmanned spacecraft; Montreal's Expo '67 (RBF, architect of U.S.A. Pavilion) draws 50.3 million visitors in 6 months, setting record; American Institute of Architects gives RBF First Architectural Design Award; Alpha Chapter of Phi Beta Kappa (Harvard University) elects RBF to honorary membership on occasion of RBF's Class of 1917 50th reunion; late-1966 discovery of tenth moon of Saturn, Janus, verified; Harvard paleontologists Patterson and Howells discover human bone fragments 2.5 million years old, Kenya; RBF and AHF celebrate 50th wedding anniversary; full infectious DNA virus, representing five to six genes, synthesized by Goulian and Kornberg; fossil of world's oldest reptile discovered (Romer); RBF attends Doxiadis' Delos Symposium #5; Nirenberg demonstrates that identical genetic code combinations have the same results in mammal, amphibian, and bacterium in determining protein structure; human heart transplant (Barnard); design drawings, economic analyses, and model of RBF's tetrahedronal floating city project commissioned by U.S. Department of Housing and Urban Development. European Organization for Nuclear Research (CERN, Geneva) discovers seven new mesons; observes that the *squares* of their *masses* are in simple *numerical relationship*, supporting existence of "quarks" and "anti-quarks" (particles of fractional charge). RBF delivers 90 public lectures including: centennial address at American University, Beirut, Lebanon; keynote address to Austrian Architects Association; to World Congress of Architecture Students, Barcelona, Spain; 50th Anniversary Address, American Planners Association; to First World Congress of Engineers and Architects, Tel Aviv, Israel. RBF receives honorary Doctor of Engineering, Clarkson College of Technology, bringing his total of honorary doctorates to 13. The heaviest element yet known (isotope mendelevium 258) discovered by Hulet, who determines its life to be two months, compared with eight seconds for lawrencium, the second heaviest. RBF's "Star Tensegrity" granted U.S. patent; Johnson and Kosygin meet at Glassboro, N.J.; Soviet Union celebrates 50th anniversary; DuPont develops new chromium dioxide magnetic tape, doubling information storage capacity; RBF differentiates human brain and mind when speaking as Harvey Cushing Orator to annual congress of 2000 members of American Association of Neuro-Surgeons' meeting in Chicago; bone fragments and plant fossils found under Antarctic ice.

1968   Apollo 8 crew first men to orbit Moon; treaty for peaceful use of outer space adopted; Tet offensive, Vietnam; direct airline service between U.S.A. and U.S.S.R. initiated; Martin Luther King assassinated, April 4; Robert Kennedy assassinated, dies June 6; RBF elected to National Academy of Design and the World Academy of Arts and Sciences; Pulsars first detected; crowding of electromagnetic spectrum leads to development of airborne system to process 280,000 voice channels in bandwidth formerly handling 28,000; U.S. scientists fit 12 million unconnected transistors into 1-inch-square wafer—all demonstrating RBF's concept of significant evolutionary trending of the more-with-less performance per pounds and volumes of materials and energy used per each function; degrees granted in colleges and universities increase 100-fold in 100 years in U.S. from 9372 in 1869 to 866,000 in 1968; RBF appointed Distinguished University Professor at Southern Illinois University, one of three so honored in the institution's 99-year history; international monetary crises caused by faltering British pound and French franc; Columbia University student rebellion; police and antiwar demonstrators clash at Democratic National Convention in Chicago; students riot in France; UN nonproliferation treaty enacted; Soviets invade Czechoslovakia; volume of technical and scientific literature on weather and climate is twice that of eight years ago; RBF and Shoji Sadao receive First Architectural Design Award from American Institute of Architects for the Expo '67 Dome; RBF receives Gold Medal, National Institute of Arts and Letters, and British Royal Gold Medal of Architecture from Her Majesty the Queen, on recommendation of the Royal Institute of British Architects; RBF receives honorary doctorates from Dartmouth College, University of Rhode Island, Ripon College, and New England College; ribonuclease molecule synthesized; RBF's 1934 Dymaxion Car #2 displayed at Museum of Modern Art, N.Y.C; *Playboy* publishes RBF's "City of the Future."

1969   RBF leads his first public World Game workshop at New York Studio School, testifies on World Game before U.S. Senate Subcommittee on Intergovernmental Relations at invitation of Chairman Edmund Muskie of Maine; man lands on Moon, July 20, seen live around the world by 600 million viewers in 49 countries; RBF delivers Jawaharlal Nehru Memorial Lecture on "Planetary Planning," New Delhi, India; NASA launches first remote-sensing satellite, senses global temperature patterns, proves the revolutionary impact of satellites in weather forecasting. Beatle-mania in music, worldaround; Harvard scientists isolate the basic unit of heredity, a single gene, of 3000 genes of *E. coli*, an intestinal bacterium, making possible detailed study of mechanisms of gene control—enzyme synthesized for the first time; first paperback publication of RBF's *Utopia or Oblivion: The Prospects for Humanity* (Bantam); RBF attends Doxiadis' Delos Symposium #7; American Association of Humanists awards RBF Humanist of the Year Citation; Woodstock Music and Art Festival, gathering of 300,000 young people; Eisenhower dies; Charles DeGaulle resigns; North Vietnam President Ho Chi Minh dies; Ted Kennedy's "Chappaquiddick" incident; SALT talks begin in Helsinki; large oil spill, Santa Barbara, Calif.; Sidney Rosen's *Wizard of the Dome—R. Buckminster Fuller, Designer of the Future* published by Little, Brown; RBF is Hoyt Fellow, Yale University; receives Citation of Merit, U.S. Department of Housing and Urban Development; RBF receives honorary doctorates from University of Wisconsin, Boston College, and Bates College; RBF is architect of the Samuel Beckett Theatre of St. Peter's College, Oxford, England; deciphering of structure of gamma globulin, U.S.A. Newly emergent technologies: integrated circuits, fiber optics, microwaves, fluidics.

1970   Soviet Venera 7 soft-lands on Venus and transmits temperature and atmospheric pressure data for about 15 minutes; first Earth Day celebrated; world's oldest edge-ground axes discovered on the island of New Britain (as found earlier in New Guinea and Australia), indicating that as many as 30,000 years ago man was crossing open water and carrying on trade as described in RBF's speculative prehistory account; as gifts of students' gratitude during his visits to their universities, RBF receives Stone Age ground axes from both Australia and Finland; U.S. scientists announce the discovery of 17 amino acids, the "building blocks of life," in meteorite that fell on Australia in 1969; RBF attends Doxiadis' Delos Symposium #8; RBF is awarded an honorary "Donship" as Fellow of St. Peter's College, Oxford University; first commercial flight of Boeing 747 jumbo jet, which is built of over 500,000 precision-machined parts and carries nearly 400 passengers; completion of gene synthesis, University of Wisconsin; RBF's *I Seem To Be a Verb* is published by Bantam; *The Buckminster Fuller Reader* is published in Great Britain (Jonathan Cape, Ltd.; Penguin Books, paperback); European Economic Community finance ministers agree on plans for economic and monetary union by 1980; element #105 (proposed name, hahnium) 13th man-made element, U.S.A.; Detroit's oldest extant architectural firm endows the RBF Chair at the School of Architecture, University of Detroit; by 1970 there is one computer for every 4000 people in the U.S.A. (twice the per capita ratio of any other nation); 109 million telephones in the United States carry 141 billion phone conversations per year; Nauru, in the Pacific, becomes the 128th country to join the phone network (more than 96 percent of the world's telephones can be reached from the U.S.—including for the first time direct transatlantic dialing); world-around there are 231 million TVs and 620 million radios; Bell Labs announces a newly developed low-cost pocket-sized infrared laser semi-conductor device that can carry hundreds of thousands of telephone messages, TV signals, etc., at room temperature while powered by ordinary flashlight batteries; largest fully steerable dish radio telescope (328-foot diameter), West Germany; oxygen process (BOP) now accounts for half of all U.S. steelmaking; first liberal abortion law in U.S. goes into effect in New York State; Dr. Salvador Allende becomes first freely elected Marxist president in Western Hemisphere; U.S. voting age lowered to 18; National Guardsmen kill four Kent State students during protest of U.S. invasion of Cambodia; National Chapter of Alpha Rho Chi Fraternity installs RBF as its Master Architect for life; RBF is visiting professor at International University of Art, Venice and Florence, Italy; Thor Heyerdahl and crew successfully sail from Morocco to Barbados in a papyrus boat, *Ra II;* RBF makes 86 important addresses, receives honorary doctorates from Minneapolis School of Art, Park College, Brandeis University, Columbia College, and Wilberforce University.

1971 First synthesis of the hormone responsible for human growth, University of California; *New York Times* prints RBF's telegram to Senator Edmund Muskie on the entire "Op-Ed" page, March 27; People's Republic of China admitted to United Nations; U.S.A.'s Mariner 9 spacecraft orbits Mars—the first man-made object to orbit another planet; Russians accomplish Mars landing with their Mars 2 mission; "Old Man River's City" project, with RBF as architect, presented to East St. Louis community; twin World Trade Center towers succeed Empire State Building as world's tallest (since 1930)—there are now 14 buildings in U.S. taller than 1915's world's-tallest, Woolworth Building; commissioned by *Toronto Star* newspaper, RBF heads "Project Toronto" proposal for future design of the city; international treaty banning nuclear weapons from ocean floor signed; U.S. Supreme Court upholds right to publish Pentagon Papers; Governor Nelson Rockefeller orders Attica (N.Y.) prison riot quelled—42 killed; Pakistan-India war; NBC-TV broadcasts one-hour transnational program on RBF, "Buckminster Fuller on Spaceship Earth," produced by Robert Snyder (Allegra Fuller Snyder's husband); dedication ceremonies held for the Southern Illinois University Religious Center; Geoscope, oriented precisely on the Earth's 90th meridian, designed by RBF and Shoji Sadao; RBF receives honorary doctorate from Southeastern Massachusetts University; *Life, Christian Science Monitor,* and *Rolling Stone* publish major articles on RBF.

1972   Unmanned Luna 20 Soviet spacecraft returns to Earth with Moon soil samples; Pioneer 10, U.S. interplanetary probe launched to pass by Jupiter (early 1979) on barely possible outer planetary "grand tour"; Apollo 16 Moon voyage; U.S. scientific satellite Copernicus launched to study evolution of stars, seek new energy source in deep-space X rays; special 40th anniversary issue of *Architectural Forum* is dedicated to RBF and his work; England's *Architectural Design* magazine devotes its entire issue to "Buckminster Fuller Retrospective"; *Playboy* interviews RBF; Nixon visits China and U.S.S.R.; U.S.A. devalues dollar; Bangladesh created; UN Conference on the Human Environment (Stockholm, Sweden); RBF calls for "Declaration of Interdependence" in 1976-Bicentennial Year for U.S.A., at Bryn Mawr College; Black September terrorists assassinate Israeli Olympic athletes, Munich; U.S.A.–U.S.S.R.-puppeted Indochina air war accelerates; RBF attends Doxiadis' Delos Symposium #9; 2.6-million-year-old skull (discovered by Richard Leakey in 1971 in Kenya) appears to be closer to modern man than either *Australopithecus* or the later *Homo erectus*; Bay Area Rapid Transit (computer-programmed subway train) in San Francisco is first new transit system in U.S.A. since 1907; RBF becomes "World Fellow in Residence" at a consortium of Philadelphia-area institutions—University of Pennsylvania, Bryn Mawr, Haverford, and Swarthmore colleges, and the University City Science Center; in "Operation Deep Freeze" U.S.A. installs entire research station of several buildings beneath large stainless steel and aluminum geodesic dome at exact South Pole of Earth; population growth of U.S.A. nears zero (as explained by RBF as a corollary to electrical-power-generation level); RBF's *Intuition* is published by Doubleday, which also publishes *Buckminster Fuller to Children of Earth* with text by RBF, compiled and photographed by Cam Smith; Nixon re-elected; RBF receives honorary doctorates from Grinnell College, University of Maine (Orono), and Emerson College; RBF awarded the Founders Medal of Austin College; RBF consultant to Design Science Institute and advisor to Earth Metabolic Design; crisis for periodicals—*Life* ends 36 years of publication.

1973 As "World Fellow in Residence," RBF establishes his publications
      and research office and archives in Philadelphia at University City
      Science Center; RBF and AHF move to apartment at Society Hill
      Towers, at 200 Locust St., Philadelphia; RBF attends 10th Doxiadis'
      Delos Symposium; Hugh Kenner's *Bucky: A Guided Tour of Buck-
      minster Fuller* is published by William Morrow; *The Dymaxion
      World of Buckminster Fuller* by RBF and Robert Marks is reissued
      in paperback by Doubleday; U.S.A. launches orbiting space station.
      RBF patents "Floating Breakwater" and "Tensegrity Dome,"
      achieving an ephemeralization ratio of 200 geodesic domes for
      weight of one present-day equivolumed fireproof building; RBF is ar-
      chitect with Shoji Sadao in the completion of design project for In-
      ternational Airports of New Delhi, Bombay, and Madras, India,
      under administration of Prime Minister Indira Gandhi; year of Wa-
      tergate and the contrived "energy crises" (reminiscent of U.S. eco-
      logical revolution of 1966–72, which had resulted in legislated
      restrictions against atomic energy, strip mining, high sulphur fume
      fuels, DDT, etc.); Watkins Glen Rock Festival with 600,000 people
      is largest gathering in American history; RBF delivers 124 public
      lectures; RBF receives "Award of Merit" from the Philadelphia Art
      Alliance, delivers keynote address at the 1973 Milton S. Eisenhower
      Symposium at Johns Hopkins University; RBF a founding member
      of United States Committee for the United Nations University; Ja-
      pan constructs two weather geodesic radomes atop rim of Mount Fu-
      ji's summit and issues memorial stamp, "Pearl in the Crown of Fuji-
      San,"; Chicago Museum of Science and Industry mounts major
      traveling exhibit of RBF artifacts, which travels in two years to Min-
      neapolis Institute of Art, Ontario Science Center, Franklin Institute
      in Philadelphia, Bronfman Center in Montreal, California Museum
      of Science and Industry in Los Angeles, Des Moines Center of Sci-
      ence and Industry, East St. Louis Senior High School; RBF honored
      as Brockington Visitor at Queens University, Kingston, Ontario,
      Canada; RBF receives honorary doctorates from Nasson College,
      Rensselaer Polytechnic Institute, and Beaver College.

1974 Molecular biologists call for a temporary ban on research combining
      animal, viral, and bacterial DNA, fearing development of uncontrol-
      lable strains of biological-warfare agents; primates are successfully
      vaccinated for the first time in cancer experiments; radio telescope
      beams message to star cluster Messier 13 in search for intelligent be-
      ings, many light-years away; *Mind's Eye of Buckminster Fuller* by
      Don Robertson (Vantage) and *Buckminster Fuller at Home in Uni-*

verse by Alden Hatch (Crown) are published; Comet Kahoutek not as spectacular as predicted; "close-in" pictures of Venus, Mercury, and Jupiter; astronauts spend 85 days in space aboard U.S. space station Skylab; RBF on 37th complete circuit of Earth as he gives record 150 major public addresses; Nixon becomes first American President to resign (in wake of Watergate); *New York Times* publishes RBF article on wind energy; element #106 synthesized; India becomes sixth nation to explode a nuclear device; Turkish jumbo jet crashes, killing 346, in aviation's worst disaster; fighting continues in Ireland, Middle East, Cyprus; after 40-year prohibition Americans are given right to own gold bullion; U.S. Treasury auctions gold, weakening the world-wide gold market; RBF gives commencement addresses and receives honorary doctorate degrees from the University of Notre Dame, St. Joseph's College, Pratt Institute, University of Pennsylvania, and McGill University; RBF speaks to Department of State's Foreign Service Institute; world food crops poor—bad weather threatens widespread famine; U.S. unemployment rises to 6.5 percent; crude oil prices quadruple; RBF granted New York State Architect's License; world's-tallest Sears Tower constructed in Chicago (title held by N.Y.C. buildings for nearly 100 years, starting with Flatiron Building); RBF Chicago Museum of Science and Industry and U.S. Foundation for the Arts traveling exhibit continues at five major museums in U.S. and Canada. After Arab oil embargo U.S. oil companies report huge fourth-quarter profits over previous year: Exxon up 59 percent, Mobil up 68 percent, Texaco up 70 percent, etc. Supranational think tank, the Club of Rome, submits *The Limits to Growth,* citing accelerating linear population growth curves as proof of "not enough life support to go around" on our now-acknowledged-to-be-small, spherically finite planet (a restatement of Malthusian thinking of 1810).

1975   *Synergetics,* RBF's half-century work on the geometry of nature's own coordinate system—the isotropic vector matrix that models both the physical and metaphysical aspects of Universe—published by Macmillan (876 pages, in collaboration with E. J. Applewhite, with preface and article by Harvard mathematician Arthur Loeb); molecular biologists write guidelines for recombinant genetic engineering; Exxon surpasses General Motors as world's biggest industrial corporation; 300 largest and richest U.S.A. corporations have become transnational operations—move engineered by Wall Street lawyers; RBF University Professor Emeritus at Southern Illinois University and University of Pennsylvania; supermicrobe that can digest crude oil developed by recombinant DNA to deal with increasingly frequent oil spills; RBF made International President of the World Society for Ekistics; taxes rise faster than food, housing, or transportation costs; Medard Gabel and World Game Workshop publish *Energy, Earth and Everyone* (Doubleday) with introduction by RBF; cracks found in Illinois atomic reactor cause shutdown of 23 similar reactors; new particles suspected of association with the property "charm" discovered; first intimate pictures of surface of Venus transmitted by Soviet soft-landing probes; RBF patents "Floating Breakwater" and "Non-Symmetrical Tension-Integrity Structures"; U.S. population drops below Zero Population Growth; *New York Times Magazine* features RBF in article by Hugh Kenner; RBF makes 39th circuit of planet Earth; RBF makes 43 continuous hours of color videotaped "thinking-out-loud" sessions at Bell Laboratories Studios in Philadelphia; Satellite brings educational TV to 2400 villages in India; American and Soviet astronauts meet in orbit during Apollo-Soyuz cooperative space link-up; RBF testifies before the U.S. Senate Committee on Foreign Relations; RBF presented Planetary Citizens Award by United Nations, Distinguished Service Award Medal by Beech Aircraft, and Certificate of Honor, City and County of San Francisco; major articles on RBF appear in *New York Times Book Review, Domus* (Italy), *Metropolis* (France), *Monday* (Canada), *Wall Street Journal,* and *Newsweek*; Canada opens world's largest airport, Montreal; RBF invested as a Fellow in American Institute of Architects and speaks at their national convention; fossil remains of the oldest hominids yet (3.35 to 3.75 million years) found near Olduvai Gorge by Mrs. Leakey; communist indigenous governments in Vietnam, Laos, and Cambodia withstand invasion forces in 30-year-long war; marketing of home video recorders, home TV projection systems begins; videodisc systems tested. RBF attends 11th Delos Symposium (old "Delians"—dear friends of RBF—Dinos Doxiadis, Sir Robert Matthew, Arnold Toynbee, C. F. Waddington, all die); major figures in Watergate scandal found guilty, January 1; RBF speaks for Department of State's Senior Seminar in Foreign Policy; unemployment rises to over 9 percent; RBF receives 39th honorary degree from Hobart and William Smith colleges; New York City narrowly avoids bankruptcy as $3 billion becomes due.

1976   RBF conceives and designs Synergetics exhibit for opening of Smithsonian/Cooper-Hewitt Museum of Design and a limited edition of silkscreens, "Synergetics Poster Series"; Viking mission lands two U.S. spacecraft on Mars, while two parent craft monitor the planet from orbit in man's first extraterrestrial planetary exploration; North and South Vietnam officially reunited, with Hanoi as capital; Chou En-lai (January 8) and Mao Tse-tung (September 8) die, leading to a power struggle for leadership in China, won by the pragmatists— purge of orthodox Maoists ensues and "Gang of Four," led by Mao's widow, arrested; M.I.T. scientist constructs first synthetic gene; RBF participates in convention to draft and sign a Declaration of Principles and Rights for American Children; 26 die from "Legionnaire's Disease" at American Legion Convention in Philadelphia (50 years after American Legion Convention in Philadelphia opposed successfully U.S. Senate's ratification of Geneva Accords outlawing chemical and biological warfare weaponry internationally); formal guidelines regulating recombinant DNA research issued by National Institutes of Health, scientific groups urge world-around regulation; RBF proposes Geoscope for Montreal Expo '67 Dome, which remains structurally undamaged after fire burns off vinyl skin; RBF interviewed by CBS-TV for U.S. Bicentennial show (July 4, 1976); RBF conceives and designs limited edition of metal sculpture "Jitterbug," demonstrating 4-D wave generation—spheres-becoming-spaces, spaces-becoming-spheres; proton found to be made of three layers, each of which has a different spin; Carter-Ford debates, first U.S. presidential debates in 16 years, interrupted by 28-minute technical blackout, September 23, Philadelphia; China's largest series of nuclear tests showers Philadelphia with fallout; Jimmy Carter elected President; publication of *And It Came to Pass—Not to Stay,* RBF's 15th book (Macmillan); RBF cited as "Philadelphian who has brought honor to Philadelphia" at Golden Slipper Charity dinner; largest stony-meteorite fall in recorded history in Kirin, China; RBF is First Annual Distinguished Lecturer, College of Engineering, Villanova University; RBF receives Messing Award from St. Louis University Library Association; worst disaster of modern times— 700,000 die in Chinese earthquake, July 28; worst English drought in history reaches crisis; nationwide flu vaccinations halted on October 12, following deaths of several people; repressive conservative regimes strengthen their hold in South America as military coup takes over in Argentina and a coup opposes reformist regime in Peru; progress in unification of general relativity, quantum mechanics, and thermodynamics leads to prediction that miniature black holes (10^{15} grams) created early in history of Universe are exploding, yielding burst of gamma rays that should be observable; establishment of detailed climatic chronology from sediment cores produces virtually conclusive proof that the cycles of ice ages on Earth are caused by variations of Earth's orbit; National Science Foundation studies possibility of converting $300 million spy ship *Glomar Explorer* to a scientific research vessel for use in Deep Sea Drilling Project; RBF receives Development of Consciousness Award on September 20 from International Meditation Society; sex differences in brain hemisphere specialization reported, with specialization present in males by age of 6 but not in females until about age 13; RBF testifies at U.S. House hearing on "The Recovery of the City"; World's largest solar furnace at Odeillo, France, attracts American interest through defense and energy-related contracts; RBF speaks at Habitat—UN Conference on Human Settlements, Vancouver, British Columbia, Canada; "Now House" exhibited; RBF continues as World Fellow in Residence, Philadelphia; consultant to Architects 3 in Penang, Malaysia; tutor in Design Science, International College, Los Angeles; International President of World Society for Ekistics; RBF interviewed for CBC by Margaret Trudeau; July 23—RBF signs limited edition of world's first tetrahedronal book, *The Tetrascroll* which was conceived, illustrated, and written by him, and published by Tayana Grossman's Limited Editions Press.

1977   RBF designs and develops two prototype geodesic domes—"Pinecone Dome" and "Fly's Eye Dome"; RBF writes *Synergetics 2* (to be published in 1979); RBF's "Tetrascroll" exhibited at Museum of Modern Art in New York and Philadelphia Museum of Art; "Jitterbug" sculpture exhibited in New York, Washington, D.C., Florida, and Ohio; and RBF Retrospective Exhibit at Ron Feldman Gallery in New York includes "Synergetic Geometry Posters" and "Tetrascroll"; five million Hindus celebrate January 19 as the holiest day in history (according to Hindu astrologers, the auspicious moment when Sun, Moon, and stars are at the same positions as at the creation of the Universe); American astronomers discover a swarm of satellites around Uranus, making it the planet with the most satellites; oil first flows in the Alaska pipeline; largest oil spill ever in the Ekofisk, 150 miles northeast of Scotland; gene-splitting technique to attack human disease, University of California; cruise missile, neutron bomb, and charged particle beam weapons are discussed and secretly researched; Carter drops B-1 strategic bomber program; worst aviation disaster in history at Santa Cruz de Tenerife, Canary Islands, involves two 747s, 577 dead; a 25-hour blackout leads to extensive looting and vandalism, N.Y.C.; Explorer satellite studies Sun emissions while in orbit from one of the Sun-Earth libration points;

first explicit demonstration of a burn within the target core in fusion reaction; Bell Labs tests fiber optics for telephone transmission, using gallium-arsenide lasers; Department of Energy added to Cabinet with James Schlesinger, former defense secretary and AEC chairman, as new head; February 11 proclaimed "Buckminster Fuller Day" by governor of Massachusetts and mayors of Boston and Cambridge; RBF is first witness at U.S. Senate Select Committee on Small Business hearings on alternative energy. RBF receives awards: First Annual Heald Award at Illinois Institute of Technology, Eleanor Roosevelt Humanitarian Award from League for the Hard of Hearing, Stevens Honor Award from Stevens Institute of Technology, "The Golden Plate" Award from the American Academy of Achievement. Gandhi government of India defeated because of sterilization programs and replaced by devout Hindu Desai; Djibouti, last remaining European colony in Africa, granted independence; Polaroid announces instant movie picture system; RBF presents keynote address at "Toward Tomorrow Fair," University of Massachusetts, Amherst; RBF makes Far East lecture tour sponsored by U.S. State Department and United States Information Agency; John Mitchell first U.S. Attorney General to go to jail; RBF writes "Fifty Years Ahead of My Time," for *Saturday Evening Post*; E. J. Applewhite's *Cosmic Fishing* recounts the writing of *Synergetics*; RBF interviewed for BBC-TV "Twentieth Century Series"; President Carter pardons Vietnam War draft evaders as one of his first acts in office; China frees 100,000 political prisoners and expands trade with Japan, Europe, and the U.S., while relations with Russia, Cuba, and Vietnam worsen—ideological guidelines with respect to industry, science, education and the armed forces are liberalized; RBF completes term as International President, World Society for Ekistics; Chinese claim to have predicted three of six major (magnitude 7) earthquakes in the previous year. RBF, Philadelphia's "World Fellow in Residence," continues as University Professor Emeritus at Southern Illinois University and University of Pennsylvania; consultant to Architects 3, Penang, Malaysia; and tutor in Design Science, International College, Los Angeles. U.S. Census Bureau announces that for the first time a majority of Americans live in the Sunbelt states of the South and West; U.S. Commerce Department announces a trade deficit of $26.7 billion for the year (four times that of 1976)—oil, machinery, cars, coffee, and sugar accounted for the 22-percent increase in imports; U.S. exports increased only 4.6 percent over previous year; the Club of Rome publishes *Mankind at the Turning*

Point, perhaps influenced by RBF's theories, retracting their pessimistic *Limits to Growth* theories restating Malthus, published two years earlier.

1978   World's first test-tube baby born in England (a case also reported, but not confirmed, in India)—the healthy baby girl provokes worldwide interest and controversy; two Soviet cosmonauts spend record 140 days in orbit aboard Solyut 6 space station; Soviet nuclear-powered reconnaissance satellite disintegrates over northwestern Canada; RBF's *Synergetics Folio* published in limited edition in Singapore; biggest snowstorm in the history of the northeastern United States; $1.4-million roof of Hartford Coliseum collapses only hours after audience of 5000 leaves, and investigation blames failure on 4.8 inches of wet snow and "design deficiencies" (RBF's geodesic domes can handle Arctic snow load-burials of over 300 pounds per square foot); as lopsided balance of trade devalues U.S dollar against other currencies, Bank of Japan buys $1 billion of U.S. currency but is unable to prevent dollar from reaching new postwar low against yen; $112 million awarded in antitrust suit filed against Eastman Kodak; People's Republic of China begins crash program to industrialize with Western help; researchers continue to probe for solar-weather links, and a "global electrical circuit" is proposed as a possible coupling mechanism—as proposed in 1969 by RBF to N.Y.C. World Game workshop, and recounted in this book as a strategy with much potential and of utmost priority in World Gaming; U-25B, the joint U.S.A.–U.S.S.R. magneto-hydrodynamics project begins generating electricity and feeding it into the Moscow power grid; last smallpox case in the world—first instance of complete disease eradication in recorded history; first U.S. maximum-safety (P4) facility for recombinant DNA experiments opened at Fort Detrick (Maryland) as the N.I.H. eases their guidelines; RBF speaks to World Congress of the New Age in Florence, Italy, and presents his model of Einstein's $E = mc^2$ equation; speaks to members of Congress as part of Clearinghouse on the Future series; speaks at "Holistic Health" conference in Washington; speaks at Sun Day Celebration in Carbondale, Ill.; speaks at Aspen Healing Arts Conference; is keynote speaker at Annual Conference of the Society for College and University Planning; is keynote speaker for Colorado Energyfest (Alternative Energy Fair) in Golden, Colo.; presents Peter Goldmark Memorial Lecture at Electromedia Conference in Copenhagen, Denmark. Athena Lord's *Pilot for Spaceship Earth—B.F.*—published by Macmillan for young readers; President Carter mediates peace talks at Camp David, Md, between President Sadat of Egypt and Prime Minister Begin of Israel; U.S. government sells $4.8 billion worth of jet warplanes to Egypt, Israel and Saudi Arabia; Japan and China conclude $20-billion trade pact; worldwide population growth rate begins to decline, confirming RBF's industrialization prognostications; theory that all open universes develop to an anisotropically twisted "heat death" published, perhaps confirming RBF's theories that closed global system may serve as syntropic, integrating centers, countering the "heat death" trending; first federally funded commercial wind generator begins two years of tests in Clayton, N. M.; ten spacecraft visit Venus in December, including five atmosphere probes and an orbiter, and two Soviet landing craft; the all-microwave Seasat launched to study ocean surface, but fails amid some controversy after providing 99 days of data; RBF testifies before U.S. Senate Foreign Relations Committee and describes satellite use in taking daily inventories of everything from world resources to public opinion polls world-wide; RBF writes "Accommodating Human Unsettlement," *Town Planning Review,* and "Energy Economics"; RBF does half-hour program on Will Durant's *Lessons of History* on NBC-TV series; insulin production by bacteria is approached by two groups using recombinant DNA; national demonstration to close Rocky Flats Colorado Nuclear Arsenal in largest antinuke demonstration in U.S. to date; Mayor Moscone and Supervisor Milk assassinated in San Francisco; UN special session on World Disarmament opens; RBF gives Vikram Sarabai Memorial Lecture and conducts workshop on "Synergetics and Development" at Nehru Foundation for Development, Ahmedabad, India; RBF scholar in residence, University of Massachusetts, attends informal gathering of world leaders at D'Arros in the Seychelles; "RBF Day" jointly proclaimed in Minnesota by governor and mayors of St. Paul and Minneapolis; RBF interviewed on ABC News "Directions" program with Dean Morton of Cathedral of St. John the Divine, N.Y.C.; interviewed on NBC-TV noon "News Break" with Lee Phillips and Mort Crim, on "Voice of America" with Bill Reed; Honda advertisement with RBF, geodesic dome and Honda car run nationally; RBF interviewed by *Centerpiece* magazine; April and October bring heaviest periods of trading in history of New York Stock Exchange (65 million shares traded in a day), when institutional and foreign investors buy in record numbers to bolster up continually weakening dollar and after U.S. Treasury announces it will sell some of U.S. gold reserve and Federal Reserve announces it will tighten up credit; U.S. to grant sovereignty to Panama Canal Zone in December 1999; Pope Paul VI dies August 6, newly elected Pope John Paul I dies September 29 after reign of only 34 days, then first non-Italian pope in 456 years, John Paul II, chosen; first transatlantic balloon flight in history, August 17; United Airlines orders $1.6 billion worth of Boeing medium-size jets—largest order in aviation history—mostly Boeing 767s at $40 million each.

1979   RBF speaks at 6000-audience, Art Deco Radio City Music Hall at Rockefeller Center—largest movie theater with largest stage in world—to be refurbished after year-long conservation movement rescues it from destruction; March 28 "radiation accident" and "near-meltdown" at Three Mile Island nuclear-power facilities near Harrisburg, Pa., lead to re-evaluation of nuclear-power program—with 83 reactors operating and four times that many in the construction or planning stages; RBF in extensive visit to People's Republic of China finds officials and people anxious to industrialize using "Design Science Revolution"; Egypt-Israeli Peace Treaty signed in U.S. with President Carter as mediator; plane crash of DC-10 in Chicago leads to grounding and evaluation of DC-10 wing strut design; man-powered *Gossamer Albatross,* using new lightweight, superstrength space-technology alloys and Mylar, flies across English Channel—demonstrating RBF's theory that ever-improving scientific technology will produce ever-more-effective results with ever-less investment of weight and volume of materials, ergs of energy, and seconds of time for the performance of a particular function; Skylab (84-ton U.S. space station) leaves orbit and crashes in Western Australia; Pioneer 10 and 11 send pictures of Jupiter, revealing never-before-seen rings and the first extraterrestrial volcanic activity on Io, one of Jupiter's four large moons and perhaps its most interesting; RBF's *Synergetics 2* published by Macmillan—contains amplification of and collateral material for RBF's over-50-year-long conception, gestation, and manifestation of nature's coordinate system that encompasses both physics and metaphysics; prototyping of Fly's Eye Dome. *Ho-Ping: Food for Everyone* and *Earth, Energy and Everyone* by Medard Gabel and RBF-initiated World Game Laboratory published by Doubleday (these volumes encompass world resource inventories of food and energy and World Game strategies using present resources and our ever-increasing know-how and technological capabilities for solving critical problems in the shortest time possible); Chrysler Corporation asks for $4 billion in federal aid to avoid bankruptcy as General Motors (introducing its 1980 X-body cars a half-year early) begins a $70-billion retooling program to compete with smaller, more efficient, and fast-selling Japanese and West German cars; RBF interviewed by Andy Warhol's *Interview* magazine and by *Quest* magazine; RBF's prostate surgery, Bangor, Me.; RBF invested into the Order of Knights of St. John of Jerusalem and Priory of King Valdemar the Great in Copenhagen, Denmark; RBF presents keynote address at Mind Child Architecture Conference at New Jersey Institute of Technology, speaks at Flag Day Ceremony, June 14, Betsy Ross House, Philadelphia; *Buckminster Fuller on Education* published by University of Massachusetts Press; RBF receives Philadelphia's John Scott Award and the United Steelworkers of America's Raymond A. Dart Award; price of gold soars to $800 an ounce from $37 an ounce at the opening of the decade; international crises in Iran and Afghanistan; large-scale model demonstrating principle of tensegrity—discontinuous compression–continuous tension—unveiled at bank in Dayton, Ohio.

1980   Crises in Iran and Afghanistan continue—U.S. rescue of Iranian hostages fails; Mount St. Helens, long-dormant Washington State volcano, erupts with hundreds-of-megatons-of-TNT force killing scores in the area; U.S. and 50 supporting nations boycott Moscow Olympic Games ostensibly because of U.S.S.R. invasion of Afghanistan; RBF honored by exhibition and gold medal from American Academy of Arts and Letters; *Buckminster Fuller: An Autobiographical Monologue/Scenario,* edited and documented by Robert Snyder, published by St. Martin's Press; Los Angeles Bicentennial leases 50-foot-diameter Fly's Eye Dome for its theme building; RBF and AHF move to Pacific Palisades, Calif., February 29; $1.5 billion federally-guaranteed loan to struggling Chrysler Corporation approved as new 1981 K-body small cars go into production; Japan passes U.S. in automobile production (by large margin) for first time; RBF travels to Brazil and views implementation of industrialization strategies he first described in 1942 (see Chapter 9, pp. 293–308). RBF awarded 45th honorary doctorate by Alaska Pacific University; RBF speaks to International Dome Conference at Winooski, Vt.; Russian tidal energy project—largest power project in human history; RBF appointed to presidential commission to follow-up *Global 2000 Report* on crisis in energy and the global environment; RBF appointed to Congressional committee on the future. Robert Grip–Christopher Kitrick edition of RBF's Dymaxion Sky-Ocean World Map issued—largest, most accurate whole Earth map in human history.

Index

Human power structures; National sovereignty
Illiteracy. *See:* Literacy: Illiteracy; Speech patterns
Immigration. *See:* Migration & immigration
Immortality. *See:* Life is not physical
"In." *See:* World power structure, "outs" vs "ins"
In & out, 55
   See also: Orientation; Up & down
Inbreeding
   of nations & tribes, 11
   of nationalities, 218
   of special capabilities, 6–7
   specialization fomented by, 8, 215
   See also: Cross-breeding; Divide & conquer; Genetics; Nation; Specialization: Overspecialization
Incas, 49
Income tax, 80, 83
   See also: taxes
Incorporated (Inc.), xxi
   See also: Fundamental risk enterprise
India
   airports designed for, 57, 78
   hydroelectric program of, 205–6
   irrigation canal of, 208
   See also: Rivers of Asia
Indian Ocean
   crossing of, by Phoenicians, 34
   early humans on, 5–6
   early ships of, 24
   origins of ocean trade on, 22–24
   U.S.S.R. access to, 188, 193, 194, 196
   See also: Geopolitics; Line of vital supply; World ocean
Individual human. *See:* Human individual
Indonesia
   banking in, 13, 15
   population density of, 20
   See also: Bali
Industrial Revolution, 53
Indus River, 20
   See also: Rivers of Asia
Industrialization
   as class-one evolution, 240
   as comprehensive, 53–54
   as exterior metabolic system, 250
   defined, 130
   financing of, 77

first tool of, 240
in Los Angeles, 278
in Japan, 109–10, 299
navy yard, 239
of U.S., 82–84, 85, 86
of U.S.S.R., 138, 191, 288–91
vs business, 130
See also: Evolution: Class-one evolution; Ford, Henry; Mass production; Naval prognosticating science & art; Production tools
Industry
   need for helium, 221
   need for water, 221
   See also: World resources inventory
Infinite: Infinity. *See:* Finity & infinity
Information
   as awareness of "otherness," xi–xii
   relevant & irrelevant, 240
   critical, 232
   See also: Design as orderly pattern; Secret (critical information); Sensing; Syntropy & entropy
Information access
   audio-visual documentation on RBF for, 134–35
   future, 263
   library for, xxxv, 331–32
   memory bank for, 160
   newsclippings on RBF for, 134–37, *135*
   through interactive video, xxxv, 26, 223, 224, 253, 265–66, 267
   video encyclopedia for, 264
   See also: Communication; Communication satellite; Computer; Education; Geoscope; Pattern reading; Remote sensing; Secret (critical information); Television
Information display, 168–69, 180–84
   omnidirectional, 168, 172–74, 179–80
   television, 231
   See also: Computer; Dymaxion Sky-Ocean Map; Geoscope; Model: Modelability; Pure science isolations chart; Synergetics; Television
Information-gathering, 161, 199
   as critical necessity, 161
   as function of humanity, xxxvi
   data rates of, 231, 235, 238–39, 284
   in class-one evolution, 230
   in space program, 247